STATISTICS
FOR THE
BEHAVIORAL SCIENCES

STATISTICS FOR THE BEHAVIORAL SCIENCES

FOURTH EDITION

B. Michael Thorne
Mississippi State University

J. Martin Giesen
Mississippi State University

McGraw Hill

Boston   Burr Ridge, IL   Dubuque, IA   Madison, WI   New York
San Francisco   St. Louis   Bangkok   Bogotá   Caracas   Kuala Lumpur
Lisbon   London   Madrid   Mexico City   Milan   Montreal   New Delhi
Santiago   Seoul   Singapore   Sydney   Taipei   Toronto

McGraw-Hill Higher Education

*A Division of The **McGraw-Hill** Companies*

STATISTICS FOR THE BEHAVIORAL SCIENCES, FOURTH EDITION

Published by McGraw-Hill, a business unit of The McGraw-Hill Companies, Inc., 1221 Avenue of the Americas, New York, NY 10020. Copyright © 2003, 2000 by The McGraw-Hill Companies, Inc. All rights reserved. No part of this publication may be reproduced or distributed in any form or by any means, or stored in a database or retrieval system, without the prior written consent of The McGraw-Hill Companies, Inc., including, but not limited to, in any network or other electronic storage or transmission, or broadcast for distance learning.

Some ancillaries, including electronic and print components, may not be available to customers outside the United States.

This book is printed on acid free paper.

9 0 DOC/DOC 1 0 5 4 3 2 1

ISBN-13: 978-0-07-283251-8
ISBN-10: 0-07-283251-7

Vice President and editor-in-chief: *Thalia Dorwick*
Publisher: *Ken King*
Editorial coordinator: *Georgia Gero-Chen*
Senior marketing manager: *Chris Hall*
Senior project manager: *Marilyn Rothenberger*
Production supervisor: *Enboge Chong*
Senior media technology producer: *Sean Crowley*
Art director: *Jeanne M. Schreiber*
Art editor: *Robin Mouat*
Interior designer: *Richard Kharibian*
Cover designer: *Cassandra Chu*
Illustration: *Lotus Art*
Compositor: *G&S Typesetters*
Typeface: *10/12 Palatino*
Printer: *R. R. Donnelley Sons Company/Crawfordsville, IN*

Library of Congress Cataloging-in-Publication Data

Thorne, B. Michael (Billy Michael), 1942–
    Statistics for the behavioral sciences / B. Michael Thorne, J. Martin Giesen.—4th ed.
      p. cm.
    Includes index.
    ISBN 0-07-283251-7
    1. Social sciences—Statistical methods. 2. Psychometrics. I. Giesen,
J. Martin. II. Title.
HA29. T54 2002
300_.1_5195—dc21   2002141442
www.mhhe.com

To Wanda, my wife and friend,
and to my children, Dean and Erin.
B.M.T.

To my parents, teachers, friends,
and students who have helped me learn.
J.M.G.

Brief Contents

Contents

Choosing the Correct Inferential Test   370

Preface

Like the third edition, we had four goals: First, we sought to preserve and improve the features of previous editions that, based on our experience and feedback, have been beneficial to new learners of statistics. Second, we strove for clear and enhanced conceptual presentations. Third, we included additions and adjustments that recognize advances and changes in statistics for the behavioral sciences. Finally, we tried to do all these things without losing sight of our overall goal: a simplified textbook that maintains essential content.

Special Features and Enhancements

This edition contains a number of special features and enhancements that set it apart from its competition.

Getting Started Right—How to Think About Learning Statistics and How to Avoid Being Anxious About the Subject. Like the previous editions, we use *the metaphor of learning a second language* to introduce students to statistics. Just like learning Spanish or French, learning statistics requires developing a new vocabulary and discovering how to combine terms and phrases into longer and more useful "sentences." Like language students, students of statistics often find they are already familiar with many of the basic concepts and simply have to learn new "words" for them. Also like language students, statistics students find they benefit from immersion in the new subject and from regular practice.

Another similarity is that students often enter their first statistics course with some fear and anxiety, worrying that they may not have the necessary background for success. Many students are traumatized by textbooks that introduce too many statistical concepts and formulas too quickly. In this book, we show that statistics can be approached and appreciated on different levels. We aim for comprehension on two levels: (1) the practical level, involving the ability to use statistical tests and methods in applied settings, and (2) the intuitive level, involving a feel for the principles underlying statistical procedures. Again, our goal has been to write a simplified text without sacrificing essential content. At all times, we have kept in mind the student with less mathematics training. In fact, the statistical procedures in this book require little more than addition, subtraction, multiplication, division, and some elementary high-school algebra. Almost all students, well pre-pared in math or less well prepared, can succeed on the levels at which this book is aimed. Just as students *can* learn a second language with good instruction and regular practice, students *can* learn statistics.

Practice Using Statistical Tests and Immediate Feedback Exercises: Checking Your Progress. Our emphasis is on teaching students to use statistical tests and procedures. To this end, almost all newly introduced techniques are illustrated with two completely solved examples. Sections labeled "Checking Your Progress" do what the name implies—allow students to check their ability to use the technique they've just read about. Additional exercises at the end of each chapter fur-ther strengthen the students' computational skills; the exercise sets have been in-creased for this edition.

Engaging Illustrations of Chapter Concepts and Tips to Avoid Common Errors. Many chapters begin with a brief vignette that illustrates the chapter's ma-terial, engages the students, and alleviates anxiety. Beginning with Chapter 5, most chapters also have a section called "Troubleshooting Your Computations." These sections identify some of the common errors that can result if the chapter tech-niques are misapplied and show students what to do about them. Frequently, the troubleshooting sections help students recognize an obviously incorrect answer and provide suggestions about finding and correcting the problem.

Summaries of Major Sections on Descriptive and Inferential Statistics and Help Choosing the Right Test. Following a short introductory chapter, the text is divided into two parts. In Part I, Descriptive Statistics, Chapters 2–6 cover ba-sic measurement concepts and statistical vocabulary, the frequency distribution, graphing, measures of central tendency, and measures of dispersion and standard scores. There is a **brief summary** of Part I following Chapter 6. It is highlighted by a bleed tab to make it easy to locate.

In Part II, Inferential Statistics, Chapters 7–15 cover probability, the normal distribution, confidence intervals and hypothesis testing, significance testing with two sample means, one-way analysis of variance with post hoc comparisons, two-way analysis of variance, correlation and regression, and several popular non-parametric inferential tests (i.e., chi square, Mann–Whitney U, Wilcoxon T, and Kruskal–Wallis H). There is a **brief summary** of inferential techniques after Chap-ter 15. This summary is followed by a decision tree in a section called "Choosing the Correct Inferential Test." Bleed tabs on both the summary and the decision tree make them easy to locate as well.

Arrangement of Topics, Changes in Emphasis, and Introduction to Bayesian Statistics. We follow the arrangement of chapters from the third edition (e.g., the correlation and regression chapter is at the end of parametric inferential tests). The grouped frequency distribution is de-emphasized and boxed in the chapters con-taining it (i.e., Chapters 3–6), reflecting its infrequent application in the behavioral sciences. The probability chapter initiates the survey of inferential statistics, as be-fits the importance of probability theory for the inferential tests. The chapter also has been expanded from its coverage in the second edition, with the addition of various ways of thinking about probability (e.g., subjectively, theoretically, empirically) and an introduction to Bayesian statistics. The probability chapter ends with a brief look at the binomial distribution, which ties in well with the following chapter on the normal probability distribution.

A Step-By-Step Approach to Hypothesis Testing and Added Emphasis on Writing Good Conclusions. Chapter 9—devoted to confidence intervals and a first look at hypothesis testing (the one-sample t test)—introduces a verbal, problem context-oriented interpretation of confidence intervals. The chapter also introduces a seven-step procedure for testing the null hypothesis. The final step emphasizes the importance of writing good conclusions following the American Psychological Association style manual guidelines. Examples provide model conclusions that fully explain results in the research context of the problem. The seven-step procedure with model conclusions is employed throughout the remainder of the text to guide students through the hypothesis-testing process, which is often perceived as counterintuitive. Conclusion writing—an emphasis frequently requested by our colleagues—is reinforced by end-of-chapter exercises.

New Topics and Controversies. Chapter 9 ends with a brief, intuitive look at meta-analysis and an equally brief examination of the current debate on the value of hypothesis testing ("Should Hypothesis Testing Be Abandoned?").

Relating Procedures and Increasing Understanding by Using "Key Concepts." In many places in this text, there is more sophisticated discussion without losing sight of the simplicity for which previous editions were known. For example, the key deviation of the score minus the mean $(X - \overline{X})$ is identified in the chapter on measures of dispersion. This key deviation is carried through and expanded in the coverage of analysis of variance. The key deviation concept is extended to regression as the deviation of a score from its predicted value. The idea of a pooled or common variance has been added to the chapter devoted to the two-sample t test, and this concept carries through to mean square within groups in analysis of variance. In the correlation and regression chapter, there is a section on "Correlation, Variance, and Covariance" that ties the formula for the Pearson r to the familiar concept of variance and introduces variance's relative—the covariance.

Integrated Testing Procedures for ANOVA and a Simplified Consistent Method for Post Hoc Testing. In this text, the post hoc tests following ANOVA are included in the ANOVA chapter rather than being consigned to the succeeding chapter. Also, the order of presentation of the post hoc tests is reversed, with the Fisher LSD presented before the Tukey HSD and in greater detail. Finally, the equation for computing LSD and the procedures for reporting the results of the analysis have been modified to make them parallel to the comparable HSD discussion.

Showing Relationships Between Procedures and Research Questions—Introducing the General Linear Model. The correlation chapter mentions correlation coefficients other than the Pearson r and the Spearman r_s—specifically, the point biserial correlation and the phi coefficient. The chapter closes with a brief discussion of how the inferential techniques covered can be subsumed and related to one another under the general linear model.

Helpful Appendixes. Five appendixes at the end of the book provide important resources for students. Appendix 1 is a brief math–algebra review for students who need to refresh their math skills. Appendix 2 is a glossary of statistical terms. Appendix 3 contains the symbols and the most important computational formulas in the book, organized by chapter. Appendix 4 contains the tables needed for the inferential tests, and Appendix 5 provides answers to the odd-numbered exercises at the end of each chapter.

Additional Helpful Materials Complete the Package

Available with our text is an *Instructor's CDROM* containing answers to all the even-numbered exercises in the text, a sample syllabus with formulas, *Solutions Manual* with complete calculations from formula to final answer for every problem in the text, including the "Checking Your Progress" exercises, and a test bank of problems the instructor can use either for in-class exercises or for constructing tests. Also available is a comprehensive online learning center with additional resources for students and instructors including a free interactive study guide with self tests for unit mastery, additional problems and chapter reviews.

If an instructor wants to place more emphasis on computer use in his or her course, we recommend consideration of *Ready, Set, Go! A Student Guide to SPSS for Windows* by Thomas Pavkov and Kent Pierce. This practical user's manual for SPSS for Windows focuses on the types of problems covered in our text and online learning center.

Let Us Hear From You. We want your teaching experience using *Statistics for the Behavioral Sciences* to be as successful as possible. If you have comments, questions, or suggestions, please contact us by e-mail (bmt2@ra.msstate.edu).

We would like to thank the previous reviewers of this book: Nancy Anderson, Liberty University; Xuanning Fu, Brigham Young University, Hawaii; Paul C. Price, California State University, Fresno; Sarah C. Sitton, St. Edward's University; and Todd D. Zakrajsek, Southern Oregon State University.

We are grateful to the literary executor of the late Sir Ronald A. Fisher, F.R.S., Dr. Frank Yates, F.R.S., and Longman Group Ltd., London, for permission to reprint portions of Tables IV and VII from their book *Statistical Tables for Biological, Agricultural and Medical Research* (6th ed., 1974).

CHAPTER 1

The Language of Statistics

Statistics are all around us. We use them every day, perhaps without realizing we are doing so. Statistics help us make sense of the information we receive about events in our community, nation, and world. Consider the following typical day in the life of a young American woman:

After waking up, Maria makes herself a cup of coffee and turns on a morning news show. One of the stories is about recent college admissions. The reporter says that 8 of 10 students who score in the 90th percentile or above on the SAT are admitted to the colleges of their choice. Because Maria is working to save enough money to go to college, she is particularly interested in this report. She wonders whether her scores will be good enough to get her into the school she wants to attend or whether, despite the fact that she scored in the 90th percentile, she will be one of the 20% who are not accepted by their first-choice school.

On her way out the door, Maria grabs the morning newspaper. While riding to work on the bus, she reads that car thefts have risen 67% nationally in the last 25 years. The article states that in New York and Miami, 1 of every 29 cars is reported stolen. In addition, the dollar losses from car thefts have jumped 134% in the same 25-year period. She figures that part of the greater increase in dollars lost is caused by the rapid rise in car prices. She then wonders how much insurance costs have escalated. Maybe she won't be able to get a car any time soon.

That night, Maria relaxes with the sports section of the paper. An avid baseball fan, she wants to know the results of last night's game. She is thrilled to read that the pitcher on her home team gave up only two runs in eight innings, lowering his earned run average to 1.80. The first baseman went 4 for 4 with two home runs, raising his batting average from .287 to .301. The team won and went over the .500 mark for the first time this season, moving into third place in the division.

You may not be a baseball fan, and you may have read different stories in today's paper, but, like Maria, you are surrounded by statistics. Most people who use statistics are average citizens, not professional statisticians. Whether their purpose is personal or professional, though, most people need and benefit from a basic understanding of statistics. That is what this book is designed to provide.

WHAT IS STATISTICS?

Before we look more closely at Maria's day, let's consider the term **statistics.** What does it really mean? Actually, the term is used in two different ways. We use it to refer to the summary numbers, or **indices,** that result from an analysis of **data** (numbers). An example is the summary number, or statistic, that expresses a grade point average or baseball batting average.

We also use the word *statistics* to refer to all the procedures and tools used to organize and interpret facts, events, and observations that can be expressed numerically. Throughout this book, we demonstrate how to make sense of facts, events, and observations by converting them into numbers and organizing and analyzing them by using the tools of statistics.

We use the term *statistics* in both these senses in this book. You will know from the context which use is intended.

WHY STUDY STATISTICS?

Personal Reasons

Maria's day illustrates two important points about statistics. The first has already been stated: We are surrounded by statistics. We encounter statistics in the newspaper, on television, in magazines, and in conversation. We are a statistical society. In fact, all civilizations, ancient and modern, have been statistical societies.

As a student, you are no doubt interested in your average grade in a course. Your average grade is a statistic. What's the weather going to be like tomorrow? If the TV weather reporter says that there is a 70% chance of rain, you'll probably take your umbrella with you. The likelihood of showers, expressed as a 70% chance, is a statistic.

What is the latest news in scientific studies? What food additives have been found to increase the probability of cancer, and by how much? What is the effectiveness rate of various contraceptives? What does it mean to say that heart disease is the leading cause of death in the United States, but injuries, homicide, and suicide are responsible for more potential years of life lost? How successful is the latest AIDS drug? Statistical techniques used to answer such questions also give information on *how sure we are* about our answers. Is the Sugar-Busters diet effective in bringing about weight loss? Will a flu shot really prevent *you* from contracting the flu? Statistical techniques are used to organize and analyze the results of the studies conducted to answer these questions. The statistical analysis can also tell us how sure we are—the **degree of certainty**—of our conclusions.

Furthermore, to evaluate such studies critically, you need to understand the statistical methods and procedures that were used to arrive at the stated conclusions. A working knowledge of statistics is essential in sorting out the diverse claims and counterclaims that you encounter in daily life. Although this text and a first course in statistics will not make you a professional statistician, they will help you become an informed consumer of statistics.

The second point illustrated by Maria's story is that we are all amateur statisticians. Because of our continual exposure to statistics, we have developed a practical and working knowledge of rudimentary statistical concepts. For example, most of us understand the probabilities associated with coin tosses and card games. As with other practical knowledge, it tends to be incomplete and is often misused or misunderstood, but it is knowledge nonetheless. In this book, we hope to build on your current understanding of statistics, filling in the gaps in your knowledge and enhancing your ability to use statistics to describe and understand the world around you.

Professional Reasons

Statistics has more than everyday uses, of course. It is also an essential tool for people who study and do research in the social and behavioral sciences. To understand why this is so, consider this typical definition of psychology: Psychology is the scientific study of behavior and cognition. The term *scientific* refers to the fact that psychologists perform experiments, manipulate variables, make objective observations, and quantify their results. Just as important, however, is the word *behavior.* Examples of behavior studied by psychologists are the disk-pecking behavior of pigeons, language production in humans, change in attitude after hearing a persuasive speech or commercial, and heart rate as a response to a threatening situation.

What is there about behavior that requires the use of statistical procedures? Behavior is ordinarily quite variable, and this is what makes statistical procedures necessary. *Statistical* methods are designed for information and data that are variable. Consider, for example, an experiment designed by a colleague of ours to evaluate the flexibility and adaptability of visual perception. Our colleague asks his students to wear special goggles that reverse what a person sees. Everything is upside down and backward: Right appears left, left appears right, up is down, and down is up. Each student is then asked to play catch with the professor using a small rubber ball. As you can imagine, the results are often hilarious. After a time, however, most students' visual systems accommodate, and they begin to see normally. Despite the goggles, they are able to throw and catch the ball.

Our colleague measures the length of time it takes each student to begin to throw and catch normally after putting on the goggles. This measure is an index of the adaptability of each student's visual system. Some students adapt quickly; others experience vertigo and don't adapt at all. The majority fall somewhere in between.

What accounts for this variability—the differences in the amount of time it takes students to adapt? It may be that some students have more coordination than others. Maybe some students are affected by performing in front of the class, whereas others aren't. Perhaps the professor gets better at throwing and catching with the students as the demonstration goes on, so that students coming toward the end appear to do better. No doubt you can think of some other factors that might influence the outcome of this experiment.

In short, there is variability not only among the subjects of a study but in the characteristics of the study and in the procedures used to measure the subjects' behavior. The variability that characterizes all living things is one of the main reasons we need statistics.

When we measure some stable object or phenomenon with great precision and under rigidly controlled conditions, we have little need for statistics beyond certain basic descriptive measures. The process occurs almost exactly the same way every time. We can report our results in one or a few numbers that anyone can appreciate. In chemistry or physics, for example, instruments are often so precise and the processes underlying an observation so well known that variability is practically nonexistent. Unfortunately, as the goggles experiment illustrates, things are not so precise in psychology. Instruments of measurement are often very crude; psychologists frequently do not have control over all extraneous conditions; and psychologists are rarely aware of all the factors that could affect the subjects' performance. Psychologists and other behavioral scientists need ways to describe their data and methods that will help them relate their results to the "real world." Statistics was created to deal with uncertainty and variability. Thus, behavioral scientists especially need to study statistics.

Our Goals

As you can see, we consider the study of statistics to be important for a number of reasons. We have written this text with several goals in mind. First, we want to help you learn the basic vocabulary, procedures, and logic of statistics. Second, we want to assist you in becoming a better everyday consumer of statistical information. Third, we want to show you how to improve your ability to read and understand the professional literature—journal articles, for example—in the behavioral sciences. Finally, we want to give you the tools with which to calculate and interpret statistics on data you or others collect, whether as part of a lab class or as part of your job.

STATISTICS AS A SECOND LANGUAGE

At the level that most of us understand it, mathematics involves using "proven" rules for the manipulation of numbers. The fact that there are mathematical laws governing these manipulations is comforting. By contrast, statistics is composed of indices and procedures—some from the laws of mathematics and probability, and some that have evolved over time, sometimes by trial and error, because they have "worked" to convey certain information. Much of our choice is influenced by culture and convention—that is, what is commonly done by other people in our field. So even though statistics uses numbers, it isn't completely mathematical; it is more like a language. In statistics, there are conventions that must be learned, and the best way to learn them is by practice.

Our first step will be to present a vocabulary of statistics, including the concepts of central tendency, variation, probability, and other descriptive statistics introduced in the first several chapters of the text. Later, basic statistical "grammar" and "syntax" will be introduced. This is where you will learn to combine the indices of central tendency and variation to draw inferences and make decisions about hypotheses.

Approaching the study of statistics as a second language should help you learn the basic concepts. In the course of this book, we will try to help you acquire an intuitive feel for the rationale behind the various statistics. However, a more sophisticated understanding will have to await more advanced course work. This parallels the way we master a second language. After one course in Spanish, we probably will not be comfortable conversing in Spanish. Moreover, so long as Spanish is a second language, we will never be as fluent as a native speaker, and even after many courses, we will probably always experience some anxiety and uncertainty.

In statistics, don't let that anxiety and uncertainty inhibit your progress. As with a second language, the most important way to learn statistics is to do it. Practice, repetition, and daily use are essential and lead to comfort, confidence, and greater understanding. Our best advice in mastering statistics is to immerse yourself in the material. Do the homework, use the study guide, and practice, practice, practice.

WHAT YOU NEED TO USE THIS BOOK SUCCESSFULLY

This is not a mathematics text. However, it does require some mathematical skill. The statistical calculations in this book will involve computations of squares and square roots as well as the use of summation and simple algebra. Because this level of skill is required to enter most colleges, you probably already have all the math skills you will need to understand this text. Nevertheless, if you haven't had a math class in a number of years or if you substituted business math for high school algebra, you may want to read Appendix 1 to review your math skills.

An indispensable tool for the beginning statistics student is a good, relatively simple, and inexpensive pocket calculator. There are many different brands on the market, and features vary almost as widely as the different model types. We recommend a full-size pocket calculator with large keys, at least an eight-digit display, four basic functions (add, subtract, multiply, divide), a square root function, a percentage function, at least one memory function, and a clear current entry key separate from a clear total key. Most calculators have all these functions except possibly the separate clear current entry key.

One other recommendation is that you purchase a light-powered calculator rather than a battery-operated one. Over the years, we have observed the inevitable operation of Murphy's law: If something *can* go wrong, it *will.* Battery-powered calculators seem especially prone to fail during exams or at midnight (when all the battery stores are closed) the day before the homework assignment is due.

Many calculators are considerably more sophisticated than the one recommended here. Some of these are quite useful for statisticians because they compute a number of important statistics directly. However, for our purposes, a simple calculator is preferable because it will be easily mastered.

Perhaps most important to your success in statistics is your orientation to the material. Most students can easily master statistics as long as they are willing to confront the material and to practice. More than most disciplines, statistics requires regular use. Don't assume that studying statistics once a week while watching television will suffice. Follow a regular study schedule—and practice!

By practice we mean that you should work problems outside of class. We would encourage you to read your textbook actively, with a calculator, pencil, and scratch paper beside you. When you encounter a "Checking Your Progress" section, you should check your progress by working the problem that is presented. If you have difficulty with it, reread the previous section to find where you went awry. Remember: You will learn statistics by doing, not by reading the text with your mind disengaged or by sitting passively through your instructor's lectures.

That raises another issue—class attendance. Although it should go without saying, we urge you to attend class regularly. We often have had students who did not achieve the grade (and knowledge) from our statistics courses that they should have achieved, primarily because they cut too many classes. Your instructor is your guide on the statistical journey; missing class can cause you to lag behind or to become lost along the way. Also, because we realize that statistics is generally a class that most students are not excited about taking, we have never understood why all students don't work as hard as possible in the course in order to ensure that they do not have to repeat it. From our experience, students who are forced to repeat the course are frequently the ones who have poor class attendance. Don't sabotage yourself by cutting class.

We would be remiss if we didn't at least acknowledge that many of you probably have a certain degree of anxiety associated with this course. Although this is not a mathematics text, statistics is a math-related discipline; we will present equations, and you will learn how to use them to solve problems. One of us even tells his students to consider formulas to be their friends because equations tell exactly what to do—they provide guides that, if followed successfully, will lead students safely and confidently through the wilds of the statistical jungle. We hope we can convince you that the dangers you will have to overcome are not all that foreboding. We believe that your anxiety, although understandable, is to some extent unwarranted; although statistics may not be easy for some of you, it is something at which virtually all of you can succeed and may find more interesting than you expect. With diligence and practice, you can achieve comfort, confidence, and understanding. We have led many students through introductory statistics, and we can do the same for you, if you will give us the chance. Read the text, attend class regularly, do homework, and we believe you will achieve the result you desire— successful completion of your first statistics course.

SUMMARY

Statistics refers either to summary numbers resulting from data analysis or to the procedures used to organize and analyze facts numerically. We are all amateur statisticians, but we need to extend and sharpen our understanding because we are increasingly surrounded by statistics in our everyday lives.

This text has four goals: to teach you the basic vocabulary, procedures, and logic of statistics; to help you become a better consumer of statistical information; to teach you how to read and understand the professional literature in the behavioral sciences; and to enable you to calculate and interpret statistics on data that you or others collect.

It is helpful for us to approach statistics as we would a second language. This orientation places more emphasis on practice than on proof and does not demand immediate fluency, focusing instead on a progressive understanding.

To use this text successfully, you will need a basic understanding of mathematical operations and algebra, a good inexpensive calculator, and a willingness to practice.

EXERCISES

1. How was statistics defined for this course? Why should you take a statistics course?
2. What are the three things you will need for this course?
3. Read the instructions that accompanied your pocket calculator and work through the examples provided. Learn to use the memory function.
4. Think about your day's activities, and list as many examples as you can of statistics that you have encountered.

5. Read and study Appendix 1 ("Brief Math–Algebra Review"). Use this material and your calculator to work Exercises 1–15 at the end of this appendix.

6. Review several recent news magazines or newspapers. Find examples of statistics that are of interest to you or may affect your life. Find two examples in each of the following areas: economics/finance, medicine/health, education, science/technology, and sports.

7. Review the reasons we offered for why you should study statistics. Which of the reasons do you find most appealing and why?

8. Go online on the Internet to Psychwatch.com or conduct an Internet search for "psychology news." Review the current psychology news stories. List five examples in different topic areas and indicate the statistics used in these examples.

9. How can knowing about statistics and research methods affect your ability to find employment in psychology-related areas? Go to Monster.com or some other job search site and search it for jobs in the behavioral sciences. Examine 10 jobs requiring a bachelor's degree in one of the behavioral sciences. Write a brief description of the job responsibilities, noting how statistics and/or research methods are involved.

DESCRIPTIVE STATISTICS

Our most common experience with statistics is descriptive. It is so common, in fact, that we usually don't think about the information we receive as "statistical." Descriptive statistics involves using indices, usually numerical, to summarize larger amounts of data so that they become easier to understand and digest. News reports are full of statistics. The weather forecaster on television may say that today's temperature is 67 °F, 10° lower than normal for this time of year. The sports pages of a newspaper are loaded with box scores, batting averages, strokes under par, and yards per rushing attempt. The business section gives us stock prices, the Dow Jones average, and the interest rates of T-bills.

A working knowledge of descriptive statistics is useful for two reasons. First, given the huge amount of statistical information we are exposed to each day, it is important that we be good consumers of statistics. It will help us properly interpret the wealth of statistical information around us. Second, at some point we are likely to be in the position of presenting statistical information, and we need to know which statistics are appropriate to use and how to determine them.

In this part of the book, we discuss several different kinds of descriptive statistics. In Chapter 3, we discuss how to organize data in a frequency distribution. A frequency distribution is a simple way to summarize a lot of numerical information in an orderly way; it also allows for the computation of other statistics such as the median. One common use of frequency distributions is to summarize scores on class exams. Scores are listed from highest to lowest, with the numbers of people scoring at each level indicated.

Chapter 4 deals with the graphing of data. Graphs give a pictorial representation of data. They are useful as a kind of snapshot of information. There are many different types of graphs, and there are rules for graphing as well. We discuss all these issues in the chapter.

Chapter 5 presents measures of central tendency—indices of the "center" or "most typical" score in a set of scores. If we were required to select one score that would be most representative of a set of scores, what would it be? Most people think of the average, or mean. There are others, however, such as the median and the mode. We discuss these statistics as well as the situations most appropriate for their use.

When we are describing our data, it is important to know not only the most typical score but also the "width," "spread," or dispersion of a set of scores. Distributions with the same measures of central tendency might differ greatly in the dispersion of the scores. In Chapter 6, we present several indices used to describe dispersion.

In Chapter 1, we introduced the metaphor of statistics as a second language. In terms of that metaphor, descriptive statistics are the vocabulary. They are the words and phrases of the language called statistics. Learning the vocabulary of statistics is a necessary first step before learning the inferential uses of statistics, just as learning the vocabulary of any language precedes learning the grammar and syntax. After completing Part 1, you will be a more sophisticated consumer of statistical information. You will also be better able to communicate with others using the language of statistics.

2

Definitions and Scaling

Do you prefer the routine and predictable? Do you value a life of security, comfort, and peacefulness? Or do you like excitement, change, and risk? Would you rather experience "life on the edge"? According to work initiated by Marvin Zuckerman in the 1970s, if you prefer excitement and change, you are considered a sensation seeker (SS). If you prefer predictability and security, you are considered a non–sensation seeker (non-SS).

A great deal of research has been performed on the concept of sensation seeking, including the development of a scale, known as the SS Scale, to measure it. Among other attributes, sensation seekers are hypothesized to have a low threshold for boredom; we expect them to be more easily bored than non–sensation seekers. If we wanted to investigate this hypothesis, we could have the students in our classes respond to the SS Scale and use their scores to divide the students into SS and non-SS groups. Based on our experience with the students in class, we could then categorize them into people who are "easily bored" and people who are "not easily bored." If our hypothesis is correct, we would expect more "easily bored" than "not easily bored" students to fall into the SS group and more "not easily bored" than "easily bored" students to fall into the non-SS group.

This is just one of several ways we might work with data and hypotheses about sensation seekers and non–sensation seekers. In this chapter, we introduce some of the terms that scientists and statisticians use when they design research, decide what kind of data they want to collect, and plan how they will organize the data that result from their studies. Although many terms will be introduced and defined throughout this book, some terms are so basic and pervasive that they need

11

to be identified at the outset. After defining these basic terms, we discuss the measurement scales that statisticians use to make sense of their data.

STATISTICS: SOME BASIC VOCABULARY

The terms that will be formally defined in this section are *variable* (*dependent* and *independent*), *population, parameter, sample, statistic,* and *sampling.*

Variable

A current edition of *Webster's Dictionary* says that a **variable** is anything that is likely to change, and synonyms include *changeable, inconstant,* and *fluctuating.* Thus, a variable is anything that can take on different values or amounts over a period of time. As scientists, we are interested in variables because it is through observing the ways things vary together that we can, for example, better describe personality traits, make sense of interactions between people, and build models of the world.

What are some things that vary? We could begin with the size of textbooks, the heights of students in a class, or the dosage of a given drug prescribed by a doctor to different patients. Blood pressure varies from person to person and within a person from time to time. The same is true for IQ scores. In psychology, there are many different types of variables—personality traits, reaction times, test scores, degree of extraversion versus introversion, hyperactivity in children, and galvanic skin response (a measure of the skin's electrical conductivity), to name just a few.

In experimental research, there are two important classes of variables. The **independent variable** is the variable that is controlled, or manipulated, by the researcher. The **dependent variable** is the variable that the researchers observe to see whether it changes as a result of changes in the independent variable. The dependent variable's scores or values *depend* on—or may vary because of—changes in the independent variable. In the behavioral sciences, the dependent variable is the measurement of an organism's behavior. In our colleague's experiment with the goggles (see Chapter 1), the goggles were the independent variable that was used to manipulate the students' visual systems. The time it took the students to adjust to the goggles was the dependent variable.

In a typical experiment, we might be interested in the effect of various drugs on driving ability. To study this, we might administer different drugs (the independent variable) to separate groups of people. Then we would measure driving ability (the dependent variable) by recording reaction time (the time it takes a person to react to a suddenly occurring stimulus) or the number of steering wheel adjustments in a simulated driving test.

Sometimes the independent variable isn't something that can be manipulated directly. In psychology, this is encountered most often when the independent variable of interest is an existing attribute of a person, such as gender, height, IQ, sensation seeking, or self-esteem. In these cases, people are typically assigned to groups representing different levels of the independent variable based on an assessment. The experimenter is thus manipulating the independent variable through group assignment or classification. We could compare males with females, short people with tall people, high IQ with low IQ, and so on. At the beginning of this chapter, we proposed selecting people high or low on a scale of sensation seeking (our independent variable) and comparing their tolerance for boredom (our dependent variable).

Population and Parameters

As psychologists studying sensation seeking, we are interested in more than just the level of boredom among SS and non-SS students in our classes. We would like our results to generalize to a broader group of individuals of whom our students are representative. We may want our findings to be applicable to all college students, to all adults in the United States and Canada, or to all students at a particular university. This group, which our subjects represent and to which we want to generalize, is called a population.

If pressed for a definition from everyday life, most of us would probably say that a population is a very large group of things, living or nonliving. Actually, this is not a bad definition except that we shouldn't put a size restriction on the term. Populations can be any size at all, from very large to very small. Thus, a **population** is a complete collection of anything, no matter what the size of the collection.

Even though populations may be small, most researchers are primarily interested in large populations. Specifically, they are often interested in **parameters,** numerical summary characteristics of populations. Consider the population consisting of all the students at your school. The average ACT or SAT score is an example of a population parameter. Unfortunately, it is usually too difficult, time consuming, and/or costly to measure large populations. If you want to know, for example, how many households in America watched a particular TV show last week, can you really afford to call or write them all to get the answer? If you want to know how much support a political candidate has nationwide, is it feasible to ask every voter? No, and for this reason most research relies on sample data.

Sample, Statistic, and Sampling

A **sample** is a portion or subset of the population, and a measurable characteristic of a sample is called a **statistic.** Again, think of the population of all the students at your school. Your statistics class is a sample, and the average ACT or SAT score in your class is a statistic. A major application of statistical procedures, such as those described in this text, is to use sample statistics to make inferences about populations and population parameters. From your sample of American households, you could make inferences about the popularity of a TV program, and from your sample of voters, you could make inferences about your candidate's chances of winning. (Making inferences is discussed in more detail later in this chapter.)

Sampling is the process of selecting a sample from the population. Although entire books have been written on the topic of sampling, here we will just briefly consider the most common sampling procedures.

If we intend to generalize the results from our sample to the population from which it came, we need to select a sample in such a way that it is **unbiased.** The sample should accurately reflect the population from which it came—be a kind of "scale model" of the population. A **biased** sample is one that is not representative of the population of interest.

A famous example of biased sampling occurred during the 1936 U.S. presidential election. The *Literary Digest* sent postcards to people selected from telephone directories and automobile registration lists, asking whether people would vote for Alf Landon or Franklin Delano Roosevelt. They received over 2.5 million responses, with the overwhelming majority preferring Landon. The *Literary Digest* went to press predicting Landon the winner. FDR won handily. The sample of voters was unrepresentative because it contained too many affluent people—voters who could afford telephones and automobiles during the Great Depression—relative to the U.S. population at the time.

One way to get a representative sample is with random sampling. **Random sampling** is a sampling method in which each member of the population theoretically has an equal chance of being selected into the sample. Random sampling is sometimes called **random and independent sampling** or just **independent sampling,** where *independent* means that picking one person or object for a sample has no effect on the probability of selecting another person or object. Random sampling is also **sampling with replacement,** which simply means that each individual selected from the population is returned to the population before the next selection. In **sampling without replacement,** each chosen individual is not returned to the population before the next selection.

Why is replacement necessary? Think about the definition of a random sample. If individuals are not replaced as they are drawn from the population, the probability of each later selection is increased because the population is decreased by 1 each time. For example, suppose we have a population of 1,000 individuals. The probability of selecting any one person for our sample is $\frac{1}{1000}$ before we make our selection, and if we replace that person, the probability continues to be $\frac{1}{1000}$. However, if the person is not replaced, the population no longer has 1,000 individuals and the probability of selecting a particular individual on the second selection is $\frac{1}{999}$. Obviously, if the population is large, replacement or nonreplacement will have little effect.

To illustrate random sampling, suppose we are interested in the population consisting of all full-time students at a university. Because of the size of the population, we decide to select a random sample of 100 students. For our sample to be truly random, each student must have an equal chance of being included; that is, we can't just go to the student union and select the first 100 students who walk through the door. It may be that some students never go to the student union, and the probability of their selection would be zero.

One way to obtain a random sample would be to put each student's name on a slip of paper, put all the slips into a big drum, and mix the slips thoroughly. Then we would select 100 names, one at a time, with replacement and remixing after each selection. An easier procedure would be to enter all the student ID numbers into a computer and then program the computer to select 100 numbers randomly with replacement.

Of course, even with completely random sampling, it is still remotely possible to obtain a nonrepresentative sample. Suppose the computer has randomly selected 100 students from the university. We convert the ID numbers to names and discover that 90 of the subjects are females even though we know that only 40% of the student body are women. If gender is not a factor in what we're studying, then the unrepresentative nature of our sample may be unimportant. However, if we're interested in height, experience playing football, or any of the myriad things on which we might reasonably expect males and females to differ, the unrepresentative sample may give us spurious results.

If we know in advance that different groups in the population differ in the characteristic we're interested in measuring, then **stratified random sampling** may be preferable to random sampling. Suppose we are interested in individuals under 5 feet 5 inches in height and we suspect that women are more likely to fit this description than men. If we want our sample results to truly reflect the population and we know that 40% of the student body are women, then we should specify in advance of sampling that our sample will contain 40 females. The 40 females are then randomly selected from the population of females. Thus, the population has been stratified into males and females, and within the strata random samples are taken.

SCALES OF MEASUREMENT

Statistics involves using tools to make sense of numbers (data). **Measurement** is the assignment of numbers or labels to objects or events. The rules that we use to assign numbers to objects or events are called **scales** or **scales of measurement.** The particular scale used often suggests the statistical tool we should employ.

There are four measurement scales we need to consider. In order of complexity from least to most, they are the nominal scale, the ordinal scale, the interval scale, and the ratio scale.

Before we consider the four measurement scales in detail, we can simplify our task by considering two basic types of data: measurement data and frequency data. Measurement data are derived by some kind of true measurement process. Examples are grades on a test, speed at answering a question, or scores on the ACT or SAT. By contrast, frequency data consist of counts, totals, or frequencies. Examples are the number of votes cast for each candidate in an election or the number of people in your class who like broccoli and the number who don't. As we will see, nominal scale data are generally frequency data, whereas ordinal, interval, and ratio scale data involve *at least some* form of measurement.

The Nominal Scale

The word *nominal* comes from the Latin word for "name," and a **nominal scale** does just that. It provides a name, or label, for different objects or events. If numbers are assigned in a nominal scale, they serve only to identify or classify, and it would make little sense to manipulate them mathematically. For example, the numbers assigned to horses before a race serve only to identify particular animals and tell us nothing about the order of finish in the race, the size of the horses, the amount of money each has won, or any other measurable characteristic. Nominal scaling is somewhat of a misnomer, as it does not locate items along some dimension but merely labels them. In this sense, it is not true measurement.

There is nothing inherent in nominal scales that requires that numbers be assigned. Examples of nominal scales that we are all familiar with are plentiful. Shirt manufacturers spend vast sums of money on advertising to ensure product differentiation, and we could probably assign our shirt wardrobe to categories such as Izod, Polo, Arrow, Sears, Guess, Salvation Army, and so on. Rat researchers in psychology may be interested in comparing rat strains, and the different strain names constitute another type of nominal scale. Again, nominal scales are used for identification purposes only.

We must be alert to the fact that numbers are commonly used in a nominal fashion. When they are, common arithmetic and statistical operations, such as computing an average (mean), are not appropriate. For example, the assignment of room numbers in a building is a use of a nominal scale. Suppose you have classes in rooms 103, 235, and 300. Is there any reason to compute your average room number? No, the only function of the numbers is a qualitative one: to identify a spatial location.

In the example at the beginning of the chapter, students were categorized into "easily bored" or "not easily bored." This is an example of a nominal scale. Other frequently encountered nominal data include gender, Social Security numbers, license plate numbers, and street addresses.

In trying to convey information using nominal scales, the best that can be accomplished is to count the frequency (number) of members or observations in each category. Thus, in terms of types of data, this information is *frequency data*. For example, we might count the number of girls and the number of boys in an elementary school class or the number of people voting yes or voting no on a piece of legislation. The numbers assigned by a nominal scale differentiate the objects or events that they categorize. Thus, room 103 is different from room 235, and horse 1 in a race is not the same as horse 5.

The Ordinal Scale

The numbers assigned by an **ordinal scale** not only serve to identify objects or events—that is, have a nominal function—they also tell us the **ranking,** or **rank ordering,** of each object or event. In other words, ordinal scale values tell us which object or event is greater than another. Although crude, these are measurement data.

Classifying our students into "easily bored" and "not easily bored" groups allows us to say which group is more easily bored. We could also produce a more detailed ordinal scale by ranking our students from most to least easily bored. Ben, who shuffles into class, finds a seat in the back of the room, and immediately falls asleep, would receive the lowest rank. Stephanie, who has laserlike intensity, sits in the front row, and even understands our jokes, would rank highest. The rest of our students would be ranked in between.

As another example of ordinal scale data, consider a race with 10 entrants. Their order of finish is an example of an ordinal scale in which the number 1 is assigned to the winner, 2 is given to the second-place finisher, and so on. Here the numbers tell us about the relative performance of the runners, with 1 performing better than 2, 2 better than 3, and so on; however, we don't know how much better or worse the performance of each was relative to the others. Although the numbers assigned are directly related to the time taken to complete the race and provide a rank ordering of the finishers, the ranks alone don't tell us how much better 1 was than 2. The ordinal scale doesn't give us this information.

The Interval Scale

The third type of scale is the **interval scale.** On an interval scale, each unit is assumed to be equal to each other unit on the scale. In psychology, scores on standardized tests, such as IQ, are examples of interval scales. The interval scale has the categorizing and ranking properties of the nominal and ordinal scales, respectively, and also has the property of having equal intervals between the scores. Data on this scale are true measurement data. Celsius and Fahrenheit temperature scales are examples of interval scales. Water at 50° Celsius is different from water at 25 °C (nominal): It has more of the characteristic (heat) being measured (ordinal) and is the same number of units from 25 °C as 25 °C is from 0 °C (interval). Unfortunately, we cannot say that 50 °C is twice as hot as 25 °C because the Celsius scale has an arbitrarily determined zero point, as does the Fahrenheit scale. Thus, 0° on either scale does not mean an absence of temperature. Zero on the Kelvin scale, however, does mean an absence of temperature. Figure 2-1 illustrates this point.

One position is that ratings should be used only to determine a ranking of the individual relative to other individuals; that is, that the level of measurement should be assumed to be at best an ordinal scale. The other position is that ratings—including such variables as unstandardized examination scores—have some interval properties. This information would be discarded in the process of converting ratings to rankings. Because throwing away information is generally a bad thing to do, we should assume that ratings represent interval-level measurement but be cautious with our interpretations. For example, we would not want to say that a student who gave a rating of 4 on a 5-point scale to the statement "I enjoyed this class" did in fact enjoy the class twice as much as a student who gave a rating of 2. We would also not want to say that a person who scored 100 on a history exam knew twice as much about history as another student who made 50 on the exam.

In this book, we will take the position that rating scales can cautiously be assumed to be interval-level measurement and recommend using common sense in

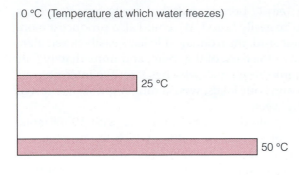

25 °C

50 °C

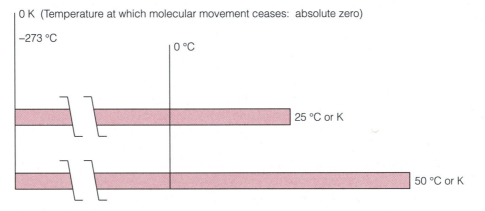

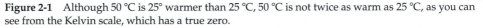

Figure 2-1   Although 50 °C is 25° warmer than 25 °C, 50 °C is not twice as warm as 25 °C, as you can see from the Kelvin scale, which has a true zero.

making interpretations. This position seems to be most consistent with how data from rating scales are frequently treated in the research literature in psychology and other behavioral sciences.

The Ratio Scale

The **ratio scale** has all the properties of the preceding scales in addition to having a true zero. Thus, data on this scale represent the highest level of true measurement. The Kelvin scale is a ratio scale. Other ratio scales specify time, length, height, and weight. Thus, it is meaningful to say that 2 hours is twice as long as 1 hour and that a person weighing 130 pounds is half as heavy as someone weighing 260 pounds. We are using the ratio scale in psychology when we measure the running speed of rats in a maze or the incidence of head banging in autistic children. In our example of sensation seeking and boredom, if we had measured the minutes and seconds it took for each of our students to become bored, we would have been using a ratio scale. Even though it is the most useful scale from a mathematical standpoint, examples of the ratio scale are hard to find outside the physical sciences. In fact, variables studied in the behavioral sciences often cannot be proved to have all the characteristics of interval scales.

The statistical tools introduced in this text are neutral concerning the origin of the numbers to which they are applied. It makes no difference to a statistic such as t whether the numbers to which it is applied come from an interval scale, a ratio scale, or even a nominal scale. The statistic can be used to manipulate the numbers, and an arithmetically correct answer will be obtained. The problem is one of interpretation; if we feed nonsense into an equation, we will get nonsense as the result. Thus, it is essential that we be aware of the type of data we have before we begin to compute statistics.

Remember that the type of data (frequency data vs. measurement data) limits the kind of arithmetic and statistical operations that may be performed meaningfully on the numbers. For example, summing and averaging are meaningless when performed on nominal (frequency) data, whereas most arithmetic operations are appropriate for interval data. Throughout the book, as we discuss each statistic, we will point out what type of data is necessary for proper computation and interpretation.

TWO BASIC USES OF STATISTICS

Statistics texts are often divided according to the two basic uses of statistics. You are certainly familiar with using statistics to describe data. This division of statistics is called, appropriately enough, **descriptive statistics.** When you compute your average test score in a course, you have computed a descriptive statistic. Most of the statistics we encounter daily—in the newspaper, for example—are descriptive statistics. Graphs also describe data and are another way to use descriptive statistics. Descriptive statistics can be used to describe numerically the variability in data.

It's often not enough just to describe data, however. A very important use of statistics for the scientific researcher involves making inferences from data. This branch of statistics is called **inferential statistics.** As an example of inferential statistics, imagine that you are interested in seeing whether the color of a toothpaste tube affects toothpaste preference. To test the effect of tube color, you ask 100 people to brush their teeth with a new toothpaste. Half receive the product packaged in a white tube; the other half brush with the same product from an orange tube. Afterward, the subjects are asked to rate their experiences on a scale from 1 to 10.

Suppose that the average rating assigned to toothpaste in the white tube is 8 and the average rating for toothpaste in the orange tube is 5. What does this difference mean? If you have collected good data by running this study correctly, you might infer that people prefer white tubes of toothpaste. Statistics that are used to draw conclusions about hypotheses are inferential statistics.

The purpose of inferential statistics is to allow us to draw conclusions, or inferences, about a larger group based on the results from some portion of it.

Another important thing that inferential statistics does for us is to tell us how certain—how accurate or confident—we are in the conclusions we draw. Several inferential techniques are discussed in Part 2 of this book.

SUMMARY

A variable is anything that may take on different values or amounts. The independent variable in an experiment is the variable manipulated and controlled by the experimenter to determine its effect on the dependent variable. In the behavioral sciences, the dependent variable is the measurement of behavior.

A population is a complete collection of anything, and a parameter is a numerical characteristic of the population. A sample is a subset of the population; a measurable characteristic of a sample is called a statistic. Sampling is the process of selecting a sample from the population. Random sampling is a method in which each member of the population has an equal chance of being selected. In stratified random sampling, the population is divided into relevant groups (strata), and then random samples are taken from each group.

Measurement is the assignment of numbers or labels to objects or events. A nominal scale assigns a name or label to different objects or events; that is, it provides identification and generally provides frequency data. Numbers assigned with an ordinal scale both identify and rank-order each object or event. Interval and ratio scales have all the properties of the ordinal scale in addition to providing equal intervals between scores. Finally, a ratio scale has a true zero point, in addition to the properties of an interval scale. Ordinal, interval, and ratio scales provide measurement data.

Descriptive statistics consists of tools used to describe or to illustrate data. Examples of descriptive statistics are averages and graphs. Inferential statistics permits us to draw conclusions with known certainty about a large group based on results from some subset of the group.

EXERCISES

1. Differentiate between each of the following pairs:
   a. independent and dependent variables
   b. population and sample
   c. parameter and statistic
   d. sampling with and without replacement
   e. descriptive and inferential statistics
2. Name the type of measurement scale that each of the following represents:
   a. Centigrade scale

    b. Kelvin scale

    c. room numbers

    d. the order of finish of contestants in a decathlon

    e. ratings of your college president's effectiveness

    f. scores on a sociology test

    g. blood pressure

    h. gender

3. As part of a study examining growth patterns, your task is to determine the average height and weight of all children in the fifth grade in your county. In planning your study, try to use as many of the terms (e.g., *sample, population, parameter*) and methods (e.g., *random sampling*) covered in this chapter as possible.

4. Briefly define the following:

    a. data

    b. random sampling

    c. variable

    d. sampling

    e. unbiased sample

5. Three groups of schoolchildren receive three different types of reading instruction for a school year. At the end of the year, student reading performance is measured. Identify the independent variable and the dependent variable in this study.

6. A researcher wants to examine the effects of alcohol intake on the driving ability of male college students. She equally and randomly assigns 30 volunteers to one of four treatment conditions: no alcohol, a low dose of alcohol, a moderate dose of alcohol, and a high dose of alcohol. Thirty minutes after the students ingest the appropriate substance, each student plays a video driving game in which the number of crashes is registered. Identify the independent variable and the dependent variable in this study.

7. In order to test the effectiveness of hypnotic analgesia, 10 deeply hypnotized volunteers are compared with 10 unhypnotized participants on the amount of time each person can hold his or her hand in a bucket of ice water. What are the dependent and independent variables in this experiment?

8. Consider the entire student enrollment of your college or university this semester (or quarter). Give an example of the circumstances under which this would be considered a population. When would it be considered a sample?

9. If your college enrollment is considered a sample, as in the previous question, is it a random or nonrandom sample?

10. A random sample drawn from a small town in Wyoming is used to produce an estimate of the percentage of the U.S. population that is Hispanic. How would you criticize this sampling procedure?

The Frequency Distribution

 Not long ago, a colleague posted the results of a class quiz on the bulletin board outside his office. The posting consisted simply of the students' codes (known only to them and the professor) and the points earned on the quiz. The posting looked like this:

Code	Score	Code	Score
BU	4	PU	8
JB	8	EZ	10
LC	10	JY	9
KS	9	TO	5
MD	2	AJ	9
BE	0	KO	8
IF	6	MM	3
OH	8	SS	4
IP	9	MT	2
XL	7	JR	1
PQ	7	TS	9
IS	6	JN	8
IT	6		

If you were a student in the class, what would you make of these data? Other than your own score, what information would you try to find out? You would probably look for the low and high scores and try to determine how your own score fell relative to those of your classmates. In other words, you would construct a crude distribution in your mind. Frequency distributions, the main topic of this chapter, are a more formal means of accomplishing this same task.

Frequency distributions are a simple way to organize and describe data. If we took the quiz scores and tried to organize them, we might first arrange them in descending order. In other words, it would be helpful to arrange them in order of value, listing them from the highest to the lowest. It would make just as much sense to list them from lowest to highest (ascending order), but by convention it is done the other way around. At any rate, after listing the scores from highest to lowest, we have the following:

X	X
10	7
10	6
9	6
9	6
9	5
9	4
9	4
8	3
8	2
8	2
8	1
8	0
7	

Note that at the top of each column of numbers is the capital letter X. The reason for this is that X is used in statistics to stand for (symbolize) a **score**. In this particular example, we have 25 Xs or scores, the highest being 10 and the lowest 0. This arrangement of scores is more informative than the previous one because we have now identified the highest and lowest values. We can also see the distance between the highest and the lowest scores, often referred to as the *range*.

However, we still have a problem with this arrangement of the 25 scores: It is too bulky and takes up too much space. How might we condense the data?

DEFINING THE FREQUENCY DISTRIBUTION

Looking at the scores, we see that two students received a perfect score of 10 on the quiz, five students earned a 9, five earned an 8, and so on. Instead of listing each score of 10 and each score of 9 and each score of 8, we can save space without losing any information if we list each different score only once and make a note beside it of how many times it occurred. This new arrangement, in which the scores are listed in order from highest to lowest and the number of times each score occurs is placed beside it, is known as a **frequency distribution.** A score's **frequency,** symbolized by f, is defined as the number of times the score occurs.

X (Score)	f (Frequency)
10	2
9	5
8	5
7	2
6	3
5	1
4	2
3	1
2	2
1	1
0	1

Using quiz data, we get the above frequency distribution. It is more informative than our original listing of scores because it allows us to tell at a glance the highest and lowest scores. In addition, we can readily see which scores occurred most frequently by referring to the numbers in the frequency column.

At this point, another example may help to clarify the construction of the frequency distribution. In a field experiment, 23 monkeys were observed over a 1-week period, and the number of times each engaged in threatening behavior toward another monkey was recorded. Thus, the scores indicate the number of incidents of threat for each monkey in the colony. The monkeys were observed for 30 minutes each day.

From the definition of the frequency distribution, we first arrange the scores in order numerically and then put beside them the number of times each score occurred. The result is as follows:

X	f	X	f
15	1	7	3
14	0	6	2
13	0	5	2
12	0	4	4
11	0	3	2
10	1	2	2
9	1	1	2
8	2	0	1

The highest incidence of aggression among the monkeys was a score of 15, and the lowest was a score of 0. Notice that in constructing the frequency distribution, we included the scores occurring with a frequency of 0. Although we could save even more space by omitting scores that have a frequency of 0, doing so would change the "look" of the distribution and convey a false impression to the casual observer. For example, all the categories between 15 and 10 have a frequency of 0, and we certainly could save space by leaving them out. However, to do so would result in a distribution that might appear to have less dispersion than it actually has. Furthermore, categories with a frequency of 0 often enter into calculations, as when we calculate percentiles, which are based on the frequency distribution. For these reasons, scores should be omitted from a frequency distribution only under very special circumstances.

---

⑤ CHECKING YOUR PROGRESS

For an additional exercise in constructing a frequency distribution, assume that the following numbers represent the number of trials required by each of 50 graduate students to learn a list of nonsense syllables:

> 22, 27, 9, 18, 9, 10, 21, 10, 19, 20, 7, 15, 8, 19, 25, 26, 20, 26, 18, 18, 12, 11, 26, 19, 23, 25, 19, 24, 17, 16, 24, 8, 23, 14, 14, 24, 18, 20, 17, 17, 20, 17, 21, 13, 16, 24, 13, 16, 21, 19

Construct a frequency distribution for these numbers.

See Box 3-1 for a description of a *grouped frequency distribution*.

Continuous Variables and Discrete Variables

A **continuous variable** is a variable whose measurement can take an infinite number of values. For example, time is a continuous variable; the passage of time may be broken into an infinite number of units. Between one minute and the next, we could subdivide the seconds into milliseconds (thousandths of a second) or even microseconds (millionths of a second). Weight is also a continuous variable. Suppose a student named Andrew weighs 122 pounds according to his scale. However, scales are very crude; his weight might really be 122.15 pounds or 122.1497 pounds or anything near that. The number of final decimal places is limited only by the accuracy of the machine. Gaps in the measurement of a continuous variable (the gap between 122 and 123 pounds, for example) are caused by the crudeness of our measurement and are *apparent* rather than *real*.

In addition to continuous variables, there are **discrete variables,** variables capable of assuming only specific numbers or values. Number of children in a family is a discrete variable, because only whole numbers are possible. Can you imagine

Box 3-1 The Grouped Frequency Distribution

One of the main purposes of constructing a frequency distribution is to get a clearer idea of what form or shape the distribution actually assumes. Knowing the shape of the distribution is an important part of summarizing our data. For example, we can look at the frequency column and tell which scores occur with the highest frequency and where the scores tail off—that is, have low frequencies. If we have a fairly large range of scores, however, it may be hard to discern any trend in the frequencies; that is, we may have difficulty seeing any bunching of the scores or any tailing off. In addition, listing each individual score may require an inordinately long column. One answer to these problems is to condense the data still further into a grouped frequency distribution.

In a **grouped frequency distribution,** the total range of scores is divided into a number of mutually exclusive (nonoverlapping) and collectively exhaustive (contiguous, or "touching") intervals. Each interval will contain the same number of score units (i.e., be the same width). To illustrate, let's consider a frequency distribution of the test scores made by a large number of students in an introductory psychology class.

At the end of the course, students in a large general psychology class are asked to define 50 commonly encountered terms in psychology. Each student receives a score indicating the number of correctly defined items. Here is the resulting frequency distribution:

X	f	X	f	X	f	X	f
45	2	37	5	29	11	21	2
44	3	36	6	28	13	20	3
43	2	35	4	27	8	19	0
42	4	34	7	26	7	18	1
41	3	33	7	25	3	17	1
40	5	32	8	24	6	16	0
39	6	31	10	23	1	15	2
38	3	30	9	22	0	14	1

Let's construct a grouped frequency distribution. To begin, we need to find i, the width of each class interval. We can determine the interval width, defined as the number of score units in the interval, by dividing the range of the distribution (R) by the number of class intervals (ci) desired. Suppose we want to have approximately 10 intervals (a useful rule of thumb is that a grouped frequency distribution should have between 10 and 15 class intervals).

$$i = \frac{R}{\text{number of ci's}} = \frac{45 - 14}{10} = \frac{31}{10} = 3.1$$

or 3 score units, rounding to the nearest odd integer, which we do to ensure whole numbers for interval midpoints.

Starting with the nearest multiple of i less than the lowest score in the data set (that multiple is 12), we add $i - 1$ to it, which gives us $12 + (i - 1) = 12 + (3 - 1) = 12 + 2 = 14$. Thus, the limits of the lowest interval are from 12 to 14, and the interval has three score units: 12, 13, and 14.

Continuing, we have 15 as the lower limit of the second lowest interval. Adding $i - 1$, or 2, to 15 gives the upper limit of the second interval, which is 17. The limits and frequencies for the complete grouped frequency distribution are as follows:

ci	f
45–47	2
42–44	9
39–41	14
36–38	14
33–35	18
30–32	27
27–29	32
24–26	16
21–23	3
18–20	4
15–17	3
12–14	1

Once the class intervals have been determined, we refer to the original frequency distribution to find the frequency for each interval. Thus, the class interval from 12 to 14 contains only a single score, 14, so there is a frequency of 1 for that interval. The same process is applied to all intervals, as shown in the f column.

Compared with the original frequency distribution, the shape and trends are easier to see. For example, we can see that more than half of the students scored between 27 and 35 and that there are fewer scores toward the low end of the distribution than toward the high end.

Despite the clearer picture of the distribution and despite the compactness of the grouped distribution, we have lost something by constructing it; we no longer know the exact location of each score. For this reason, in any problems involving the grouped frequency distribution, the assumption is typically made that all the scores in an interval are evenly spaced across it, which may or may not be true. Consider the interval from 33 to 35. There are three score values in the interval, which has a frequency of 18; even distribution requires six of each score value. If you look at the original frequency distribution, you will see that both 33 and 34 occurred 7 times and 35 occurred 4 times. Thus, in order to get a better overall picture of the distribution, we sacrifice some specific information about the original data.

a family with 2.16 kids? Answers on a true-or-false test are another example of discrete variables. You either miss a question or you don't, and fractional credit is impossible.

Real Limits and Apparent Limits

Let's consider the frequency distribution of a continuous variable such as weight, in which the scores are given as whole numbers. The scores are the initial weights of 50 anorexia patients enrolled in a weight-gain program.

X	f	X	f
115	1	104	2
114	0	103	3
113	1	102	5
112	2	101	7
111	2	100	2
110	2	99	1
109	3	98	1
108	2	97	0
107	4	96	2
106	4	95	2
105	3	94	1

Because the weights appear as whole numbers, there are really gaps between each of the scores in the distribution. For example, between the weights of 110 and 111, there are infinitely many possible values, if we had measured the weights more precisely. Although we have recorded two patients with weights of 110 pounds, one might really have weighed 110.4 and the other 110.3, 110.42 and 110.33, or 110.424 and 110.333, and so on.

The scores that we have listed, which have gaps between them, are called **apparent limits.** It is possible to construct a frequency distribution in which there are no gaps between the scores—one with **real limits,** in other words. In practice, real limits are obtained by subtracting a half *unit* from the apparent limit and adding a half *unit* to the apparent limit. The unit refers to the accuracy of our measurement, how we have rounded. In the frequency distribution we are considering, each score is given in whole numbers; each unit difference between scores is exactly 1 point. Thus, the real limits of the weight of 110 pounds are from 109.5 to 110.5 pounds (110 − 0.5, 110 + 0.5), and the entire frequency distribution could be rewritten accordingly.

The example we've considered was the simplest case, the one in which the scores are given as whole numbers. What happens if our initial number contains a fraction? The rule remains the same: Subtract a half unit and add a half unit. Only the unit has changed. For example, suppose that the weights were expressed in tenths at the outset. What would be the real limits for a weight of 110.5 pounds? The unit in this case is a tenth (0.1, expressed as a decimal) and a half of the unit is

(0.1)(0.5) = 0.05. Thus, the real limits of a weight of 110.5 pounds are 110.45 and 110.55 (110.5 − 0.05 = 110.45; 110.5 + 0.05 = 110.55).

---

⑤ CHECKING YOUR PROGRESS

Reconstruct the frequency distribution of the weights of the anorexic patients, using real limits rather than apparent limits. Assuming we have weighed the patients more accurately, what are the real limits of the following weights?

a. 102.473

b. 105.5525

c. 110.2

For the second part of the exercise, the answers are 102.4725 to 102.4735, 105.55245 to 105.55255, and 110.15 to 110.25.

PERCENTAGE OR RELATIVE FREQUENCY AND CUMULATIVE FREQUENCY DISTRIBUTIONS

So far, we have considered only the most basic of frequency distributions—distributions consisting of scores and their frequencies. However, it is often practical to have frequencies presented as percentages of the total sample and in cumulative fashion. **Percentage frequencies** are useful for comparing distributions that have unequal sample sizes. Let's look now at how a percentage frequency distribution (often called a relative frequency distribution) is obtained using the data from the distribution of quiz scores at the beginning of the chapter.

X	f	%age
10	2	8
9	5	20
8	5	20
7	2	8
6	3	12
5	1	4
4	2	8
3	1	4
2	2	8
1	1	4
0	1	4
	N = 25	100

Note that the frequencies have been summed and the result given as $N = 25$, where N stands for the sum of the frequencies, or the total sample size. (N comes from the word *number*, as in the number of observations.) One way to convert the frequencies into percentages is to divide them by N and then multiply by 100. We can state this procedure as a formula:

FORMULA 3-1   *Percentage from frequency*

$$\%age \text{ (percentage)} = \frac{f}{N}(100)$$

For example, 5 students had scores of 9 on the quiz. Using Formula 3-1, we find that the percentage is

$$\%age = \frac{f}{N}(100) = \frac{5}{25}(100) = (.2)100 = 20.$$

The other frequencies have also been converted and are listed in the distribution table.

The **cumulative frequency distribution** helps us interpret the frequency distribution and is useful in helping us find the median, a statistic discussed in Chapter 5. To construct the cumulative frequency distribution, we start with the distribution's lowest score and accumulate frequencies as we ascend. For any score, the cumulative frequency tells us the frequency of that particular score plus the sum of the frequencies of scores below the one we are considering. It may sound more complicated than it really is. An easy way to think about the cumulative frequency is to think of it as a *subtotal*. The subtotal is calculated at each frequency as we ascend. Let's examine a frequency distribution that's been converted into a cumulative frequency distribution. This has been done with our quiz data, and the result is as follows:

X	f	Cum f	Cum %age
10	2	25	100
9	5	23	92
8	5	18	72
7	2	13	52
6	3	11	44
5	1	8	32
4	2	7	28
3	1	5	20
2	2	4	16
1	1	2	8
0	1	1	4
	$N = 25$		

To construct the Cum f (cumulative frequency) column, we start with the frequency in the lowest interval, add to it the f in the next lowest interval, add to that the frequency in the third interval from the bottom, and so on, ending with 25, or the total sample size. What does Cum f tell us? Looking at the score of 5, for example, the Cum f of 8 tells us that 8 students had scores of 5 or less on the quiz. Thus, for any score, the Cum f tells us how many students achieved that score or a lower score on the quiz.

The cumulative percentages making up the **cumulative percentage distribution** are also shown. These were obtained in the same way as the percentage frequencies; that is, each Cum f was divided by N and the result multiplied by 100:

> **FORMULA 3-2** *Cumulative percentage from cumulative frequency*
>
> $$\text{Cum \%age (cumulative percentage)} = \frac{\text{Cum } f}{N}(100)$$

The Cum %age column indicates the percentage of scores that fall at or below a particular score. For example, 52% of the scores fall at or below a score of 7, and 92% fall at or below a score of 9.

↻ CHECKING YOUR PROGRESS

Using the distribution of monkey threat behavior, construct a percentage frequency distribution, a cumulative frequency distribution, and a cumulative percentage distribution. The frequency distribution is as follows:

X	f
15	1
14	0
13	0
12	0
11	0
10	1
9	1
8	2
7	3
6	2
5	2
4	4
3	2
2	2
1	2
0	1

To help you check your work: For the score of 7, the %age frequency is 13.04, Cum f = 18, and Cum %age = 78.26.

SUMMARY

The frequency distribution is a preliminary method for describing data. In this method, the scores (symbolized by the letter X) are ranked from highest to lowest, with the number of times each score occurs listed beside it. The number of times each score occurs is called its frequency (symbolized by the letter f).

A continuous variable is one whose measurement can assume an infinite number of values. Gaps in measuring a continuous variable are apparent rather than real, and we can close the gaps between scores on a continuous variable by subtracting a half unit from the score and adding a half unit to the score. Discrete variables are variables that are capable of assuming only specific numbers or values.

In addition to frequency distributions, we constructed percentage frequency and cumulative frequency as well as cumulative percentage distributions. In a percentage frequency distribution, frequencies for each interval are converted to percentages using the equation

$$\%age = \frac{f}{N}(100).$$

To construct the cumulative frequency distribution, we start with the frequency in the distribution's lowest interval, add to that the frequency in the next lowest interval to form subtotals, and continue to accumulate frequencies throughout the distribution. The equation

$$Cum\ \%age = \frac{Cum\ f}{N}(100)$$

is used to convert cumulative frequencies to percentages.

EXERCISES

1. Thirty-five soccer players were challenged to do as many sit-ups as possible in 2 minutes. Here are their scores:

37	48	29	50	13
34	47	29	40	16
27	45	25	38	18
28	33	20	35	14
23	15	18	33	38
50	11	16	25	40
44	12	13	20	14

    Use the data to construct frequency, cumulative frequency, percentage frequency, and cumulative percentage distributions.

2. Students in a speech class are given a test at the beginning of the semester that assigns a number representing their public speaking anxiety. Higher numbers

indicate greater anxiety. Use the scores to construct frequency, cumulative frequency, percentage frequency, and cumulative percentage distributions.

20	18	10	11
9	16	11	16
8	16	11	15
10	14	15	15
17	14	15	9
12	7	12	
12	7	11	

3. At the end of the semester, the students in the speech class are again given the public speaking anxiety instrument. Again, use the scores to construct frequency, cumulative frequency, percentage frequency, and cumulative percentage distributions. The reason there are fewer scores is that three students dropped the course.

3	13	5	6
14	13	4	4
7	9	12	9
7	9	11	8
11	8	11	9
12	8	9	

4. What are the real limits of each of the following?

   a. 7

   b. 15.55

   c. 23.828

   d. 5.63

5. Thirty-seven people got off a bus and were going into a diner when a car rounded a corner at a high rate of speed and smashed into the rear of the bus. As part of the accident report, each witness was asked independently to estimate the speed of the car before it struck the bus. Seven persons claimed they did not see the incident, and 30 people gave the following estimates:

35	40	28	40	60
25	45	30	40	55
55	37	45	35	50
40	50	40	38	45
70	30	40	30	48
25	30	35	32	37

Construct a frequency distribution, giving the real limits of each score. Also construct percentage frequency, cumulative frequency, and cumulative percentage distributions.

6. In a simple reaction-time test, a person tries to catch a ruler between thumb and forefinger after it has been released suddenly by another person. The following are scores generated with the test in a statistics class:

Females			Males		
5	13	7	5	5	9
9	9	9	6	6	6
2	5	6	8	8	6
9	7	10	4	6	6
7	11		7	3	

Construct separate frequency distributions for the females and males. Combine the scores and construct a frequency distribution for the class.

7. In an experiment on exercise physiology, the pulse rates of 30 male athletes are recorded before they jog a mile. Here are the pulse rates in beats per minute:

57	53	49	52	46
40	55	57	48	49
43	56	48	49	41
44	51	51	43	48
60	52	46	42	58
56	51	45	49	49

Construct a frequency distribution. Give the real limits for each score and a cumulative percentage distribution.

8. After jogging a mile, the pulse rates of the male athletes in Exercise 7 are as follows:

67	81	76	76	78
70	72	81	85	74
72	76	82	69	68
76	73	74	80	81
79	84	73	71	65
78	74	73	85	74

Construct a frequency distribution as in Exercise 7, and compare the distributions between the two exercises.

9. For Exercise 8, what is the Cum f for a pulse rate of 74? 80?

10. For Exercise 8, what is the Cum %age for a pulse rate of 72? 82?

11. Define the following terms:
    a. continuous variable (give two examples)
    b. frequency distribution
    c. discrete variable (give two examples)
    d. cumulative frequency

Graphing Data

Teresa, a coffee lover, picked up the student newspaper and was confronted with the headline "Coffee Prices Soar: Students Steam." The story went on to say that unseasonable temperatures in Brazil and other coffee-growing countries had resulted in a shortage of coffee beans. This produced a dramatic increase in wholesale coffee prices that was now being reflected in the price of a cup of coffee at the student union and coffee shops near the university. The newspaper had conducted a survey of per-cup coffee prices at local establishments, and the article included an impressive graph of the findings (see Figure 4-1). Shocked and depressed, Teresa decided that she would have to reduce her daily coffee consumption from seven cups to five cups.

In Chapter 3, we considered one preliminary way to describe data, the frequency distribution. In this chapter, we acknowledge the old adage that a picture is worth a thousand words and discuss graphing as a descriptive technique. We also discuss how some graphs—such as the coffee graph—are misleading and how they can be corrected.

Although there are many different types of graphs, in this text we consider only the ones most commonly used by behavioral scientists: the frequency polygon, the cumulative frequency polygon, the histogram, the bar graph, the stem-and-leaf plot, and the line graph. Let's begin with a look at some graphing conventions.

RULES FOR GRAPHING

A frequent criticism of statistics is that statistics can be used to mislead; that is, you can "lie" with statistics. Because it is certainly possible to misrepresent data

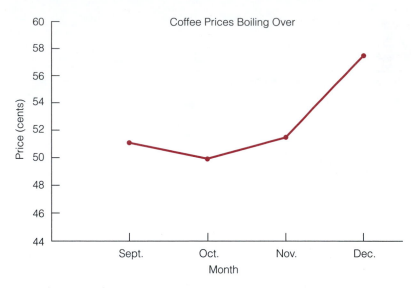

Figure 4-1 Coffee prices over a 4-month period.

graphically, in this section we present some graphing conventions designed to help prevent flagrant misrepresentation. The first convention concerns the relative lengths of the X axis (the horizontal axis, or the **abscissa**) and the Y axis (the vertical axis, or the **ordinate**). Specifically, the distance between the points on the axes should be chosen so that the Y axis is approximately three fourths as long as the X axis. This is sometimes called the three-quarters rule. Let's look at an example of what can happen when the three-quarters rule is violated.

A list of 10 nonsense syllables has been learned to the point at which it can be repeated without error. For each nonsense syllable on the list, the number of times it was given incorrectly before it was given correctly is recorded. We will plot the list position of the nonsense syllable (1–10) on the X axis and the number of incorrect trials until it was given correctly on the Y axis. The length of the Y axis will be varied to give different impressions of the data. The graphs are shown in Figure 4-2.

It is apparent that each graph in the figure creates a different impression. The middle portion of the curve in Figure 4-2c is greatly magnified by the expansion of the Y axis relative to the X axis, whereas just the opposite is true for Figure 4-2a. Figure 4-2b corresponds to the three-quarters rule.

Another type of misrepresentation can result when the values on the Y axis don't begin with 0 and when the units on the Y axis are very small and don't reflect reasonable variations in the data. Look at Figure 4-3a; it appears that the value of silver is plummeting. The graph in Figure 4-3b reveals a truer picture. Values on the Y axis generally should begin with 0. It is also apparent from the graph in Figure 4-3a that very small units on the Y axis maximize differences.

These types of misrepresentations can be seen in the graph of coffee prices in Figure 4-1. Using the three-quarters rule and starting the Y axis at 0 gives a very

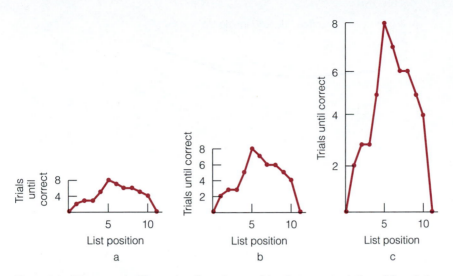

Figure 4-2 Three graphs illustrating distortion resulting from manipulation of the relative lengths of the X and Y axes. The middle graph conforms to the three-quarters rule. The graphs show, as a function of list position, the number of times the nonsense syllables were given incorrectly before they were given correctly.

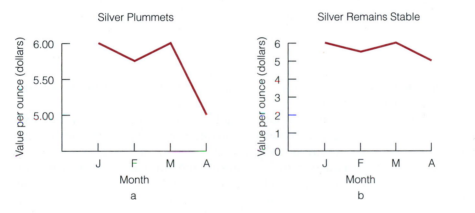

Figure 4-3 The price of silver, showing the effect of omitting 0 on the Y axis and using small units.

different picture. As can be seen in the properly constructed graph in Figure 4-4, retail coffee prices are "warming up," but they are hardly "boiling over."

THE FREQUENCY POLYGON

The frequency distribution, discussed in Chapter 3, is a useful way to organize data and show overall distribution. From it, we can get an idea of where the scores

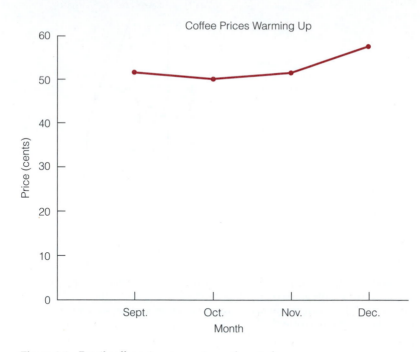

Figure 4-4 Retail coffee prices over a 4-month period.

are concentrated, readily see the highest and lowest scores, and tell where the scores are sparsely represented.

A graph of the frequency distribution—a **frequency polygon**—is even more useful in a descriptive sense. A frequency polygon is constructed by plotting the scores on the X axis and the frequency of each score along the Y axis. To illustrate, let's consider a frequency distribution of the number of repetitions required by 54 students to learn a list of nonsense syllables. The distribution is as follows:

X	f	X	f	X	f
33	1	24	5	15	1
32	1	23	4	14	1
31	1	22	4	13	1
30	1	21	3	12	0
29	1	20	3	11	1
28	2	19	2	10	1
27	3	18	2	9	2
26	4	17	2	8	1
25	5	16	1	7	1

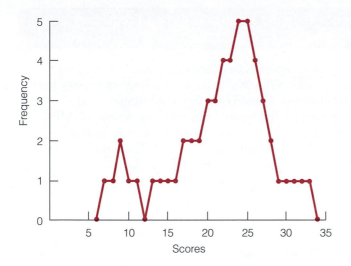

Figure 4-5 Frequency polygon based on the number of repetitions required to learn a list of nonsense syllables.

The frequency polygon depicting this distribution is shown in Figure 4-5. Examining the polygon, we can clearly see the trends in the data. The majority of scores pile up in the region of scores 24 and 25, and there is a longer tail of scores to the left side of the graph than to the right. By convention, the polygon begins and ends with a zero frequency score (see Figure 4-2 for another example).

Note that the axes of the graph have been labeled, with "Score" appearing below the X axis and "Frequency" to the left of the Y axis. It is not necessary to denote each possible score, and for this reason only selected ones have been labeled on the X axis. It is important that the axes be labeled appropriately; otherwise the graph will be meaningless. Of equal importance is the caption—in this case, "Figure 4-5 Frequency polygon. . . ." Each graph should have a caption that describes the graph and what it shows. Constructing a frequency polygon from a grouped frequency distribution is discussed in Box 4-1.

A Comparison of Distributions Using the Percentage or Relative Frequency Polygon

One of the most important uses of the frequency polygon is to compare the performance of different groups (or to compare different treatments on the same group). Suppose we are interested in the difference between introverts and extraverts in the number of friends they have. We might expect (we hypothesize) that extraverts will have more friends. To investigate this, we ask 90 people, 50 extraverts and 40 introverts, how many friends they have (assume that we couldn't find equal numbers of introverts and extraverts). The frequency distributions for extraverts and introverts are as follows:

Box 4-1   The Frequency Polygon From a Grouped Frequency Distribution

As you know from Box 3-1 in Chapter 3, frequency distributions may be based on grouped data. The only difference between the frequency polygon described in the last section and one based on a grouped frequency distribution is that for the latter we plot the frequencies over the *midpoints* (MPs) of the class intervals rather than over the scores themselves. For example, let's reconsider the grouped distribution from Chapter 3. The data are quiz scores made by students from a large introductory psychology class:

ci	MP	f
45–47	46	2
42–44	43	9
39–41	40	14
36–38	37	14
33–35	34	18
30–32	31	27
27–29	28	32
24–26	25	16
21–23	22	3
18–20	19	4
15–17	16	3
12–14	13	1

As you can see, the midpoint of each class interval is listed in the second column. The midpoint for any class interval can be found by adding $(i - 1)/2$ to the lower limit of the class interval. For example, consider the interval

	Extraverts				Introverts			
X	f	X	f	X	f	X	f
18	1	10	7	12	2	4	4
17	2	9	6	11	2	3	2
16	2	8	5	10	1	2	2
15	4	7	2	9	1	1	3
14	2	6	2	8	4	0	2
13	3	5	1	7	4		$N = 40$
12	6	4	1	6	7		
11	5	3	1	5	6		
			$N = 50$				

from 12 to 14. The interval width we used was $i = 3$, so $(i - 1)/2 = (3 - 1)/2$ $= 2/2 = 1$. Adding 1 to the lower limit of the interval gives us $12 + 1 = 13$, and this is the value shown.

The frequency polygon based on the grouped frequency distribution we have been considering is shown in Figure 4-6. As you will note, the primary difference between this figure and Figure 4-5 is that the X axis here is labeled "Midpoint of the class intervals" instead of "Score." The graph is plotted in the same way.

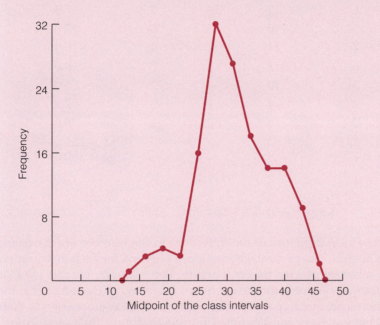

Figure 4-6 Frequency polygon based on a grouped frequency distribution of scores earned by students in an introductory psychology class.

Because there is a difference in the total N for the introverts and extraverts, we must use percentages instead of the actual frequencies. We should do this whenever we have unequal Ns in order to put groups on an equal basis. For example, what if we want to compare the number of extraverts and introverts who have eight friends? From the frequencies, it appears that more extraverts than introverts have eight friends (5 vs. 4). However, we sampled more extraverts than introverts. If we compare percentages, we see that exactly the same proportion (10%) of extraverts and introverts have eight friends.

You may recall from Chapter 3 that one way to convert each frequency into a percentage is to divide each frequency by N and then multiply by 100 (Formula 3-1). Using this procedure, we convert each of the frequencies to a percentage, with the following results:

Extraverts			Introverts		
X	f	%age	X	f	%age
18	1	2	12	2	5.0
17	2	4	11	2	5.0
16	2	4	10	1	2.5
15	4	8	9	1	2.5
14	2	4	8	4	10.0
13	3	6	7	4	10.0
12	6	12	6	7	17.5
11	5	10	5	6	15.0
10	7	14	4	4	10.0
9	6	12	3	2	5.0
8	5	10	2	2	5.0
7	2	4	1	3	7.5
6	2	4	0	2	5.0
5	1	2	$N = 40$	Total	_____
4	1	2		%age = 100.0	
3	1	2			

$N = 50$ Total   _____
%age = 100

Figure 4-7 gives a clear picture of the difference in the number of friends for introverts and extraverts. The percentage frequency polygon for each distribution is plotted on the same set of axes for comparison. For example, we can see that most of the distribution of scores for the introverts is shifted to the left of that for the extraverts. Therefore, our hypothesis that extraverts have more friends than introverts would appear to be substantiated by our findings, illustrated in Figure 4-7.

Shapes of Frequency Polygons

A frequency polygon can assume many shapes, but some are more common and therefore more interesting to us than others. The normal curve is one of the most interesting curves, both because of its properties and because so much of the data in the real world approximates it. Data we often assume to be almost normally distributed include IQ scores, heights, and weights.

The **normal curve** is defined by a mathematical equation that fixes its shape while leaving certain parameters—that is, the central point and the amount of spread about the central point—free to vary. The shape of the curve is symmetrical (the left half would fold precisely over the right half), and the tails never reach the baseline. The normal curve is often called the "bell-shaped curve." Of

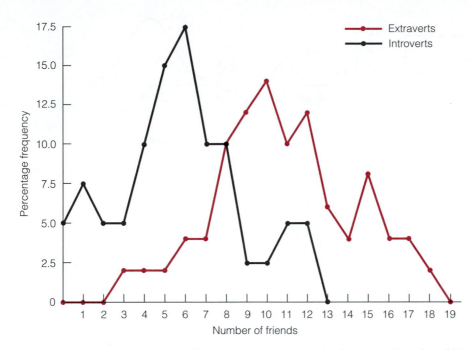

Figure 4-7   Percentage frequency polygon comparing introverts' and extraverts' number of friends.

course, many curves can be symmetrical without having the properties of the normal curve. Examples of symmetrical, nonnormal curves are shown in Figure 4-8 along with the normal curve.

Some curves that are not symmetrical are called skewed. A **skewed curve** is a curve in which a large number of scores are piled up at one end or the other, with a tail at the opposite end. If we consider the right side of the X axis to be positive (numbers increasing) and the left side to be negative (numbers decreasing), then a **positively skewed curve** is one that has its tail to the right, and a **negatively skewed curve** has its tail to the left of the X axis. Remember that the tail—not the end where the scores pile up—gives the direction of the skew. Examples of positively and negatively skewed curves are shown in Figure 4-9.

One real-life example of a negatively skewed distribution, at least from our experience, is the distribution based on the student ratings of faculty teaching performance. Most professors are given relatively high evaluations, and only a select few are rated as being very poor. Data based on ratio scales (e.g., time, speed, weight) are often positively skewed. This is because there is a smallest possible value (0), but there is no limit to how large the values may be. This often leads to scores clustering near the small values with a few large scores creating a long tail. Personal income in the United States is another example of a positively skewed distribution. The majority of people have incomes below $35,000, but a few individuals have eight- or nine-digit incomes. Human weights are an example of a normal distribution.

Figure 4-8   Examples of symmetrical curves. Curves a and b are nonnormal; curve c is normal.

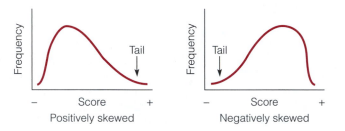

Figure 4-9   Examples of positively and negatively skewed curves.

THE CUMULATIVE FREQUENCY (OR CUMULATIVE PERCENTAGE) POLYGON

The shape of the polygon created from a cumulative frequency distribution is different from the polygon shapes we considered in previous sections. The old saying "What goes up must come down" is not true for the cumulative frequency polygon.

The **cumulative frequency curve,** or **cumulative frequency polygon,** shows the relative position of individuals in a distribution. For example, suppose 23 students in an honors class are given an IQ test, and the resulting frequency distribution of their scores is as follows (possible scores that were not actually observed, such as 169, 168, and so on, have been omitted to save space):

X	f	X	f
170	1	144	1
163	1	143	1
160	1	142	1
158	2	140	2
157	1	138	1
153	3	129	1
150	3	127	1
145	2	120	1

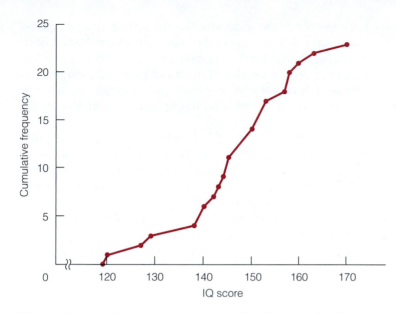

Figure 4-10 Cumulative frequency curve based on IQ scores of students in an honors class.

The cumulative frequency polygon is constructed by plotting the cumulative frequencies (or percentages) over the scores. The cumulative frequency distribution for the honors students is shown below, and Figure 4-10 depicts the resulting polygon.

X	f	Cum f
170	1	23
163	1	22
160	1	21
158	2	20
157	1	18
153	3	17
150	3	14
145	2	11
144	1	9
143	1	8
142	1	7
140	2	6
138	1	4
129	1	3
127	1	2
120	1	1

To see the relative performance of any individual on the IQ test, draw a vertical line from that person's score on the X axis up to the curve, and then draw a horizontal line from the curve across to the Y axis. The point where the horizontal line crosses the Y axis gives us an approximate idea of the number of individuals scoring at or below the score we are examining. For example, suppose we want to know the relative performance of a student who might have scored 155 on the IQ test.

First we draw a vertical line from a score of 155 on the X axis up to the point where the line intersects the curve. From this point we draw a horizontal line to the Y axis, where it intersects at a frequency of slightly more than 17. We conclude that approximately 17 persons had scores of 155 or lower and 6 persons had scores this high or higher. The procedure is shown in Figure 4-11.

We may also use the cumulative polygon to plot cumulative percentages. In the following distribution, the cumulative frequencies have been converted to cumulative percentages using Formula 3-2. The **cumulative percentage polygon** is plotted in Figure 4-12.

X	f	Cum f	Cum %age
170	1	23	100.00
163	1	22	95.65
160	1	21	91.30
158	2	20	86.96
157	1	18	78.26
153	3	17	73.91
150	3	14	60.87
145	2	11	47.83
144	1	9	39.13
143	1	8	34.78
142	1	7	30.43
140	2	6	26.09
138	1	4	17.39
129	1	3	13.04
127	1	2	8.70
120	1	1	4.35

The procedure for determining the relative location of a score in terms of the percentage of scores either above or below is precisely the same as that illustrated for the cumulative frequency polygon. For example, we could easily determine that someone with an IQ score of 155 is in approximately the 75th percentile of this particular distribution. This means that the person with an IQ score of 155 scored as well as, or better than, approximately three quarters of the class.

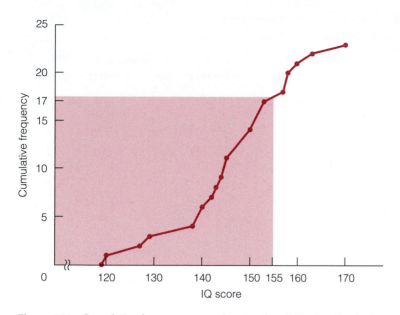

Figure 4-11 Cumulative frequency curve showing the relative location in the honors class of an individual with an IQ score of 155.

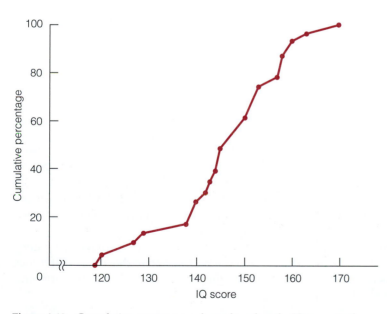

Figure 4-12 Cumulative percentage polygon based on the IQ scores in the honors class.

⟳ CHECKING YOUR PROGRESS

At a smoking clinic, each person fills out a questionnaire on smoking habits. The average number of cigarettes smoked per day for 60 people is shown in the following distribution:

X	f	X	f
60	1	26	3
55	2	25	5
53	2	24	2
50	3	23	5
47	1	20	10
45	2	18	3
40	3	15	2
35	4	12	1
30	5	11	1
28	3	10	2

Use the data to construct a frequency polygon, a cumulative frequency curve, and a cumulative percentage curve. If this is a representative sample, approximately what percentage of smokers smoke 20 or fewer cigarettes per day?

THE HISTOGRAM

Another way to graph a frequency distribution is with a histogram. In a **histogram,** a rectangular bar is drawn over each score value on the X axis, its height determined by the score's frequency. Each bar is centered above a particular score value and extends halfway between adjacent scores. A histogram based on the frequency distribution of the number of introverts with certain numbers of friends is shown in Figure 4-13.

If you compare the histogram in Figure 4-13 with the percentage frequency polygon for the introverts in Figure 4-7, you will see that the main difference between the two is that dots are plotted over the score values in the polygon and bars are used in the histogram.

⟳ CHECKING YOUR PROGRESS

Plot a histogram of the distribution of the extraverts' number of friends.

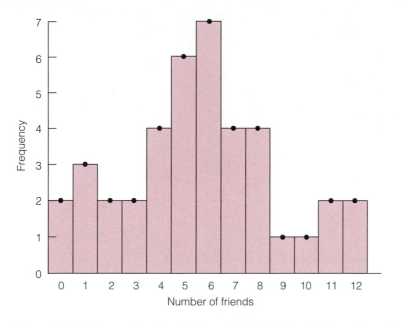

Figure 4-13 Histogram based on the frequency distribution of introverts' number of friends.

THE BAR GRAPH

The **bar graph** is a variation of the histogram used to graph nominal scale data. The scale along the X axis consists of labels that are used to identify types or categories, whereas the Y axis typically shows frequency counts or percentages in each of the categories. For example, suppose we go into a parking lot and count the number of cars falling into the categories Toyota, Mazda, Chevrolet, Ford, and so on. For each of the different categories (car manufacturers), we would have a frequency of occurrence. A bar graph could be used to show this information; that is, we would draw a bar over each category or label to indicate its frequency. The bar's width would be arbitrary, and each bar would be separated from its neighbors.

Suppose a traffic planner has determined the number of vehicles passing through five different intersections at a particular time of day. Although for identification purposes the planner may label the intersections 1, 2, 3, 4, and 5, the number assigned to any particular intersection is purely arbitrary; the planner might just as well use the street names for identification or call the intersections A through E. The data generated might be as follows: Intersection 1, 25; Intersection 2, 43; Intersection 3, 10; Intersection 4, 5; Intersection 5, 26.

The bar graph of these data is plotted in Figure 4-14. As you can see, the intersection number is shown on the X axis, and the number of vehicles (frequency) is shown on the Y axis. Also, we might have shown percentage or some other summary measure of frequencies on the Y axis. Instead of the bars touching and giving

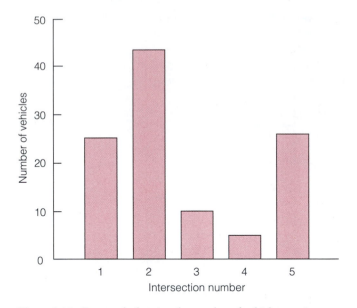

Figure 4-14   Bar graph showing the number of vehicles passing through particular intersections.

an impression of continuity, the rectangles are slightly separated. Like their width, the spacing of the bars is arbitrary.

Ꮛ CHECKING YOUR PROGRESS

In some classic research on the observational learning of aggression, psychologist Albert Bandura and his colleagues exposed children to five different models of aggression (live, film, cartoon, nonaggressive, and none). Later, the number of imitative aggressive responses made by each child was recorded. The average number of imitative responses in each condition was as follows: live model, 22; film model, 16; cartoon model, 12; nonaggressive model, 2; no model, 4. Construct a graph of these data. Label the X axis "Type of model" and the Y axis "Mean number of imitative aggressive responses."

THE STEM-AND-LEAF PLOT

Yet another way to organize and display data that has features of both a frequency distribution and a frequency histogram is to construct a **stem-and-leaf plot.** To create the display, we split each score into two parts: a stem and a leaf. The first one or two digits constitute the stem, and the last digit is the leaf. For example, a score of 91 would have a stem of 9 and a leaf of 1. Similarly, X = 153 would have a stem of 15 and a leaf of 3. Let's look at some data and actually construct a stem-and-leaf plot.

As part of a high school physical education class, the pulse rates of 30 male students were recorded before they jogged a mile. The data were as follows:

75	68	77	69	90	70
72	102	78	97	83	77
83	75	81	68	90	72
95	73	80	110	98	105
65	74	75	95	85	87

To construct a stem-and-leaf plot, the first step is to list all the different stems, from lowest to highest. In this case, the lowest pulse is in the 60s and the highest is 110. Thus, the stems are the numbers 6 through 11, and our list is

Stems

6
7
8
9
10
11

The next step is to draw a vertical line to the right of the column of stems. Then we go through the list of scores, one at a time, and put each leaf beside its stem. Starting at the left, the first score is 75; its leaf (5) is placed beside its stem (7). We continue this procedure through all the scores. The completed stem-and-leaf display is as follows:

Stem-and-Leaf Display of Student Pulse Rates

Stems	Leaves
6	5 8 9 8
7	5 2 5 3 4 7 8 5 0 7 2
8	3 1 3 0 7 5
9	5 5 0 7 0 8
10	2 5
11	0

In actuality, the stem-and-leaf display shown is a histogram in which each stem represents an interval of 10 scores. If we rotate the display so the stems become scores on the X axis of a graph, the result is a histogram with digits rather than bars over the scores. The beauty of the stem-and-leaf plot is that it is easily constructed; it has features of both a grouped frequency distribution (see Box 3-1) and a histogram; and no information is lost (i.e., we still know the exact location of each score). Here is the rotated stem-and-leaf display based on the male pulse rates:

```
        2
        7
        0
        5
        8                               Leaves
        7   5   8
        4   7   0
    8   3   0   7
    9   5   3   0
    8   2   1   5   5
    5   5   3   5   2   0

    6   7   8   9   10  11              Stems
```

ॐ CHECKING YOUR PROGRESS

Construct a stem-and-leaf plot of the male pulse rate data after exercise. The data are as follows:

85	97	110	85	128
85	95	135	80	135
91	93	125	93	120
110	100	110	97	117
125	105	115	97	118
130	80	107	110	110

Comparing Groups With the Stem-and-Leaf Plot

Another useful feature of the stem-and-leaf plot is that it can be modified to provide a graphical comparison of two groups of data. Consider the following example: Suppose that the pulse rates from the 30 students in the previous example were actually from males and females, as shown next.

Females			Males		
75	68	77	69	90	70
72	102	78	97	83	77
83	75	81	68	90	72
95	73	80	110	98	105
65	74	75	95	85	87

The first step in constructing the stem-and-leaf comparison plot is the same as before—list all the different stems from lowest to highest. Next we draw a vertical line on each side of the column of stems. Then we put the name of one group on the left side and the name of the other group on the right side, as shown here.

Females	Stems	Males
	6	
	7	
	8	
	9	
	10	
	11	

The final step is to construct the stem-and-leaf plot using the data for each group on the different sides of the stems. The only difference is that for the group on the left, the leaves accumulate to the left.

Stem-and-Leaf Display Comparing Male and Female Pulse Rates

Females	Stems	Males
5 8	6	9 8
5 4 3 5 8 2 7 5	7	0 7 2
0 1 3	8	3 5 7
5	9	0 7 0 8 5
2	10	5
	11	0

We can see that in this group of students, males and females have a different distribution of pulse rates. Males have higher pulse rates, mostly in the 80s and 90s, whereas the rates of the females are mostly in the 70s. This illustrates how the stem-and-leaf display can be modified to provide an easy way to compare groups.

THE LINE GRAPH

All of the graphs discussed to this point have been based on the frequency distribution. Although frequency polygons, cumulative frequency curves, histograms, and bar graphs are very useful in a descriptive sense, they are not the only types of graphs employed by behavioral scientists. The line graph is another type of graph often encountered on which numerical information is displayed graphically.

With the **line graph,** an independent variable is recorded on the X axis, and some measure of the dependent variable is given on the Y axis. Often the Y-axis variable has undergone some preliminary analysis before being graphed; that is, average (or mean) scores may be used instead of individual scores or frequencies of occurrence. Also, the independent or X-axis variable is assumed to be continuous, and for this reason a line is used to connect the plotted points. A common misuse of the line graph occurs when discontinuous or qualitative (nominal scale) variables, such as gender or ethnicity, are displayed on the X axis of a line graph. In these cases, lines are used to connect values of a variable that cannot meaningfully be displayed on a continuous dimension.

For example, suppose we have collected data on the average number of friends of male and female introverts and extraverts. We might try presenting the data in a line graph, such as that shown in Figure 4-15. However, this is an incorrect presentation because it implies a continuous dimension connecting males and females. In this example, males and females are categories. A more appropriate presentation would be the bar graph shown in Figure 4-16.

One of the most common uses of the line graph is to show the development of some type of behavior over time. For example, the development of learning in an organism may be shown by a line graph in which a measure of the amount of practice (time, trials, etc.) is given on the X axis and a measure of performance or behavior (number correct, percentage of correct responses, number of errors, average anxiety rating, speed of performance, etc.) is shown on the Y axis.

Let's illustrate with a specific example. In one experiment, rats were trained to press a lever to receive a food reward. The animals were trained to barpress on a variable interval schedule in which they received rewards on the average of every 30 seconds; that is, they followed a VI 30-s reinforcement schedule. The development of their performance is shown in Figure 4-17, where the average number of rewards is noted on the Y axis and the day of testing is shown on the X axis. Each day's training session was 20 minutes.

As you can see from the graph, the performance of the animals improved over the first 4 days of testing; that is, their average number of reinforcements increased each day. Performance on the last 3 days of testing was essentially stable.

The line graph is also useful for comparing two or more groups, as this next example illustrates. To study experimenter bias, 20 students are divided into two

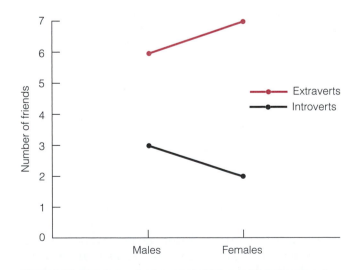

Figure 4-15   A misuse of a line graph. Males and females are not a continuous dimension. Compare to Figure 4-16.

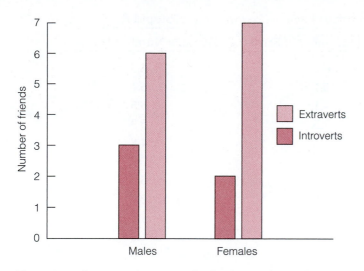

Figure 4-16   An appropriate way to display data on the number of friends of male and female extraverts and introverts. Compare to Figure 4-15.

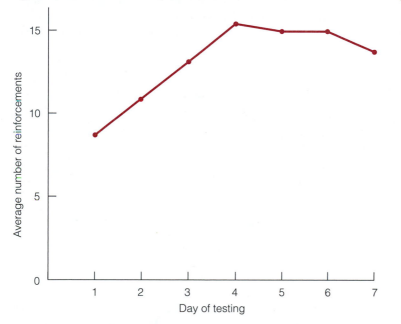

Figure 4-17   Line graph showing the average number of reinforcements per day of testing on a VI 30-s schedule.

groups of 10 students each, and each student is given a rat. One group of students is told that their rats are very bright; the other group is informed that their animals are stupid. Each of the 20 students then trains her or his rat on a simple task and records the number of daily errors. The average number of errors per day is computed for the "smart rat" group and for the "stupid rat" group. Here are the results:

	"Smart Rats"	"Stupid Rats"
Day	Average Number of Errors	Average Number of Errors
1	6.2	6.5
2	5.1	6.1
3	4.1	5.5
4	2.5	5.3
5	1.5	4.8
6	0	3.9
7	0	3.5
8	0	2.9
9	0	1.8
10	0	1.3
11	0	0

Figure 4-18 reveals that the "smart rats" improved much more rapidly than the "stupid rats." (Note that the lines go *down* because the number of errors is recorded on the Y axis.) Incidentally, in reality there was no difference in the intelligence of the rats. The only difference was in the instructions given to the students.

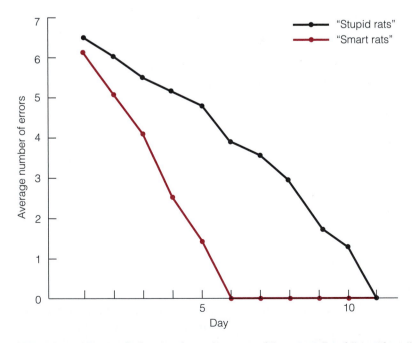

Figure 4-18   Line graph showing the performance of "smart rats" and "stupid rats" over days of training.

There are inferential statistical techniques that will allow us to decide whether or not students who trained "smart rats" came from the same population as students who trained "stupid rats."

☙ CHECKING YOUR PROGRESS

Suppose five students have learned a list of 10 nonsense syllables to the point at which they can recite the list without error. The average number of errors per repetition before learning was perfected has been determined and is as follows:

Repetition	Average Errors
1	9.6
2	7.2
3	6.1
4	5.8
5	5.2
6	4.4
7	3.5
8	2.1
9	2.3
10	1.3
11	1.1
12	0.6
13	0.0

Use the line graph to show the average number of errors per repetition.

SUMMARY

In this chapter, we have studied graphing conventions and a variety of types of graphs. One graphing convention that helps prevent misrepresentation of data is making the length of the Y axis approximately three quarters as long as the X axis. Another graphing "rule" is to have values on the Y axis begin with 0 and reflect reasonable increments in the data. This helps avoid misleading graphs.

The first type of graph introduced was the frequency polygon. To construct a frequency polygon from a frequency distribution, we list the scores across the X axis and give the frequencies on the Y axis. Each point plotted on the graph shows the frequency of a given score.

The frequency polygon is useful for comparing frequency distributions on the same set of axes. However, if the distributions to be compared have unequal Ns, then frequencies must be converted to percentages before the graph is plotted. The resulting curve is called the percentage or relative frequency polygon.

Some commonly encountered shapes of frequency polygons were described. One very important curve is the normal, or bell-shaped, curve. Nonnormal curves with tails pulled either toward the right side or toward the left side of the X axis are called skewed curves. Positively skewed curves have a tail (relatively few scores) toward the positive, or right, side of the X axis, whereas negatively skewed curves have a tail toward the negative, or left, side of the X axis.

The cumulative frequency polygon and cumulative percentage polygon were constructed by plotting the cumulative frequencies or percentages over the scores. The cumulative frequency for a score tells the total number of scores up to and including the score itself.

A frequency distribution may also be graphed with a histogram. In the histogram, a rectangular bar is drawn over each score on the X axis, with frequency of the score determined by the height of the bar. The bar graph is a variation of the histogram used to show nominal scale data. In nominal scale data, the scale along the X axis consists of labels rather than amounts of something, and the bars are separated from their neighbors.

Data can also be organized and displayed with a stem-and-leaf plot, a technique having features of both a frequency distribution and a frequency histogram. In the stem-and-leaf plot, each score is split into two parts called the stem and the leaf. The first digit(s) of the score is the stem, and the last digit(s) is the leaf; for example, for the number 85, 8 is the stem and 5 is the leaf. To construct the display, we list the stems from lowest to highest and draw a vertical line to the right of the list. Going through the scores one at a time, we then place each leaf to the right of its stem. The stem-and-leaf display results in a histogram in which each stem represents an interval of 10 scores, although other convenient intervals can be used. The advantage of a stem-and-leaf display is that no information is lost, and such a display can be modified easily to allow group comparisons.

In a line graph, an independent variable is plotted on the X axis and some measure of the dependent variable is plotted on the Y axis. Because the independent variable is assumed to be continuous, a line is used to connect the plotted points.

EXERCISES

1. Construct a frequency polygon from the following scores:

   10, 7, 12, 8, 10, 9, 10, 10, 8, 9, 11, 10, 9, 7, 8, 6, 11, 9

2. As part of the annual study of course demands at the university, the registrar computes the average number of credit hours in the natural sciences (chemistry, biology, geology, etc.) that various majors take during the academic year. The registrar discovers that in 1996, engineering majors enrolled for an aver-

age of 15 hours of natural sciences; business majors, 3 hours; psychology majors, 6 hours; and education majors, 4 hours. Construct a bar graph to represent these data.

3. Some students in an English class have been asked to unscramble 25 sentences in 10 minutes. From the frequency distribution of their scores—the number of sentences correctly unscrambled—construct a frequency polygon, a cumulative frequency polygon, a cumulative percentage polygon, and a histogram. Be sure to label your axes and to add the appropriate caption.

X	f	X	f
22	1	12	3
21	1	11	3
20	1	10	4
19	0	9	2
18	2	8	2
17	1	7	2
16	1	6	1
15	3	5	2
14	4	4	1
13	5	3	1

4. On a recent 50-point quiz, 30 educational psychology students obtained the scores presented in the following frequency distribution:

X	f	X	f	X	f
46	1	38	1	30	1
45	2	37	3	29	0
44	0	36	2	28	1
43	2	35	0	27	1
42	1	34	1	26	0
41	3	33	3	25	1
40	1	32	1	24	0
39	2	31	2	23	1

Use the frequency distribution to plot a frequency polygon, a cumulative frequency polygon, and a histogram. Tell whether the frequency polygon is skewed in appearance, and if so, in which direction.

5. As part of a class project, students surveyed classmates about their fast-food preferences. Of 90 students surveyed, the preferences were as follows: pizza, 17; hamburgers, 39; hot dogs, 12; tacos, 22. Construct a graph from these data.

6. In a study of book-carrying style of schoolchildren, at least four different styles were noted and the percentages of each sex using a particular style recorded.

The percentages were as follows:

Style	Male %	Female %
1 (side carry)	80	15
2 (front carry)	20	35
3 (both hands)	0	15
4 (balanced on hip)	0	35

Use the appropriate graph to illustrate these data.

7. Briefly define the following terms:

   a. positively skewed curve

   b. symmetrical curve

   c. negatively skewed curve

8. For each of the following graphs, define or describe the conditions under which it is used and give an example of a situation in which it would be appropriate:

   a. stem-and-leaf plot   c. bar graph

   b. histogram   d. line graph

9. What two graphing conventions are often employed to help prevent misrepresentation of data?

10. Twenty art history majors were given a list of 200 art-related words to identify. Construct a stem-and-leaf plot of the number of words each student correctly identified.

98	100	105	97	128
155	152	107	123	135
141	145	133	125	107
103	95	148	140	127

11. Use the following data from Chapter 3, Exercise 1 (35 soccer players doing as many sit-ups as possible in 2 minutes) to construct a stem-and-leaf plot that organizes the scores:

37	48	29	50	13
34	47	29	40	16
27	45	25	38	18
28	33	20	35	14
23	15	18	33	38
50	11	16	25	40
44	12	13	20	14

12. Using the data from Exercise 11, assume that the first 15 players (data in rows 1–3) are rookies. Construct a comparison stem-and-leaf plot that compares sit-up performance between rookies and more experienced players. Comment on any differences or similarities between the two displays.

13. Blood samples are drawn from a large number of young adult males and females before a study of the effects of relaxation training on HDL (high density lipoprotein, the "good" kind) cholesterol. HDL values are given here. Use the appropriate graphing technique to compare males and females.

Females				Males			
X	f	X	f	X	f	X	f
75	1	62	6	60	1	47	3
74	1	61	4	59	0	46	4
73	0	60	3	58	1	45	4
72	0	59	1	57	2	44	3
71	1	58	1	56	1	43	2
70	2	57	1	55	2	42	2
69	2	56	0	54	3	41	1
68	2	55	1	53	4	40	0
67	2	54	1	52	5	39	0
66	4	53	2	51	5	38	1
65	3	52	1	50	7	37	1
64	3	51	1	49	2	36	2
63	5	50	1	48	1	35	1

14. Students in a philosophy class are given 10-point pop quizzes on three consecutive class days, and the frequency distributions of their scores are given here. Plot a frequency polygon for each distribution, and tell whether the curve is symmetrical, positively skewed, or negatively skewed.

Monday		Wednesday		Friday	
X	f	X	f	X	f
10	3	10	1	10	1
9	6	9	2	9	1
8	5	8	2	8	1
7	5	7	3	7	2
6	4	6	4	6	2
5	3	5	7	5	3
4	2	4	4	4	4
3	2	3	2	3	5
2	1	2	3	2	6
1	1	1	2	1	5
0	1	0	1	0	2

15. Using the information in Exercise 14, for each day, what is the cumulative frequency of a student with a score of 8 on the quiz? What is the percentage frequency? What is the cumulative percentage?

Note: Exercises 16–20 are based on the assumption that if you can construct misleading graphs, you will be better able to recognize them and be sensitized and cautious about conclusions drawn from such graphs.

16. A sociological study was conducted to investigate the effect of police foot patrols on crime. Three similar metropolitan areas were selected, and the number of daily on-foot police patrols were varied in the three areas over a 15-week test period. The number of crimes reported during the period was the outcome measure of interest.

Area	Number of Foot Patrols	Crimes
A	No patrols	500
B	10 patrols	490
C	20 patrols	480

Construct a misleading bar graph showing that increasing foot patrols really "takes a bite out of crime." (Hint: Scale your Y axis from 470 to 500.)

17. Use the data in the previous exercise to construct a graph that correctly reflects the effect of patrols on crime rate. Based on the graph in this problem, what is your conclusion from the data? Use a caption that describes this graph according to your conclusion.

18. Construct two graphs for the following data, one showing that state government spending has been stable and the other showing that it has substantially increased.

Month	Amount	Month	Amount
January	$304,000	May	$305,000
February	302,000	June	307,000
March	303,000	July	309,000
April	306,000	August	311,000

19. The following data are total sales for salespersons at a national computer supply company. Construct three graphs: (a) one showing that all employees are performing at a high level, (b) one showing that all are performing poorly, and (c) one showing that Charlie should be fired.

Charlie	$86,000	Matthew	$88,100
Hanna	87,200	Ray	90,000
Noland	89,800	McNair	90,100

20. Review popular newspapers, magazines, or Web sites. Collect three examples of correctly constructed graphs. Collect three examples of misleading graphs, excluding stock, bond, and financial indices that are published daily. Why are the graphs you selected misleading?

5

Measures of Central Tendency

 Incumbent Governor Jones was locked in a hard-fought and very close election race with two challengers, candidate Smith and candidate Harris. Both challengers were emphasizing the severe economic woes of the state, particularly as they affected middle- and lower-income families. Candidate Smith asserted that the median annual family income for the state was $17,500, which was insufficient to support an acceptable quality of life. Candidate Harris took an even more negative view; he pointed out that the modal annual family income was $15,000. Governor Jones, on the other hand, pointed to an unprecedented level of prosperity for families. He argued that the average family income was over $25,000, a level more than sufficient for a good quality of life.

Is one of the candidates lying? Are the candidates using different data from which to draw their conclusions? As you can see from Figure 5-1, the answer to both questions is no. All three candidates are looking at the same data, but they are selecting different indices to represent the "typical" family. Thus, they are coming to equally correct but very different conclusions.

The argument among candidates Smith, Jones, and Harris centers around a difference of opinion about which index of income best represents the typical family. (Of course, each candidate is also using the value that best supports his position!) Harris argues that the mode is best, Smith prefers the median, and Jones counters that the mean is the preferred index.

In our use of statistics, both professionally and in our everyday lives, we regularly encounter indices in the form of median income, batting averages, modal type of house or car, and so forth. Similarly, we are often asked to summarize a set of scores with a single index that represents the "center," the "most typical," or the "average." If we wanted a single number to convey as much information as

63

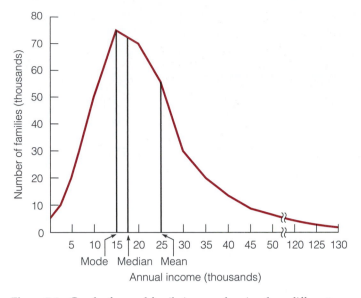

Figure 5-1   Graph of annual family income showing three different "averages."

possible about a distribution of scores, what number should we choose? In other words, what single score is most typical or representative of an entire distribution of scores? We would probably select a score near the middle or center of the distribution; that is, we would locate a measure of central tendency in the data. **Central tendency** refers to the tendency of scores in a distribution to be concentrated near the middle of the distribution.

The measures of central tendency that will be discussed in this chapter are the arithmetic mean, the median, and the mode. Each of these measures is a kind of average. (The election race example illustrated all three indices.) Of the different averages, the one that is probably the most familiar is the arithmetic average, or mean. The mean is frequently encountered in everyday life. For example, we might hear a weather report stating that the average maximum daily temperature for the month of July was 91 °F or predicting that rainfall in August will be below average, meaning below the arithmetic mean for previous years. Similarly, you are probably interested in your mean test score in a class or your overall grade point average. As you may notice from these examples, the mean is particularly useful for summarizing interval or ratio data.

Another type of average, the mode, or most frequently occurring score or category, is also encountered often. For example, we may read or hear that the subfield of psychology receiving the most graduate school applications is clinical psychology. If we sell cars, it may be valuable for us to know that the most commonly requested body style is a four-door sedan. If we're politicians, it may be important to know that the average, or modal, education level in the state is the 12th grade, which means that more voters have that level of education than any other. The mode is a particularly useful measure of central tendency for nominal scale or categorical data, although it can be found for any data.

The median, although encountered less often than the mean and mode (or perhaps more often misidentified and confused with the arithmetic mean), is nonetheless important. While watching a gymnastics meet, we might hear that a gymnast has received a median rating of 9.9 on a 10-point scale for an outstanding session on the uneven bars. Thus, 9.9 is the rating in the middle of the judges' scores; half the judges' ratings are below 9.9, and half are above 9.9. On a 4-point scale, the median grade point average of a group of students might be 2.5, with 2.5 being the score in the middle (50% above and 50% below) of the distribution. The median talent rating for a group of talent show contestants might be 8.5. The median is especially useful for summarizing rank order or ordinal scale data, although it can be used with interval or ratio scale data as well.

Let's begin our discussion of the measures of central tendency with the one that is easiest to determine—the mode.

THE MODE

The mode is the simplest of the measures of central tendency to locate; unfortunately, it is the least useful for further statistical purposes. The mode is not based on any manipulation of the original data; its determination does not require any measurement scale property of the data. The **mode** (*Mo*) is the most frequently occurring score in a frequency distribution. To determine its value, we have only to look down the column of frequencies to see which frequency is the largest and then look across to find the score that has this frequency.

The following frequency distributions, first presented in Chapter 4, give the number of friends of a group of extraverts and a group of introverts:

Extraverts				Introverts			
X	*f*	*X*	*f*	*X*	*f*	*X*	*f*
18	1	10	7	12	2	4	4
17	2	9	6	11	2	3	2
16	2	8	5	10	1	2	2
15	4	7	2	9	1	1	3
14	2	6	2	8	4	0	2
13	3	5	1	7	4		$N = 40$
12	6	4	1	6	7		$Mo = 6$, score
11	5	3	1	5	6		with the highest
			$N = 50$				frequency

$Mo = 10$, score with the highest frequency

To determine the value of the mode for these distributions, we first look down the frequency column to find the highest value. Looking across from this value to the

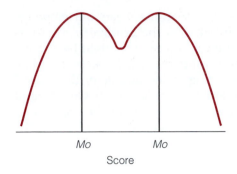

Figure 5-2   A bimodal, symmetrical distribution.

score column, we see that the mode for extraverts is 10, and the mode for introverts is 6. Thus, more extraverts had 10 friends than any other number of friends, and more introverts had 6 friends.

Unfortunately, as mentioned earlier, once we have determined the mode, there is little we can do with it beyond reporting it, because we can't use it for any further statistical purposes (such as estimation). In addition, we may not be able to decide on only one value for it; that is, our data may contain more than one score with identical high frequencies. A distribution with two modes is said to be **bimodal,** and we report both values. The authors have occasionally obtained bimodal distributions of test scores in courses we have taught; that is, some students knew the material and did well but an equal number hadn't learned the material and did poorly. A bimodal, symmetrical distribution is shown in Figure 5-2. It is also possible, although rare, to obtain distributions with three or more modes. These distributions are said to be multimodal.

Yet another disadvantage of the mode is that it is determined only by the frequency of one particular score. No other scores in the distribution are included in the determination. This makes the mode vulnerable to vagaries and variations in the sample, especially if the sample is small. A measure based on all the scores would be more useful because it would have greater stability from one sample to another drawn from a population. When we say that the mode is unstable, we mean that if we take a large number of samples from a known population and determine the mean, median, and mode for each sample, the mode will vary more than the mean or median among samples.

THE MEDIAN

The **median** (*Md*) is a point along the score scale that separates the top 50% of the scores from the bottom 50%; it is the score value at the 50th percentile. A **percentile** is the score at or below which a given percentage of the scores lie. In other words, the 50th percentile, or the median, is a point above which half the scores lie and below which half lie. The determination of the median requires that we be able to *order* our data—that the data be at least an ordinal scale of measurement. The median is often easier to determine than the mean, or arithmetic average. Although not as useful for further statistical procedures as the mean, the median is at times the best descriptive measure of central tendency. We will come back to this last statement after we have looked at some ways to compute the median.

Locating the Median by the Counting Method: Even Number of Scores

In a frequency distribution or an array of scores ranked from highest to lowest, the median is the middle score value. This means that in a frequency distribution with an even number of scores, the median will be a number halfway between the two scores in the middle of the distribution. For example, if there are 10 scores, the median will be halfway between the two "middle scores," the 5th and 6th scores; there are 4 scores above the 6th score and 4 scores below the 5th score.

Score No.	1	2	3	4	5	6	7	8	9	10

4 scores   *Md*   4 scores

The position of the median in a frequency distribution with an even number of scores may be determined as follows:

Md = score halfway between the $(N/2)$th score and the $(N/2)$th + 1 score.

To illustrate, if you have 26 scores, the median will be between the $(N/2)$th, or $26/2 = 13$th score and the $(N/2)$th + 1, or $13 + 1 = 14$th score. However, don't forget: This procedure is designed to tell you the *location* of the median—not its value.

Let's look at some data and actually determine the median. In a study of problem solving, we have measured the number of "brainteasers" correctly solved in 10 minutes by a group of 20 students. The scores are 2, 0, 6, 5, 5, 2, 1, 7, 4, 3, 4, 6, 4, 3, 2, 0, 4, 1, 3, and 6. We want to find the median score. The first step is to arrange the scores into a standard frequency distribution:

X	f	Cum f
7	1	20
6	3	19
5	2	16
4	4	14
3	3	10
2	3	7
1	2	4
0	2	2
	$N = 20$	

We also have constructed the Cum *f* column. This column counts up the scores in order, thus determining the *positions* of the scores. For example, the 2 at the bottom of the Cum *f* column indicates that the score of 0 is in the 1st and 2nd positions in the frequency distribution. The 4 above that indicates that the 3rd and 4th scores are both 1s, and so on. Remember that the frequency for a given score tells how many positions are occupied by that score. For example, the score of 4 has a frequency of 4 and thus occupies the 11th through the 14th positions in the distribution.

Because there are 20 scores in the distribution,

$$Md = \text{score halfway between the } (N/2)\text{th and the } (N/2)\text{th} + 1 \text{ scores.}$$

$$\frac{N}{2} = \frac{20}{2} = 10\text{th score} = 3$$

$$\frac{N}{2} + 1 = 10 + 1 = 11\text{th score} = 4$$

Thus, the median is the score halfway between 3 and 4, and

$$Md = \frac{3 + 4}{2} = \frac{7}{2} = 3.5.$$

This means that a median of 3.5 brainteasers were correctly solved in 10 minutes.

Let's look at another example. Suppose we have recorded the high temperature each day during the month of February in a town in Maine. We want to know the median temperature for the month. The data are as follows (each of the scores is a temperature in degrees Celsius):

X	f	Cum f
3	1	28
2	0	27
1	0	27
0	2	27
−1	2	25
−2	3	23
−3	1	20
−4	3	19
−5	2	16
−6	1	14
−7	4	13
−8	2	9
−9	0	7
−10	2	7
−11	2	5
−12	2	3
−13	0	1
−14	1	1
	N = 28	

Because there are 28 scores,

Md = score halfway between the $(N/2)$th score and the $(N/2)$th + 1 score.

$$\frac{N}{2} = \frac{28}{2} = 14\text{th score} = -6$$

$$\frac{N}{2} + 1 = 14 + 1 = 15\text{th score} = -5$$

$$Md = \frac{(-6) + (-5)}{2} = \frac{-11}{2} = -5.5$$

Thus, the median temperature during February was $-5.5\,°C$.

⟳ Checking Your Progress

A police officer monitors the speed of automobiles passing through a school zone during school hours. In a 15-minute period, the officer records the following speeds for 36 automobiles:

X	f	X	f
33	1	23	0
32	1	22	4
31	1	21	2
30	0	20	3
29	2	19	2
28	0	18	3
27	3	17	1
26	5	16	1
25	0	15	1
24	5	14	1

Find the median.

Answer: Md = 23. The median speed was 23 mph.

Locating the Median by the Counting Method: Odd Number of Scores

Now let's look at what happens when N is an odd number. Actually this is an easier situation because we need only locate the one score in the middle of the distribution. For example, if there are 9 scores, we locate the 5th score (the one with 4 scores below it and 4 above) and report this as the median. If we have 49 scores, the median will be the 25th score (24 scores below and 24 above).

The *location* of the median may be determined by computing

$$\frac{N + 1}{2}.$$

Thus, if we have 65 scores, the median will be the

$$\frac{65 + 1}{2} = \frac{66}{2} = 33\text{rd score.}$$

Consider the following example. Twenty-five students have rated a sociology professor on a 10-point scale that assesses how well prepared the professor's lectures are. The results are as follows:

X	f	Cum f
10	3	25
9	4	22
8	6	18
7	5	12
6	3	7
5	2	4
4	1	2
3	1	1
	N = 25	

Because there are 25 scores, the median will be the $(25 + 1)/2 = 26/2 = 13$th score. In the Cum f column, we see that there are 12 scores of 7 or less and 18 scores of 8 or less. This tells us that the 13th through the 18th scores are all 8, and so the median is 8. Thus, the sociology professor has been given a median score of 8.

For another example, let's look at the scores of 59 professional golfers on the last day of a tournament. The distribution is as follows:

X	f	Cum f
80	1	59
79	0	58
78	2	58
77	2	56
76	0	54
75	3	54
74	4	51
73	5	47
72	6	42
71	9	36
70	8	27
69	6	19

(cont.)

X	f	Cum f
68	6	13
67	4	7
66	2	3
65	1	1
	N = 59	

Because there are 59 scores, the median will be the $(59 + 1)/2 = 60/2 = 30$th score. From the Cum f column, we see that there are 27 scores of 70 or less. The next 9 scores are all 71; that is, the 28th through the 36th scores are all the same. The 30th score, or median, is 71 according to the counting method.

---

⑤ CHECKING YOUR PROGRESS

A clinical psychologist specializing in behavior therapy has used systematic desensitization to treat 21 patients for removal of phobic symptoms. In systematic desensitization, the patient is first taught how to relax. Next, a fear hierarchy is constructed in which the patient ranks fearful situations relevant to the phobia. For example, if the patient has a snake phobia, the most feared situation might be handling a live snake; the second most fearful event might be handling a dead snake; and the least feared occurrence might be to encounter a garden hose coiled in the grass. After the fear hierarchy is developed and the patient learns relaxation techniques, the two are combined; the patient is asked to imagine each of the feared situations beginning with the least feared while maintaining relaxation.

The therapist has recorded the number of sessions required by each patient to achieve symptomatic relief. Unfortunately, 4 patients showed no progress after 20 sessions and were assigned an arbitrary score of 25. The data are as follows:

Number of Sessions	f	Number of Sessions	f
25	4	6	1
14	1	5	1
12	2	3	1
11	1	4	1
10	3		
9	4		
8	2		

Determine the median by the counting method.

Answer: Md = 10. A median of 10 sessions was required to achieve relief.

Before proceeding, let's summarize the steps involved in finding the median in an array of scores and in a frequency distribution by the counting method:

1. Arrange the scores into a frequency distribution if they are not already so arranged.
2. Compute N and see if it is odd or even.
3. If N is even, the median will be halfway between the two scores in the middle, which we locate by looking at the Cum f column. The *location* of the median will be halfway between the $(N/2)$th score and the $(N/2)$th + 1 score.
4. If there is an odd number of scores, the median is the one in the middle, again found by looking at the Cum f column. The *location* of the median is determined by finding the $[(N + 1)/2]$th score.

THE MEAN, OR ARITHMETIC AVERAGE

The mean, or arithmetic average, is a value that most people have been exposed to since elementary school. The **mean** is the sum of the scores in a distribution divided by the number of scores. The symbol for the mean of a sample is $\overline{X}$ (read "ex-bar"), and the definitional formula is:

FORMULA 5-1   *Mean*

$$\overline{X} = \frac{\Sigma X}{N}$$

If you have all the values for a population, you use μ instead of $\overline{X}$:

$$\mu = \frac{\Sigma X}{N}.$$

As you know, Σ (capital Greek letter sigma) means to add or sum everything following it, in this case all the Xs, or scores. For example, if the Xs were 5, 3, and 2, then ΣX, or the sum of X, would be $5 + 3 + 2 = 10$. N is the number of scores, or Xs, that are summed. In this example, $N = 3$ and $\overline{X} = 10/3 = 3.33$.

Formula 5-1 assumes a distribution in which the frequency of each score is 1. However, suppose we have the following quiz scores of 25 students: 6, 5, 5, 10, 9, 8, 0, 2, 4, 7, 7, 6, 5, 6, 6, 7, 9, 9, 8, 6, 6, 5, 2, 7, 5. We could certainly find the mean by using Formula 5-1, but this would involve adding all 25 scores to obtain $\Sigma X = 150$, from which we could then get $\overline{X} = 150/25 = 6$. With this number of scores, it would make more sense to put the data into a frequency distribution:

X	f
10	1
9	3

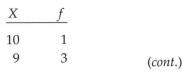

(cont.)

X	f
8	2
7	4
6	6
5	5
4	1
3	0
2	2
1	0
0	1
	$N = 25$

To find the mean for a frequency distribution, we use the following formula:

FORMULA 5-2 *Mean for a frequency distribution*

$$\overline{X} = \frac{\Sigma fX}{N}$$

Again, if you have all the values for a population, you use μ rather than $\overline{X}$.

The first step in computing the mean (or any other statistic) should always be to write the formula and look at it for a moment to see what it tells us to compute. In this case, the numerator tells us first to multiply each score (X) by its frequency (f) and then to sum the result (ΣfX). These operations give the following results:

X	f	fX
10	1	10
9	3	27
8	2	16
7	4	28
6	6	36
5	5	25
4	1	4
3	0	0
2	2	4
1	0	0
0	1	0
	$N = 25$	$\Sigma fX = 150$

The denominator of the formula is N, which is the total number of students in the class, or the total number of scores. In the case of the frequency distribution, N is the sum of the numbers in the f column. In this case, the total is 25.

Why does the formula require us to multiply each score by its frequency? Why couldn't we just sum the Xs and divide by N? Look at the distribution again. Was there just one student with a quiz score of 9? No, there were three students with that score. To find an average, we sum *all* the scores in a distribution before dividing by N, and to sum all the scores in a frequency distribution, we must first multiply each score by its frequency.

To find ΣfX, we need a column labeled fX that we can sum. Again, the values in the column are produced by multiplying each score by its frequency. Adding the values in this column results in the number 150.

The final step is to plug the values we have determined for N and ΣfX into Formula 5-2:

$$\overline{X} = \frac{\Sigma fX}{N} = \frac{150}{25} = 6.$$

The mean quiz score for the 25 students is 6.

↻ CHECKING YOUR PROGRESS

Suppose we have determined the digit span (number of digits that can be held in memory for a brief time period) in thirty-seven 4-year-olds. What is the mean digit span for our sample?

X	f
6	2
5	7
4	17
3	5
2	3
1	2
0	1

Answer: $\overline{X}$ = 3.73. The mean number of digits the 4-year-olds can hold in memory is 3.73.

Rounding Conventions

In the preceding "Checking Your Progress," you should have gotten $\overline{X}$ = 138/37 = 3.7297297. It would be quite tedious to list all digits after the decimal for each computation. Thus, we need to consider some rounding conventions. How should decimal fractions be rounded off? Should they be rounded to hundredths or tenths or not at all? If we do need to round, what rules should we use to make a rounding decision?

Rule 1: The convention adopted in this text is to round all final answers to hundredths. Thus, we will carry out computations to at least three decimal places before deciding to increase the digit in the hundredths place or to leave it alone in our final answer.

Rule 2: If we're doing a series of operations, less inaccuracy will be introduced in our final answer if we round *only* the final answer. A corollary to this rule is: Learn to use your calculator's memory function.

Rule 3: In all preliminary calculations leading up to the final answer, maintain at least three decimal places. Thus, these calculations should be rounded to the nearest thousandth.

Rule 4: In rounding the final answer, if the digit in the thousandths place is less than 5, drop it and everything that follows it. For example, if we have the number 88.764623, the number in the thousandths place (4) is less than 5, so drop it and everything that follows it. In other words, 88.764623 rounds to 88.76.

Rule 5: In rounding the final answer, if the number in the thousandths place is 5 or greater, round the preceding digit up and drop the following numbers. For example, the number 8.335221 rounds to 8.34 because the number in the thousandths place is 5.

The Mean as a Balancing Point

The mean is often called the balancing point in the distribution. In a distribution of scores, some scores have values greater than the mean and others have values below the mean. Thus, scores in the distribution differ from the mean either positively or negatively—and, of course, some may be equal to it. If we sum all the positive and negative differences from the mean (the difference between each score and the mean is symbolized by $X - \overline{X}$), the result will be 0. In statistics, differences from a standard or reference value (in this case, the mean) are known as **deviations.** This deviation—the deviation of each score from the mean—is an important concept that will remain with us through later chapters.

The reason the sum of the deviations of the scores from the mean is 0 and the reason the mean is called the balancing point in the distribution is that the sum of the positive deviations is exactly equal to the sum of the negative deviations. Symbolically, this property of the mean is expressed as

$$\Sigma(X - \overline{X}) = 0.$$

To illustrate the property, let's consider the following example. Nine students have been given 10 problems to solve, each requiring some creative ability. The number of problems solved in a 20-minute period is recorded, and the frequency distribution of the scores and the computation of the mean are as follows:

X	f	fX
10	1	10
8	2	16
7	1	7
6	1	6
5	1	5
4	1	4
3	2	6
	$N = 9$	$\Sigma fX = 54$

$$\overline{X} = \frac{\Sigma fX}{N} = \frac{54}{9} = 6$$

Imagine that the problems solved are objects placed on a seesaw. Their weights are determined by how far from the mean they are placed (Figure 5-3). As you can see, the score of 7 is 1 unit above the mean and has been given the weight of +1. There are two scores of 8, which are located 2 units above the mean and have been given the combined weight of +4. Also above the mean is the score of 10, which is 4 units from the mean and has been given the weight of +4. The four scores above the mean have a combined weight of $1 + 2 + 2 + 4 = +9$.

Because the score of 5 is 1 unit to the left of (below) the mean, it has been assigned a weight of −1; the score of 4 is 2 units below the mean and has the weight of −2; and the two scores of 3 are 3 units below the mean and together have been assigned a weight of −6. The sum of the weights below the mean is $(-1) + (-2) + (-3) + (-3) = -9$. Adding the weights above and below the mean yields $(+9) + (-9) = 0$. Thus, we see that the weights above the mean exactly equal the weights below the mean, and the mean is the balancing point for this and any other distribution.

Earlier we said that this property of the mean could be expressed symbolically as $\Sigma(X - \overline{X}) = 0$, or, by extension, $\Sigma f(X - \overline{X}) = 0$ for a frequency distribution in which the frequencies are different from 1. Let's demonstrate this now:

X	f	$X - \overline{X}$	$f(X - \overline{X})$
10	1	+4	+4
8	2	+2	+4
7	1	+1	+1
6	1	0	0
5	1	−1	−1
4	1	−2	−2
3	2	−3	−6
			$\Sigma f(X - \overline{X}) = 0$

The mean is still 6, and in the column labeled $X - \overline{X}$, the mean has been subtracted from each score and the appropriate sign retained. In the next column,

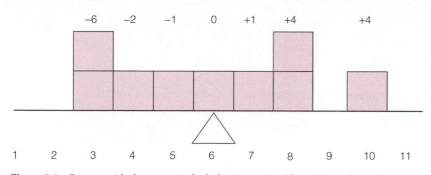

Figure 5-3 Seesaw with the mean as the balancing point. The weights above the mean exactly balance the weights below the mean.

labeled $f(X - \overline{X})$, each deviation is multiplied by its frequency. Summing this last column, we see that the sum of the deviations about the mean is indeed equal to 0. It is important to keep this property of the mean in mind when we talk in the next chapter about ways of determining the amount of variability (or deviation) in a distribution. Box 5-1 presents techniques for determining the measures of central tendency from a grouped frequency distribution.

Box 5-1   Determining the Measures of Central Tendency From a Grouped Frequency Distribution

In Box 3-1, we introduced the grouped frequency distribution as a technique for condensing data when you have a broad range of scores, and in Box 4-1 we showed how you can plot a frequency polygon from a grouped frequency distribution. In this box, we will detail how to find the mode, median, and mean from such a distribution.

Suppose we have given a test to 83 students to assess their interest toward current events. The test consists of 60 items taken from a weekly news magazine, and each student is asked to indicate interest in the item. The score for each student is the number of items marked "no interest." The grouped frequency distribution of the results is as follows:

ci	MP	f
40–44	42	4
35–39	37	5
30–34	32	11
25–29	27	18
20–24	22	7
15–19	17	11
10–14	12	13
5–9	7	14

(continued)

Box 5-1 (*continued*)

Finding the Mode

In a grouped frequency distribution, we will define the mode as the **midpoint** of the class interval with the highest frequency. As we did with the ungrouped distribution, we first find the highest frequency, which is 18 scores in the class interval from 25 to 29. Then, the mode is the midpoint of that interval, or, for this example, the $Mo = 27$. The most frequently occurring number of items marked "no interest" was 27.

Finding the Median

The method we will use for finding the median from a grouped frequency distribution is called the **interpolation** method. To find the median, we first locate the class interval containing it and then interpolate to find its exact location. The grouped distribution is repeated next, with the real limits and the Cum f added.

ci	Real Limits	f	Cum f
40–44	39.5–44.5	4	83
35–39	34.5–39.5	5	79
30–34	29.5–34.5	11	74
25–29	24.5–29.5	18	63
20–24	19.5–24.5	7	45
15–19	14.5–19.5	11	38
10–14	9.5–14.5	13	27
5–9	4.5–9.5	14	14
		$N = 83$	

To find the interval containing the median, we divide the total N by 2, giving $N/2 = 83/2 = 41.5$. From the Cum f column, we see that there are 38 scores of 19 or less and 45 scores of 24 or less; thus, the 41.5th score must be in the interval from 20 to 24 (real limits are 19.5–24.5, applying the rule to subtract a half unit from the lower limit and to add a half unit to the upper limit). To find the exact location of the 41.5th score within the interval, we apply the following formula:

$$Md = LRL + i\left(\frac{N/2 - Cum\,f}{f}\right),$$

where LRL = lower real limit of the score containing the $(N/2)$th case,

i = the width of the class intervals, or
the upper limit − the lower limit + 1,

Cum f = cumulative frequency in the interval below the one
containing the $(N/2)$th case, and

f = frequency in the interval containing the $(N/2)$th case.

For our specific example,

$$Md = 19.5 + 5\left(\frac{41.5 - 38}{7}\right) = 19.5 + 5\left(\frac{3.5}{7}\right)$$

$$= 19.5 + 5(.5) = 19.5 + 2.5 = 22.$$

The median number of items marked "no interest" is 22.

Finding the Mean

As in finding the mode, to find the mean, we use the midpoint of each class interval for X. Then, we apply the equation for the mean, which is Formula 5-2, or

$$\overline{X} = \frac{\Sigma fX}{N}.$$

ci	MP	f	fX
40−44	42	4	168
35−39	37	5	185
30−34	32	11	352
25−29	27	18	486
20−24	22	7	154
15−19	17	11	187
10−14	12	13	156
5−9	7	14	98
		$N =$ 83	$\Sigma fX =$ 1,786

$$\overline{X} = \frac{\Sigma fX}{N} = \frac{1,786}{83} = 21.52$$

Thus, the average number of items marked "no interest" is 21.52.

COMPARING MEASURES OF CENTRAL TENDENCY

As the example at the beginning of the chapter illustrates, the three measures of central tendency can have markedly different values and therefore lead to very different conclusions from the same data. Thus, it is important to understand when the use of each index is appropriate and what advantages or limitations are associated with each.

When to Use the Mode   The mode is the measure of choice in three instances: when we need the quickest possible estimate of the central tendency in the data, when we want to report the score obtained by the largest number of subjects, or when we have nominal scale or categorical data, so the computation of a median or mean is not appropriate, and yet we want to report a summarizing statistic. Thus, the mode is a good descriptive measure, but it is not used in inferential procedures. It is useful as a rough estimate of the mean and the median, and it can be used as a rough check of how accurately these latter statistics were computed.

When to Use the Median   The median is a very useful statistic and should be used when we have a fairly small distribution and a few extreme scores, when the distribution is badly skewed, or when some scores in the distribution were not actually determined (missing scores).

Because the median is based on the number of scores and not on their values, it will not be influenced by very deviant or extreme scores. To illustrate, suppose we have a distribution consisting of the scores 5, 5, 5, 5, and 35. Using our simple counting method to estimate the median, we find that it is the third score, which is a 5. The mean, on the other hand, is the sum of the scores divided by their number, or $\frac{55}{5} = 11$. As you can see, in a small distribution with extreme scores, the mean is dramatically influenced, whereas the median is not. In this case, the median is much more representative of the data.

In some studies, it may be impossible to determine an exact score for every subject. Some data that illustrate this point were obtained in a study with rats. As part of a study of the effects of diet on behavior, nine rats were trained to press a bar for a reward, and then the reward was omitted so that their bar pressing eventually ceased (extinguished). The response measure, or dependent variable, to be analyzed was the number of days it took the animals to stop responding. Because it was expected that some animals would continue to respond much longer than others, it was arbitrarily decided to terminate the participation of any animal that continued to respond beyond 15 days. Thus, if an animal were still responding at 15 days, its training would be discontinued. In actuality, however, it would not be known how long it would have taken the rat to extinguish its bar-pressing behavior if it had been allowed to continue. This sort of arbitrary cutoff point is often necessary in learning experiments.

The scores recorded for the nine subjects were 15, 15, 15, 15, 12, 6, 5, 4, 3. Because the first four scores were arbitrarily determined, the median is the most appropriate measure of central tendency. Remember, because the median depends on the number of scores and not on their values, the arbitrary cutoff scores do not affect the value calculated for the statistic. The mean, on the other hand, depends on the value of each score, so that an arbitrary ceiling depresses its value. In the example presented, the mean is 10. We know that this value is too low because each of the animals scoring 15 would have had a higher score if its participation hadn't been arbitrarily terminated. The value of the median would be 12 even if we had allowed each animal to continue until it achieved the criterion.

When to Use the Mean　　The mean is the *most useful* of the three measures of central tendency because many important statistical procedures are based on it. In addition, the mean has merit because it is *based on all the data* in the distribution and not on just a limited portion of it, as the median and the mode are. Also, the mean is a *more reliable (more stable) measure* than either the median or the mode. Specifically, if several samples are taken from a known population and each of the three measures of central tendency is computed for each sample, the mean will vary least of the three measures, followed by the median and the mode, in that order.

One of the most important uses of the mean of a sample is to estimate the population mean, symbolized by μ (Greek letter mu). (Note that Greek letters are used to symbolize population parameters; sample statistics are symbolized by letters of our own alphabet.) This process of **estimation** is a very important part of inferential statistics, and we will have more to say about it in Chapter 9. If we take several samples and calculate the mean for each, we find that the sample mean is neither always above the population mean nor always below it. If we continued this process and took successive samples from a population, the mean of the sample means (the "long-run" average) would equal the population mean. For this reason, we say that the sample mean is an **unbiased estimate** of the population mean. This property of the sample mean as an unbiased estimator of the population mean will be especially important in Chapter 9.

As the example at the beginning of the chapter illustrates, there are times when the mean is not the best measure of central tendency to report. As we noted earlier, in small samples with extreme scores or in badly skewed distributions, the mean may be a poor representative of the distribution. The same is true when we have missing scores or arbitrarily determined cutoff scores. In all of these situations, the median is the preferred measure of central tendency.

POSITIONS OF MEASURES OF CENTRAL TENDENCY ON A FREQUENCY POLYGON

In a symmetrical, unimodal distribution, the mean, median, and mode are all the same. In a skewed distribution, however, the mean is pulled in the direction of the extreme scores or tail (same as the direction of the skew), and the median is between the mean and the mode. Examples of the relative locations of the three measures are shown in Figure 5-4.

Figure 5-4   The relative locations of the three measures of central tendency in a normal distribution, a positively skewed distribution, and a negatively skewed distribution.

To further illustrate the positions of the three measures and also review computational procedures, suppose we have the highly simplified but negatively skewed frequency distribution shown here:

X	f	Cum f	fX
9	5	34	45
8	5	29	40
7	7	24	49
6	6	17	36
5	5	11	25
4	3	6	12
3	1	3	3
2	1	2	2
1	1	1	1
	$N = 34$		$\Sigma fX = 213$

$Mo = 7$, because this is the score with the highest frequency.
Md = score halfway between the $(N/2)$th score and the $(N/2)$th + 1 score:

$$\frac{N}{2} = \frac{34}{2} = 17\text{th score} = 6$$

$$\frac{N}{2} + 1 = 17 + 1 = 18\text{th score} = 7$$

$$Md = \frac{6 + 7}{2} = \frac{13}{2} = 6.5$$

$$\overline{X} = \frac{\Sigma fX}{N} = \frac{213}{34} = 6.26$$

The frequency polygon based on this distribution is plotted in Figure 5-5. On it are shown the relative locations of the measures of central tendency.

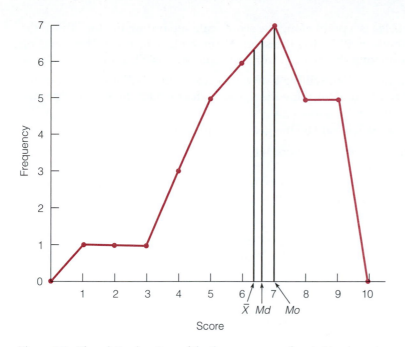

Figure 5-5 The relative locations of the three measures of central tendency in a negatively skewed distribution.

Because the mean is pulled in the direction of the tail in a skewed distribution, if we are given any two of the measures of central tendency, we should be able to guess both the shape of the distribution and the location of the missing value. For example, if we know that the mean of a distribution is 13 and the mode is 20, we will probably guess that the distribution is negatively skewed and the median is somewhere between 13 and 20. If we are told that the mode is 10 with a median of 15, then the distribution will probably be positively skewed and the mean will be above 15.

SUMMARY

Three measures of central tendency are the mode, the median, and the mean (or arithmetic average). The mode (Mo) is the most frequently occurring score in the distribution and is determined by locating the score(s) with the highest frequency. A distribution with two modes is bimodal, and both values are reported. The mode is valuable in a descriptive sense but is not useful for further statistical procedures. Because it is so easily determined, it is useful as a first approximation of the central tendency in the data. It is also useful for summarizing central tendency in categorical or nominal scale data.

The median (Md) is a point along the score scale separating the top 50% of the scores from the bottom 50%; it is the score at the 50th percentile. The counting procedure for estimating the median from a frequency distribution is as follows:

1. If N is even, the median will be halfway between the ($N/2$)th score and the ($N/2$)th + 1 score. To determine the value of the median, first locate the two scores and then take their average.
2. If N is odd, the median will be the $[(N + 1)/2]$th score.

The median is the preferred measure when the distribution is skewed or when there are missing scores.

The mean, or arithmetic average ($\overline{X}$ for a sample, μ for a population), is defined mathematically as the sum of the scores divided by the number of scores. The formula is

$$\overline{X} = \frac{\Sigma X}{N},$$

or, in the case of a frequency distribution,

$$\overline{X} = \frac{\Sigma fX}{N}.$$

The mean is the balancing point in the distribution, verified by $\Sigma(X - \overline{X}) = 0$; that is, the sum of the deviations about the mean is 0. The mean is the least variable of the three measures of central tendency and is used in many other statistical procedures. It may not be the most representative measure in situations favoring the median—that is, in which there are badly skewed distributions and/or missing scores in the distribution. The mean of a sample is an unbiased estimator of the population mean.

We also presented a set of rounding conventions:

1. Round everything to hundredths.
2. Wait until the final answer to round.
3. Maintain at least three decimal places in all preliminary calculations.
4. If the digit in the thousandths place is less than 5, drop it and everything that follows.
5. If the number in the thousandths place is 5 or more, round up the preceding digit and drop all following numbers.

In a symmetrical distribution with only one mode, the mean, median, and mode will all have the same value. In a skewed distribution, however, the mean will be pulled in the direction of the tail, and the median will be between the mean and the mode.

❊ *Troubleshooting Your Computations*

No matter how simple the statistic, computational errors are possible. How will you know (or suspect) that an error has been made?

The most basic piece of advice we can give is this: *Be aware of what constitutes a reasonable answer.* Try to estimate the type of answer that makes sense for the given problem. For example, if you are computing a measure of central tendency for a sample distribution, the value you obtain should be not only in the distribution of scores you have but also in the *center* (more or less) of the distribution. Thus, before starting to plug numbers into an equation, look at the distribution of scores and try to guess a value for the statistic desired. In this way, if you make a mistake and obtain an impossible answer for the distribution, at least you'll recognize it.

If you are working with a frequency distribution, be sure to take the frequencies into account; that is, be sure to use the appropriate formula (e.g., $\Sigma fX/N$ rather than $\Sigma X/N$) and to multiply each score by its frequency before summing. A common error is to add the scores (Xs) without multiplying each score by the corresponding frequency. One rule worth remembering is to never sum the scores (Xs) in a frequency distribution.

The mode is so easy to determine that mistakes are difficult to make. Be sure to report the *score* with the highest frequency rather than the highest frequency itself.

Finally, to help prevent computational errors, perform all computations twice, being sure you get the same answer each time.

EXERCISES

1. A sports psychologist worked with a basketball team to improve the players' free-throw shooting. One technique she used was visualization. She asked each player, before taking the shot, to imagine the entire act of shooting, including the path of the ball and the sound it would make as it passed through the net. To see how good the team was before introducing the procedure, she had each of the 20 players take 25 shots, and she recorded the number of successful shots each one made. The data are given here:

X	f	X	f
24	1	15	0
23	0	14	0
22	2	13	0
21	3	12	1
20	2	11	0
19	4	10	2
18	1	9	2
17	0	8	1
16	1		$N = 20$

For these data, determine each of the measures of central tendency, tell which you think is most appropriate for this situation, and say what you can about the shape of the distribution based on the three measures.

2. After a week of practicing with the visualization technique, the 20 players again shot 25 free throws, and the sports psychologist recorded the number of successful shots:

X	f	X	f
25	1	18	0
24	1	17	0
23	1	16	1
22	4	15	0
21	4	14	1
20	3	13	0
19	3	12	1
			$N = 20$

Compute the measures of central tendency.

3. Determine the median and the mean for each of the following:

a. 27, 33, 10, 9, 6, 7, 11, 23, 27

b.

X	f	X	f
150	5	108	3
148	5	65	5
145	8	64	5
133	7	62	5
110	4	37	3

c.

X	f	X	f
5	2	−3	3
4	3	−10	2
3	4	−15	3
2	1	−30	2

4. Which measure of central tendency is most appropriate when

a. you have extreme scores or missing scores?

b. you need a quick estimate?

c. you need the value that will be most consistent from sample to sample?

5. a. A unimodal distribution with $Mo = 30$ and $\overline{X} = 25$ is an example of a _____ skewed distribution.

b. If $\overline{X} = 27$ with $Md = 22$, this will probably be a _____ skewed distribution.

6. A developmental psychologist is interested in the attention of infants to human faces. To study this, he shows infants either a set of geometric figures or a photograph of a human face. He then records the number of seconds the infants look at the stimuli (geometric figures or faces) without looking away

for more than 5 seconds. Infants who attend for more than 100 seconds are given a score of 100. The data are as follows:

Geometric Figures		Faces	
Number of Seconds	f	Number of Seconds	f
27	1	100+	3
25	2	52	2
21	3	46	4
20	3	33	2
18	5	24	3
16	2	21	2
15	3	19	3
14	1	18	2
12	1	13	1

Determine the three measures of central tendency. Which is the most appropriate for this experiment? Suppose we discard the data for the three infants who attended for more than 100 seconds. Recalculate the measures of central tendency and tell which is most appropriate.

7. In Chapter 1, we described a classroom demonstration in which students tried to catch a ball while wearing goggles that reversed the visual field. The frequency distribution of the number of successful catches out of 10 trials for 20 students is given here:

X	f
10	1
9	0
8	2
7	1
6	1
5	2
4	2
3	4
2	5
1	1
0	1
	$N = 20$

Determine each of the measures of central tendency.

8. In this chapter, we stated that the mean is the balancing point in the distribution. Make up a simple example to illustrate this important property of the mean.

9. To determine a baseline of smoking activity, 30 smokers at a smoking-cessation clinic were observed for a day and the number of cigarettes each smoked was counted. Find the mean, median, and modal number of cigarettes smoked.

X	f	X	f	X	f
43	1	38	2	33	3
42	1	37	1	32	2
41	0	36	6	31	1
40	1	35	5	30	1
39	2	34	4		

10. Using the rounding rules introduced, round the following:
    a. 43.85492
    b. 2.875
    c. 3.33333
    d. 73.66666

11. The following data represent the number of sentences correctly unscrambled by students in an English class. Determine each of the measures of central tendency.

X	f	X	f
23	1	13	5
22	0	12	4
21	1	11	4
20	1	10	3
19	0	9	2
18	2	8	2
17	1	7	1
16	1	6	2
15	3	5	1
14	3		

12. Every semester one of us asks the students in his class how many children there are in their families. Find the measures of central tendency for this semester's results.

X	f
5	3
3	8
2	18
1	4

13. Every semester one of us administers a simple reaction-time test in his class; he holds a ruler between the thumb and forefinger of each student, drops it

suddenly, and the mark on the ruler where the student catches it is his or her score. The scores are given in whole numbers. If a student misses the ruler entirely, he or she receives an arbitrary score of 13. Determine the measures of central tendency for the males in this semester's class, whose scores are given here. Which is the most appropriate measure, and why is that the case?

X	f
13	1
7	4
6	2
5	2
4	2
3	1

14. For the same reaction-time test, the scores of the females are listed here. Find the measures of central tendency and tell which is most appropriate and why.

X	f	X	f
13	3	6	6
11	1	5	2
10	2	4	1
9	3	3	1
8	3	2	1
7	4		

15. Combine the frequency distributions of the males and the females shown in Exercises 13 and 14 into one distribution and compute the measures of central tendency for the whole class.

16. In a class on social problems, 30 students are given a scale that measures their attitudes toward a politician lying about money; higher scores represent less favorable attitudes. Determine the measures of central tendency.

X	f
10	3
9	4
8	5
7	7
6	2
5	2
4	1
3	3
2	1
1	1
0	1

17. In the same class as in Exercise 16, the students' attitudes about a politician lying about a sexual affair while in office are assessed. Determine the measures of central tendency.

X	f
8	1
7	1
6	2
5	3
4	4
3	5
2	6
1	5
0	3

18. As they are leaving a bar, 20 patrons take a test to determine their blood alcohol levels. Determine the measures of central tendency from the values given.

0.05	0.08	0.09	0.12
0.03	0.07	0.11	0.14
0.09	0.12	0.10	0.06
0.10	0.02	0.10	0.02
0.08	0.00	0.07	0.00

Measures of Dispersion and Standard Scores

One of our colleagues does research on the ways people solve arithmetic problems "in their heads." His approach is to ask people to solve different types of problems (such as how close together are two numbers to be added) and to measure the frequency of errors and the amount of time taken to solve the problem. In analyzing his data, he has observed that some people are highly consistent in the number of errors they make across sets of problems. If they make few (or many) errors on one set of problems, they tend to make few (or many) errors on the next set. Our colleague has also observed that there are people who are very inconsistent. They may make few errors on one set of problems but many errors on the next. The mean (or median or modal) number of errors for both types of participants is the same, but the spread of scores differs markedly. Examples of the types of distribution produced in this situation are presented in Figure 6-1. As you can see, the indices of central tendency are identical, but they do nothing to convey the differences in the shapes of these distributions. It is clear that we need an index of the spread, width, or distribution of scores if we are to adequately describe our data.

In Chapter 2, we talked about the two basic uses of statistics: to describe data and to make inferences from them. In Chapters 3, 4, and 5, we discussed different ways to describe data: by organizing them into a frequency distribution, by graphing them, and by determining a number in the central part of the distribution to summarize the data. To have a complete description of our data, we must also have a measure of the spread of the distribution, or its **dispersion.** There are three terms used frequently throughout this chapter to refer to the spread of the scores around the mean in a distribution. They are *dispersion, deviation,* and *variability.*

Another example will help clarify the need for measuring the variability in the data. Suppose we look at the amount of rainfall in 1 year for two cities and find

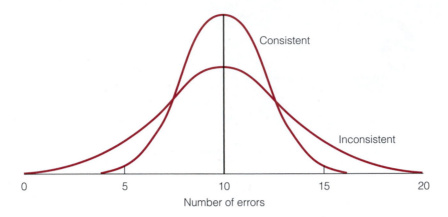

Figure 6-1   Graph of the spread of scores for consistent and inconsistent problem solvers.

that each received a total of 150 inches, or a mean of 12.5 inches a month. Just knowing the mean will tell us nothing about how the rainfall was distributed during the year. We might find that in one city the climate was extremely dry for 10 months, with most of the 150 inches coming during a 2-month period. By contrast, a small amount of rain fell on the other city almost every day. If we simply reported our measure of central tendency, there would be no way to distinguish the two cities in terms of rainfall. What we need is a measure of dispersion, deviation, or variability. In this chapter, we discuss four such measures: the range, the average deviation, the variance, and the standard deviation.

THE RANGE

The range is similar to the mode in that it is easy to determine. Although it is useful in a descriptive sense, it is not used in statistical tests in this text. The **range** is the difference between the highest score (*HS*) in the distribution and the lowest score (*LS*).

> **FORMULA 6-1**   *Range of a distribution*
>
> $$R(\text{range}) = HS - LS$$

The range is a quick and useful way of communicating the spread of a distribution. A course instructor, for example, might announce that the average score on the midterm was 72, with a high score of 98 and a low of 40. By giving the high and low scores, the instructor is indicating the range. Suppose we have obtained the IQ scores of most of the population in the United States and have found a low score of 0 and a high score of 200. The range is from 0 to 200 or $200 - 0 = 200$. In

Exercise 3c at the end of Chapter 5, a distribution was given in which the high score was 5 and the low score was −30. What was the range? In this case,

$$R = HS - LS = 5 - (-30) = 5 + 30 = 35.$$

The range is a useful measure if we are interested only in a basic approximation of the variability in the data. However, because the range is based on only two scores in the distribution, and these are the two extremes, it is obviously not a very sophisticated measure. It is entirely possible to have two distributions with the same range but different variabilities. Consider the following two distributions of scores in math classes:

Class A: 13, 23, 33, 43, 53, 63, 73, 83, 93, 100

Class B: 13, 85, 85, 86, 87, 87, 88, 88, 89, 100

In each case, the range of scores is from 100 to 13, or 87. However, the scores are much more evenly distributed across the range in Class A than in Class B. In fact, if we omitted the two extremes in Class B, its range would be only 4 (89 − 85).

This example illustrates a major problem with the range as a measure of dispersion. If the extreme scores are not representative of the distribution (as in Class B), the range will be unrepresentative as well. Now let's consider a statistic to measure dispersion based on the "best" measure of central tendency.

THE AVERAGE DEVIATION

One way of quantifying the dispersion of a set of scores is to use the distance between scores and the center of the distribution. As noted in Chapter 5, we are again using the important concept of *deviation*. Because the mean, as we discussed in Chapter 5, is the "best" measure of central tendency, we can create an index of dispersion by subtracting the mean from each score $(X - \overline{X})$. The greater the spread, or dispersion, of a set of scores, the greater these distances should be, on average. Thus, we can create an index called the **average deviation** (AD)—the average amount that each score in a distribution deviates from the mean. To do this, we first calculate the deviation of each score from the mean $(X - \overline{X})$, then sum these deviations $[\Sigma(X - \overline{X})]$, and finally divide by the number of scores:

$$\frac{\Sigma(X - \overline{X})}{N}.$$

The problem with this procedure is that the negative deviations of the scores below the mean exactly balance the positive deviations of the scores above the mean, so their sum is 0, as we found in Chapter 5. If we used this procedure, we would find that the average deviation was always 0. Clearly, this would not be very useful, and we must try another method—one that finds the sum of the deviations without getting 0 every time.

There are actually several methods for doing this; one requires the summation of the absolute values of the deviations. The **absolute value** of a number (symbolized by parallel vertical lines on either side of the number; e.g., $|-3|$) is the value of the number itself, without regard to sign. The absolute value of -5 is just 5, and the absolute value of $+5$ is likewise 5. The absolute value of the difference between a score and the mean is simply the number of units, or distance, between them regardless of whether the score is above or below the mean. Because it is the distance and not the direction that captures the spread of the scores, it is appropriate to replace $(X - \overline{X})$ with $|X - \overline{X}|$. Therefore, the formula for computing the average deviation of a sample is:

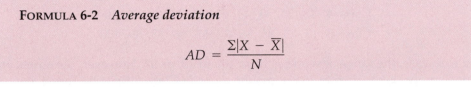

FORMULA 6-2   *Average deviation*

$$AD = \frac{\Sigma|X - \overline{X}|}{N}$$

The formula for computing the average deviation for a frequency distribution is:

FORMULA 6-3   *Average deviation for a frequency distribution*

$$AD = \frac{\Sigma f|X - \overline{X}|}{N}$$

Although the average deviation tells us the average amount that each score in a distribution deviates from the mean of the distribution, its application is limited because absolute values have little use in other statistical procedures. However, there is another way to avoid the problem of negative signs when finding the deviation of each score from the mean: We can simply square each of the deviations, because a minus times a minus is a plus. We discuss this in the next section.

THE VARIANCE AND THE STANDARD DEVIATION

The Variance

In the previous section, we discussed the average deviation. In the formulas for *AD*, we avoided obtaining 0 when we summed the deviations from the mean by taking the absolute value of each deviation before summing. Unfortunately, as we noted, the resulting statistic is not very useful for further procedures.

Another way to avoid getting 0 each time we sum the deviations is to square the deviations before summing; that is, we could sum the squared deviations and divide by their number. This would give us the **variance**—the average of the squared deviations. Here are the formulas for the population variance, symbolized by σ^2 and read "little sigma squared":

FORMULA 6-4 *Population variance (definitional formula)*

$$\sigma^2 = \frac{\Sigma(X - \mu)^2}{N}$$

FORMULA 6-5 *Population variance for a frequency distribution (definitional formula)*

$$\sigma^2 = \frac{\Sigma f(X - \mu)^2}{N}$$

Remember from Chapter 2 that a population is a broad group of individuals to which we want to generalize our results. Most populations are very large. For example, we might be interested in all college students enrolled in statistics courses in the United States, or all graduating high school seniors, or all people with hypertension.

Usually, we know population values in one of three situations. In the first, the value is defined by probability, such as our knowledge that in the population of coin tosses, heads occur 50% of the time. In the second, we may have extensive data on a variable, such as our knowledge from census data that the mean family size in the United States is 3.1. In the third, scales may be constructed so they have defined parameters, such as IQ tests that have a mean (μ) of 100. More often, we are faced with the necessity of estimating population parameters from sample statistics. This process of estimation is the foundation of inferential statistics, which we begin discussing in Part 2 of this book.

We can begin the process of estimation in this chapter by developing an equation to estimate population variance from sample values. The question is: Can we use Formulas 6-4 and 6-5, with appropriate changes in symbols to reflect sample values rather than population values, to determine a sample statistic that is an unbiased estimator of σ^2? Unfortunately, the answer is no.

Recall that in Chapter 5 we said the sample mean ($\overline{X}$) shows no systematic tendency to deviate from the population value (μ), and thus $\overline{X}$ is an unbiased estimator of μ. This it not true in the case of the sample statistic computed from the formula for σ^2:

$$SD^2 = \frac{\Sigma(X - \overline{X})^2}{N} \quad \text{or} \quad \frac{\Sigma f(X - \overline{X})^2}{N}.$$

The resulting statistic tends to produce estimates that generally are smaller than σ^2 and is thus biased. If we use SD^2 to estimate σ^2, we will tend to underestimate the population value.[1] The solution to the problem requires a slight modification of the defining formula for σ^2 for use with samples to compensate for the tendency for SD^2 to be smaller than σ^2. The resulting statistic is called s^2, the sample variance.

Instead of dividing the sum of the squared deviations by N, we will divide by $N - 1$. Because $N - 1$ is less than N, the resulting fraction will always be larger; that is, s^2 will be slightly larger than SD^2. The defining formulas for s^2 are as follows:

FORMULA 6-6   *Sample variance (definitional formula)*

$$s^2 = \frac{\Sigma(X - \overline{X})^2}{N - 1}$$

FORMULA 6-7   *Sample variance for a frequency distribution (definitional formula)*

$$s^2 = \frac{\Sigma f(X - \overline{X})^2}{N - 1}$$

Understanding the Variance   The defining formulas (6-6 and 6-7) for the sample variance are the expressions we should examine and think about to get a feel for the meaning of the variance. First, we note that the formulas make use of the *key deviation* $(X - \overline{X})$, the deviation of each score from the group mean. As we stated, these deviations are squared so that positive and negative deviations will not cancel each other out when summed. The numerator of the fraction is a sum of the squared deviations (also called the "sum of squares"); the denominator is one less than the number of deviations that are summed. We can think of the formulas for the variance as kinds of averages—the *average of the squared deviations of the scores about their mean.* Thus, the variance is an average of how the scores are dispersed from the "center" of the scores.

Now let's use Formula 6-6 to compute a sample variance. As a preliminary to a study of the effects of antihistamines on driving ability, researchers determined the number of movements of the steering wheel in a 1-minute simulated driving exercise for 11 normal people. The data and computations are as follows:

---

[1]Note that SD^2—a formula for the sample variance based on the population formula for σ^2—is used in many texts as a "descriptive statistic" measure of variance. Although this formula may be suitable for producing a measure of sample variance as a descriptive statistic, it always needs to be corrected to the unbiased formula when used as an inferential statistic to estimate σ^2. To avoid this complication, we have introduced the unbiased formula for the sample variance.

Steering Adjustments	$X - \overline{X}$	$(X - \overline{X})^2$
25	7.09	50.27
24	6.09	37.09
23	5.09	25.91
22	4.09	16.73
20	2.09	4.37
18	0.09	0.01
17	−0.91	0.83
16	−1.91	3.65
14	−3.91	15.29
10	−7.91	62.57
8	−9.91	98.21
$\Sigma X = 197$		$\Sigma(X - \overline{X})^2 = 314.93$

$$\overline{X} = \frac{\Sigma X}{N} = \frac{197}{11} = 17.91$$

$$s^2 = \frac{\Sigma(X - \overline{X})^2}{N - 1} = \frac{314.93}{11 - 1} = \frac{314.93}{10} = 31.49$$

To compute s^2, the researchers first found the mean by summing the X column (197) and dividing by N (11) to get 17.91. Next, they obtained the values in the $X - \overline{X}$ column by subtracting the mean from each score. Squaring each of the deviations and summing the resulting column, $\Sigma(X - \overline{X})^2$, gave the total 314.93. To obtain s^2, they divided 314.93 by $N - 1$ (10) to get the sample variance of 31.49.

If we wanted to use Formula 6-7 to compute s^2 from a frequency distribution, we would need to add one more step before summing the squared deviations. We would need to multiply each of the squared deviations by its frequency; that is, we would need an additional column headed $f(X - \overline{X})^2$.

In addition to the definitional formulas, there are *computational* or *raw score* formulas. These formulas require fewer computations than the definitional formulas and are easier to use when computing the statistics with a pocket calculator. The computational formulas are derived from and produce equivalent values to those obtained from the definitional formulas:

FORMULA 6-8   *Sample variance (computational formula)*

$$s^2 = \frac{\Sigma X^2 - \dfrac{(\Sigma X)^2}{N}}{N - 1}$$

> **FORMULA 6-9** *Sample variance for a frequency distribution (computational formula)*
>
> $$s^2 = \frac{\sum fX^2 - \dfrac{(\sum fX)^2}{N}}{N - 1}$$

Consider an example. As part of a study on Down's syndrome, the number of physical abnormalities has been determined for a group of 23 children diagnosed with this syndrome. Let's use Formula 6-9 to compute s^2 for the distribution:

X	f	fX	fX²
14	1	14	196
13	2	26	338
12	3	36	432
11	3	33	363
10	5	50	500
9	3	27	243
8	2	16	128
7	1	7	49
6	2	12	72
5	1	5	25
	$N = 23$	$\sum fX = 226$	$\sum fX^2 = 2{,}346$

$$s^2 = \frac{\sum fX^2 - \dfrac{(\sum fX)^2}{N}}{N - 1} = \frac{2{,}346 - \dfrac{(226)^2}{23}}{23 - 1} = \frac{2{,}346 - \dfrac{51{,}076}{23}}{22}$$

$$= \frac{2{,}346 - 2{,}220.70}{22}$$

$$= \frac{125.30}{22} = 5.70$$

Using Formula 6-9, we first need to determine values for three terms: N, $\sum fX$, and $\sum fX^2$. Note that in order to find $\sum fX^2$, we need to multiply the values in the X column by the corresponding numbers in the fX column. Equivalently, we could have squared the values in the X column and then multiplied by the frequencies.

Note that fX^2 means $f(X^2)$—the X value is squared before multiplication by the frequency. Many students make the mistake of thinking that all they have to do is square the values in the fX column to obtain the numbers under the heading fX^2. But by squaring the values in the fX column, they really have found f^2X^2; that is, they have squared the frequencies as well as the scores. This is not what is needed. Remember the following:

$$(fX)^2 = f^2X^2 \neq fX^2$$

but

$$(fX)(X) = fX^2 \quad \text{or} \quad (f)(X^2) = fX^2.$$

🌀 CHECKING YOUR PROGRESS

In Exercise 13 at the end of Chapter 5, we gave a frequency distribution of dropped-ruler test scores for the males in a statistics class. From the distribution repeated here, use Formula 6-9 to compute the sample variance.

X	f
13	1
7	4
6	2
5	2
4	2
3	1

Answer: s² = 6.52.

The Standard Deviation

The variance is in squared units; now let's look at a statistic that has the same units as the distribution from which the variance has been computed. The **standard deviation** is simply the square root of the variance. This will always be true whether we are considering the population standard deviation ($\sigma = \sqrt{\sigma^2}$) or the sample standard deviation ($s = \sqrt{s^2}$). It's really not a new formula. Another way to say this is that the standard deviation is the square root of the sum of the squared deviation of the scores from the mean divided by the number of scores. The standard deviation is the square root of the average squared deviation, or, more simply once again, the square root of the variance. For a population, the definitional formulas for the standard deviation (symbolized by σ) are:

FORMULA 6-10 *Population standard deviation (definitional formula)*

$$\sigma = \sqrt{\frac{\Sigma(X - \mu)^2}{N}}$$

> **FORMULA 6-11**   *Population standard deviation for a frequency distribution (definitional formula)*
>
> $$\sigma = \sqrt{\frac{\Sigma f(X - \mu)^2}{N}}$$

As we found with the variance, the sample statistic computed from the formula for the population standard deviation results in a biased estimate of σ. For this reason, we again modify the population equations slightly to compensate. As before, we divide the squared deviations by $N - 1$ rather than by N. The defining formulas for s, the sample standard deviation, are:

> **FORMULA 6-12**   *Sample standard deviation (definitional formula)*
>
> $$s = \sqrt{\frac{\Sigma(X - \overline{X})^2}{N - 1}}$$

> **FORMULA 6-13**   *Sample standard deviation for a frequency distribution (definitional formula)*
>
> $$s = \sqrt{\frac{\Sigma f(X - \overline{X})^2}{N - 1}}$$

Let's use a simple distribution to illustrate the use of the definitional formula for s. Suppose we have a distribution consisting of the scores 20, 19, 14, 12, and 10. What is s for this distribution?

X	$X - \overline{X}$	$(X - \overline{X})^2$
20	+5	25
19	+4	16
14	−1	1
12	−3	9
10	−5	25
$\Sigma X = 75$		$\Sigma(X - \overline{X})^2 = 76$

$$\overline{X} = \frac{\Sigma X}{N} = \frac{75}{5} = 15$$

$$s = \sqrt{\frac{\Sigma(X - \overline{X})^2}{N - 1}} = \sqrt{\frac{76}{5 - 1}} = \sqrt{\frac{76}{4}}$$

$$= \sqrt{19} = 4.36$$

The first step is to find the mean (15) and then to subtract the mean from each score ($X - \overline{X}$). Next we square the deviations and sum the squared deviations (76). Then we divide the sum of the squared deviations by $N - 1$ (4) to get the variance (19). Finally, we find the square root of the variance, 4.36, which is the standard deviation.

Let's use a raw score or computational formula to compute another example of s. As you will see, the formulas are precisely the same as the ones we introduced for variance (Formulas 6-8 and 6-9) except that we take the square root as the final step. When the frequencies are all 1, the computational formula for s is:

FORMULA 6-14 *Sample standard deviation (computational formula)*

$$s = \sqrt{\frac{\Sigma X^2 - \frac{(\Sigma X)^2}{N}}{N - 1}}$$

By using Formula 6-14, we avoid the steps of computing the mean, subtracting the mean from each score, and squaring the difference. These steps are time consuming and prone to error, especially when the numbers are computed to several decimal places. Even when the numbers are simple, however, Formula 6-14 is easier. To illustrate, let's use Formula 6-14 in the previous example:

X	X^2
20	400
19	361
14	196
12	144
10	100
$\Sigma X = 75$	$\Sigma X^2 = 1{,}201$

$$s = \sqrt{\frac{\Sigma X^2 - \frac{(\Sigma X)^2}{N}}{N - 1}} = \sqrt{\frac{1{,}201 - \frac{(75)^2}{5}}{5 - 1}} = \sqrt{\frac{1{,}201 - 1{,}125}{4}}$$

$$= \sqrt{\frac{76}{4}} = \sqrt{19} = 4.36.$$

Note that the computational formula gives us precisely the same result as before. For a frequency distribution, the computational formula is:

FORMULA 6-15   *Sample standard deviation for a frequency distribution (computational formula)*

$$s = \sqrt{\frac{\Sigma fX^2 - \dfrac{(\Sigma fX)^2}{N}}{N-1}}$$

As an example, let's say we test 10 students to see how many scrambled sentences they can correctly rearrange. The data and the computation of the standard deviation are as follows:

X	f	fX	fX²
13	1	13	169
12	1	12	144
11	2	22	242
10	1	10	100
9	3	27	243
6	1	6	36
4	1	4	16
	N = 10	ΣfX = 94	ΣfX² = 950

$$s = \sqrt{\frac{\Sigma fX^2 - \dfrac{(\Sigma fX)^2}{N}}{N-1}} = \sqrt{\frac{950 - \dfrac{(94)^2}{10}}{10-1}} = \sqrt{\frac{950 - \dfrac{8,836}{10}}{9}}$$

$$= \sqrt{\frac{950 - 883.6}{9}} = \sqrt{\frac{66.4}{9}}$$

$$= \sqrt{7.38} = 2.72$$

As before, we need to determine values for N, ΣfX, and ΣfX^2. The variance, or s^2, is 7.38. The square root of 7.38, or 2.72, is the standard deviation.

Visualizing the Standard Deviation

Now that we have gone through the computational steps of calculating the sample standard deviation, what do we actually have? Can we graphically depict the number we have computed? Fortunately, yes. To illustrate, let's take another example of a frequency distribution, calculate the standard deviation, and plot s on the X axis of the frequency polygon plotted from the frequency distribution. Suppose we administer the same scrambled-sentences test to a class of 56 introductory psychology students and obtain the following distribution of scores:

X	f	X	f
19	1	10	6
18	1	9	6
17	1	8	5
16	1	7	4
15	2	6	3
14	3	5	2
13	5	4	3
12	5	3	1
11	6	2	1

You should treat this as a "Checking Your Progress" exercise and find s^2 and s. The answers are $s^2 = 14.18$ and $s = 3.77$, with $\overline{X} = 10$.

Using the values from the frequency distribution, we can plot the frequency polygon shown in Figure 6-2. Then we can mark off the X axis of the polygon on either side of the mean in standard deviation units, which in this case would have a width of 4 raw-score units (the value we calculated for s rounded to a whole number for ease in plotting).

The standard deviation can be visualized as another unit of measurement on the X axis of a frequency polygon; that is, the raw-score units we used to plot the polygon constitute one scale, the raw-score scale. However, we can also plot the standard deviation scale on the X axis, and this also is shown in Figure 6-2.

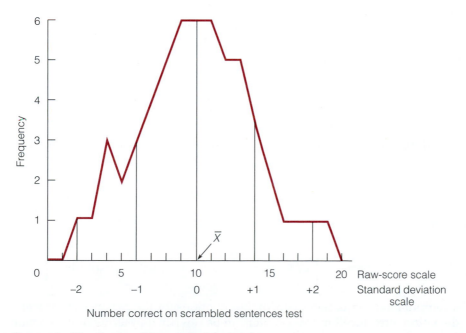

Figure 6-2   Visualization of the standard deviation.

Later in the chapter, we will refer to the values on the standard deviation scale as either standard scores or z scores. Note that in the distribution shown, a raw score of 14 lies 1 standard deviation unit above the mean (mean + $1s$ = 10 + 4 = 14), whereas a score of 6 lies 1 standard deviation unit below the mean (mean − $1s$ = 10 − 4 = 6).

Approximating the Standard Deviation   From our teaching experience, most students seem to have little "feel" for what is a reasonable value for the sample standard deviation. As a result, errors in applying the formulas, particularly Formula 6-15, can produce dramatically erroneous values for s that the student fails to recognize. Fortunately, there is a simple way to approximate (or guess) s for the kind of distributions you are likely to encounter in problems, which is to divide the range of scores in the distribution by 4; that is,

$$s_{approx} = \frac{R}{4}.$$

If you have a large, symmetrical distribution, a somewhat better approximation will be the range divided by 6.

Applying our formula for approximating s to the examples of s we've actually calculated, we find for the 10 students and scrambled-sentences example that s_{approx} = $R/4$ = (13 − 4)/4 = 9/4 = 2.25, whereas the value we computed for s was 2.72. For the distribution of scores based on a class of 56 students, s_{approx} = $R/4$ = (19 − 2)/4 = 17/4 = 4.25; our computed s was 3.77. Obviously, the value you get for s_{approx} often will not be exactly equal to the actual value of s. However, it will be in the ballpark and should prevent you from reporting wildly erroneous values, which it is possible to obtain with certain types of computational errors. Our advice is to make it a habit to compute s_{approx} before computing s so you have a target to aim at. If your obtained value for s is dramatically different from your s_{approx}, at least you will know that you need to look for where you went awry.

The Sum of Squares   The numerator of the equation for variance is sometimes called the **sum of squares,** or SS; that is,

$$SS = \Sigma(X − \overline{X})^2 \qquad [\Sigma f(X − \overline{X})^2 \text{ for a frequency distribution}]$$

for the definitional equations, and

$$SS = \Sigma X^2 − \frac{(\Sigma X)^2}{N} \qquad \left[\Sigma f X^2 − \frac{(\Sigma f X)^2}{N} \text{ for a frequency distribution} \right]$$

for the computational equations. Any of the equations for the variance or the standard deviation introduced in this chapter can be rewritten in terms of the sum of squares. For example, Formula 6-8 would become

$$s^2 = \frac{SS}{N-1}, \text{ where } SS = \Sigma X^2 - \frac{(\Sigma X)^2}{N}.$$

Similarly, Formula 6-15 could be written

$$s = \sqrt{\frac{SS}{N-1}}, \text{ where } SS = \Sigma f X^2 - \frac{(\Sigma f X)^2}{N}.$$

The sum of squares appears in several equations in future chapters, and we will note it when appropriate.

Taking Stock—Variance and Standard Deviation Formulas By this time, you may look at the population and sample formulas for variance and the standard deviation and be concerned about the apparent number of different formulas. As you become accustomed to working with variances and standard deviations, you will realize that you need to remember only two things: First, you should know the defining formula (for "thinking") and the computational formula (for "easy computing") for the *sample variance* (s^2). Second, remember that the standard deviation is the square root of the variance ($s = \sqrt{s^2}$). These are the tools you will use most often.

STANDARD SCORES (*z* SCORES)

Earlier, we discussed visualizing the standard deviation as a width measure on the X axis of a frequency polygon. As mentioned, the scores plotted on the standard deviation scale are called either standard scores or z scores. Thus, a **standard score,** or *z* **score,** is the deviation of a raw score from the mean in standard deviation units. A z score tells us how far from the mean a raw score is in standard deviation units. In addition, the sign of the z score tells us the direction of the score relative to the mean: Negative z scores correspond to raw scores below the mean, and positive z scores indicate scores above the mean.

An example may help to illustrate the definition. Suppose we have a symmetrical distribution with a mean of 10 and a standard deviation of 2. How many standard deviation units away from the mean is a raw score of 14? The problem and its solution are shown in Figure 6-3. As you can see, the X axis of our frequency polygon has been divided into both raw-score units and standard-score, or z-score, units. It is apparent that 14 is 2 standard deviation units above the mean; that is, it has a z score of +2. Similarly, the z score for 8 is −1, for 6 is −2, and so forth.

Remember that the standard deviation is a kind of uniform amount that each score in a distribution deviates from the distribution's mean. A z score compares a score's deviation with the "center" (or mean), which represents no deviation. For example, a z score of +2 means that the raw score is twice as deviant as a raw score with a z of +1. The advantage of z scores is that the units or "steps" represented

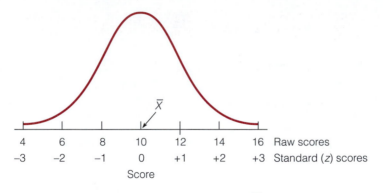

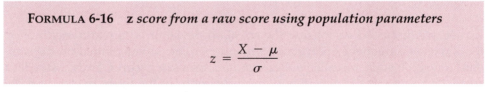

Figure 6-3 Hypothetical frequency polygon with $\overline{X} = 10$ and $s = 2$, illustrating the standard-score (z-score) scale.

by each unit of z are based on the standard deviation for *that* distribution. This allows us to use z scores to compare the position of scores in distributions with very different means and standard deviations. In other words, a z score of +2 (or −2, for that matter) indicates that a particular raw score is very deviant or unlikely, regardless of the distribution from which it came.

There are two simple formulas for converting raw scores to z scores. On those infrequent occasions when we have population parameters of the standard deviation and the mean, we use Formula 6-16 to find z scores:

**FORMULA 6-16   z *score from a raw score using population parameters*

$$z = \frac{X - \mu}{\sigma}$$

More commonly, we have sample statistics, and we use Formula 6-17 to find z scores:

**FORMULA 6-17   z *score from a raw score using sample statistics*

$$z = \frac{X - \overline{X}}{s}$$

Suppose we have a sample with a mean of 7.53 and a standard deviation of 2.37, and we wish to find the z score for a raw score of 3.22. With Formula 6-17, it is quite simple:

$$z = \frac{X - \overline{X}}{s} = \frac{3.22 - 7.53}{2.37} = \frac{-4.31}{2.37} = -1.82.$$

Thus, 3.22 is 1.82 standard deviation units *below* the mean.

Box 6-1   Solving the z Score Formula for X

$$z = \frac{X - \overline{X}}{s}$$

Multiply both sides of the equation by s to clear the fraction:

$$zs = \left(\frac{X - \overline{X}}{s}\right)s.$$

The s terms cancel on the right side, leaving

$$zs = X - \overline{X}.$$

Add $\overline{X}$ to both sides of the equation:

$$zs + \overline{X} = X - \overline{X} + \overline{X},$$

which simplifies to

$$zs + \overline{X} = X.$$

Reversing terms gives the final form of the equation:

$$X = zs + \overline{X}.$$

We will also find it useful to be able to do the reverse—that is, to convert any z score to a raw score. For example, suppose we want to know what score is 2.5 standard deviation units above the mean in the distribution with a mean of 10 and a standard deviation of 2. In this case, we are told that $z = +2.5$, because the definition of z is how far a raw score is from the mean in standard deviation units. Examination of Figure 6-3 reveals that the score 2.5 standard deviation units above the mean is halfway between the scores of 14 and 16—that is, 15. Again, however, we run into problems when the mean and standard deviation are not so easy to work with. For this reason, it is handy to have a formula similar to Formula 6-17 for converting z scores to raw scores—and we do. We simply solve Formula 6-17 for X rather than for z. With the simple algebraic manipulations shown in Box 6-1, we derive Formulas 6-18 and 6-19:

FORMULA 6-18   *Raw score from a z score using population parameters*

$$X = z\sigma + \mu$$

> **FORMULA 6-19**   *Raw score from a z score using sample statistics*
>
> $$X = zs + \overline{X}$$

For example, what is the score that lies 2.4 standard deviation units below the mean? In this case, $z = -2.4$ (negative z score, indicating that it is below the mean), $\overline{X} = 10$, and $s = 2$. Thus,

$$X = (-2.4)(2) + 10 = -4.8 + 10 = 5.2.$$

Therefore, a score of 5.2 lies 2.4 standard deviation units below the mean.

⟳ CHECKING YOUR PROGRESS

Suppose we have measured the heights of all the basketball players in the National Basketball Association and have found that the average height is 77 inches, with a standard deviation of 2.2. What is the z score for a player 73 inches tall? 83 inches? What is the height of a player who is 2.6 standard deviation units below the mean?

Answer: $z = -1.82$; $z = 2.73$; $X = 71.28$. The player who is 73 inches tall is 1.82 standard deviation units below the mean; the player who is 83 inches tall is 2.73 standard deviation units above the mean; the player who is 2.6 standard deviation units below the mean is 71.28 inches tall.

One very important application of z scores is in comparing raw scores that are in different units; that is, z scores can be used as a common unit of comparison. For example, we might be confronted with the question of which is a higher score, 620 on the verbal SAT or 27 on the verbal part of the ACT. This is like asking which is more money, 9,000 lire or 50 francs. We can answer the money question by converting both lire and francs to dollars. There are about 5 francs to the dollar and 1,500 lire to the dollar, so we can convert the lire to dollars by dividing 9,000 by 1,500 and the francs to dollars by dividing 50 by 5. Our lire convert to $6 and our francs to $10, so 50 francs is more than 9,000 lire.

For our test scores, we can determine whether 620 on the verbal SAT is higher than a verbal ACT score of 27 by converting both to z scores. Suppose that the verbal ACT has a population mean of 25 and a standard deviation of 2.5. Then for an ACT score of 27,

$$z = \frac{X - \mu}{\sigma} = \frac{27 - 25}{2.5} = \frac{2}{2.5} = 0.8$$

For verbal SAT scores, $\mu = 500$ and $\sigma = 100$; thus for an SAT score of 620,

$$z = \frac{X - \mu}{\sigma} = \frac{620 - 500}{100} = \frac{120}{100} = 1.2.$$

The verbal SAT score is 1.2 standard deviation units above the mean, whereas the verbal ACT score is only 0.8 standard deviation units above the mean. Thus, the SAT score is higher.

Note that both examples involved division by a constant. In the case of the money, we divided by the number of lire or francs in a dollar. For the test scores, we divided by the number of units in a standard deviation.

SUMMARY

Several measures of the spread, or dispersion, of data were discussed in this chapter. The simplest measure, but the least useful for further computations, is the range: $R = HS - LS$, where HS is the highest score and LS is the lowest score in the distribution.

The second measure presented was the average deviation, defined as the average amount that each score in a distribution deviates from the mean of the distribution. The formulas used to compute the average deviation from sample data are

$$AD = \frac{\Sigma|X - \overline{X}|}{N} \quad \text{and} \quad AD = \frac{\Sigma f|X - \overline{X}|}{N} \quad \text{(for a frequency distribution)}.$$

Actually, a more useful pair of statistics is the variance and the standard deviation.

The variance is defined as the sum of the squared deviation of the scores from the mean divided by the number of scores—that is, the average of the squared deviations. The definitional formulas for population variance are

$$\sigma^2 = \frac{\Sigma(X - \mu)^2}{N} \quad \text{and} \quad \sigma^2 = \frac{\Sigma f(X - \mu)^2}{N} \quad \text{(for a frequency distribution)}.$$

There are two definitional formulas for an unbiased estimate of σ^2 based on sample values. They are

$$s^2 = \frac{\Sigma(X - \overline{X})^2}{N - 1} \quad \text{and} \quad s^2 = \frac{\Sigma f(X - \overline{X})^2}{N - 1} \quad \text{(for a frequency distribution)}.$$

Modification of the definitional formulas results in computational formulas for s^2 that should be used when computing the statistic with a hand calculator. The formulas are

$$s^2 = \frac{\Sigma X^2 - \frac{(\Sigma X)^2}{N}}{N - 1} \quad \text{and} \quad s^2 = \frac{\Sigma f X^2 - \frac{(\Sigma f X)^2}{N}}{N - 1} \quad \text{(for a frequency distribution)}.$$

The standard deviation is defined as the square root of the average squared deviation or the square root of the variance, and the definitional formulas for the population standard deviation are

$$\sigma = \sqrt{\frac{\Sigma(X - \mu)^2}{N}} \quad \text{and}$$

$$\sigma = \sqrt{\frac{\Sigma f(X - \mu)^2}{N}} \quad \text{(for a frequency distribution)}.$$

The definitional formulas for the sample standard deviation that provide an unbiased estimate of σ are

$$s = \sqrt{\frac{\Sigma(X - \overline{X})^2}{N - 1}} \quad \text{and}$$

$$s = \sqrt{\frac{\Sigma f(X - \overline{X})^2}{N - 1}} \quad \text{(for a frequency distribution)}.$$

The computational or raw-score formulas for s are

$$s = \sqrt{\frac{\Sigma X^2 - \dfrac{(\Sigma X)^2}{N}}{N - 1}} \quad \text{or}$$

$$s = \sqrt{\frac{\Sigma f X^2 - \dfrac{(\Sigma f X)^2}{N}}{N - 1}} \quad \text{(for a frequency distribution)}.$$

You can have good command of measures of dispersion by knowing the defining formula and computational formula for the sample variance (s^2) and knowing that the standard deviation is the square root of the variance ($s = \sqrt{s^2}$). The standard deviation can be visualized as another width measure on the X axis of a frequency polygon. A useful approximation of s can be computed by dividing the range by 4.

The numerator of the equation for the variance is sometimes called the sum of squares (SS). The definitional formulas are

$$SS = \Sigma(X - \overline{X})^2 \quad \text{and} \quad SS = \Sigma f(X - \overline{X})^2 \quad \text{(for a frequency distribution)}.$$

The computational formulas are

$$SS = \Sigma X^2 - \frac{(\Sigma X)^2}{N} \quad \text{and}$$

$$SS = \Sigma f X^2 - \frac{(\Sigma f X)^2}{N} \quad \text{(for a frequency distribution)}.$$

The equations for the standard deviation and variance can be rewritten in terms of the sum of squares.

A *standard score,* or *z score,* is defined as the deviation of a raw score from the mean in standard deviation units. The definitional formula for the *z* score using population parameters is

$$z = \frac{X - \mu}{\sigma}.$$

The formula to convert any sample raw score to a *z* score is

$$z = \frac{X - \overline{X}}{s}.$$

To convert a *z* score back to a raw score, the formulas are

$$X = z\sigma + \mu \qquad \text{using population parameters}$$

and

$$X = zs + \overline{X} \qquad \text{using sample statistics.}$$

❊ *Troubleshooting Your Computations*

This chapter dealt with statistics that are computationally more involved than anything encountered in Chapter 5. For this reason, we need to consider carefully some possible clues to trouble or to frequently made errors.

It is very important when computing *s* or any other statistic to have a "feel" for the right answer. For example, if you have a fairly large, symmetrical distribution, *s* will be somewhere near one sixth of the range, or about one fourth of the range for most of the data you will encounter. If you have scores that are rather tightly bunched, then *s* will be small relative to the case in which the scores are widely dispersed. If you obtain a value for *s* that is nearly the same as, or larger than, the range, you have made a gross computational error.

You must always get positive values for s and s². Often, students obtain a negative number under the radical while computing *s* and then overlook it before reporting their final answer. In most of these cases, the value of $\Sigma f X^2$ [$\Sigma f(X^2)$] has been improperly computed. At any rate, if you get a negative value for one of the measures of dispersion, it is incorrect.

Remember to take the frequencies into account when working with a frequency distribution. Finally, when computing *s*, be sure to extract the square root.

EXERCISES

1. Given that $\Sigma X = 1{,}000$, $N = 100$, and $\Sigma X^2 = 10{,}400$, what are s^2 and s?
2. Find s^2 and s for the following distribution of scores: 10, 9, 8, 7, 6, 5, 4, 3, 2, 1.
3. Find s for the following data: $\Sigma X^2 = 210$, $\Sigma X = 30$, $N = 15$.
4. Find s for the following data: $\Sigma X^2 = 416$, $\Sigma X = 48$, $N = 18$.
5. Given the following frequency distribution, find R, s_{approx}, $\overline{X}$, s^2, and s:

X	f
9	4
8	6
7	7
6	8
5	7
4	3
3	3
2	1
1	1

    In addition, plot the frequency polygon from these data and mark off the X axis in units of s. Round s to a whole number for ease in plotting.

6. On an examination in a statistics course, the scores were as follows:

    27, 36, 42, 12, 18, 15, 23, 13, 9, 26, 21, 20, 17, 14, 21, 15, 14, 2, 14, 19

    Determine R, s^2, and s.

7. Over a 3-year period, a clinical therapist recorded the number of sessions required by phobic patients to achieve relief from their symptoms. The frequency distribution of the data is shown here. Find R, s_{approx}, s^2, and s.

X	f
22	1
20	2
19	2
18	3
15	4
13	4
11	2
10	1
9	2
8	1

8. Under distracting conditions, 30 people learn a list of 10 nonsense syllables. The experimenter records the number of repetitions of the list each person

requires before he or she achieves an errorless trial. The results are shown here. Find s^2 and s for the distribution.

X	f		X	f
38	1		25	3
36	2		24	2
34	3		22	2
33	2		18	2
31	1		17	1
29	3		16	1
28	4		10	1
26	2			

9. In a study of mental arithmetic, each of 20 participants responded to 100 problems. The number of errors is shown here. Find R, s^2, and s.

5	7	3
4	8	2
9	0	6
3	4	8
8	6	2
2	10	6
6	7	

10. For the 20 participants in Exercise 9, the average amount of time taken to solve each problem was also recorded (in seconds). Find R, s^2, and s.

8.2	1.1	2.3
4.0	5.2	2.7
6.2	1.8	1.9
2.3	4.7	1.4
1.8	2.6	3.1
3.4	3.7	2.9
3.0	4.1	

11. Identify each of the following:

   a. σ^2

   b. σ

   c. μ

   d. s^2

   e. s

   f. R

12. The average ACT score for a class of 33 students is 21.65, with $s = 2.83$. Convert each of the following to z scores: 19, 25, 33. What ACT score is 1.5

standard deviation units below the mean? What score is 2 standard deviation units above the mean?

13. For the Wechsler Adult Intelligence Scale (WAIS), $\mu = 100$ and $\sigma = 15$. Find the z score for an IQ of 92; for an IQ of 127. Find the IQ score corresponding to a z score of 1.1; to a z score of -0.5.

14. Quiz scores have been obtained for 50 students in a history class. The sum of scores for the class (ΣX) was 366.5, with $\Sigma X^2 = 2,836.39$. What is the z score for a raw score of 9? For a raw score of 4? What is the raw score corresponding to a z score of -1.65? Of 1.55?

15. A group of 10 college sophomores was trained on a computer video game. The reward consisted of points needed to fulfill an experimental participation requirement. A special reward schedule (fixed interval, FI) was used during the game. According to the schedule, the participant received reinforcement for points scored after a set period of time. The number of total points earned by each student during a 20-minute period is shown here. Compute R, s^2, and s.

Student No.	Points Earned
1	55
2	74
3	83
4	43
5	25
6	38
7	44
8	49
9	54
10	137

16. On her first test in algebra, Mary earned a score of 75, and she made an 85 on her first psychology test. If the average score on the algebra test was a 68, with $s = 7$, and the average on the psychology test was 91, with $s = 6$, is Mary doing better in psychology or in algebra?

17. In a problem at the end of Chapter 5, data were given representing the number of children in families of students in one of our statistics classes. Use the data, repeated here, to compute R, s^2, and s.

X	f
5	3
3	8
2	18
1	4

18. Compute the major measures of dispersion for the distribution of dropped-ruler test scores for males given in Exercise 13 in Chapter 5; the distribution is presented here.

X	f
13	1
7	4
6	2
5	2
4	2
3	1

19. A distribution of dropped-ruler scores for females was presented in Exercise 14 in Chapter 5. From the distribution presented here, compute R, s_{approx}, s^2, and s.

X	f		X	f
13	3		6	6
11	1		5	2
10	2		4	1
9	3		3	1
8	3		2	1
7	4			

20. Use the distribution of students' attitudes about lying politicians to determine the major measures of dispersion. After you have computed s, use it and $\overline{X}$ to convert a raw score of 4 to a z score; convert 8 to a z score. What is the raw score that is 1.3 standard deviation units above the mean? What score is 1.5 standard deviation units below the mean?

X	f
10	3
9	4
8	5
7	7
6	2
5	2
4	1
3	3
2	1
1	1
0	1

REVIEW OF DESCRIPTIVE STATISTICS

Chapters 3–6 have dealt with techniques to organize and describe data. We began Chapter 3 by presenting a collection of data that, initially at least, was just a random array of numbers. From this array, we constructed a *frequency distribution,* which is a listing of the scores from highest to lowest with each score's frequency of occurrence beside it.

Chapter 4 explored graphing techniques commonly used by behavioral scientists. Most of the graphs were based on the frequency distribution, and the ones illustrated included the frequency polygon, the cumulative frequency (or percentage) curve, the histogram, and the bar graph. In the *frequency polygon,* scores are given on the baseline or *X* axis, whereas frequencies appear on the *Y* axis. The *histogram* is similar to the frequency polygon except that a bar is drawn above each score, with its height indicating the score's frequency. The *bar graph* is used to show categorical data or data in which the scale on the *X* axis consists of labels rather than actual measurements.

The *stem-and-leaf plot* is a simple way to organize and display data with features of both the frequency distribution and the frequency histogram. To construct the stem-and-leaf plot, we split each score into two parts; the first one or two digits are called the stem and the next digit is called the leaf. Rotating the stem-and-leaf plot produces a histogram with digits over the scores rather than bars. The stem-and-leaf plot can also be used to compare two different distributions in side-by-side fashion.

In a *line graph,* an independent variable appears on the *X* axis, whereas some measure of the dependent variable appears on the *Y* axis. A common use of the line graph is to show the development of some behavior over time.

Chapters 5 and 6 discussed techniques used to determine single numbers describing important characteristics of a frequency distribution. In Chapter 5, we discussed the mode, median, and mean, each of which is both a measure of central tendency and a type of average. The *mode* is the most frequently occurring score in a distribution and is useful mainly as a first guess about the data's central tendency.

The *median* is the score in the middle of the distribution—the score above which half of the scores lie and below which half lie. It is the score at the 50th percentile and is the best measure of central tendency when the distribution is badly skewed or when there are missing scores in the data.

The *mean,* or arithmetic average, is the sum of the scores divided by their number. It is the balancing point in the distribution; the sum of the deviation of scores around it is equal to zero. In addition, the mean is the most stable measure of central tendency from sample to sample, and it is used in a variety of other statistical procedures.

Chapter 6 presented techniques to determine the amount of spread of scores in a distribution. The techniques discussed were the range, the average deviation, the variance, and the standard deviation. The *range* is the difference between the highest and lowest scores in a distribution and is useful mainly as a descriptive measure.

The *average deviation* is the average amount that each score in a distribution deviates from the distribution's mean. Because its computation involves taking the absolute value of deviations, the average deviation is not used in other statistical operations. However, because it is an average deviation, the discussion of AD provides a useful prelude to the discussion of two important types of average deviation: the variance and the standard deviation.

The *variance* is the average squared deviation, whereas the *standard deviation* is the square root of the average squared deviation—the square root of the variance, in other words. The baseline of a frequency polygon can be marked off in standard deviation units in addition to raw score units.

In Chapter 6, a *z score* or *standard score* was defined as the deviation of a raw score from the mean in standard deviation units. A *z* score tells you how far and in what direction a raw score is from the mean in standard deviation units. One important use of *z* scores is in making comparisons of raw scores between distributions that have different means and standard deviations.

Another technique that is often included under the umbrella of descriptive statistics—the correlation coefficient—will be covered in Chapter 13. One reason for not including it here is to preserve the continuity between *z* scores, an intuitive look at probability, the normal curve, and confidence intervals and hypothesis testing. At this point, it will be sufficient to say that the *correlation coefficient* measures the degree to which two variables are related to each other. Thus, when we say that two things are correlated (for example, the weight of a car and gas mileage or time spent studying and grades on tests), we mean they go together. Another reason for considering correlation later is that it is hard to imagine computing a correlation and using it in a purely *descriptive* manner—not making any inference beyond the sample at hand. For example, if you found a correlation between class attendance and final grade in statistics for this semester's class, it is almost certain that you are thinking that this is true for other and future classes—an inference.

INFERENTIAL STATISTICS

We have now spent several chapters examining the descriptive uses of statistics. Although descriptive statistics may be more common, social scientists are often much more interested in the inferential use of statistics. Inferential statistics helps us make inferences about a larger population from a sample. In doing so, we are usually testing hypotheses. Thus, inferential statistics helps us decide whether there is support (or lack of support) for a scientific hypothesis. It allows us to make scientific judgments and to determine their degree of certainty. It also tells us how likely we are to be in error when we draw conclusions from our data. As a set of powerful scientific tools, inferential statistics has played a part in much of the scientific development of the 20th century.

As you will see, many types of inferential statistics involve combinations of the descriptive statistics we have already discussed. So in most cases, we will be using "old friends" in new ways to make decisions about hypotheses. In this part of the book, we discuss several inferential statistics, but we begin with a discussion of probability in Chapter 7. Probability is the foundation of statistics. Our statistical judgments are couched in probabilistic terms; that is, we draw conclusions from data based on the likelihood, or probability, of certain kinds of error. A basic understanding of probability is at the core of statistics.

In Chapter 8, we discuss a very important probability distribution, the normal distribution. In the chapter, we develop techniques that we can use to answer questions about a population from which we have taken a sample, if we can assume that there is a normal distribution of our variable of interest in the population. The two major problem types considered in the chapter involve finding scores when we know areas (or probabilities) and finding areas (or probabilities) when we know scores. The methods developed to solve the problems in this chapter will allow us to move easily into the two topics discussed in Chapter 9.

In Chapter 9, we introduce confidence intervals and simple hypothesis testing. We show how to compare sample values to expected values of populations, given a very simple experimental design. This procedure involves using z scores, with which you are already familiar, as well as a related index called the t score.

Chapter 10 extends the one-sample case to two samples—situations in which population values are not available or are unknown. In the simplest case, we compare an experimental group to a control group or we compare scores on a pretest to scores on a posttest to determine the effectiveness of a manipulation or treatment. This procedure involves using different forms of the t test.

Chapter 11 carries the logic of t tests to more than two groups or testing times. For example, we might want to examine the effect of several levels of a treatment or the impact of a treatment at several points in time. The appropriate statistic in these situations is called one-way analysis of variance. Once we have completed our overall analysis of variance and have found that there is at least one meaningful difference, post hoc comparisons allow us to determine more completely the exact pattern of relationships involved. If the one-way ANOVA is not significant, post hoc comparisons are not performed.

Chapter 12 introduces two-way analysis of variance, which extends the one-way analysis of variance to situations that simultaneously incorporate two independent variables instead of one. Two-way analysis of variance is a very powerful and widely used statistical technique, which we will address in an intuitive way.

Chapter 13 discusses correlation, a powerful statistical tool that is descriptive and also allows us to make inferences about the population from which we have drawn a sample. Correlation allows us to describe the strength of the relationship between two sets of scores, such as IQ scores and test scores. Based on the strength of this relationship, we can use scores on one variable to predict scores on the other.

Unfortunately, we often do not have the type of data needed for t tests or analysis of variance. Other techniques have been developed that can be used in these situations. One is chi square, which uses data in categories for which we have only frequencies of occurrence. In Chapter 14, we learn how to calculate chi square.

Chapter 15 presents other alternatives to t tests and analysis of variance that are not as well known as chi square. These alternatives include the Mann–Whitney U test, the Wilcoxen signed-ranks test, and the Kruskal–Wallis one-way analysis of variance for ranked data.

When you complete this part, you will be well equipped to perform many of the most common statistical analyses. In addition, you should be able to read and understand much of the research literature in the behavioral sciences.

Probability

Many years ago, a wily statistics professor taught his class a valuable and expensive lesson about probability. On the first day of the semester, he offered the class a challenge. He bet that at least two people in the class had the same birthday. If he was wrong, he would pay $5 to each student who accepted the challenge. However, if he was correct and two or more people in the room did have the same birthday, each student who took the bet would owe him $5.

Students looked around the room at their 25 or so classmates. It seemed highly unlikely that 2 people in the room would have the same birthday. After all, there were so few students in the room (25) and so many possible birthdays (365). It seemed to many that the odds were heavily in their favor.

A number of high rollers put $5 out on their desks. Then the students began giving the month and day of their birth. After only a few birthdays had been given, a young woman exclaimed, "That's my birthday!" Ouch! Students who bet were $5 poorer, and the professor was $75 richer. "If you're hoping that I'll cancel the bet, you're mistaken," he said. "You must all learn to understand and respect the probabilities of events. Misunderstanding can be expensive!"

In this example, what forces of probability were operating? How could the students be so wrong? Had they stopped to think more carefully, they would have seen their error in judgment.

Here is how it works. The first person in the class (of 25) has 24 others with whom to match, out of 365 possible birthdays, so the chances of a "hit" on the first person are 24/365. For the second person, one birthday is expended, so he or she might match one of 23 others out of 364 remaining possibilities for a 23/364 chance.

121

For the third person, the chances are 22/363. Across all 25 people in the class, the chances are actually very good (better than 55%) that at least two people will have the same birthday. The professor knew this and profited.

In the preceding chapters, we discussed a number of ways to describe data, including arranging a frequency distribution, graphing, computing measures of central tendency, and determining measures of the spread, or dispersion, in the data. We are now almost ready to develop methods for testing statistical hypotheses.

Statistical hypotheses are predictions about populations based on sample results. Although we work with samples, we are often not interested in a sample itself, but rather in what the sample tells us about the population from which it came. Unfortunately, a sample is not the same as a population; it is a subset of the population and may or may not be an accurate reflection of it. Thus, when we hypothesize about a population based on a sample, we are making an "educated guess." Because our hypothesis is based on a good (random) sample, we think it is a good guess or estimate—but how good or accurate is it? With the help of probability, we can determine the degree of certainty we can have in our conclusions.

As mentioned earlier, this chapter marks the beginning of our study of inferential statistics. The techniques introduced in the next several chapters will enable you to apply decisions made from sample data to the population presumably reflected in the sample. The essence of inferential statistics is in attaching a probability to the predictions and estimates of population parameters based on sample statistics. It is for this reason that we need to begin by briefly exploring what is meant by the term *probability*, some ways of thinking about probability, and a few of probability's simpler rules.

THINKING ABOUT PROBABILITY

Most of us intuitively use or at least encounter the idea of probability every day of our lives. For example, we may listen to the radio weather report and hear that the probability of rain is 20%. On the basis of this information, we may decide not to take an umbrella or raincoat with us, or, if we are more cautious, we may elect to be safe rather than sorry. If we decide to reduce our intake of red meat, it may be because we have heard that the probability of heart disease is lower for people with a low fat intake in their diets.

In other words, we are constantly assessing probabilities, whether we do it consciously or not, whether we are right or wrong. Many of our actions are based in part on these assessments—that is, whether we feel an event is likely or unlikely to occur. Our *feelings* about the probability of an event's occurrence may be based on pure speculation or intuition, on previous experience with similar events, or on a knowledge of theoretical outcomes.

There are times, as seen in the example at the beginning of the chapter, when our intuitive ideas about probability are incorrect. In the movie *The World According to Garp*, based on John Irving's novel with the same title, Garp—played by Robin Williams—is obsessed with the idea that a plane will crash into his house.

In order to protect himself from this fate, he buys a house that was rebuilt after previously being destroyed by a plane crash. Will Garp thus be protected from his greatest fear? A sizable body of research has developed on the ways in which people's estimates of probability can go awry and on the factors that influence these estimates. Consider *gambler's fallacy*, the mistaken belief that the probability of a particular event changes with a long string of the same event. Garp is probably subject to this fallacy. Other more mundane examples are easy to find. Suppose an unbiased coin (one in which a head or tail is equally likely to appear on any given flip) is flipped nine times, with a head appearing each time. What is the probability of a tail coming up on the tenth flip? The answer is that the probability of either a head or a tail is exactly the same as it was on the first flip: 1/2, or .5. The string of heads has in no way increased or decreased the likelihood of a tail appearing, even though we may subjectively feel that this has happened. Coins have no memory. Similarly, after a string of failures, people often say, "I'm due for some good luck." Also, baseball announcers frequently refer to a batter with a long hitless streak as someone who is "due." These are all examples of gambler's fallacy.

For our purposes, the **probability** of an event is defined as the proportion of times an event would occur if the chances for occurrence were infinite. In other words, the probability of an event is equal to the number of ways *that* event can occur divided by the number of ways *any* event of that type can occur. Probability is symbolized by p; the probability of a specific event, such as a head on a coin flip, is p(head). Also, probability may be expressed as the *percent chance* of some event. Percent chance is simply probability expressed as a percentage. For example, $p = .3$ is the same as a 30% chance of occurrence.

To illustrate the definition, let's consider what the probability is of obtaining a head from the toss of an unbiased coin. If the coin were flipped an infinite number of times, on half of the flips a head would appear and on the other half a tail would appear. The ratio of the number of times the event (a head) occurs to the total number of events is 1/2, or .5, or 50%.

Similarly, suppose we have one die (singular of *dice*). What is the probability of any particular number of spots from 1 to 6 appearing on any particular roll, assuming the die is unbiased? Because the die has six sides and each side is equally likely to appear, the probability of any particular number of spots is 1/6.

Sometimes, rather than talking about the occurrence of an event, we wish to consider the likelihood of the event's not occurring—its nonoccurrence, in other words. If there's a .3 probability of rain, then there is a .7 probability of no rain today. The probability of an event and the probability of the event not occurring must add to 1.0.

Probability and the Individual

When it comes to what will happen to *you*, probability means probability, not certainty. Regardless of what the probabilities are for some event, there is no guarantee that a *specific event* will turn out according to the expected probabilities. You may know that with your GRE scores your chance of being accepted for graduate study in clinical psychology at a particular university is 85%. This probability does not guarantee *your* admission, however. You may not be accepted, and your friend with a lower GRE score who has a 35% chance of admission may be accepted. For students with both scores, some are admitted and some are not. Probabilities should be thought of as long-run patterns, not as guarantees about what will happen to you as an individual.

Theoretical Probability

Theoretical probability is the way events are supposed to work—in theory, or in terms of *formal* probability. In this realm, situations and events are perfect. Our dice are perfectly formed, and the rolls of the dice are totally unbiased. The deck of cards is perfectly shuffled each time the poker game begins. As a consequence, theoretical or formal probabilities can be derived with great precision. You can undoubtedly find books explaining systems to "beat the odds" at your favorite casino in Las Vegas, but what happens when you get there and actually try out the system may not be the same as what was described by the *theory* of your system.

Real-World Probability

Anyone who can count can become an expert of sorts in **real-world**—or *empirical*—**probability.** This kind of probability is the basis for many assessments of chance that affect our lives. Insurance companies base their rates, to a large extent, on empirical probabilities. For example, if your home is in "tornado alley," then your home insurance rates will be high, because insurance companies have collected data over many years indicating that homes in this part of the country receive windstorm damage more often than homes in other areas. Similarly, regardless of the driving record of any particular teenage male, all teenage male drivers pay much higher car insurance rates than other classes of drivers because of the accident rates of teenage male drivers as a group.

Other examples include the batting averages of baseball players, the free-throw percentages of basketball players, and similar sports statistics that are used to predict the future behavior of individuals. These probabilities are based on past behavior and counting. This type of probability has been called *relative frequency* probability because the occurrence of events (e.g., number of hits) has been tallied relative to the number of opportunities for the event to occur (e.g., number of times at bat). Statisticians become concerned when theoretical probabilities and empirical probabilities do not match up well. In some of the situations, we may suspect that the dice are loaded; in others, that probability theorists need to recheck their theories.

Subjective Probability

We all develop guesses about how likely events are to occur. These guesses can be based on theory (logical analysis), empirical knowledge (experience), and subjective factors such as our attitudes or motivations. **Personal probabilities** are formed on the basis of our own personal, unique perspectives—they are **subjective.**

Personal, subjective probabilities may be largely right or largely wrong. We already saw an example of subjective probability assessment in the vignette at the beginning of this chapter. The students who decided to take the professor's bet on birthdays were engaging in a subjective probability assessment when they reasoned that the students were few and the number of birthdays many—hence, the odds seemed to be in their favor. Similarly, people subject to gambler's fallacy, like Garp, are operating on the basis of subjective probabilities.

Overreliance on subjective probabilities can be detrimental. You may know someone who, in spite of good empirical probability data indicating safety, refuses to fly. You also may know someone who systematically enters lotteries and the Publisher's Clearinghouse sweepstakes even though the chance of winning is astronomically small.

Subjective probabilities are also used in an area called Bayesian statistics. In **Bayesian statistics,** subjective probabilities form a starting point for assessing a subsequent probability. The idea is that we start with an initial (prior) probability assessment. To this we add new information about the event or situation. This new information allows us to refine our initial probability "given" the new data to arrive at a subsequent (or "posterior") probability assessment that is more informative than our initial assessment. For a discussion of Bayesian statistics beyond the scope of this text, consult P. J. Bloomers and R. A. Forsyth, 1977, *Elementary Statistical Methods in Psychology and Education*, 2nd ed., Lanham, MD: University Press of America, Inc.

Bayes's alternative method of making statistical inferences is the really controversial part of his contribution to statistics and is embraced by a minority of statisticians today. The classical approach to inference tells us to make our decision about the outcome of our experiment (effect or no effect) based just on our data, without making any prior assumptions. The Bayesians would have us use the data from our experiment to adjust our prior, possibly subjective, beliefs. The Bayesian view draws its appeal from its seemingly logical use of prior (subjective) probabilities. However, this is also its weak point: Prior probabilities may be wrong or distorted, and data from the same experiment can lead to very different conclusions when different researchers start with different initial beliefs. We will have more to say about Bayesian statistics later in the section on conditional probability. For now, we will take a look at two primary rules of probability: the addition rule and the multiplication rule.

RULES OF PROBABILITY

The Addition Rule

On any particular flip of an unbiased coin, what is the probability of obtaining either a head *or* a tail? Because there are no other possibilities, the probability is 1, or 100%; that is, we will always observe either a head or a tail when we flip the coin. As you can see, to obtain the probability of either a head *or* a tail on one flip, the probabilities of the two possibilities have been summed:

$$p(H) = .5,$$
$$p(T) = .5,$$
$$p(H \text{ or } T) = .5 + .5 = 1,$$

where $p(H)$ is the probability of a head, $p(T)$ is the probability of a tail, and $p(H$ or $T)$ is the probability of a head or a tail.

What is the probability of getting either 1 or 2 on one roll of our unbiased die? Because the probability of getting either number is 1/6, the probability of obtaining either a 1 or a 2 is the sum of their individual probabilities:

$$\frac{1}{6} + \frac{1}{6} = \frac{2}{6}, \text{ or } .33.$$

In other words, 1/3 of the time we would get either a 1 or a 2.

One more example: Suppose you're a graduate student doing research with guinea pigs. You have 10 guinea pigs; 4 are cinnamon brown (CB), 3 are black and white (BW), and 3 are all white (AW). The 10 animals are in one large cage, and you've been asked to take one out. What is the probability that you will draw either a BW or an AW? The probability of getting a BW is 3/10; the probability of getting an AW is the same, 3/10. The probability of getting either a BW or an AW is 3/10 + 3/10 = 6/10, or .6.

These simple examples illustrate the **addition rule of probability**, which states that for mutually exclusive random events, the probability of either one event or another event equals the sum of the probabilities of the individual events. Because the events being combined here include the logical keyword *or*, the addition rule of probability is often called the "OR rule" of probability. The addition rule is expressed symbolically in Formula 7-1, where A and B represent two independent events:

FORMULA 7-1   *Addition rule of probability*

$$p(A \text{ or } B) = p(A) + p(B)$$

The Multiplication Rule

In the previous section, we considered what might happen with only one flip of a coin or one roll of a die. What rule of probability can we apply when dealing with a series of events?

For example, suppose we roll one die twice. What is the probability of obtaining a pair of 1s? All of the possible events that we might observe are shown in

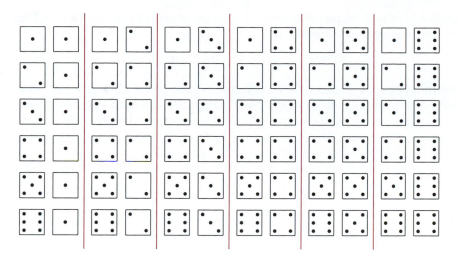

Figure 7-1 All possible events that might be observed following two throws of one unbiased die.

Figure 7-1. Note that in the 36 possible events, there is only one way for two consecutive rolls of 1 to occur. Thus, the probability is 1/36. The same result could also be obtained by multiplying the individual probabilities. In this case, the probability of obtaining a 1 on the first roll is 1/6, and the probability of a 1 on the second roll is also 1/6. The product of the individual probabilities is $1/6 \times 1/6 = 1/36$.

As another example, what is the probability of getting heads in three successive flips of an unbiased coin? Using the multiplication procedure, the product of the individual probabilities is $1/2 \times 1/2 \times 1/2 = 1/8$. This is the same answer that would be obtained if all the possible events were described. The possible events are HHH, HHT, HTT, TTT, TTH, THH, THT, and HTH. As you can see, there is only one way that three heads can occur out of the eight possibilities for three flips of an unbiased coin, and the probability is 1/8.

What about our cage of guinea pigs? What is the probability of drawing three BW guinea pigs if you put the guinea pig back after each draw—in other words, if you sample with replacement? Again, it is the product of the individual probabilities or $3/10 \times 3/10 \times 3/10 = .3 \times .3 \times .3 = .027$.

Stated formally, the **multiplication rule of probability** says that the probability of two or more independent events occurring on separate occasions is the product of their individual probabilities. It is expressed symbolically by Formula 7-2, where $p(A, B)$ is the probability of the occurrence of both A and B:

FORMULA 7-2 *Multiplication rule of probability*

$$p(A, B) = p(A) \times p(B)$$

Because the events being combined here include the logical keyword *and*, the multiplication rule of probability is often called the "AND rule" of probability.

Any number of other independent events could be added to this expression. For example, for three events, we would have

$$p(A, B, C) = p(A) \times p(B) \times p(C).$$

With **independent events,** the occurrence of one event does not alter the probability of any other event. For example, whether or not a head appears on one toss of a coin does not alter the probability of a head appearing on a succeeding toss. Similarly, if there are 10 guinea pigs in a cage, 3 BW, 3 AW, and 4 CB, the probability of selecting a BW is 3/10 initially. If a BW is selected on the first draw and replaced, the probability of selecting a BW on the second draw is still 3/10. Sampling with replacement does not change the probabilities for subsequent events.

However, what if we sample without replacement? What if we're dealing with *nonindependent events*? For example, suppose we've drawn a 6 from a deck of cards and have not replaced it. What is the probability of our drawing another 6? The probability of drawing the first 6 was 4/52, or 1/13, or .077, but the probability of drawing a second 6 depends on the first draw. After one 6 has been taken from the deck and not replaced, there are now only three 6s left in a 51-card deck, for a probability of 3/51, or .059. The probability of drawing a pair of 6s in two draws is therefore .077 × .059 = .0045.

This example is an illustration of **conditional probability,** the probability of an event given that another event has already occurred. Conditional probability is expressed symbolically by $p(B \mid A)$ (read "probability of B given A"). As we have seen, determining the probability for a sequence of events involves the multiplication rule for independent events. The difference here is that the probability of B depends on A. Thus, Formula 7-2 can be modified to reflect nonindependent events:

> **FORMULA 7-3**   *Probability of a sequence of nonindependent events*
>
> $$p(A, B) = p(A) \times p(B \mid A)$$

For three events, the equation becomes

$$p(A, B, C) = p(A) \times p(B \mid A) \times p(C \mid A, B).$$

Let's look at another example that illustrates conditional probability with nonindependent events. Suppose we select an AW guinea pig on the first draw from the cage and do not put it back. What is the probability that we will draw another AW? The probability of drawing the first AW was 3/10, but the probability of drawing another is 2/9. Thus, the probability of selecting AW guinea pigs on consecutive draws is

$$p(AW, AW) = p(AW) \times p(AW \mid AW) = .3 \times .22 = .066.$$

The birthday example at the beginning of the chapter illustrates a series of conditional probabilities. The calculations necessary to solve this problem—determining the probability of any 2 people out of 25 having the same birthday—are quite complicated, because we have to compute the probability of the same day (out of 365 days) being named by 2 or more of the 25 people. Nevertheless, the principle of conditional probability is the same.

More on Conditional Probability

Conditional probability can help us assess probabilities of events in the world around us by providing a way to add information to probabilities we already know. Let's take Formula 7-3 and rearrange it to give us the formula for conditional probability—that is, the formula for the probability of B given A or $p(B \mid A)$. Formula 7-3 is $p(A, B) = p(A) \times p(B \mid A)$. Now, if we divide both sides of the equation by $p(A)$ and reverse the terms, this gives us the formula for conditional probability, which is

$$p(B \mid A) = \frac{p(A, B)}{p(A)}.$$

We gave an example earlier that used the multiplication rule (the AND rule) to show that the probability of getting 1s on two rolls of a die was 1/36; that is,

$p(\text{"1 on first roll" and "1 on second roll"}) =$

$$p(\text{"1 on first roll"}) \times p(\text{"1 on second roll"}) = 1/6 \times 1/6 = 1/36.$$

Now, let's consider the conditional probability of a 1 on the second roll *given* that we obtained a 1 on the first roll. According to the conditional probability formula,

$$p(\text{1 on second roll} \mid \text{1 on first roll}) = \frac{p(\text{1 on first roll}) \times p(\text{1 on second roll})}{p(\text{1 on first roll})}$$

$$= \frac{1/36}{1/6} = 1/6.$$

At first, this may seem like probabilistic sleight-of-hand: In the first instance, the answer is 1/36, whereas in the second (conditional) situation, the answer is 1/6. Remember that in the first example, we simply rolled the die twice. In the second example, *we added more information*—the known condition that a 1 was obtained on the first roll. If we know this, chance operates only on the second roll.

   This example also tells us that events B and A are independent. The probability of a 1 on the first roll is independent of the probability of a 1 on the second roll. The formula for conditional probability can be used to determine whether two events are independent; that is, if $p(B \mid A) = p(B)$, then events A and B are independent. Let's see how this works. By the definition of conditional probability,

$$p(B \mid A) = \frac{p(A, B)}{p(A)}.$$

Now, we will apply the multiplication rule to $p(A, B)$. This gives

$$p(B \mid A) = \frac{p(A) \times p(B)}{p(A)}.$$

As you can see, the $p(A)$s in the numerator and denominator cancel each other, leaving

$$p(B \mid A) = p(B).$$

We conclude from this that events A and B are independent.

On an intuitive level, if $p(B \mid A) = p(B)$, then the "given" occurrence (or non-occurrence) of A has nothing to do with the occurrence of event B, and this is what happened in our die-rolling example. The occurrence of a 1 on the first roll has no effect on the occurrence of a 1 on the second roll. Hence, we have proved what we already knew—that rolls of a die are independent events.

Let's look at an example in which the events are *not* independent. In the College of Arts and Sciences at our university, the probability of randomly selecting a female student is event B, with $p(B) = .526$ (that is, slightly more than half of our A&S majors are women), and "psychology major" is event A, with $p(A) = .0744$ (that is, about 7.5% of A&S students are psychology majors). We also know that $p(\text{"female" and "psychology major"}) = .0564$. Assuming that a person majoring in psychology is selected, what is the probability that the person is a female?

$$p(\text{"female"} \mid \text{"psychology major"}) = \frac{p(\text{"female," "psychology major"})}{p(\text{"psychology major"})}$$

$$= \frac{.0564}{.0744} = .758$$

We knew initially that $p(\text{"female"}) = .526$ in arts and sciences. We then added the information that the person selected was a psychology major. It turns out that the events "female" and "psychology major" are *not* independent, which means that we gain information by knowing that the person selected was a psychology major. We can now say that the probability of selecting a female has increased to .758, if we know that the person selected is a psychology major. This example should give you an added appreciation of what conditional probability can add in terms of increasing the accuracy of predictions.

Bayesian Statistics

Thomas Bayes (1702–1761) was an English clergyman and mathematician who initiated using probability to help establish a mathematical basis for statistical inference. The preceding formula for conditional probability is a simple version of Bayes's original formula or theorem (see Box 7-1). This theorem indicates how conditional probabilities relate to one another.

Box 7-1 Safer Boating Through Bayesian Statistics

We will consider an example of how Bayes's theorem helps us make improved predictions. Here is Bayes's theorem:

$$p(B \mid A) = \frac{p(A \mid B)p(B)}{p(A \mid B)p(B) + p(A \mid \text{not } B)p(\text{not } B)}$$

Several states have recently enacted boating safety education programs. Consider event B to be a "serious boating accident in the next year" and event A to be a "course in boater safety education." We want to know the probability of event B (boating accident) given event A (boating safety course). In other words, what is $p(B \mid A)$?

First we make the following assumptions:

$$p(B) = p(\text{boating accident}) = .09,$$
$$p(\text{not } B) = p(\text{no boating accident}) = 1 - .09 = .91,$$
$$p(A \mid B) = p(\text{safety course } given \text{ boating accident}) = .5,$$
$$p(A \mid \text{not } B) = p(\text{safety course } given \text{ no boating accident}) = .8.$$

From Bayes's theorem, the probability of a boating accident (B) *given* that our captain has taken the safety course (A) is

$$p(B \mid A) = \frac{(.5)(.09)}{(.5)(.09) + (.8)(.91)} = \frac{.045}{.773} = .058.$$

For any randomly selected captain, the probability of a boating accident is .09. If we have the additional information that the captain has taken the safety course, we can revise the probability of a boating accident downward to .058. If we are passengers on a night cruise in shark-infested waters, our appreciation may grow for this reduction of more than 35% in the chance of an accident.

Box 7-1 gives an example of Bayes's theorem applied to predicting boating accidents. In the example, we see how using Bayes's approach, we can predict that the percent chance of a boating accident will fall from 9% to 5.8%, if we know ahead of time (the "prior" probability) that the boat driver has taken the U.S. Power Squadron boater safety education course.

The Bayesian approach to probability and statistics is controversial and, although often discussed, it has not been widely adopted. One problem with the approach—and it's not a small one—involves how to get good estimates of the "prior" probabilities needed in Bayes's formula. Using a "subjective probabilities" approach to assessing prior probabilities has been a point of conflict with statisticians who are dedicated to the empirical or relative frequency approach to probability. Nevertheless, Bayesian statistics, in the form of Bayesian decision theory, has found acceptance and application in business and governmental decision making. In these applications, the needed prior (or subjective) probability estimates are provided by expert opinion. For further information on this topic, see J. Neter, W. Wasserman, and G. A. Whitmore, 1978, *Applied Statistics,* Boston: Allyn and Bacon.

THE BINOMIAL PROBABILITY DISTRIBUTION

In the previous section, you were exposed to a simple and abbreviated introduction to probability theory. It is now time to consider a simple theoretical probability distribution—the binomial.

The **binomial distribution** is based on events in which there are only two possible outcomes on each occurrence, and its construction is often illustrated by coin-flipping examples. To begin, suppose that we flip an unbiased coin three times. As before, the possible outcomes we might observe are HHH, HHT, HTT, TTT, TTH, THH, THT, and HTH. One way to look at the possible outcomes involves calling the heads "hits" and the tails "misses" (alternatively, "successes" and "failures"). Using this approach, the following table can be constructed:

Possible Outcomes of an
Unbiased Coin Flipped
Three Times

Outcome	No. of Hits (X)
HHH	3
HHT	2
THH	2
HTH	2
HTT	1
THT	1
TTH	1
TTT	0

A frequency distribution can be constructed from the table as follows:

X	f
3	1
2	3
1	3
0	1

From the frequency distribution, we can plot a frequency polygon. This was done in Figure 7-2.

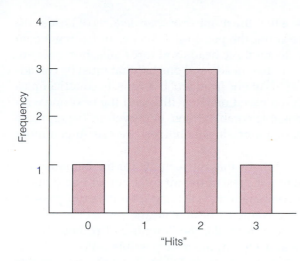

Figure 7-2   Number of ways that "hits" may occur when an
unbiased coin is flipped three times.

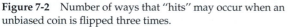

"Hits"	Frequency	Probability
3	1	.125
2	3	.375
1	3	.375
0	1	.125

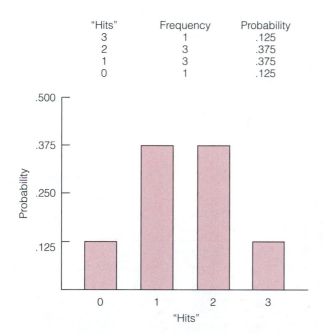

Figure 7-3   Probability associated with each number of "hits."

Finally, we can convert the frequencies into probabilities and plot these rather
than the frequencies. This is shown in Figure 7-3.

We can note from Figures 7-2 and 7-3 that the bar graph in each case is symmetrical. This will always be true for the binomial distribution when $p = .5$.

We can also see by this example that the number of *combinations* of heads and tails must be considered when we count the possible outcomes of tossing a coin three times. There is only one way to get three heads and three tails, but there are three ways—three combinations—of two heads and one tail that must be considered. The same is true for combinations of one head and two tails. In small samples such as the one we've just considered based on three flips and the next one with four flips, we can easily list the possible combinations. However, in larger, more complicated problems, the enumeration of all possibilities becomes much more difficult.

It is with these more difficult situations that the formula for the binomial distribution becomes essential. We will not present the formula but will note that it contains two parts: a "number of combinations" part and a "number of possible outcomes" part. For example, if we wanted to calculate the probability of two heads in three flips using the binomial formula, the "number of combinations" part would give us the answer 3 and the "number of possible outcomes" part would give us the answer 8; thus, the probability is 3/8 or .375. Of course, in this particular example, we were actually able to count the outcomes. In more complex probability problems, we must use formulas for combinations and permutations of events in order to arrive at solutions.

Let's take our example a step further. What are the possible outcomes if we flip our unbiased coin yet a fourth time? The possible outcomes are as follows:

HHHH	HHHT	HHTT	HTTT	TTTT
	HHTH	HTHT	THTT	
	HTHH	HTTH	TTHT	
	THHH	THHT	TTTH	
		THTH		
		TTHH		

The frequency distribution of hits and the probabilities of the hits are as follows:

Hits	f	p
4	1	.0625
3	4	.2500
2	6	.3750
1	4	.2500
0	1	.0625
	16	1.0000

A bar graph depicting the probability of hits is shown in Figure 7-4.

The construction of polygons similar to the ones illustrated in Figures 7-3 and 7-4 using successively larger values of N would reveal two very important features of the binomial distribution: (1) when $p = .5$, the distribution is symmetrical, and (2) as N increases in value, the distribution more closely approximates the *normal probability distribution*. Because of this approximation of the normal distribution by the binomial distribution, the normal distribution is often substituted for the

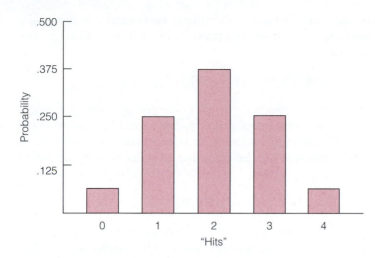

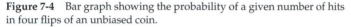

Figure 7-4 Bar graph showing the probability of a given number of hits in four flips of an unbiased coin.

binomial distribution in evaluating binomial data. For this reason, the next chapter will be devoted to the discussion of the normal distribution.

SUMMARY

Probability is defined as the proportion of times an event would occur if the chances for occurrence were infinite, or as the ratio of the number of times the event occurs to the total number of events. Gambler's fallacy is the mistaken notion that the probability of a particular event changes with a long string of the same event.

In terms of whether something will happen to you as an individual, probability is not certainty—unless the probability is 1.0 or 0. From the standpoint of the individual, probabilities should be considered long-run patterns, not guarantees of what will happen. By contrast, theoretical probability refers to the way things are supposed to work according to the formal rules of probability. Probability based on empirical data—real-world probability—is sometimes called relative frequency probability because the occurrence of events has been tallied relative to the total number of opportunities for the events to occur. Subjective probabilities are probabilities formed on the basis of our personal perspectives. Subjective probabilities are used in an area called Bayesian statistics.

Two simple rules from probability theory are the addition rule and the multiplication rule. The addition rule states that the probability of either one event or another event is equal to the sum of the probabilities of the individual events. It is expressed symbolically as

$$p(A \text{ or } B) = p(A) + p(B).$$

The multiplication rule states that the probability of two or more independent events occurring on separate occasions is the product of their individual probabilities. Its symbolic expression is

$$p(A,\ B) = p(A) \times p(B).$$

Events are independent if the occurrence of one event does not alter the probability of any other event. Conditional probability is the probability of an event given that another event has already occurred. It is expressed symbolically as $p(B \mid A)$, and the multiplication rule can be modified to reflect nonindependent events:

$$p(A,\ B) = p(A) \times p(B \mid A).$$

Conditional probability is a contribution by the 18th-century mathematician, Thomas Bayes. The conditional probability of some event B given that event A has occurred is equal to the probability that events A and B have occurred divided by the probability of event A. The formula is only a rearrangement of the formula we gave for the multiplication rule modified to reflect nonindependent events:

$$p(B \mid A) = \frac{p(A,\ B)}{p(A)}.$$

Bayes's theorem is useful because it gives us a way to add new information to our initial probability assessments, making our subsequent probability assessments more informative. Bayes's approach also gives an alternative method for making inferences. His method suggests that research results should be used to adjust prior subjective beliefs about the topic of investigation—an approach that has generated much controversy.

A simple probability distribution called the binomial distribution was described. The binomial distribution is based on events in which there are only two possible outcomes on each occurrence. As N increases, the binomial distribution becomes more and more similar to the normal curve distribution, and the normal distribution is often used to evaluate binomial data.

EXERCISES

1. A standard deck of playing cards has 52 cards, so the probability of drawing any particular card is 1/52. In five consecutive draws (without replacement) from a standard deck of playing cards, what is the probability of obtaining a royal straight flush (10, jack, queen, king, ace) in hearts?

2. Define the following:
   a. gambler's fallacy
   b. addition rule
   c. multiplication rule

3. Toss a coin, roll one die, and draw one card from a standard deck. What is the probability of getting the following combination: tails, 4, king?

4. What is the probability of drawing either an ace or a king on any single draw? What is the probability of drawing either a heart or a spade? What is the probability of drawing an ace and a king on two consecutive draws?

5. What is the probability of drawing aces on four consecutive draws without replacement?

6. The probability of exposure to a virus in a blood transfusion is .001 at a particular hospital. A man who had a blood transfusion at that hospital is later tested for the presence of the virus, and the test is negative. The probability that the test will result in a false negative (i.e., that it will fail to detect the presence of the virus) is .01. What is the probability that the man was exposed to the virus and that the screening test failed to detect it?

7. Harry has just taken a 20-question true–false test for which he has not studied. Assuming random guessing, what is the probability that Harry will miss all 20 questions?

8. Give two examples each of formal probability, relative frequency probability, and subjective probability.

9. You have just bought a ticket for the Chamber of Commerce lottery, and your friend has bought two tickets. You read in the local paper that 500 tickets were sold, and the winner will be chosen tomorrow.

    a. What is the probability that you will win?

    b. What is the probability that your friend will win?

    c. What is the probability that either you or your friend will win?

    d. What is the probability that you and your friend will win?

10. Assume that a lottery was conducted in a small office and only 10 tickets were sold; you and a friend each bought 1 ticket. Two winners will be selected. What is the probability that your friend will get the first prize and you will get the second? What is the probability that you will get the first prize and your friend will get the second?

11. Given the situation in Exercise 10, what is the probability that you two will receive both prizes?

12. What is the probability of three heads in five flips of a fair coin? Of four heads?

13. A study was made of outcomes from psychotherapy and education—whether the client had a college degree. The results of the study are summarized in the following table of probabilities:

		College Degree		
		Yes	No	Total
Psychotherapy Outcome	Good	.30	.12	.42
	Poor	.15	.43	.58
	Total	.45	.55	1.00

    a. What is the probability that a person will have success in psychotherapy?

    b. Given that a person is a college graduate, what is the probability that the person will have a good psychotherapy outcome?

    c. Does added information about education aid in predicting psychotherapy success?

14. Given the same data as in the previous exercise,

    a. What is the probability that a person will have a college degree?

    b. Given that a person has a good psychotherapy outcome, what is the probability that he or she has a college degree?

    c. Does added information about outcome of psychotherapy aid in predicting education?

    d. Are education and psychotherapy success independent?

CHAPTER **8**

The Normal Distribution

Nearly all college-bound high school students take a standardized college admissions test. The two most common are the SAT and the ACT. You may recall the day you received your scores in the mail. They were accompanied by a report containing several tables with scores and percentiles and instructions about how to interpret your scores. You were probably able to figure out whether you had scored high enough to qualify for your preferred college or for certain college programs (e.g., honors programs). You may have wondered, though, how the tables were constructed and how your test scores were converted into percentiles.

The statistical tool used for these procedures is the *normal distribution*, which is a sort of statistical Rosetta stone. Discovered in Egypt by Napoleon's troops in 1799, the Rosetta stone contained a message written in both hieroglyphics and Greek. Scholars were unable to decipher hieroglyphic inscriptions until the Greek translation on the Rosetta stone allowed them to break the code.

We aren't troops in a foreign country, and learning statistics isn't like deciphering hieroglyphics. However, like the Rosetta stone, the normal distribution allows us to make several different translations: from scores to percentiles and probabilities, from probabilities and percentiles to scores, and from scores in one set of units to scores in other units.

The **normal distribution,** also called the **normal curve** or *bell curve* because of its shape, is often attributed to the brilliant German mathematician, Karl Friedrich Gauss (1777–1855). Thus, it is sometimes called the *Gaussian distribution.* Actually, the mathematical equation that generates the normal curve was introduced by Abraham De Moivre (1667–1754) in 1733.

In the normal curve, shown in Figure 8-1, the horizontal axis represents possible scores on some measure such as IQ, and the vertical axis represents the

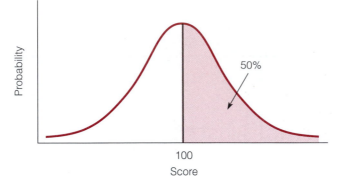

Figure 8-1   Normal curve illustrating the percentage area above the IQ score of 100.

probability of occurrence of the scores. In this chapter, we will learn to use the normal distribution to make translations and to answer questions such as the ones posed in the preceding example about SAT and ACT scores.

The normal distribution is among the handiest tools of statistics. It allows us to attach probabilities to events (or scores) and vice versa. For example, using the normal distribution, we can determine the likelihood of encountering a person with an IQ of 180 or more, or we can calculate the score corresponding to the 25th percentile on a standardized reading test so that we can select students for a special reading program. In the example of college admissions tests, we could dispense with the tables provided and calculate the exact SAT or ACT score corresponding to the 90th percentile. The normal distribution is a useful tool indeed—but what does the normal distribution really mean?

When we say that a measure is normally distributed, we are making a statement about the probability of scores across the range of the horizontal axis—lower scores to the left, intermediate scores in the middle, and higher scores to the right. In the normal distribution, extreme scores, either high or low, have low probabilities and are rare; scores in the midrange have higher probabilities and are more frequent. In other words, to say that a measure is normally distributed simply means that the scores are "piled up" in the middle and rare at the high or low extremes.

Contrary to what most people believe, including many statisticians, most data that we encounter are not normally distributed. In fact, some of our best data, numbers based on ratio scales (e.g., time and distance), are typically positively skewed. Some measurements, however, such as height, weight, and IQ, *are* normally distributed, and many empirical distributions (distributions based on actual measurement and observation) are similar enough to the normal distribution for us to treat them as if they were normal distributions. Moderate departures from "normality" usually don't disturb the statistical conclusions that we make. Thus, in answering questions about the distribution of scores, we will treat our frequency distributions as if they had the shape of the normal curve.

The normal distribution is the limiting case for a number of other distributions we will discuss. In Chapter 9, for example, we will consider a distribution composed of sample means. As the samples whose means comprise the sampling distribution increase in size, the distribution becomes more nearly normal. In Chapter 14, we will discuss the distribution of chi square, which approaches a normal distribution as N increases. Thus, even if we are working with distributions other than the normal curve, we can often assume a normal distribution with large samples. Further, through the process of sampling, all data, no matter what their original form, can be made to correspond to a normal distribution. This process is the basis of the sampling distribution of means, which we will discuss in Chapter 9.

CURVES AND PROBABILITY

All distributions of scores can be thought of as **probability distributions;** that is, a distribution represents the probabilities associated with scores in addition to the scores themselves. Think of the area under a portion of the distribution as representing the probability associated with the scores falling in that area.

    For example, we can think of the curve in Figure 8-1 as representing all (100%) IQ scores. If we select a person at random and measure his or her IQ using the Stanford–Binet test of intelligence, what is the likelihood that it will be above 100? (The Stanford–Binet was constructed to give a mean of 100, with a standard deviation of 16.) As you can see in Figure 8-1, 50% of the distribution of IQ scores fall above 100; therefore, the probability is 50%. What is the probability of selecting a person with an IQ below 100? Again, it is 50%.

    What is the chance of choosing a person with an IQ above 120? The small shaded portion in Figure 8-2 represents the area of the curve corresponding to an IQ above 120. If we could determine the proportion of the curve that is shaded, we would have the answer to our question. Determining this proportion usually involves two steps using the normal distribution. The first step is to convert our

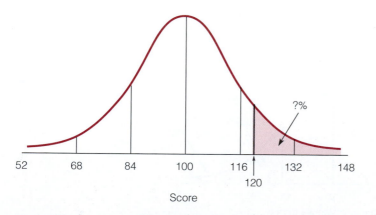

Figure 8-2 Normal curve illustrating the problem of finding the percentage area above an IQ score of 120.

scores to units of the standard normal distribution. This is accomplished by converting our raw scores to z scores. The second step is to use the z scores in conjunction with Table A in Appendix 4 to determine an area (proportion of the curve) that will answer our question. These steps will be discussed more fully later. Before we go any further, however, we must apply these ideas about probability to the normal curve.

CHARACTERISTICS OF THE NORMAL CURVE

We've alluded frequently in previous chapters to the properties of the normal curve. Actually, there are many possible normal curves, each differing in its values for the mean and standard deviation. For a given mean, the larger the standard deviation, the greater the spread of scores; that is, although each normal curve is bell shaped, as the standard deviation increases, the curve becomes flatter.

Normal curves all share certain characteristics. First, each normal curve is symmetrical; if you draw a line down the middle and fold the right half of the curve over the left half, the two halves will coincide. Second, each normal curve is unimodal, and its mean, median, and mode all have the same value. Third, the tails of each curve never quite reach the X axis; they stretch to minus infinity ($-\infty$) on the left side and plus infinity ($+\infty$) on the right.

The **standard normal curve** is a special example of the normal distribution in which the mean is 0 and the standard deviation is 1. If we draw the standard normal curve and mark off the X axis in standard deviation units, the result is the curve shown in Figure 8-3. Notice that some percentages are entered on the curve. For example, between the mean and 1 standard deviation unit above the mean there is the notation 34.13%. What does this mean?

Although the standard normal curve never quite reaches the X axis, in practice we treat it as though it did. Thus, if we assume that the total area under the curve (the area between the curve and the X axis) is 100%, then 34.13% of the total area under the curve lies between the mean and 1 standard deviation unit above the

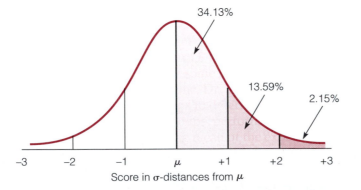

Figure 8-3   The standard normal curve with several areas labeled.

mean. Because the curve is symmetrical, the same thing is true to the left of (below) the mean as well. Continuing, we find that 13.59% of the area lies between 1 and 2 standard deviation units on either side of the mean. Summing these two areas on each side of the mean, we find that 47.72% (34.13% + 13.59%) of the area lies between the mean and 2 standard deviation units on either side of it. Finally, we see that only 2.15% of the total area under the normal curve lies between 2 and 3 standard deviation units above or below the mean. Combining all the areas, we can see that almost the entire normal curve (99.74%) is contained between ±3 standard deviation units of the mean.

In other words, almost the entire normal curve is bounded by 6 standard deviation units. You may recall from the "Troubleshooting" section in Chapter 6 that if you have a fairly large, symmetrical distribution, s is going to be somewhere near one sixth of the range. Now you know why.

Because the normal curve is symmetrical, we really need to consider only one side of the distribution; the values on the other side will be identical. Fortunately for us, the areas under the normal curve have been determined for many different standard deviation units from the mean and are given in Appendix 4, Table A. However, the distances from the mean in the table are based on the *standard* normal curve, which has a mean of 0 and a standard deviation of 1. It is unlikely that we will ever encounter a sample in which the mean is exactly 0 and the standard deviation is 1. Thus, we will avail ourselves of the table by converting our score values into standard scores, or z scores.

REVIEW OF z SCORES

We discussed standard scores, or z scores, in Chapter 6. At that time, a z score was defined as the deviation of a raw score from the mean in standard deviation units; that is, a z score tells us how far from the mean a score is in standard deviation units and in which direction. Negative z scores indicate that the score is below the mean, and positive z scores correspond to scores above the mean.

Recall the formulas for converting raw scores to z scores:

FORMULAS 6-16 AND 6-17   *z scores from a raw score*

$$z = \frac{X - \mu}{\sigma} \quad \text{or} \quad z = \frac{X - \overline{X}}{s}$$

For converting z scores back to raw scores, we introduced Formulas 6-18 and 6-19:

FORMULAS 6-18 AND 6-19   *Raw score from a z score*

$$X = z\sigma + \mu \quad \text{or} \quad X = zs + \overline{X}$$

Let's consider an example to refresh our memories about the use of these formulas. Suppose we find for a sample of women that the average shoe size is 8.25, with a standard deviation of 1.17. What will be the z score, or standard score, corresponding to a shoe size of 10.5? Using Formula 6-17, we have

$$z = \frac{X - \overline{X}}{s} = \frac{10.5 - 8.25}{1.17} = \frac{2.25}{1.17} = 1.92.$$

Based on this sample, a woman who wears a size 10.5 shoe will be 1.92 standard deviation units above the mean.

Continuing with the same example, what size shoe will be worn by a woman who is 2.25 standard deviation units below the mean? In this case, we have been given the z score, $z = -2.25$, and we are asked to convert it to a raw score. Using Formula 6-19, we have

$$X = zs + \overline{X} = -2.25(1.17) + 8.25 = -2.63 + 8.25 = 5.62.$$

Thus, the shoe size corresponding to a z score of -2.25 is 5.62. This woman will probably have to try on a $5\frac{1}{2}$ and a 6 to get a pair of shoes that fits!

---

⑤ CHECKING YOUR PROGRESS

Use the example of women's shoe sizes ($\overline{X} = 8.25$, $s = 1.17$) to determine the z score for a size 6. What shoe size lies 2.5 standard deviation units above the mean?

Answer: $z = -1.92$; $X = 11.18$. A shoe size of 6 corresponds to a z score of -1.92, and size 11 is 2.5 standard deviation units above the mean.

USING THE NORMAL CURVE TABLE

Now that we know how to convert a raw score into a z score and vice versa, what do we do with this knowledge? We can use it to give us access to the normal curve table, which can provide information about the population from which our sample was drawn.

Let's examine the portion of the normal curve table (Table A) that is shown in Table 8-1. From the normal curve table, we can find the percentage of the total area under the curve for a particular z score. Column A contains z scores to the nearest hundredth. In column B, we can find the percentage for the area between the mean and any particular z score we have. In column C, the table gives us the remaining area under the curve beyond our z score.

Let's look at a specific z score to see what information we can extract from the table. We'll use a z score of 0.52. To determine the percentage area under the curve between the mean and a z score of 0.52, we look down column A until we locate

TABLE 8-1

Reproduction of a portion of Table A, the normal curve table: Areas under the normal curve (in percent). The complete table is found in Appendix 4.

(A) z	(B) area between mean and z	(C) area beyond z	(A) z	(B) area between mean and z	(C) area beyond z	(A) z	(B) area between mean and z	(C) area beyond z
0.00	00.00	50.00	0.40	15.54	34.46	0.80	28.81	21.19
0.01	00.40	49.60	0.41	15.91	34.09	0.81	29.10	20.90
0.02	00.80	49.20	0.42	16.28	33.72	0.82	29.39	20.61
0.03	01.20	48.80	0.43	16.64	33.36	0.83	29.67	20.33
0.04	01.60	48.40	0.44	17.00	33.00	0.84	29.95	20.05
0.05	01.99	48.01	0.45	17.36	32.64	0.85	30.23	19.77
0.06	02.39	47.61	0.46	17.72	32.28	0.86	30.51	19.49
0.07	02.79	47.21	0.47	18.08	31.92	0.87	30.78	19.22
0.08	03.19	46.81	0.48	18.44	31.56	0.88	31.06	18.94
0.09	03.59	46.41	0.49	18.79	31.21	0.89	31.33	18.67
0.10	03.98	46.02	0.50	19.15	30.85	0.90	31.59	18.41
0.11	04.38	45.62	0.51	19.50	30.50	0.91	31.86	18.14
0.12	04.78	45.22	0.52	19.85	30.15	0.92	32.12	17.88
0.13	05.17	44.83	0.53	20.19	29.81	0.93	32.38	17.62
0.14	05.57	44.43	0.54	20.54	29.46	0.94	32.64	17.36
0.15	05.96	44.04	0.55	20.88	29.12	0.95	32.89	17.11
0.16	06.36	43.64	0.56	21.23	28.77	0.96	33.15	16.85
0.17	06.75	43.25	0.57	21.57	28.43	0.97	33.40	16.60
0.18	07.14	42.86	0.58	21.90	28.10	0.98	33.65	16.35
0.19	07.53	42.47	0.59	22.24	27.76	0.99	33.89	16.11
0.20	07.93	42.07	0.60	22.57	27.43	1.00	34.13	15.87
0.21	08.32	41.68	0.61	22.91	27.09	1.01	34.38	15.62
0.22	08.71	41.29	0.62	23.24	26.76	1.02	34.61	15.39
0.23	09.10	40.90	0.63	23.57	26.43	1.03	34.85	15.15
0.24	09.48	40.52	0.64	23.89	26.11	1.04	35.08	14.92
0.25	09.87	40.13	0.65	24.22	25.78	1.05	35.31	14.69
0.26	10.26	39.74	0.66	24.54	25.46	1.06	35.54	14.46
0.27	10.64	39.36	0.67	24.86	25.14	1.07	35.77	14.23
0.28	11.03	38.97	0.68	25.17	24.83	1.08	35.99	14.01
0.29	11.41	38.59	0.69	25.49	24.51	1.09	36.21	13.79
0.30	11.79	38.21	0.70	25.80	24.20	1.10	36.43	13.57
0.31	12.17	37.83	0.71	26.11	23.89	1.11	36.65	13.35
0.32	12.55	37.45	0.72	26.42	23.58	1.12	36.86	13.14
0.33	12.93	37.07	0.73	26.73	23.27	1.13	37.08	12.92
0.34	13.31	36.69	0.74	27.04	22.96	1.14	37.29	12.71
0.35	13.68	36.32	0.75	27.34	22.66	1.15	37.49	12.51
0.36	14.06	35.94	0.76	27.64	22.36	1.16	37.70	12.30
0.37	14.43	35.57	0.77	27.94	22.06	1.17	37.90	12.10
0.38	14.80	35.20	0.78	28.23	21.77	1.18	38.10	11.90
0.39	15.17	34.83	0.79	28.52	21.48	1.19	38.30	11.70

Source: This table is from R. P. Runyon and A. Haber, *Fundamentals of Behavioral Statistics* (Third Edition, Addison-Wesley, 1976, pp. 377–379). Copyright © 1976 by Addison-Wesley. Reprinted with permission of The McGraw-Hill Companies.

0.52. Adjacent to this, in column B, is the number 19.85. This tells us that between the mean of a normal distribution and a z score of 0.52 lies approximately 20% of the normal curve. A glance at column C reveals that slightly over 30% (30.15, to be more precise) of the area under the curve is beyond a z score of 0.52. The z score and associated areas are shown in Figure 8-4.

What about negative z scores? Because the normal curve is symmetrical, there is no need to reproduce both halves. For this reason, only the right half is reproduced in the table. If we were asked to find the area under the curve between the mean and a z score of −1.06, we would look up 1.06 and report that the area was 35.54% of the area under the curve. Remember that a negative z score indicates we are dealing with a portion of the distribution below the mean. *The areas themselves are always positive.*

We can also use the normal curve table to determine the z score associated with a particular area of the curve. For example, suppose we want to know the z score that has 17% of the area under the curve above it—in other words, the z score cutting off the upper 17% of the curve. The problem is shown graphically in Figure 8-5.

Looking at Table 8-1, we can see that for any z score, the values given in columns B and C will always sum to 50%. If we know one value, we can always find the other by subtracting from 50%. We can look in column C to find the area beyond the z score we want (17%), or we can look in column B to find the area between the mean and z (50 − 17 = 33%). Either way, we find from column A that z = 0.95; that is, we see from column C that 17.11% is closer to 17% than is 16.85% (which corresponds to a z score of 0.96), and 32.89% in column B is closer to 33% than is 33.15%. Once we've found the z score, we can use Formula 6-18 or 6-19 to convert it into a raw score.

Let's stop briefly at this point to see where we are and where we are going in this chapter. So far, we have had a brief introduction to the normal curve—its importance and its characteristics. Formulas have been reintroduced, two for con-

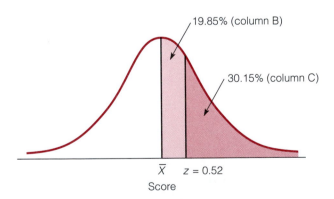

19.85% (column B)

30.15% (column C)

$\overline{X}$ z = 0.52

Score

Figure 8-4 Normal curve showing a z score of 0.52 and associated areas from Table A, a portion of which is reproduced in Table 8-1. The number 19.85% is from column B; 30.15% is from column C.

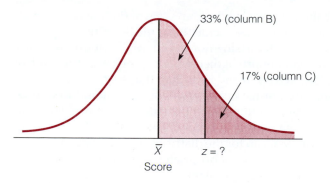

Figure 8-5   A normal curve illustrating the problem in which we want to find the z score cutting off the upper 17% of the curve.

verting raw scores to z scores and two for converting z scores to raw scores. A brief description of Table A has been presented, along with examples illustrating how to use the table to find areas under the normal curve and to find z scores cutting off specific areas.

Thus, we have covered four types of problems, and we can develop a simple way to outline each of them. First, we were given a distribution with known mean and standard deviation; given a particular score (X), we were asked to find the corresponding z score. The outline for this problem is $X \rightarrow z$. In the second type of problem, we were given z and were asked to find X, outlined $z \rightarrow X$. Second, using the normal curve table, we were given a z value and asked to find either the area between the z and the mean or the area beyond the given z. This problem is outlined $z \rightarrow$ Area. Finally, we were given an area, either between the mean and a z score or beyond a z, and were asked to find z, outlined Area $\rightarrow z$. This outline approach may appear very simple to you now, but you will find it increasingly helpful as we move through this chapter and encounter problems requiring more steps.

In the rest of the chapter, we will continue to encounter these two major types of problems: problems in which we need to find areas under the curve and problems in which we need to find scores cutting off particular areas. Moreover, because areas under the curve correspond to probabilities, we will also learn to convert scores to probabilities and probabilities to scores.

FINDING AREAS UNDER THE CURVE

Finding the Percentile Rank of a Score

If a person has a verbal SAT score of 700, what is his or her percentile rank? To begin with, **percentile rank** is the percentage of cases up to and including the one in which we are interested. Thus, our problem becomes one of finding the percentage of the population that scores 700 or less. Incidentally, the definition of percentile rank is the same whether we are discussing normal curve distributions or any other type of distribution. Even in nonnormal distributions, the percentile rank of a score is always the total percentage up to and including that score.

Before you begin working any normal curve problem, you should first draw the normal curve and label it with the information provided in the problem; you can then go on to determine the areas or scores needed. Let's assume for this problem and for any others like it that the mean for the distribution of verbal SAT scores is 500 and the standard deviation is 100. An appropriately labeled curve is shown in Figure 8-6, along with the outline for the problem.

Because we have been given a raw score (700), we must first convert it to a z score. The z score for a verbal SAT of 700 is

$$z_{700} = \frac{X - \mu}{\sigma} = \frac{700 - 500}{100} = \frac{200}{100} = 2.00.$$

From column B in Table A, we see that 47.72% of the curve falls between a z score of 2.00 and the mean. When we add this new information to the graph in Figure 8-6, we get Figure 8-7.

Because we are interested in the percentile rank of someone scoring 700, we need to find the total area at or *below* 700. We have just found that the area between 500 and 700 is 47.72%; and we already know that the area to the left of the mean is exactly 50% of the total curve. Therefore, the area below a score of 700 is 50 + 47.72 = 97.72% of the curve. We conclude that a person scoring 700 has a verbal SAT score equal to or higher than approximately 98% of the population.

Let's try another problem. What is the percentile rank of someone with a verbal SAT score of 444? Again, the first steps are to draw the normal curve and label it appropriately. This has been done in Figure 8-8. The outline for the problem is $X \rightarrow z \rightarrow$ Area.

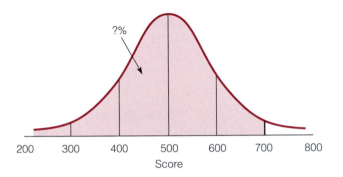

Figure 8-6   A normal curve illustrating the problem in which we want to find the percentile rank of a score of 700. The outline for the problem is $X \rightarrow z \rightarrow$ Area.

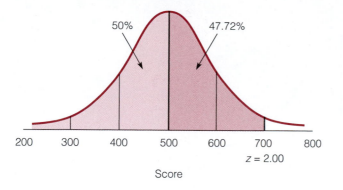

Figure 8-7 Normal curve showing an area of 47.72% (taken from Table A) between the mean and a score of 700 ($z = 2.00$).

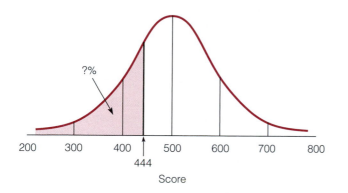

Figure 8-8 Normal curve illustrating the problem in which we want to find the percentile rank of a score of 444.

From the figure we can see that we need to find the area under the curve at or below the score of 444. To use the normal curve table, we must first convert the score of 444 to a z score:

$$z_{444} = \frac{X - \mu}{\sigma} = \frac{444 - 500}{100} = \frac{-56}{100} = -0.56.$$

The negative z score tells us that we are dealing with a score to the left of, or below, the mean. We find from the table that 21.23% of the curve lies between $z = 0.56$ (or -0.56) and the mean and that 28.77% of the curve lies beyond our z score. In Figure 8-9, this new information is added to the previous graph, and it is evident that 28.77% is the area we want. We conclude, then, that the percentile rank of someone with a verbal SAT score of 444 is 28.77, or that the person scores as well as or better than about 29% of the population.

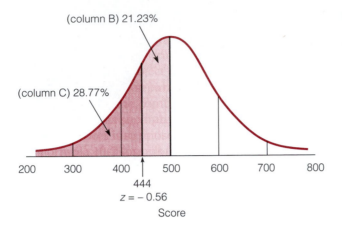

(column B) 21.23%

(column C) 28.77%

444
$z = -0.56$

Score

Figure 8-9   Normal curve on which has been entered the information from Table A that 21.23% of the curve lies between the mean and the score of 444, whereas 28.77% lies below the score.

⟲ CHECKING YOUR PROGRESS

As a final exercise in determining percentile rank, suppose we trained 1,000 rats to run from one end of a 6-foot straight alley runway to the other. On the final run for each animal, we recorded the speed of the run in feet per second. The mean running speed for the 1,000 rats was 2.4 feet per second, with a standard deviation of 0.8 foot per second. What is the percentile rank of a rat that traverses the runway at a speed of 3.7 feet per second? 1.8 feet per second?

Answer: 94.84%; 22.66%. The rat that runs 3.7 feet per second is faster than 94.84% of its fellow rats; the rat that runs 1.8 feet per second equals or exceeds only 22.66% of its fellow rats.

Finding the Percentage of the Normal Curve Above a Score

To find the percentile rank of a score, we had to find the percentage of the normal curve *below* the score. A related problem is to find the percentage of the curve above a particular point. Earlier in the chapter, we asked what the likelihood was of an IQ score above 120. To answer the question, we must find the percentage of the IQ distribution falling above 120. As in the previous section, we will first draw the normal curve, this time with a mean of 100 and a standard deviation of 16, and locate the area we want to find. This problem is pictured in Figure 8-10, and the outline is again $X \rightarrow z \rightarrow$ Area.

As before, we have been given a raw score (120) and must first convert this score into a z score so we can use the normal curve table:

$$z_{120} = \frac{120 - 100}{16} = \frac{20}{16} = 1.25.$$

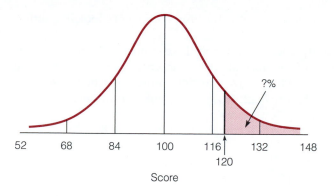

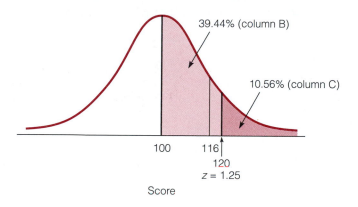

Figure 8-10 Normal curve illustrating the problem of finding the percentage area above an IQ score of 120.

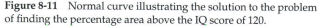

Figure 8-11 Normal curve illustrating the solution to the problem of finding the percentage area above the IQ score of 120.

From Appendix 4, Table A, we find that 39.44% of the curve lies between the mean and a z score of 1.25 and that 10.56% of the curve lies beyond this z score. The new information has been entered into the original diagram of the normal curve, and we can see from Figure 8-11 that the area we want is 10.56%. We conclude that approximately 11% of the population has IQ scores above 120.

Finding Percentage Frequency

Another useful piece of information about the normal curve is that the percentage area under the curve is the same thing as percentage frequency. In other words, when we find a percentage area under the curve, we can take that percentage of the total sample size to find how many subjects have scores in the area. For example, if we administer an IQ test to 250 randomly selected individuals, we would expect 10.56% of them to score 120 or above. How many would score 120 or above?

The answer is 10.56% of 250, or 26.4 (realistically, 26) people. Let's look at another example.

How many of our randomly selected 250 would we expect to score above 80? As before, we draw a diagram of the normal curve and enter the information we have. Then we examine it to see whether we can determine the area we want to find. The problem is shown in Figure 8-12. Now, the problem outline is $X \rightarrow z \rightarrow$ Area $\rightarrow$ Number.

To use the normal curve table, we first convert the IQ score of 80 into a z score:

$$z_{80} = \frac{80 - 100}{16} = \frac{-20}{16} = -1.25.$$

From Table A, we find that 39.44% of the normal curve lies between the mean and a z score of −1.25. Adding this information to Figure 8-12 results in Figure 8-13.

Because 50% of the normal curve lies above the mean, the total area above an IQ score of 80 is 50 + 39.44 = 89.44%. However, this is not what the question asks

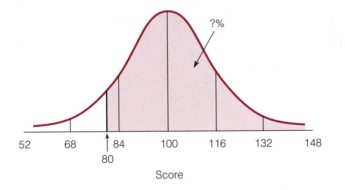

Figure 8-12   Normal curve illustrating the problem of finding the area above an IQ score of 80.

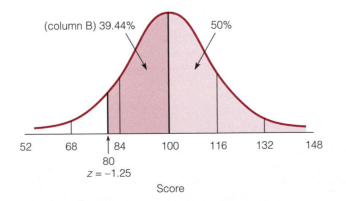

Figure 8-13   Normal curve showing that the area from the mean to the IQ score of 80 is 39.44%.

us to find. We want to know how many people from the group of 250 are likely to score 80 or above. Thus, we need to find 89.44% of 250. Using a pocket calculator, we find that

$$250 \times 89.44\% = 223.6$$

or, another way,

$$250 \times 0.8944 = 223.6.$$

In other words, we would expect about 224 people to score 80 or above.

↺ CHECKING YOUR PROGRESS

Remember our 1,000 rats trained on a straight alley runway? The mean running speed was 2.4 feet per second, with a standard deviation of 0.8 foot per second. On the basis of the normal curve distribution, if we trained 300 more rats, how many could we expect to have running speeds of 3.28 feet per second or more?

Answer: 13.57% of 300 = 40.71 or 41 rats (When dealing with living organisms such as rats and people, it makes sense to round the answer to the nearest whole number.)

Finding an Area Between Two Scores

We have learned how to find a percentage area below a score (percentile rank of the score) and how to determine an area above a score. What about determining a percentage area (or frequency) between two scores? For example, suppose we are asked to find the number of people in a random sample of 1,000 that have IQ scores between 90 and 120.

The problem, then, is to determine the area between the scores of 90 and 120 and to convert this area to a frequency based on $N = 1,000$. The outline of the problem is again $X \rightarrow z \rightarrow$ Area $\rightarrow$ Number, but there are now two steps involved. To use the normal curve table, we must first convert the two raw scores (90 and 120) to z scores. The z score for 90 is

$$z_{90} = \frac{90 - 100}{16} = \frac{-10}{16} = -0.625,$$

which rounds to -0.63. (Remember that when the last digit is 5 or more, we round up.) The z score for 120 is

$$z_{120} = \frac{120 - 100}{16} = \frac{20}{16} = 1.25.$$

From the normal curve table, we find that 23.57% of the curve lies between the mean and a z score of −0.63 and that 39.44% of the curve lies between the mean and a z score of 1.25. Figure 8-14 tells us that the total area from 90 to 120 is

$$23.57\% + 39.44\% = 63.01\%.$$

The last step is to find 63.01% of 1,000, which is

$$1,000 \times 63.01\% = 630.1, \text{ or } 630.$$

Thus, about 630 people would have IQ scores between 90 and 120. Note that drawing a sketch such as Figure 8-14 helps you to visualize the problem and enables you to see easily that the two areas must be added together to arrive at the correct solution. We have found that drawing such sketches of normal curve problems will help you understand the problem better and will enable you to avoid errors in combining areas.

A slightly more difficult problem involves finding an area between two scores when both are on the same side of the mean. To illustrate, suppose we want to know the number of people in a sample of 1,000 that have IQ scores between 110 and 125. Again, the problem outline is $X \rightarrow z \rightarrow$ Area $\rightarrow$ Number. As before, our task is to find the area between the two scores (110 and 125) and then to convert the area into a frequency. The z scores are

$$z_{110} = \frac{110 - 100}{16} = \frac{10}{16} = 0.63,$$

$$z_{125} = \frac{125 - 100}{16} = \frac{25}{16} = 1.56.$$

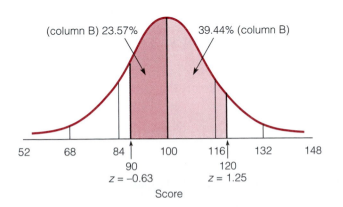

Figure 8-14 Normal curve on which have been entered areas obtained from Table A between 90 and the mean (23.57%) and between 120 and the mean (39.44%).

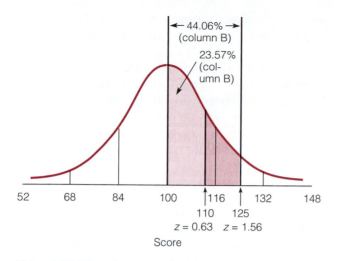

Figure 8-15 Normal curve on which have been entered the areas from the mean to 110 (23.57%) and from the mean to 125 (44.06%).

Between the mean and a z score of 0.63 lies 23.57% of the curve, and between the mean and a z score of 1.56 lies 44.06% of the curve. From Figure 8-15, it is clear that the area we are seeking is

$$44.06\% - 23.57\% = 20.49\%$$

of the area under the curve. Finally, 20.49% of 1,000 is

$$1,000 \times 20.49\% = 204.9, \text{ or } 205.$$

Thus, about 205 people would have IQ scores between 110 and 125.

Note that we took both of the areas from column B to solve this problem. We could also have taken both areas from column C, again subtracting the smaller area (5.94% for a z score of 1.56) from the larger area (26.43% for $z = 0.63$). 26.43 − 5.94 = 20.49%, which is the same value we obtained earlier. Whenever both of your scores are on the same side of the mean, just remember to get both of your areas from the same column, either B or C, and to subtract the smaller area from the larger to find the area between the two scores. Once again, you can see how helpful it is to sketch the problem. It easily shows what areas need to be subtracted to arrive at the correct answer.

CHECKING YOUR PROGRESS

Suppose 2,000 students have taken a test in introductory psychology, and we are told that $\overline{X} = 73.5$ and $s = 9.8$. What percentage of the students made scores between 70 and 90? How many scored between 80 and 95? Between 50 and 60? If a grade of D was given for scores of 60 to 69, how many students earned a D?

Answer: 59.41%, 481 students, 151 students, 478 students. The percentage of students scoring between 70 and 90 was 59.41%. There were 481 students scoring between 80 and 95, 151 students scoring between 50 and 60, and 478 students earning a D.

Probability and Areas Under the Curve

As we noted at the beginning of the chapter, the normal distribution, as well as other distributions, is a probability distribution. Although we have been discussing percentage areas under the curve up to this point, we could just as easily have talked about probabilities. In fact, we can convert the percentage areas in the normal curve table to probabilities using Formula 8-1.

> **FORMULA 8-1   *Probability from percentage area***
>
> $$p(\text{probability}) = \frac{\%\ \text{area}}{100}$$

For example, if the percentage area under the curve between 2 and 3 standard deviation units of the mean is 2.15, then the probability of someone having a score in this area is

$$\frac{2.15}{100} = .0215.$$

Let's look at a specific problem.

Suppose we are asked to determine the probability that a person picked at random would have an IQ score of 136 or above, given that the mean IQ is 100 with a standard deviation of 16. After constructing the curve in Figure 8-16, and outlining the problem $X \rightarrow z \rightarrow \text{Area} \rightarrow \text{Probability}$, we see that the immediate problem is to determine the percentage area above a score of 136.

As before, the first step is to convert the raw score into a z score:

$$z_{136} = \frac{136 - 100}{16} = \frac{36}{16} = 2.25.$$

According to the normal curve table, 48.78% of the normal curve lies between the mean and $z = 2.25$, with just 1.22% of the curve lying beyond that z score. Figure 8-17 is constructed to incorporate the new information.

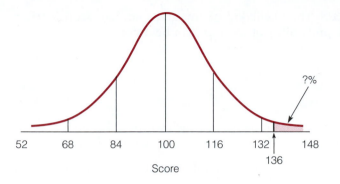

Figure 8-16 Normal curve illustrating the problem of finding the probability of an IQ score of 136 or above.

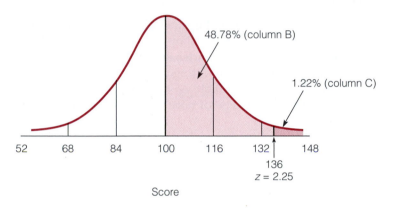

Figure 8-17 Normal curve showing the percentage area between the mean and an IQ score of 136 (48.78%) and the area above 136 (1.22%).

This area of 1.22% above a score of 136 can be converted to probability with Formula 8-1:

$$p = \frac{\% \text{ area}}{100} = \frac{1.22}{100} = .0122.$$

Because the range of probability values is from 0 to 1, a value of .0122 expresses a low probability event, one that occurs only a little over 1 time in 100. It is unlikely that we would encounter someone with an IQ score of 136 or higher.

---

⑤ CHECKING YOUR PROGRESS

Considering the 2,000 psychology students again, with a mean test score of 73.5 and $s = 9.8$, what is the probability that someone scored 95 or above? 60 or below?

Answer: $p = .0143$, $p = .0838$. The likelihood of any given student scoring 95 or above is .0143, whereas the probability of scoring 60 or below is .0838.

Brief Summary

We have now completed our look at problems in which we are asked to find areas under the normal curve. The specific examples considered were as follows:

1. Finding the percentile rank of a score, percentile rank defined as the total area below the score
2. Finding the area above a score
3. Finding the area between two scores

In addition, we saw that percentage area was the same thing as percentage frequency and that probability was percentage divided by 100.

In general, the procedure for finding areas under the curve consists of drawing the curve and labeling it appropriately, converting any raw scores to z scores, and then consulting the normal curve table (Table A) to find the area(s) needed. It is now time to discuss the second major type of normal curve problem: finding a score defining an area under the curve.

FINDING SCORES CUTTING OFF AREAS

Finding the Score That Has a Particular Percentile Rank

So far, we have considered cases in which we have been given a particular score and asked to find some area under the curve. What if we reverse the procedure and locate a score that corresponds to some particular area of the curve? Suppose you needed to achieve a verbal SAT score at or above the 80th percentile to be considered for the honors program at your preferred university. What score would that be? When doing these problems, remember to always begin by drawing a picture showing the information you have and what is needed. The outline for this problem is Area $\rightarrow z \rightarrow X$.

As illustrated in Figure 8-18, the problem is to locate the score having a percentile rank of 80—that is, where 80% of the curve lies below the score. We know immediately that the score is above the mean because it has a rank higher than 50%. Thus, we must look in the normal curve table for a z score that has 30% of the curve between it and the mean ($80\% - 50\% = 30\%$).

We will begin by looking for 30% in column B of the table, and when we find the closest number to it, we will look in column A for the z score. The closest number to 30% in column B is 29.95, which is the area between the mean and a z score of 0.84. Therefore, we will use 0.84 as the appropriate z score.

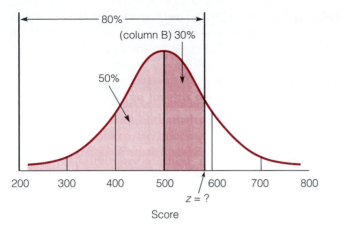

Figure 8-18 Normal curve illustrating the problem of finding the score at the 80th percentile. The outline for the problem is Area → z → X.

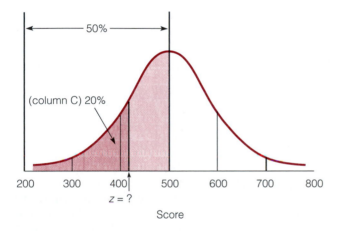

Figure 8-19 Normal curve showing the problem of finding the score at the 20th percentile.

Now that we have the z score at the 80th percentile, all that remains is to convert it to a raw score using Formula 6-18:

$$X = z\sigma + \mu = (0.84)100 + 500 = 84 + 500 = 584.$$

Thus, a person at the 80th percentile on the verbal SAT has a score of approximately 584. Let's try another problem of the same general type to be sure we have the technique.

What is the verbal SAT score at the 20th percentile? Put another way, what verbal SAT score cuts off the lowest 20% of the population? The problem is shown in Figure 8-19; the outline is again Area → z → X.

To find the z score that cuts off the lowest 20% of the distribution, we can either look for 20% in column C (the area beyond the z score we need) or look for 30% in column B (the area between the mean and z). The closest number to 20% in column C is 20.05, which corresponds to a z score of −0.84. Why is z a negative value? The answer is that we are looking for a score that is below the mean; negative values of z indicate scores below the mean. Let's convert our z score into a raw score:

$$X = z\sigma + \mu = (-0.84)100 + 500 = -84 + 500 = 416.$$

In conclusion, anyone scoring below 416 on the verbal SAT would be in the bottom 20% of the population.

↻ CHECKING YOUR PROGRESS

Consider once again the 2,000 students who took standardized tests in introductory psychology. The average score for this group was 73.5, with a standard deviation of 9.8. What score would a student have to make to be in the upper 15% of the distribution? Lower 30%?

Answer: 83.69 or above; 68.40 or below. To be in the upper 15%, a student would have to score 84 or above; to be in the lower 30%, a student would have to score 68 or below.

Finding Deviant Scores

In another type of problem, we might be asked to determine IQ scores so deviant or unlikely that they occur 10% or less of the time. In a way, this is a trick question, because the direction of the deviance from the mean is not stated. Because the direction is unspecified, we are actually dealing with both ends of the normal curve and not just the top or bottom half. An appropriately labeled diagram of the normal curve for this type of problem is shown in Figure 8-20. The outline for the problem is Area → z → X.

Notice in the figure that because the direction was not stated, the deviant 10% of the curve has been split into two equal parts, with 5% above the mean and 5% below it. Extremely high IQ scores are as unlikely as extremely low ones. If we had not divided the 10% in half and had instead put 10% at the upper end and 10% at the lower end, then the z scores located would be those defining, or cutting off, the deviant 20%. Whenever we encounter a problem in which the direction of the deviance is not given, we must halve the given area before labeling both ends of the curve.

The problem now becomes one of finding a z score when we know a percentage area under the curve and converting this z score into a raw score. As before, we can either look for 5% in column C or look for 45% in column B. Because z =

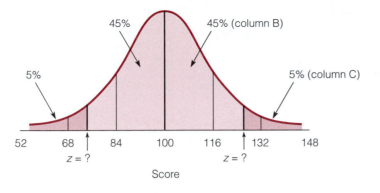

45%   45% (column B)

5%   5% (column C)

52   68   84   100   116   132   148
$z = ?$ $z = ?$

Score

Figure 8-20   Normal curve illustrating the problem of finding the scores cutting off the deviant 10% of the distribution.

1.64 cuts off an area of 5.05% and $z = 1.65$ cuts off an area of 4.95%, the z score that cuts off 5% appears to be exactly halfway between 1.64 and 1.65. If it were exactly halfway, our rule of rounding would dictate the use of 1.65 (1.645 rounds to 1.65). However, the z score is actually slightly closer to 1.64 (it's 1.6449 to four decimal places). The only other situation we'll encounter like this is the one where the z score cuts off the deviant 1% of the distribution. In that case, the z scores to use are ± 2.58.

For now, however, we have determined that the z scores that cut off the deviant 10% of the population are ± 1.64. The final step in the problem is to convert these two z scores into raw scores:

$$X = z\sigma + \mu = (\pm 1.64)(16) + 100 = \pm 26.24 + 100 = 73.76 \text{ and } 126.24.$$

Thus, the IQ scores that are so unlikely that they occur 10% or less of the time are those less than 74 and greater than 126.

Let's try another example. What IQ scores are so abnormal that they occur 5% or less of the time? This problem is shown graphically in Figure 8-21.

As before, the deviant 5% has been split, with 2.5% at either end of the curve. From column C, we find the z score cutting off 2.5% to be exactly 1.96 (± 1.96 for both tails). We now convert the z scores to raw scores:

$$X = z\sigma + \mu = (\pm 1.96)(16) + 100 = \pm 31.36 + 100 = 68.64 \text{ and } 131.36.$$

Thus, the IQ scores so unlikely that they occur 5% or less of the time are those less than 69 and greater than 131.

↻ CHECKING YOUR PROGRESS

In our example of 2,000 introductory psychology students, the mean score on a test was 73.5, with a standard deviation of 9.8. What scores are so deviant that

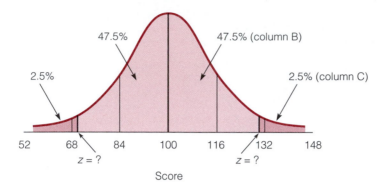

Figure 8-21 Normal curve illustrating the problem of finding the scores cutting off the deviant 5% of the distribution.

they occur 1% or less of the time? Below what score would a student be in the bottom 10% of the class?

Answer: 48.22 or less, 98.78 or more; 60.96 or less. The scores occurring 1% or less of the time are 48 or less and 99 or more. (Remember to use ±2.58 rather than ±2.57.) A score of 61 or less would put a student in the bottom 10% of the class.

Probability and Deviant Scores

The problem of finding deviant scores that we have been considering can be related to probability. For example, when we asked, "What scores are so abnormal that they occur 5% or less of the time?" we could have as easily expressed the problem in terms of probability. We could have phrased it as follows: "What scores are so abnormal that their probability of occurrence is .05 or less?" The first step in this problem, even before drawing the normal curve, is to convert the probability value to a percentage value so that we can use the normal curve table. Thus,

$$p = \frac{\% \text{ area}}{100}$$

and $\% \text{ area} = (p)(100) = (.05)(100) = 5\%.$

Now, the problem becomes the same as in the previous section: "What scores are so abnormal that they occur 5% or less of the time?" Of course, the procedure for solving it at this point and the answers that we get are the same as before. Let's consider another problem of the same type.

Suppose we want to find the IQ scores that are so unusual their probability is .20 or less. The outline of the problem is Probability → Area → z → X. The first step is to convert the probability (.20) to a percentage area by multiplying it by 100. The result is a percentage area of 20%, which we split in half to put 10% at the upper end and 10% at the lower end of the normal curve. This is shown in Figure 8-22.

We look up 10% in column C of the normal curve table and find it associated with z scores of ±1.28. Finally, the z scores are converted to raw scores as before:

$$X = z\sigma + \mu = (\pm 1.28)(16) + 100 = \pm 20.48 + 100 = 79.52 \text{ and } 120.48.$$

Thus, the IQ scores so unlikely that they occur with a probability of .20 or less are 80 or below and 120 or above.

↻ CHECKING YOUR PROGRESS

Returning to our 2,000 psychology students (mean score of 73.5, $s = 9.8$), what scores were so abnormal that their probability of occurrence was .15 or less?

Answer: 59.39 or below, 87.61 or above. Scores of 59 or below together with scores of 88 or above occurred with a probability of .15 or less.

Brief Summary

Like all normal curve problems, the most important steps in finding scores defining areas are to draw and label an appropriate normal curve and give the outline for the problem. Following the outline, the next step requires finding an area in either column B or column C of Table A to find the z score associated with it. The z score, taken from column A, is then converted to a raw score using the formula $X = zs + \overline{X}$ or $X = z\sigma + \mu$.

If the direction of the deviation of the score from the mean is not given, then we need to find scores at both ends of the distribution. To do this, we must first

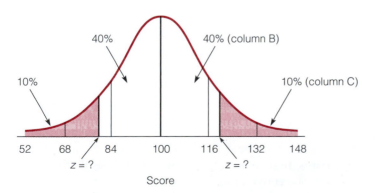

Figure 8-22 Normal curve illustrating the problem of finding the scores cutting off the deviant 20% of the distribution (IQs occurring with a probability of .20 or less).

split the deviant area in half, putting half on each tail of the curve. In this case, the z score taken from Table A is both positive and negative ($\pm$). If you're given a probability rather than an area, be sure to convert it to percentage area before labeling the normal curve.

SUMMARY

The normal curve is a unimodal, symmetrical curve on which the measures of central tendency are identical. The bell shape of the normal curve means that scores in the middle of the range of the measure occur much more often, whereas scores at the extremes are progressively less frequent (less likely or probable). Additionally, the tails of the normal curve never quite reach the X axis. For a given mean, the larger the standard deviation, the flatter the curve. The standard normal curve is a normal curve with a mean of 0 and a standard deviation of 1. Several techniques were introduced for deriving information from the standard normal curve distribution. Even if the actual distribution of scores in a sample taken from some population is not normally distributed, we can still apply the characteristics of the normal curve as long as we can assume normality in the population from which the sample was taken. For much of the data in the social sciences, this is a valid assumption.

The actual techniques for obtaining information from the normal curve table are relatively simple. You should have no difficulty as long as you remember that (1) the normal curve table gives the area under the curve from the mean to the z score you look up (column B) and the area under the curve beyond your z score (column C) and that (2) half of the area under the curve lies on one side of the mean and the other half on the other side of the mean (i.e., the normal curve is symmetrical).

Here are the steps to follow in attacking the kinds of problems discussed in this chapter:

1. Draw a small diagram of the normal curve and enter any information available.

2. Use the diagram to try to decide what area(s) or score(s) you want to find.

3. Give the outline for the problem. The two most involved outlines we encountered were

   a. $X \rightarrow z \rightarrow$ Area $\rightarrow$ Number

      or

   b. Probability $\rightarrow$ Area $\rightarrow z \rightarrow X$.

   All other problems were simplifications of these two types.

4. For part 3a, given raw scores, first convert these into z scores so that you can use the normal curve table. The conversion formula is

$$z = \frac{X - \overline{X}}{s} \quad \text{or} \quad z = \frac{X - \mu}{\sigma}.$$

5. For 3b, given some area under the curve, look up the appropriate area in either column B or column C of the normal curve table and then find the z score from column A that is associated with it. Usually, you will want to convert this z score to a raw score using the formula

$$X = zs + \overline{X} \quad \text{or} \quad X = z\sigma + \mu.$$

6. If you are asked to find scores so deviant or so unlikely that they occur less than a certain percentage of the time, look at both ends of the distribution. Divide the percentage area in half and label your diagram accordingly.

❈ *Troubleshooting Your Computations*

Most of the errors made in solving normal curve problems come from not understanding what you are being asked to find. To avoid this problem, first draw a small curve, fill in any information you are given, and try to label it so that you can actually see what you need to find. Give the outline for the problem. This is designed to give you a quick overview of the steps in the problem-solving process. When you have your final answer, ask yourself whether it is reasonable in terms of the drawing. For example, if the area you are seeking is very small, your final answer should be correspondingly small. If you are seeking a score below the mean, your final answer should be a value less than the mean.

A frequently made error is failure to complete the problem so the final answer is not in the correct form. For example, if the problem requires a frequency (e.g., number of persons with a certain range of scores), then any percentage area you find must be converted to a frequency. If the problem asks for the final answer as a probability, first find the percentage area and then divide it by 100 to convert it to a probability.

Also, if the problem of finding deviant scores is stated in terms of probability, you must first convert the probability to percentage area (i.e., multiply it by 100) before continuing the problem. Finally, from our experience, the most common error students make in problems dealing with the percentile rank of a score—finding the percentile rank of a score or finding a score at a given percentile—is that they forget the definition of percentile rank. Remember: The percentile rank of a score is the total area *below* the score, not the area above it, the area between the score and the mean, and so on.

EXERCISES

1. What are the characteristics of the normal curve? How does the standard normal curve differ from other normal curves?

2. Using the formula for a z score, derive the formula for converting a z score into a raw score.

3. We know that a reading test has a mean ($\overline{X}$) of 10 and a standard deviation (s) of 2. Using the normal distribution, answer the following questions:

   a. What is the percentile rank corresponding to a score of 11.2?
   b. If we tested 1,000 randomly selected students, how many would be expected to score 5 or lower?
   c. What reading score corresponds to a percentile rank of 75%? 30%?
   d. What is the probability of a score of 13 or higher?

4. The verbal part of the Graduate Record Exam (GRE) has a mean (μ) of 500 and a standard deviation (σ) of 100. Use the normal distribution to answer the following questions:

   a. If we wanted to select only students at or above the 90th percentile, what verbal GRE score would we use as a cutoff?
   b. What verbal GRE score corresponds to a percentile rank of 15%? 55%?
   c. What is the percentile rank of a verbal GRE score of 628? 350?
   d. If we randomly selected 1,500 students who had taken the verbal GRE, how many would we expect to score lower than 250? Higher than 750?

5. In an introductory psychology class, 83 students have taken a sociability rating scale. The possible ratings are from 1 to 7 with a low score indicating low sociability and a high score indicating high sociability. The average rating has been 4.23, with $s = 1.02$. Using the normal curve table, answer the following:

   a. What is the percentile rank of a student with a rating of 3.11?
   b. How many of the 83 students had scores between 4.88 and 5.62?
   c. What scores are so deviant that they occurred 1% or less of the time?
   d. How many students had scores of 2.55 or less? 6.11 or more?
   e. What is the score at the 83rd percentile?
   f. What is the probability of a score of 3.5 or less?

6. The police department of a major city has found that the average height of their 1,250 officers is 71 inches, with a standard deviation of 2.3 inches. Using the normal curve table, answer the following:

   a. How many officers are at least 75 inches tall?
   b. How many officers are between 65 and 72 inches tall?
   c. If an officer is at the 35th percentile in terms of height, how tall is she or he?
   d. Assuming an equal amount of service, the top 10% of the police officers in terms of height also make higher salaries than their less favored fellow officers. How tall does an officer have to be to get a better salary?
   e. What is the probability of encountering an officer who is 66 inches tall or less?
   f. What heights are so deviant that their probability of occurrence is .05 or less?

7. In an introductory English class, 100 students were given 20 words to define. The data from this test were approximately as follows: $\Sigma X = 1,000$, $\Sigma X^2 = 10,400$. Answer the following:

    a. What is the percentile rank of a person defining 9 words correctly?

    b. How many people scored above 13?

    c. What percentage of the class scored between 7 and 11?

    d. What scores are so deviant that less than 7% of the class made them?

8. Two hundred elementary school students took a 50-question math test. Their answers produced the following data: $\Sigma X = 6,000$, $\Sigma X^2 = 185,000$. Answer the following:

    a. What is the percentile rank of a score of 37? Of 22?

    b. How many students scored below 21? Above 35?

    c. How many students scored between 27 and 34?

    d. What scores are so deviant that less than 5% of the class attained them?

9. On the final exam in a large statistics class, the average score was 76 with a standard deviation of 7. Assuming a normal population, what scores were so deviant that their probability of occurrence was .01 or less? What was the probability of a score of 60 or less?

10. Data collected by the highway patrol indicate that the average speed on a stretch of interstate is 63 mph, with a standard deviation of 15. What is the likelihood of observing a vehicle traveling 80 mph or more? 45 mph or less? If a police officer observed 953 vehicles in an afternoon, how many of them (rounded to the nearest whole vehicle) would be traveling 90 mph or more?

11. A faculty member collected data on the length of faculty meetings in her department over a 3-year period. The average was 110 minutes, with a standard deviation of 25 minutes. Over the next 40 meetings, how many would be expected to last 1 hour or less? If faculty members start leaving when a meeting runs more than 2.5 hours, what is the probability of a walk-out at the next meeting? What meeting lengths are so extreme that they are likely to occur 5% of the time or less?

12. Do students ever make up information for an assignment? You be the judge. Students in an applied psychology class were sent out to observe 100 cars and report how many of the drivers were wearing seat belts. Each student reported the number of drivers he or she saw wearing seat belts as his or her score. The mean for the class was 65, with a standard deviation of 7. One student, who had a reputation for not doing his assignments, reported seeing only 42 belted drivers. Assuming the student actually counted, use the normal curve table to determine the probability that he observed 42 or fewer seat belt users. Based on this probability, do you suspect he made up the number rather than actually counting?

CHAPTER 9

Confidence Intervals and Hypothesis Testing

 Eva is watching the news the night before election day. A local television station is reporting the results of a poll it commissioned on voter support for a bond issue to rehabilitate local school buildings. The news anchor reports that 45% of the voters favor the bond issue, 40% are against it, and 15% are undecided. The anchor also reports that there is a margin of error of 3%. Eva thinks she knows how the 45% was determined; registered voters were asked for their position on the bond issue, and 45% said they supported it. However, where did the 3% come from? Eva thinks that it probably means the 45% is an estimate and might be off by 3% either way, but she wonders how it was determined that the margin was 3% and not 5% or some other amount.

Many of us, in learning the results of a poll, have had similar experiences. Intuitively, we understand that most of the statistics we are given are only estimates because they are based only on some portion (a sample) of the larger group of interest (population). It also makes sense that estimates may miss the true (population) value by some amount. Rarely will estimates exactly match the population value. In this chapter, we will discuss the process of estimation and how to determine the range within which our estimates should fall.

In Chapter 8, we discussed the properties of the normal distribution and how to use the normal distribution table to find areas under the curve. We also discussed the use of the normal curve table to determine scores associated with particular areas. In this chapter, we will discuss two distributions—the sampling distribution of means and the t distribution—that can be used to solve variants of the same two types of problems encountered in Chapter 8 (finding areas when we know scores and finding scores when we know areas). Specifically, we will discuss the use of the new distributions to construct confidence intervals (intervals of values around the sample mean) and to test hypotheses about the population from which our sample was drawn. We look first at the sampling distribution of means.

THE SAMPLING DISTRIBUTION OF MEANS

In the social sciences, the problem most often faced by investigators is one of estimating a population value from a sample value. When we collect our data, we rarely have the luxury of knowing population parameters. For example, if we conduct a study of the effects of a new drug on hypertension, there are no existing population values of the effect of the drug—after all, the drug is new. Thus, we must estimate those population values from our sample.

In Chapter 5, we said that the mean of a sample is an *unbiased estimate* of the population mean. What do we mean by *unbiased*? In a nutshell, it means that if we draw a sample from a population and calculate the sample mean ($\overline{X}$), it will, on average, be the same as the population mean (μ).

Sometimes the sample mean will be higher than the population mean, and sometimes it will be lower, but it will never be consistently high or consistently low. It is this property of the sample mean that makes it an unbiased estimate of the population mean.

We also know intuitively that the larger the sample we use in estimating the population value, the closer our sample mean is likely to be to the population mean. Let's take the example of coin tosses. Suppose we toss a coin 10 times. Although we expect the proportion of heads to be the population mean, 50%, we will not be surprised if the proportion is 30% or even 80%. After all, we did the experiment (10 tosses) only once. However, if we do the experiment 100 times, we expect the mean of sample results to approach the population value of 50% much more closely—perhaps at 48% or 56%. If we do the experiment 1,000 times, we expect our sample mean to be an even more accurate estimate of the population value.

The point of this example is to describe the derivation of a new type of distribution, the **sampling distribution of means.** The sampling distribution of means *is constructed by drawing a sample of a certain size (say, N = 20), calculating the mean of the sample, repeating the process for a large number of samples, then plotting the resulting means in the form of a frequency polygon.* The resulting distribution of means is the sampling distribution of means. It will be approximately "normal" in shape and have as its mean the mean of the population from which the samples were drawn. This population is often referred to as the *parent population.* The use of the sampling distribution underlies several inferential statistical techniques.

If we arrange the sample means from our coin toss experiment into a frequency distribution and then plot a frequency polygon from the resulting distribution, what are the properties of this frequency polygon?

To begin, we note that the vast majority of sample means differ from each other. In general, it is unlikely that any two successive samples will have precisely equivalent means. Further, any one sample mean is more likely to differ from the population mean than be equal to it. However, and this is the *first property* of the sampling distribution of means, the mean of all the sample means (symbolized by $\mu_{\overline{X}}$, which is read "mu sub ex bar") equals the mean of the parent population (μ).

The *second property* of this distribution is that the larger the size of each sample selected from the population, the more nearly the sampling distribution of means will approximate the normal curve. This property is a simplified version of the **central limit theorem.**

The *third property* is that the larger the size of each sample selected from the population, the smaller the standard deviation of the sampling distribution of means. The standard deviation of the sampling distribution of means is called the **standard error of the mean;** it is symbolized by $\sigma_{\overline{X}}$, which is read "little sigma sub ex bar." Mathematically, $\sigma_{\overline{X}}$ is equal to the population standard deviation divided by the square root of the sample size:

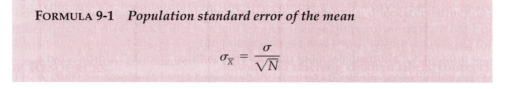

FORMULA 9-1   *Population standard error of the mean*

$$\sigma_{\overline{X}} = \frac{\sigma}{\sqrt{N}}$$

To understand the third property of the sampling distribution of means, think of it this way: The larger the size of each sample we take from the population, the closer the sample mean will be to the mean of the population. Thus, we are more likely with large samples to obtain a distribution of scores that accurately reflects the population situation. With large samples, there is less deviation of the sample means from the population mean—that is, less variability about the population mean. The smaller variability with larger samples is reflected in a smaller standard error.

Why do we call $\sigma_{\overline{X}}$ a standard error? It seems to be a contradiction—"standard" and "error." Remember that a standard deviation is based on deviation scores ($X - \overline{X}$), which are the distances between scores and the mean. In the case of the sampling distribution, these deviation scores are the distances between a sample mean and the population mean. Because $\overline{X}$ is intended to estimate μ, the distance between $\overline{X}$ and μ ($\overline{X} - \mu$) is an "error"; it is the amount by which the sample mean "missed" its mark. However, because these errors are the basis of a "standard" deviation (of the sampling distribution), we call it "standard error."

To summarize, we have imagined the construction of a frequency polygon from the distribution of sample means that were calculated from successive random samples of a given size (N) drawn from a parent population. This frequency polygon is called the *sampling distribution of means* (also written *sampling distribution of* $\overline{X}$). The shape of the polygon is symmetrical and is approximately normal with large samples. The mean of the sampling distribution of means ($\mu_{\overline{X}}$) is equal to the parent population mean (μ), and the standard deviation (called the standard error) becomes smaller as the sample size increases. A pictorial summary of the derivation and properties of the sampling distribution of means is shown in Figure 9-1.

Step 1: Successive random samples of a given size are drawn from a population, and a mean is computed for each sample.

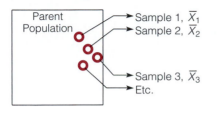

Step 2: A frequency distribution is constructed from the sample means.

X	f
$\overline{X}_1$	1
$\overline{X}_2$	1
$\overline{X}_3$	1
•	•
•	•
•	•

Step 3: A frequency polygon is drawn from the frequency distribution. Two properties are shown—that $\mu_{\overline{x}} = \mu$ and that the distribution is symmetrical.

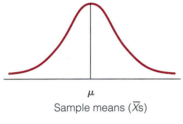

μ

Sample means ($\overline{X}$s)

Step 4: Diagram illustrates the property that the standard deviation (the standard error) decreases with increases in N.

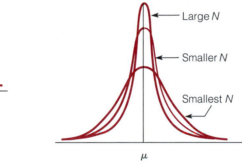

Large N

Smaller N

Smallest N

μ

Figure 9-1   A sequence of drawings illustrating the derivation and properties of the sampling distribution of means.

Figure 9-2 illustrates the properties of the sampling distribution of means, with emphasis on the property that the sampling distribution will approximate the normal curve with larger sample sizes, regardless of the shape of the parent population distribution. Note the position of the arrows on the horizontal axis for each population and sampling distribution. This illustrates the first property of the sampling distribution of means. Also notice in the figure that the dispersions of the sampling distributions decrease as the sample size (N) used for each increases. As the sample size increases, the sampling distributions become more narrow and more sharply peaked, as well as more like a normal curve.

Before leaving our discussion of the sampling distribution of means, it will be useful to define a z score for the new distribution. In Chapter 6, a z score was defined as the deviation of a raw score from the mean in standard deviation units, and the formulas were $z = (X - \overline{X})/s$ and $z = (X - \mu)/\sigma$. These formulas for z

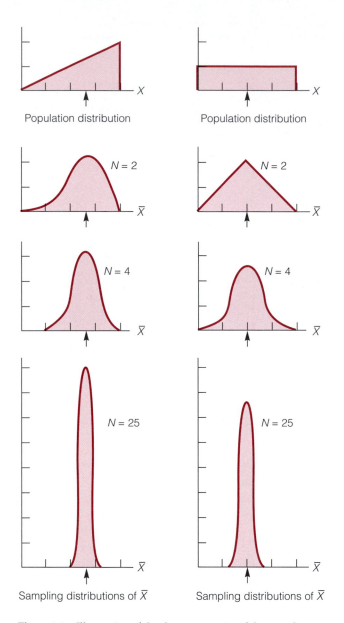

Population distribution

Population distribution

$N = 2$

$N = 2$

$N = 4$

$N = 4$

$N = 25$

$N = 25$

Sampling distributions of $\bar{X}$

Sampling distributions of $\bar{X}$

Figure 9-2 Illustration of the three properties of the sampling distributions of means, emphasizing the distribution's tendency to approximate normality with increases in sample size, no matter what the shape of the parent population distribution. Adapted from *Statistics for Modern Business*, 6th edition, by L. L. Lapin. © 1996. Reprinted with permission of Brooks/Cole Publishing, a division of Thompson Learning. Fax 800-730-2215.

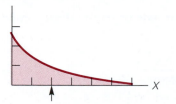

Population distribution

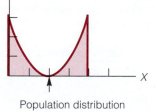

Population distribution

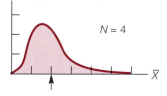

$N = 2$

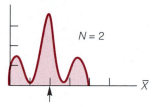

$N = 2$

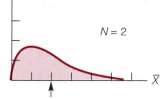

$N = 4$

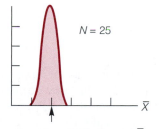

$N = 4$

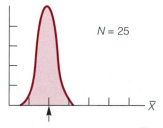

$N = 25$

Sampling distributions of $\overline{X}$

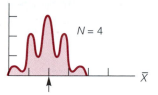

$N = 25$

Sampling distributions of $\overline{X}$

follow a general pattern for forming a z score for a variable or score. The general definition for any z *score can be written*

$$z_{score} = \frac{score - mean \text{ of } scores}{standard \text{ deviation of } scores}$$

In the case of X scores (or the variable X) from our parent population, we have already seen that

$$z_X = \frac{X - \mu}{\sigma}.$$

Using the general definition, we will write a z score for the sampling distribution of means. The score or variable of the sampling distribution of means is $\overline{X}$—that is, the sampling distribution is made up of means ($\overline{X}$s). The mean of the scores (mean of the $\overline{X}$s) equals μ. We know this by the first property of the sampling distribution of $\overline{X}$. The standard deviation is the standard error of the mean ($\sigma_{\overline{X}}$). Thus, a z score for the sampling distribution of means is found by the following formula:

FORMULA 9-2   z score for a sample mean

$$z_{\overline{X}} = \frac{\overline{X} - \mu}{\sigma_{\overline{X}}}$$

Note that the standard error of the mean ($\sigma_{\overline{X}}$) is equal to $\sigma/\sqrt{N}$ (Formula 9-1). We know this because of the third property of the sampling distribution of means. Thus, we could also write the formula for a z score for a sample mean as

$$z_{\overline{X}} = \frac{\overline{X} - \mu}{\sigma_{\overline{X}}} = \frac{\overline{X} - \mu}{\dfrac{\sigma}{\sqrt{N}}}.$$

The z score obtained for the mean of a sample can be used in all the ways we used z scores in Chapter 8. The only difference is that we are talking about a sample mean instead of a raw score. For example, a sample of 25 student applicants to a graduate program has a mean verbal GRE score of 550. We know that the verbal GRE has a mean of 500 and a standard deviation of 100. We can find the percentile rank of this sample by following a procedure that parallels the one we used in Chapter 8. First, we draw a curve, as in Figure 9-3, which indicates the information we have and the information we need to know. This time we need to be sure to label the horizontal axis with $\overline{X}$, as we are now drawing a curve to represent a sampling distribution of means. Note that we are seeking the total area below the score of 550, because the percentile rank of a score is the area up to and including the score. Second, we find $\sigma_{\overline{X}}$ by using Formula 9-1:

$$\sigma_{\overline{X}} = \frac{\sigma}{\sqrt{N}} = \frac{100}{\sqrt{25}} = \frac{100}{5} = 20.$$

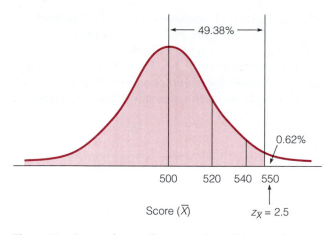

Figure 9-3 A normal curve illustrating the problem in which we want to find the percentile rank of a sample mean of 550.

Third, we calculate a z score using Formula 9-2:

$$z_{\overline{X}} = \frac{\overline{X} - \mu}{\sigma_{\overline{X}}} = \frac{550 - 500}{20} = \frac{50}{20} = 2.5.$$

Finally, we refer to Table A in Appendix 4 to find the percentage of scores below a z score of 2.5. Column C gives us 0.62% in the upper tail, but we want all the area below, so we must subtract 0.62% from 100%. Alternatively, we can take 49.38% from column B and add it to 50%. Either way, we find that the percentile rank of a sample mean of 550 is 99.38. Thus, our sample mean of 550 is at approximately the 99th percentile.

Note that we can use the procedures developed in Chapter 8 to solve any of the types of problems we learned to work in the previous chapter. For example, in addition to finding the percentile rank of a score, we could also use the z score computed with Formula 9-2 to find the probability of a deviant score. Using the information in the previous problem, suppose we wanted to know the probability of a sample mean of 550 or higher. We found that the z score for 550 was 2.5 and that the area above 550 from column C in Table A was 0.62%. To convert this area to probability, all we have to do is to divide it by 100 (Formula 8-1). Thus, the probability of a sample mean of 550 is very low ($p = .0062$).

In Chapter 8, we learned to calculate a raw score corresponding to a percentile rank by transforming the z-score formula. We can also calculate a value for $\overline{X}$ corresponding to a percentile rank by using Formula 9-3: $\overline{X} = z(\sigma_{\overline{X}}) + \mu$. Notice how it parallels the formula used for the raw scores: $X = z(\sigma) + \mu$.

FORMULA 9-3 *Sample mean from population values (computational formula)*

$$\overline{X} = z(\sigma_{\overline{X}}) + \mu$$

Extending our verbal GRE score example, suppose we wished to find the sample mean value corresponding to the 25th percentile. As with raw scores, we would proceed by first finding the appropriate z score in Table A. We look up 25% in either column B or C and find it associated with $z = 0.67$ (-0.67 because it is below the mean). Then we would calculate the value of $\sigma_{\overline{X}}$. In this case, we already know that $\sigma_{\overline{X}} = 20$. Then we simply substitute the values into Formula 9-3:

$$\overline{X} = -0.67(20) + 500 = -13.4 + 500 = 486.6.$$

The sample mean verbal GRE score at the 25th percentile is approximately 490.

ESTIMATION AND DEGREES OF FREEDOM

The use of z scores for sample means is appropriate when we know the population mean and population variance. Our problem is that we rarely know both of these values, so we must estimate the population values from our sample. As we've noted, we can use our sample mean ($\overline{X}$) to estimate the population mean (μ), because $\overline{X}$ is an unbiased estimate of μ. Similarly, as we defined it in Chapter 6, the sample standard deviation (s) is an unbiased estimate of the corresponding population value.

In Chapter 6, in order to obtain an unbiased estimate of the population variance (or standard deviation) from our sample values, we divided the sum of squared deviations by $N - 1$ rather than by N because of the tendency of the sample statistic with N in the denominator to underestimate either σ^2 (or σ). This expression, $N - 1$, is called *degrees of freedom*. **Degrees of freedom (*df*)** is defined as *the number of values in a set of scores that are free to vary after certain restrictions are placed on the data.* For example, if we are given the sum of 5 scores, only 4 of the scores are "free to vary," because the given sum determines the value of the 5th score.

Here's a simple exercise we use in class to demonstrate the definition of degrees of freedom. Do you remember the important property of the mean that the sum of the deviations of scores from it is always equal to zero? Well, that's the restriction that we place on our data—that the sum of the deviations of our sample scores from the sample mean is equal to zero. Keeping that restriction in mind, suppose we have a distribution consisting of just 5 scores. Further, suppose that we ask five students in class to each tell us a deviation of one of the scores from the mean, with no further information; that is, the students know neither the mean nor any of the distribution's 5 scores!

After some coaxing, we obtain the following values from the first four students: $+5, +3, +2, -12$ (this last we got after reminding the students that some of the values would be below the mean). Now, the key question is: What is the 5th deviation? The answer is that it is $+2$ and only $+2$, and it can't be anything else. The reason is that the sum of the first 4 deviations is -2, and the restriction is that the sum of the deviations is 0; hence, the value of the 5th deviation must be $+2$ for the total to be 0.

Now, given the restriction that the sum of the deviations is equal to zero, how many of the deviations were free to vary? The answer is 4, which is, as you've probably already realized, $N - 1$, because N was 5.

Actually, the concept of degrees of freedom is more involved, but we have more than scratched the surface with our discussion. For our purposes, it is sufficient to note that df for the problems we will encounter in this chapter is $N - 1$.

Back to our problem of estimating population parameters: Earlier in this section we reminded you that we introduced s, the sample standard deviation, as an unbiased estimate of σ, the population standard deviation. We can use s to obtain an estimate of the standard error of the mean, $\sigma_{\overline{X}}$, simply by substituting s for σ in the equation for $\sigma_{\overline{X}}$. This gives us Formula 9-4, which enables us to compute $s_{\overline{X}}$, which is called the **estimated standard error of the mean.**

> **FORMULA 9-4** *Estimated standard error of the mean*
>
> $$s_{\overline{X}} = \frac{s}{\sqrt{N}}$$

We can carry this substitution of estimated values for population values one step further. As seen in Formula 9-2, we can compute a z score for a sample mean. Then we can use the z score to find a percentile rank or probability. If we don't have the population value of the standard error, we must once again substitute our unbiased estimate ($s_{\overline{X}}$). However, in using the estimated standard error of the mean, we encounter a problem. Remember that estimates contain error. Sometimes the estimates are high, sometimes they are low, but rarely are they identical to the population value. This means that the indices we compute that include $s_{\overline{X}}$, such as $\overline{X} - \mu/s_{\overline{X}}$, also contain variability, or error, and they no longer conform to the normal (z score) distribution. Instead, they correspond to what is called a *t* **distribution** and so are called *t* scores.

The t distribution is often called Student's t distribution, because the mathematics of the distribution were actually derived by William Sealy Gosset (1876–1937), who published under the pseudonym "Student." Actually, the motivation for Gosset's work came from the Guinness brewing company in Ireland. Guinness wanted to know what kind of barley to use to make their product less variable. As part of his experimentation, Gosset discovered the t distribution for use with small samples and unknown population variability. Gosset's reason for using the pseudonym was to keep the Guinness company from having to admit to the occasional bad batch. (For capsule sketches of figures important for the development of statistics, see A. Aron and E. N. Aron, 1994, *Statistics for Psychology*, Englewood Cliffs, NJ: Prentice-Hall, Inc.)

Remember that a z score is an exact value, and the normal curve is a distribution of these exact units. However, a t score is an estimate, and a t distribution incorporates the variability, or error, that these estimates contain. Remember that when we estimate the standard error ($s_{\overline{X}}$), we are employing a particular sample size (N) to obtain that estimate. In fact, the N chosen is the basis for that particular sampling distribution of means. This means that for every sample size (N), we obtain a slightly different t distribution. The degree of the error we have mentioned depends on the sample size—more specifically, on $N - 1$, the degrees of freedom. Thus, we do not have one t distribution as we do with the z distribution; we have a *family* of t distributions—one for every degree of freedom $(N - 1)$. The larger the sample size, the less the "error" relative to the z distribution. Stated another way, the t distribution is the normal distribution with "error added." Because the amount of error contained in an estimate becomes smaller as the sample size becomes larger, the t distribution becomes more and more similar to the normal distribution as sample size increases. *A t score is simply an estimated z score.* So now we have a new statistic called a t, which can be computed using Formula 9-5:

FORMULA 9-5   t *score*

$$t_{\overline{X}} = \frac{\overline{X} - \mu}{s_{\overline{X}}}$$

We use t scores in the same way we use z scores; that is, $t_{\overline{X}}$ tells us how far a score $(\overline{X})$ is from the mean (μ) in estimated standard error units.

Now that the sampling distribution of means has been defined and some of its properties discussed, what can we do with it and with the related distribution of t? As in Chapter 8, we will discuss two basic problems: (1) conducting a one-sample t test (analogous to finding areas when we know scores) and (2) constructing a confidence interval (analogous to finding scores when we know an area). Let's begin with confidence intervals.

CONFIDENCE INTERVALS

Suppose an experimental psychologist wants to do a learning study with newborn children to establish the average rate at which a neonate can turn his or her head in response to a brief tone followed by a pleasant event (e.g., a sip of sugar-flavored water). It is impossible to measure the population of neonates, so the scientist randomly selects a sample of 23 infants and assesses their learning skills. The criterion of learning is set at five consecutive head turns and the score for each child is the number of pairings of the tone with the flavored water before reaching the criterion. From the data collected, a mean number of trials to criterion of 46.33 is computed. What does this figure mean in terms of the population of neonates? If the study were done time and again with random samples of 23 babies, would the results always be similar to this? What is the mean of means, or the population mean (μ)?

Unfortunately, we can't answer the last question. However, one of the things we learned in Chapter 5 was that the mean of a sample, $\overline{X}$, shows no systematic tendencies in relation to the mean of the population, μ, and for this reason it is said to be an unbiased estimate of μ. Thus, we can use the sample mean as an estimate of μ. When we do this, we must realize that it is very unlikely that any given sample $\overline{X}$ will exactly equal μ. Is there any way to increase our chances of capturing the population value? Yes, and it involves designating a range of values rather than only one value in guessing about the location of μ. The range of values is called a confidence interval. A **confidence interval (CI)** is a range of values within which we are reasonably certain the population mean lies. *Margin of error* is one common use of confidence intervals.

In the example at the beginning of the chapter, Eva wondered how pollsters had established a 3% confidence interval (margin of error) for their voter survey. Confidence intervals are useful in establishing a range of scores within which we can safely expect a population value to occur; they are also useful in making decisions about hypotheses.

How confident do we want to be in our guess about the value of μ? Do we want to be 80% sure, or 90%, or 63%, or what? Ninety percent probably sounds pretty good, and most of you would probably balk at anything less than this. Statisticians, however, striving for accuracy, have traditionally tended to favor either 95% or 99% certainty. For this reason, we will limit our discussion to the derivation of 95% and 99% confidence intervals. Think of it this way: If we establish a range of values around our sample mean within which we are 95% or 99% sure μ is contained, it is very unlikely—5% or 1%, respectively—that μ will be outside the range. It is not impossible, but highly unlikely.

Now that we have decided how confident we want to be, let's derive a formula for 95% and 99% CIs. To do this, we need to think about one of the last types of problems covered in Chapter 8—finding scores that were so deviant they occurred less than 5% or 1% of the time. The same problem was also expressed as finding the scores that occurred with a probability of .05 (or .01) or less. To find these scores, we first drew a normal curve, divided the 5% (or 1%) in half, and labeled each end of the curve appropriately. We then looked in the normal curve table to find the z scores cutting off the deviant percentage of the curve and converted these scores to raw scores using the equation $X = zs + \overline{X}$. The problem of finding the deviant scores occurring 5% or less of the time ($p \leq .05$) is shown graphically in Figure 9-4.

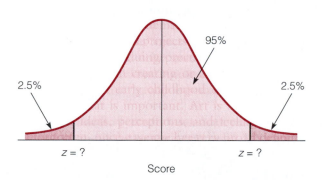

Figure 9-4   Normal curve showing the problem of finding the scores cutting off the deviant 5% of the distribution, or the scores between which 95% of the curve lies.

Note from the graph that while we sought the scores cutting off the deviant 5% (or 1%) of the normal curve distribution, we simultaneously found the scores enclosing the central 95% (or 99%) of the distribution. In other words, we already have a technique for finding the 95% or 99% CIs. All we need to do is slightly modify the equation for converting a z score to a raw score to take into account the new distribution introduced in this chapter, the sampling distribution of means.

Consider the situation where our samples are infinite in number. In this limiting case, the sampling distribution of means is normally distributed and the formulas for finding the 95% and 99% CIs are $X = \pm z\sigma_{\overline{X}} + \mu$ or $X = \pm 1.96\sigma_{\overline{X}} + \mu$ for the 95% CI and $X = \pm 2.58\sigma_{\overline{X}} + \mu$ for the 99% CI. The z scores of ± 1.96 and ± 2.58 are the scores cutting off the deviant 5% and 1% of the normal curve, respectively.

However, the most typical case is the one in which we have to use the estimated standard error of the mean ($s_{\overline{X}}$) because we don't know the population value. Because we still don't know either μ or $\sigma_{\overline{X}}$, we will estimate their values with $\overline{X}$ and $s_{\overline{X}}$, respectively. The equations just introduced now become $X = \pm t_{.05}s_{\overline{X}} + \overline{X}$ for the 95% confidence interval and $X = \pm t_{.01}s_{\overline{X}} + \overline{X}$ for the 99% CI. Instead of using the z scores of ± 1.96 and ± 2.58, we need to determine the corresponding values of t.

The values of t are both positive and negative because we are looking for scores on either side of $\overline{X}$. We add the appropriate subscripts, depending on whether we are finding the 95% CI or the 99% CI. The appropriate subscripts with t are $t_{.05}$ (the t scores that cut off the deviant 5% of the distribution or occur with a probability of .05 or less) and $t_{.01}$ (the t scores that cut off the deviant 1% or occur with a probability of .01 or less). Putting all of this together, the formulas for the 95% and 99% CIs are:

FORMULA 9-6   *95% confidence interval for the population mean*

$$95\% \ CI = \pm t_{.05}s_{\overline{X}} + \overline{X}$$

FORMULA 9-7   *99% confidence interval for the population mean*

$$99\% \ CI = \pm t_{.01}s_{\overline{X}} + \overline{X}$$

Looking at these formulas, we see that we have already encountered two of the three terms needed and shouldn't have any difficulty determining them:

$$s_{\overline{X}} = \frac{s}{\sqrt{N}} \quad \text{and} \quad \overline{X} = \frac{\Sigma X}{N}.$$

However, where do we get the t scores?

To determine the relevant values of t, we refer to Table B in Appendix 4, which lists the t scores that cut off either the deviant 5% or the deviant 1% of the distribution (as well as the deviant 10% and 2%), depending on sample size. Ordinarily, when we talk about the deviant 5% or 1% of the distribution, we are considering both ends of the distribution. Another way to express this idea is to say that we are considering *both tails* of the distribution of t scores. A portion of the table of t scores has been reproduced in Table 9-1.

Table 9-1 contains *critical values* of t—that is, values of t that cut off deviant portions of the distribution. Remember that we said the t distribution was really a family of curves, one for each degree of freedom. This is why our table contains only certain critical values of t, instead of areas under the curve for every value, as we have with the z distribution, of which there is only one. It wouldn't be practical to have a full t-distribution table for every possible degree of freedom value. The t-values table, then, is a summary of the critical values of t that we will need for many degrees of freedom.

Note the heading "Level of Significance for Two-Tailed Test," with instructions on how to obtain significance levels for a one-tailed test. Next there is a row of four different percentages with appropriate probability values listed below. The numbers in each column below the probabilities are the values of t that cut off the deviant percentage of the distribution indicated by the value heading that column. As with the normal curve table, only the positive half of the curve is given, so for a two-tailed test, which is a test that considers both ends or tails of the distribution of the test statistic, each of the values of t in the table is assumed to be both positive and negative. A one-tailed test considers only one end of the distribution.

TABLE 9-1

A portion of Table B showing values of t cutting off deviant portions of the sampling distribution of means, depending on the degrees of freedom. The complete table may be found in Appendix 4.

	Level of Significance for Two-Tailed Test (For One-Tailed Test, Halve the Following Percentages)			
df	10% ($p = .10$)	5% ($p = .05$)	2% ($p = .02$)	1% ($p = .01$)
1	6.3138	12.7062	31.8207	63.6574
2	2.9200	4.3027	6.9646	9.9248
3	2.3534	3.1824	4.5407	5.8409
4	2.1318	2.7764	3.7469	4.6041
5	2.0150	2.5706	3.3649	4.0322
6	1.9432	2.4469	3.1427	3.7074
7	1.8946	2.3646	2.9980	3.4995
8	1.8595	2.3060	2.8965	3.3554
9	1.8331	2.2622	2.8214	3.2498
10	1.8125	2.2281	2.7638	3.1693

Note: From *Handbook of Statistical Tables* (pp. 28–30), by D. B. Owen, 1962, Reading, MA: Addison-Wesley. Copyright 1962 by Addison-Wesley Publishing Company, Inc. Adapted with permission of Addison-Wesley Longman.

At the far left in the table there is a column of numbers with the heading "*df.*" As previously stated, the t distribution is really a family of distributions that change shape as a function of sample size. This sample size is reflected in degrees of freedom. Because the t distribution changes shape with changes in degrees of freedom, we must know df to look up the critical value of t. For example, if we have a sample of size $N = 46$, $df = N - 1 = 46 - 1 = 45$, and the t scores cutting off the deviant 5% of the distribution are ± 2.0141 (from Appendix 4, Table B).

Remember that t more closely approximates z as sample size increases. As a confirmation, look at the t value at the very bottom of the 5% column in Table B and compare it to the corresponding 5% z score from Table A. Both are 1.96.

Let's turn now to finding some confidence intervals. At the beginning of this section, we described a learning experiment with newborn children in which the average number of trials to criterion was 46.33 for a sample of size $N = 23$. Suppose that $s = 6.51$. What is the 95% CI for μ? We have

$$95\% \text{ CI} = \pm t_{.05} s_{\overline{X}} + \overline{X},$$

$$\overline{X} = 46.33,$$

$$s_{\overline{X}} = \frac{s}{\sqrt{N}} = \frac{6.51}{\sqrt{23}} = \frac{6.51}{4.80} = 1.36.$$

From Table B, the t scores cutting off the deviant 5% of the distribution with $df = N - 1 = 23 - 1 = 22$ are ± 2.0739. Thus,

$$95\% \text{ CI} = \pm 2.0739(1.36) + 46.33 = \pm 2.82 + 46.33 = 43.51 \text{ to } 49.15.$$

The range of values within which we are 95% sure μ is contained is from 43.51 to 49.15. (The CI in this type of equation is often expressed with the mean first— 46.33 ± 2.82—rather than last; either way—43.51 to 49.15 or 46.33 ± 2.82—is acceptable.) The 99% CI can be obtained in the same way, with the values of t being ± 2.8188. The 99% CI is from 42.50 to 50.16.

What happens to the confidence interval when the level of confidence goes up? Think of capturing μ in the confidence interval as being like catching a butterfly in a net. If you want to increase your chances of catching the insect, you use a larger net. This is what happens when we increase our confidence level, say from 95% to 99%, and our interval *increases* in size. Thus, you can see that the 99% CI is wider (has a greater range of values) than the 95% interval. Why is this? Mathematically, it is because the t scores cutting off the deviant 1% are larger than the scores cutting off the deviant 5%. The deviant 1% of the t distribution is further from the mean than the deviant 5%; hence, it is represented by a larger t score. Also, intuitively, a larger range of values is needed for us to be 99% sure we've captured μ.

Interpretation Statement for a Confidence Interval

One topic we want to introduce in this chapter is the practice of writing conclusion statements for confidence intervals and for hypothesis-testing problems. These conclusion statements have two goals: One is to write the conclusion in words that tell us—and any reader of the conclusion—what the problem or investigation is all about, including what is being measured. A second goal is to convey the results in a way that someone unfamiliar with our problem—the "person in the street"—can read the conclusion and have a reasonably good understanding of our results. We will call this a *conclusion in the context of the problem*. Fortunately, the conclusion for a confidence interval is easy to write and provides a general model. For our previous example, the conclusion in the context of the problem is as follows: *We can be 95% confident that the mean number of trials to criterion for neonates to learn to turn their heads in response to a tone is at least 43.51 and at most 49.15 trials.* For the 99% CI, simply substitute the values from that computation and change the percent confidence level at the beginning of the statement.

Another Confidence Interval Example

Let's try another example. In a study to determine the amount of REM (rapid eye movement) sleep engaged in by young adults, 35 volunteers were monitored in a sleep lab over a 1-week period. The average amount of REM sleep per night was 96 minutes, with an estimated standard deviation of 22 minutes. What is the 95% CI? We have

$$95\% \text{ CI} = \pm t_{.05} s_{\overline{X}} + \overline{X},$$

$$s_{\overline{X}} = \frac{s}{\sqrt{N}} = \frac{22}{\sqrt{35}} = 3.72,$$

$$t_{.05}(df = N - 1 = 35 - 1 = 34) = \pm 2.0301,$$

$$95\% \text{ CI} = \pm 2.0301(3.72) + 96$$

$$= \pm 7.55 + 96$$

$$= 96 \pm 7.55 \text{ or } 88.45 \text{ to } 103.55.$$

The conclusion in the context of the problem is: We can be 95% confident that the average amount of REM sleep per night for young adults is at least 88.45 and at most 103.55 minutes.

Note that the critical values of t for 34 df are not actually shown in Table B and that the value used was that for $df = 35$. If the sample size is larger than 30, the table is incomplete and the actual value of t may not be given. In this case, we use the value for the most nearly correct df.

For given values of $\overline{X}$ and s and at a given level of confidence, you will find that the size of a confidence interval is larger with smaller samples. This makes sense intuitively if you consider that the larger the sample, the more sure we are that the sample is an accurate reflection of the population. Hence, we don't need as large a range of values around $\overline{X}$ to be nearly certain we've captured μ. Mathematically, larger samples give us more precision—they result in smaller values of $s_{\overline{X}}$ and smaller t scores from Table B, both of which result in a narrower range of values for the confidence interval.

Because the distribution of t more and more closely approximates the normal curve as N increases, many instructors use z scores rather than t scores to construct confidence intervals when N is greater than some arbitrary number, such as 50. In our opinion, this results in unnecessary confusion; therefore, we will continue to use t scores, regardless of the size of N.

Understanding the Level of Confidence

Before we leave the topic of confidence intervals, we want to discuss briefly the meaning of the confidence level statement—that is, what we mean when we say that we are 95% or 99% confident about our interval capturing μ (the true population mean). To begin with, the confidence interval statement *is not* a probability statement. The data have already been collected; the "dice have been rolled," so to speak. The confidence interval *is* an inference and it *is* also an estimate—an *interval estimate*—of the value of the population mean. The confidence level speaks to the degree of certainty we have in making this interval estimate. More specifically, when we state our 95% confidence interval for μ, although each interval either does or does not contain μ, we are saying that if we repeated our research 100 times, and each time computed a new confidence interval, then 95 of the 100 intervals would capture the population mean (μ). This is the sense in which we are 95% confident that our interval contains μ.

ᕾ CHECKING YOUR PROGRESS

Suppose the digit span (number of digits a person can hold in short-term memory) of 31 adults has been measured, with the result that $\Sigma X = 220.41$ and $\Sigma X^2 = 1{,}705.72$. What are the 95% and 99% CIs for μ?

Answer: 95% CI = 6.32 to 7.90; 99% CI = 6.05 to 8.17. We are 95% confident that the adult population digit span is at least 6.32 and at most 7.90 digits and 99% confident that it is from 6.05 to 8.17.

HYPOTHESIS TESTING: ONE-SAMPLE t TEST

In our discussion of confidence intervals, we used a distribution that is approximately normal with larger samples in order to establish a range of values within which we have a certain degree of confidence that μ is contained. Another use to which we can put the distribution of t is to test hypotheses about the value of μ.

Let's consider a specific example and develop a testing procedure from it. A researcher is interested in the effect of amphetamine on recent memory. To test this, she has 25 adult volunteers swallow a small dose of amphetamine, wait 30 minutes, and take a digit-span test. The researcher finds that the mean digit span for the subjects is 7.53, with $s = 0.97$. Further, she knows on the basis of many previous studies that the average adult digit span is 7. If we assume that $\mu = 7$, what is the probability of selecting a sample of size $N = 25$ from the population (all adults) whose sample mean is as deviant as 7.53?

How likely (or unlikely) is this sample mean? Using the procedure developed earlier in this chapter for finding the probability of a deviant score, we first calculate a t score for the sample mean of 7.53:

$$s_{\overline{X}} = \frac{s}{\sqrt{N}} = \frac{0.97}{\sqrt{25}} = \frac{0.97}{5} = 0.194,$$

$$t = \frac{\overline{X} - \mu}{s_{\overline{X}}} = \frac{7.53 - 7.00}{0.194} = \frac{0.53}{0.194} = 2.73.$$

This t score of 2.73 indicates that a mean of 7.53 is 2.73 $s_{\overline{X}}$ units above a mean of 7 on the sampling distribution of means with $N = 25$. This is shown graphically in Figure 9-5.

Originally, we wanted to know the probability of obtaining an average digit span as deviant as 7.53, assuming that $\mu = 7$. Note that 7.53 is 2.73 estimated standard error units *above* the mean; but the score 2.73 units *below* the mean $[7 - (2.73)(0.194) = 7 - 0.53 = 6.47]$ is equally deviant, and the original problem really asked us to find the area of the curve above 7.53 and below 6.47. We therefore could have added the areas and converted to probability, and we would have determined the probability of obtaining a score as deviant as 7.53, given that $\mu = 7$.

However, because we are dealing with the t distribution, not with the normal curve, we cannot easily determine the exact probability associated with $t = 2.73$. Because there is a family of t distributions, the only way to determine exact probabilities is to have a complete table (similar to Table A in Appendix 4) for each degree of freedom. These tables alone would fill an entire book. (Books devoted to statistical tables, such as t, can be obtained in most university libraries.)

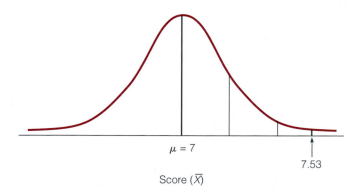

$\mu = 7$

7.53

Score ($\overline{X}$)

Figure 9-5   Sampling distribution of means from samples of size $N = 25$ ($df = 24$). Score of 7.53 is 2.73 $s_{\overline{X}}$ units above the mean of 7.

Table B in Appendix 4 is incomplete. It includes the *t* values most frequently used in hypothesis testing and the degrees of freedom for which the *t* distribution differs most from the normal distribution. However, this condensed version does not allow us to attach exact probabilities to all *t* scores. We can, though, compare our computed *t* score with table values known to cut off the deviant 10%, 5%, 2%, or 1% of the distribution for a given sample size converted to degrees of freedom. The levels at which we're testing *t* are called alpha (α) levels. In general, we will be most interested in the 5% ($\alpha = .05$) and 1% ($\alpha = .01$) alpha levels.

For the example we have been considering, we found *t* to be 2.73 and *df* = $N - 1 = 25 - 1 = 24$. From Table B, we see that the *t* scores cutting off the deviant 5% and 1% of the sampling distribution of means when the size of each sample is 25 (*df* = 24) are 2.0639 and 2.7969, respectively. Because our obtained *t* is more deviant than the critical value at the 5% level (the *t* score cutting off the deviant 5% of the distribution), the logical thing to do is to reject the assumption that the sample came from the adult population, where the average digit span is $\mu = 7$. In other words, we reject the assumed value for μ at the $\alpha = .05$, or 5%, level.

Thus, the observed mean of 7.53 is very unlikely if the population mean is 7. The researcher concludes that her treatment had an effect. The average digit span of people who have taken amphetamine is probably not the same as the average digit span of normal adults. She doesn't know what μ is for amphetamine-treated subjects; she only knows that it is probably not 7. Figure 9-6 illustrates what has been done with this problem.

Here is what we have done to this point: A sample has been selected from a population with an assumed mean of 7. The sample mean of 7.53 has been found to be very unlikely given the assumption that $\mu = 7$. We concluded, therefore, that the sample was probably taken from a population in which μ was not equal to 7.

Our goal is to make an assumption that the sample mean, in this example, came from the population of adults that did not take the drug, then to see whether

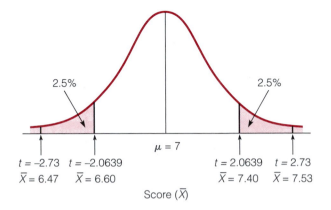

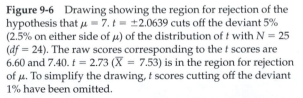

Figure 9-6 Drawing showing the region for rejection of the hypothesis that $\mu = 7$. $t = \pm 2.0639$ cuts off the deviant 5% (2.5% on either side of μ) of the distribution of *t* with $N = 25$ (*df* = 24). The raw scores corresponding to the *t* scores are 6.60 and 7.40. $t = 2.73$ ($\overline{X} = 7.53$) is in the region for rejection of μ. To simplify the drawing, *t* scores cutting off the deviant 1% have been omitted.

there is evidence against this assumption. The evidence is provided by assessing the probability of the obtained sample mean—in other words, determining how unusual or deviant the sample mean $\overline{X}$ actually is. The more unusual, more deviant, or the lower the probability, the greater the evidence *against* the assumption.

Another way to think about this process is to consider rejecting the assumption that the sample mean $\overline{X}$ is a good estimate of the "no drug" population mean. If μ falls within a defined confidence interval around $\overline{X}$, our assumption that the sample came from this population is acceptable. If μ falls outside this confidence interval, then $\overline{X}$ is not a good estimate of the "no drug" population mean, and our assumption may be rejected. In other words, we hope to reject the hypothesis that $\mu = 7$, or, in general, that $\mu = \mu_0$, where μ_0 (pronounced "mu sub naught" or "mu sub zero") is merely a symbol for some specific value that represents the "untreated" population mean—the value of μ that is the usual state of affairs. This may seem like a hopelessly convoluted approach, but there is a sound basis for it.

In the experimental approach—in fact, in any empirical approach—nothing can be proved absolutely true, because we never have all possible data. In experimental work, it is always "possible," no matter how remote, that the next piece of data will either conform to our hypothesis or it will not. Therefore, hypotheses can never be *proved* (an absolute term); they can only be *supported* (a relative term). Hypotheses can, however, be disconfirmed. If properly collected data don't match our hypothesis, then the hypothesis must be rejected, at least for the conditions and methods used. In short, scientists cannot prove something to be true; they can only build a case toward proving it to be false.

How do we extricate ourselves from this dilemma? The solution is that we support our experimental or research hypotheses by rejecting, or falsifying, alternative hypotheses. The simplest case, such as in the preceding example, involves two hypotheses. First, we have a research hypothesis that the drug will work, thus making the mean of the population from which the sample came different from the mean of the population; this hypothesis is symbolized by $H_1: \mu \neq \mu_0$ or, in the case of our example, $\mu \neq 7$. Second, we have the competing hypothesis that the drug will *not* work, in which case we should expect the mean of the sample to be an estimate (within an acceptable CI) of the population mean; this is the **null hypothesis,** symbolized by $H_0: \mu = \mu_0$. We cannot prove H_1 to be true; we can only support H_1 by rejecting H_0.

Getting back to our example, if the drug has no effect on memory, then our best prediction is that the sample came from the unaffected adult population, and the sample mean is an estimate of the mean of the population. This would be a "null" effect; hence the term *null hypothesis.* However, if the drug works, we would expect the sample mean to reflect this by falling appreciably above or below the population mean, indicating that the sample probably came from a different population—the "longer (or shorter)-digit-span-because-of-drug" population that has a *different* population mean, not the same mean as the unaffected adult population ($H_1: \mu \neq \mu_0$). We don't have to know what the mean of the "drug" population is, only that it is different from 7 (μ_0). Our definition of "appreciably" is determined by the confidence interval. If our population mean falls outside the 95% CI about $\overline{X}$, then $\overline{X}$ is not a good estimate of μ; that is, $\overline{X}$ cannot be viewed as representative of the population in which μ is the mean. Because adding the drug is the only thing we have done to the sample that makes it different from the population, we conclude that the drug is responsible for the difference.

The null hypothesis, or H_0, states that we assume the sample came from a population with mean equal to some value (μ_0), which represents the usual state of affairs:

$$H_0: \mu = \mu_0.$$

An alternative to the null hypothesis is that the sample came from a different population, which has been affected by some treatment or different condition and has *some other mean that is not equal to μ_0*. This is called the **alternative hypothesis,** or H_1. The alternative hypothesis can be either nondirectional or directional. A **nondirectional hypothesis** simply says that μ is not equal to μ_0, but it does not specify in which direction it differs. The nondirectional hypothesis is symbolized by

$$H_1: \mu \neq \mu_0.$$

This alternative hypothesis is sometimes called bidirectional (i.e., it takes into account both tails of the distribution) because the direction of the difference is not specified.

A **directional hypothesis** states the direction of the difference between μ and the sample mean; that is, H_1 may say that μ_0 is greater than μ or less than μ. Symbolically, the directional hypothesis is

$$H_1: \mu > \mu_0 \qquad \text{or} \qquad H_1: \mu < \mu_0.$$

In the example we have considered, the sample mean was found to be unlikely given the value assumed for H_0. Thus, we rejected the null hypothesis.

A phrase often used in hypothesis testing is "testing for significance." When H_0 is rejected, statisticians say that a **significant** result has been found, corresponding to either the 5% or the 1% level of significance, depending on the α level chosen.

Let's look at another example. Suppose that over a period of several years, a professor has found the average grade on the final exam for all students taking a course in economics is 75. One semester, the final exam is given and the grades are found to be slightly lower, with an average of 73.8 for a sample of size $N = 61$. The standard deviation is 8.3. The usual state of affairs is that μ_0 is 75. Assuming H_0: $\mu = 75$, what is the probability of obtaining a sample with a mean as deviant as 73.8? Is the probability low enough for the professor to reject the null hypothesis and conclude that the sample came from a different population in which the mean is different (lower!), something has changed, and perhaps a review of teaching and/or testing procedures is in order? Thus, the key to this procedure is to convert our raw score ($\overline{X}$) into a t score. By comparison with a critical t value that cuts off the deviant 5% of the distribution, our computed t score tells us how deviant our sample mean really is.

In order to work such problems, we will now introduce a seven-step procedure for hypothesis testing. This process may seem cumbersome at first, but our experience is that it gives an easy and systematic structure to follow in working hypothesis-testing problems. As we present and discuss each step, we will refer to the summary example for this problem given in Box 9-1.

BOX 9-1 Example for Testing the Null Hypothesis

Problem Statement: Over a several-year period, a professor has found that the average grade on the final exam for all students taking a course in economics is 75. One semester, the final exam is given and the grades are found to be slightly lower, with an average of 73.8 ($s = 8.3$) for a sample of size $N = 61$. Assuming H_0: $\mu = 75$, can the professor reject the null hypothesis and conclude that the sample came from a different population in which the mean is different (lower)?

1. H_0: $\mu = 75$. The population that this semester's economics class came from had a mean final exam score of 75. This had been the state of affairs over several years.

2. H_1: $\mu \neq 75$. This year's class came from a population with a mean different from 75.

3. Set $\alpha = .05$.

4. *Rejection rule:* Reject H_0 if $|t_{comp}| \geq t_{crit}$ ($t_{.05}$ for $df = N - 1$). In this case, $t_{.05}$ ($df = 60$) = 2.0003.

5. *Computation and Test Statistic:* From the statement of the problem, we know that $\overline{X} = 73.8$, $N = 61$, and $s = 8.3$.

$$s_{\overline{X}} = \frac{s}{\sqrt{N}} = \frac{8.3}{\sqrt{61}} = \frac{8.3}{7.81} = 1.06$$

$$t = \frac{\overline{X} - \mu_0}{s_{\overline{X}}} = \frac{73.8 - 75}{1.06} = \frac{-1.2}{1.06} = -1.13.$$

6. *Decision:* Because $|t_{comp}| = |-1.13| = 1.13 < 2.0003$, we fail to reject H_0, and $p > .05$.

7. *Conclusion:* A one-sample t test was performed to determine whether there has been a decrease in the average economics final exam score this semester compared to previous years. There was insufficient evidence to conclude that the mean exam score for this semester was different from 75, the mean from previous years, $t(60) = -1.13$, $p > .05$. There has not been a significant change this semester in the final exam average from previous years.

Seven-Step Procedure for Testing the Null Hypothesis

1. **State the null hypothesis in symbols and words.** The null hypothesis is written in general terms as $H_0: \mu = \mu_0$. We will always give a numerical value for μ_0 as shown in Box 9-1, Step 1. The value for μ_0 must come from the problem situation. It may be based on history, as in this example, or specified in some other way. We must have a value for μ_0 to work the problem. This value is the mean of the population from which we assume our sample came.

We want to stress the importance of putting the null hypothesis into words in the context of the problem. It's a little more trouble to do, but it will pay off in our understanding of the problem—what is actually being measured—and later when we write our final conclusions.

2. **State the alternative hypothesis in symbols and in words.** This is shown in Box 9-1, Step 2, for our example. It's easy to write. It just says "no" to the null hypothesis. The verbal statement gives what we as investigators suspect is really occurring. We are performing this test to see whether our hunch is correct. This hypothesis is also called the *research hypothesis* or *experimental hypothesis*. Our H_1 for this problem is *nondirectional*, so we state that $\mu \neq \mu_0$. If our H_1 were directional, H_1 could be either $\mu < \mu_0$ or $\mu > \mu_0$, depending on whether we expect, in this case, this year's class average to be significantly below or above the average of previous years.

3. **Choose an α level.** The α level will always be set to .05 or .01 unless there are some very special circumstances. Set $\alpha = .05$, if there are no specific instructions in the problem.

The α level serves a very important function in our procedure. Remember that we will compute a t value to tell us how deviant our sample mean $\overline{X}$ is. The α level we set *defines* how deviant the score must be in order for us to reject H_0.

4. **State the rejection rule.** See Box 9-1, Step 4. This is an explicit rule for making a decision about our null hypothesis (whether to accept or reject it). This step sets us up for making a decision once we compute t_{comp}. We are interested in the *magnitude* of t_{comp}; this is why we take the absolute value of t_{comp}. Our sample mean may be deviant (low or high) relative to the population mean (μ_0) and yield negative or positive t_{comp} values. All that we must do in this step other than writing the rule is obtain the critical table value for t (t_{crit}). From Table B, the critical value for $df = 60$ is 2.0003 at the 5% level; that is, t scores of ± 2.0003 cut off the deviant 5% of the distribution of t for samples of size $N = 61$ ($df = 60$).

5. **Compute the test statistic.** Write down what is given from the problem or data that you have. You may have to compute $\overline{X}$ and s from raw data. Note that the t_{comp} formula is the same as Formula 9-5 and that the formula for $s_{\overline{X}}$ is taken from the third property of the sampling distribution of the means. Always write down the formula first, then substitute the starting values for each symbol. Show intermediary steps and highlight or box the final answer.

6. **Make a decision by applying the rejection rule.** Because our t_{comp} is -1.13 (1.13 in absolute value), it is less than the critical value, and we cannot reject H_0. In other words, the probability is quite high of obtaining a sample of

size $N = 61$, with a mean of 73.8 from a population in which the mean is 75. Another way we could express our decision (failure to reject H_0) is to write $t(60) = -1.13$, $p > .05$. This notation will be included in the conclusion statement to come next.

7. Write a conclusion statement in the context of the problem. This statement should summarize the problem context, the decision, and the conclusion from our null hypothesis testing procedure. It should convey enough information to the reader for him or her to understand the problem context, the research question, and the conclusion drawn as a result of the testing procedure. The statement should conform to the way results are reported in a research paper. You will learn more about writing research reports when you take a course in experimental psychology or research methods.

Remember that our conclusion is an inference statement about population parameters. To emphasize the inferential nature of the critical part of the conclusion statement, it can be expanded as follows: "There was insufficient evidence to conclude that the *population* mean exam score for this semester was different from 75, the *population* mean (μ_0) from previous years." The population mean exam score for this semester is *estimated* by $\overline{X} = 73.8$. We did not write our conclusion statement in Box 9-1, Step 7, this way because the statement becomes too cumbersome when we do. Nevertheless, we need to remember that our conclusion is an inference statement and the p value tells us about degree of certainty. When p is greater than ($>$) .05, it is *not* that unusual for our sample mean $\overline{X}$ to have come from a population with mean $\mu = \mu_0$. When p is less than ($<$) .05, it exceeds the cutoff set by our α level, and we decide that it *is* very unusual for $\overline{X}$ to have been sampled from a population with $\mu = \mu_0$. In this case, we reject $H_0: \mu = \mu_0$ and conclude $H_1: \mu \neq \mu_0$, that the sample came from a population with μ equal to some value *different* from μ_0.

In Box 9-1, we have given an example of a conclusion statement (Step 7) for a situation in which we failed to reject H_0. Let's revisit our first example and provide a conclusion statement for that problem, because we did reject H_0 for it.

> **Conclusion for example investigating the effect of amphetamine on memory:** A study was conducted to determine whether a small dose of amphetamine affects recent memory as measured by digit span. A one-sample t test was performed to determine whether there was a difference in the average digit span of persons taking the drug compared to the average adult digit span of 7. The mean digit span for the drug group was significantly different from the mean adult digit span, $t(24) = 2.73$, $p < .05$. Amphetamine significantly enhances recent memory.

You may wonder how we can make the last statement in the preceding model conclusion. We tested for and found only that the drug group (population) mean was *not the same* as that for adults in general. However, the sample mean $\overline{X} = 7.53$—our best estimate of the population mean for the drug group—is *greater than* 7. Therefore, we can infer that digit span is greater for the drug group and memory is enhanced. However, there are ways to test directly for increases or decreases. These are called directional tests.

Directional Tests

In order to conduct a directional test, some alterations need to be made to our hypotheses (Steps 1 and 2) and to our rejection rule (Step 4). For a directional test, t_{comp} should have the same sign as t_{crit}. If you predict H_1: $\mu < \mu_0$, then you expect to obtain a negative t, and t_{crit} should be negative. By the same token, if you predict H_1: $\mu > \mu_0$, the t_{crit} should be positive. Also, in both cases, t_{crit} should be less extreme than for a nondirectional test, because all of the probability is placed in only one direction in the tail of the distribution. For example, suppose we are testing at the .05 level and $df = 24$. With a directional test and H_1: $\mu > \mu_0$, all the probability is placed in the right tail beyond the critical value. Using Table B in Appendix 4, $t_{.05}$ (one-tailed) = 1.7109, whereas for a nondirectional test, $t_{.05}$ = 2.0639. Thus, t_{crit} for a directional test is less extreme (smaller, closer to 0), and we do not need as large a t_{comp} to exceed the critical value. For this reason, directional tests are considered more powerful but hazardous if we cannot correctly predict the direction of our effect.

The rejection rules for directional tests are as follows:

For H_1: $\mu > \mu_0$, reject H_0 if $t_{comp} > t_{crit}$ (one-tailed).

For H_1: $\mu < \mu_0$, reject H_0 if $t_{comp} < -t_{crit}$ (one-tailed).

Returning to our general discussion of hypothesis testing, two more comments are in order. Continuing to look at Table B, we see that if we have $df = \infty$, the values required for significance are 1.96 at the 5% level and 2.58 at the 1% level. As mentioned earlier, one of the properties of the t distribution is that it approaches the normal curve as sample size increases. You may remember from Chapter 8 that the z scores cutting off the deviant 5% and 1% of the normal curve were ±1.96 and ±2.58, respectively.

Finally, note that 1.96 and 2.58 are the smallest values of t required for rejection of the null hypothesis for a two-tailed test at the 5% and 1% levels. For this reason, if any computed t is less than 1.96 in absolute value and you are performing a two-tailed test, there is no need to look in the table, because it cannot be significant.

↺ CHECKING YOUR PROGRESS

A new president has been hired at a large university and has just given his first speech to the general faculty. As the faculty members leave, 35 are randomly selected and asked to rate the speech on a scale from 1 to 7, with 1 being poor, 4 average, and 7 outstanding. The average rating is 4.4 with $s = 0.93$. Test the hypothesis that the sample was taken from a population in which $\mu = 4$.

Answer: $t = 2.55$, $df = 34$, $p < .05$, or $t(34) = 2.55$, $p < .05$. Because $p < .05$, you should reject H_0, and conclude that the president's speech was significantly above average.

Type I and Type II Errors

Hypothesis testing, as it has been discussed in this chapter, involves making an assumption about a population parameter (μ) and then determining whether or not a sample mean differs enough from the assumed value of μ to allow us to reject the null hypothesis. The actual test is performed by computing how far the sample mean deviates from the assumed μ in $s_{\overline{X}}$ units (in other words, by computing t). The computed t score is then compared with t scores known to cut off either the deviant 5% or the deviant 1% of the sampling distribution of means for a given value of df. If the absolute value of t_{comp} (computed t) is equal to or larger than the t_{crit} (critical t) at the 5% (or 1%) level of significance, the null hypothesis is rejected. By rejecting H_0, we are concluding that the probability is .05 (.01) or less of obtaining a sample $\overline{X}$ as deviant as the one we obtained from a population with the μ that we assumed. If t_{comp} is smaller than the table values, we do not reject the null hypothesis.

This process of rejecting or failing to reject H_0 is sometimes called "decision making." In statistics, as in life, sometimes we make the wrong decision. Before we consider the details of statistical decision making, let's consider some ordinary examples of decision making and the kinds of errors that can be made. Suppose you are playing poker and have been losing for a while. You might think that you are having a run of bad luck or, possibly, that your opponent is cheating. You are faced with a decision-making situation.

Let's assume first that the game really is honest. If you decide you are simply having bad luck, you have made a correct decision, and in time, your luck will change. However, what if you decide your opponent is cheating? You might accuse him or her of being dishonest. In the days of the "Wild West," you might decide you need immediate justice, draw your six-shooter, and blast your fellow card player away. Because the game was really honest, you were wrong in your decision, and you may experience some rather unpleasant consequences—hanging at sunrise, for example. This type of error in decision making is analogous to a jury convicting an innocent person. In a research context, this type of erroneous decision is analogous to making a *false claim* of effectiveness of our treatment—concluding there was a treatment effect when there really wasn't.

Now, let's look at the situation in which the poker game really is dishonest. If you decide there is cheating and shoot your opponent, you have made a correct decision, although it is certainly not an appropriate response in today's world. You have successfully *detected* the cheating and have rid the town of one more crooked gambler. On the other hand, if you decide there is no cheating, you have made a different kind of error. As a consequence, you may continue to play, losing your money, saddle, horse, and ranch. You have *failed to detect* the cheating. In a jury trial, this is analogous to declaring a truly guilty person to be innocent. In research, this error could be described as failing to find a true or real treatment effect, which may be a tragedy if the experimental treatment was an effective treatment for schizophrenia or a cure for the common cold. Thus, we have two prototype error situations: the "false claim" and the "failure of detection." Let's see how these are described and defined in the process of hypothesis testing.

One type of incorrect decision is to reject the null hypothesis when, in fact, it is true. In this case, we may conclude on the basis of our sample value that the sample was not taken from a population in which μ was what we assumed it to be when, in fact, the sample was taken from this population.

This type of judgment error (the "false claim") is known as a **Type I, or α, error** and is defined as rejecting H_0 when it is true. The levels of significance (5% and 1%) are often called α levels, and the probability of making a Type I error depends directly on α. For example, if $\alpha = .05$, then the probability of rejecting a true H_0 is .05, or 5 times in 100; that is, if we drew 100 samples from a population in which μ is what we have assumed it to be, 5 of those samples would have means deviant enough from μ for us to reject H_0. However, 5 times out of 100 is not very often, and that is why we rejected H_0 initially.

In practice, the $\alpha = .05$ level, or 5% level, of significance is widely used, and most scientists are willing to accept rejection of H_0 at the 5% level as reflecting a true difference from chance. If, however, we want to be more conservative and come closer to ensuring that we don't mistakenly reject a true H_0, we can lower the α level to .01 (1% level of significance) or even to .001, and so on. After all, we don't want to get "hanged." The problem with the ultraconservative approach is that a true difference may be discarded because it does not quite reach the required critical values caused by the small α. While decreasing the probability of a Type I error, we are simultaneously increasing the probability of a **Type II, or β, error** (a "failure of detection"), which is defined as failing to reject H_0 when it is false. Further, although the probability of a Type I error is determined by the α level, the probability of a Type II error will not be specifically known. Therefore, the investigator must choose the α level that balances Type I and Type II errors. In the social sciences, the 5% level is most often accepted as achieving this balance.

The possible consequences of hypothesis testing as outlined in this chapter are summarized in Figure 9-7. The chart reflects the two possible decisions that can be made: to reject or to fail to reject the null hypothesis, which may be either true or false. Rejection of a true H_0 results in an α error, whereas rejection of a false H_0 is correct. Failure to reject a true H_0 is correct, whereas failing to reject a false H_0 leads to a β error.

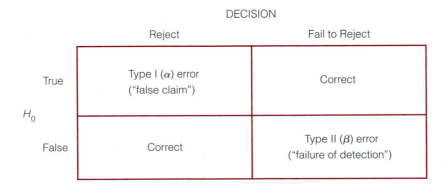

Figure 9-7   Chart illustrating the possible consequences of decision making in hypothesis testing.

The Power of a Statistical Test

In the previous section, a Type I, or α, error was defined as rejecting a true null hypothesis, and a Type II, or β, error was defined as failing to reject a false null hypothesis. Further, it was stated that decreasing the likelihood of an α error by lowering α results in an increase in the probability of a β error. Thus, by making it less likely that we will mistakenly reject a true null, we are making it increasingly more difficult to reject *any* null hypothesis, even one that is false.

A related concern is the **power** of a test, defined as the probability that our test will detect a false hypothesis. In a research context, power may be considered as the chance of detecting a real treatment effect. Power may be determined by solving the equation

$$\text{power} = 1 - \beta.$$

Unfortunately, determining the power of a test requires information that we do not have concerning the actual state of affairs in the population. We would need to know exact parameters, which are what we have been estimating from our sample values. Although we cannot determine β (and from it $1 - \beta$) without assuming a specific value for the alternative hypothesis, we can discuss some factors that contribute to the power of a test. To better understand these factors, let's consider the distributions shown in Figure 9-8.

In Figure 9-8, there are two partially overlapping distributions designated H_0 and H_1. The distribution called H_0 is what we would expect to observe if H_0 were true ($\mu = \mu_0$), whereas H_1 represents the state of affairs in which H_1 is true ($\mu = \mu_1$). Assuming that $\alpha = .05$ and that we are using a one-tailed test (one that considers only one tail of the distribution rather than both tails), a vertical line has been drawn on the graph illustrating the region of rejection of H_0; that is, any sample mean that happened to fall in the unshaded region to the right of the rejection

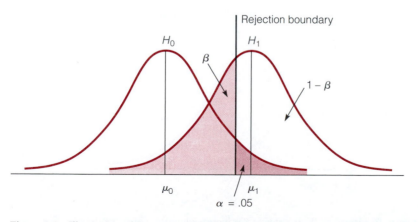

Figure 9-8   Illustration of the power of a test. The vertical line represents the lower boundary for rejection of the null hypothesis under H_0. The shaded area under H_1 to the left of the line is β, and the unshaded area to the right is $1 - \beta$, or the power of the test.

line would enable us to reject H_0. This unshaded portion of the graph is labeled $1 - \beta$, or the power of the test.

However, you can see that a substantial portion of distribution H_1 lies to the left of the rejection line. This portion of H_1 has been shaded and is labeled β. Thus, if H_1 is true, any sample drawn from H_1 with a mean in the shaded portion will not result in the rejection of H_0, which is really false. Observation of a sample in this area will result in a β error. Now let's look at the factors affecting power.

Effect of α Level on Power   As already mentioned, the value of α affects β, which in turn determines $1 - \beta$. Thus, the smaller we set the α level, the larger β will be, which in turn means that our statistical test will have less power. In constructing the line of rejection shown in Figure 9-8, α was set at .05. Suppose we make $\alpha = .01$ instead. In the new situation, shown in Figure 9-9, we can see that the shaded area β is now larger than it was with $\alpha = .05$, and the power of the test $(1 - \beta)$ has decreased.

Effect of Sample Size on Power   A second factor affecting the power of a test is the size of the sample taken from the population. Specifically, the larger the N, the greater the power of the test will be. The reason for this involves one of the properties of the sampling distribution of means: As the size of the sample increases, $\sigma_{\bar{x}}$ decreases. In other words, with larger and larger Ns, the sampling distribution becomes more and more compact. The effect of sample size on the power of a test is shown in Figure 9-10, in which the distributions have been drawn to reflect a larger N than is shown in Figure 9-8. As you can see, although the mean of each distribution is the same as before, the greater compactness results in less overlap, a smaller β, and a larger power.

Magnitude of Difference and Power   A third factor affecting power is the distance between the mean under H_0 and the true mean under H_1; that is, the greater the

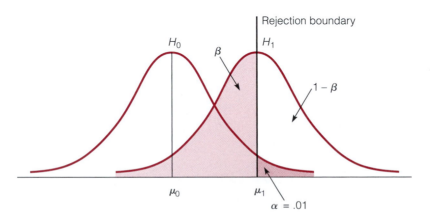

Figure 9-9   With $\alpha = .01$ instead of .05, the area of β is increased, with a corresponding decrease in the power of the test $(1 - \beta)$.

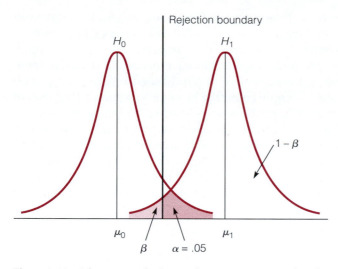

Figure 9-10 A larger sample size results in more compact distributions, a smaller region of overlap between H_0 and H_1, and a more powerful test.

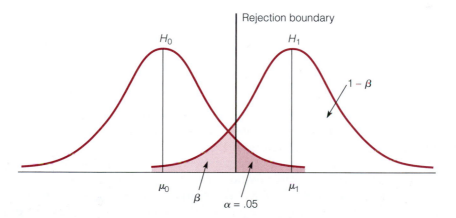

Figure 9-11 When the means μ_0 and μ_1 are farther apart, β is decreased and $1 - \beta$, or the power of the test, is increased.

discrepancy between the hypothesized value and the true value, the greater the power of the test. Figure 9-11 illustrates that power increases when the mean under H_1 is farther away from the mean under H_0 than it was in Figure 9-8.

Meta-Analysis

The size of the difference between the null hypothesis (H_0: $\mu = \mu_0$) and the alternative hypothesis (H_1: $\mu \neq \mu_0$) in standardized units, called the **effect size,** has been the point of departure for a different way of analyzing research results from large numbers of studies. Let's say that we want to review the social psychology literature on the effect of communicator credibility on persuasiveness. Although there are more sophisticated methods, the traditional approach to research literature review has been, in effect, to examine all the published research articles on communicator credibility and to simply count the number that showed significant effects. If a large majority, say 85%, of the studies showed a significant effect, in which persons of "good character" were more effective at persuading audiences than were others, then our review would conclude that empirical research had supported a claim for such an effect made by Aristotle more than 2,000 years ago. We would have to explain why 15% of the studies did not show the effect, and it's possible that studies that did not show a significant effect at the .05 level might not have been published, but our conclusion would still be basically the same: People with "good character" are more persuasive.

Meta-analysis takes a different approach, using quantitative procedures for integrating findings in a literature review. It uses the *effect size* results of studies rather than whether the results were merely statistically significant. This is like asking how large the effect of communicator credibility was rather than asking whether *any* significant effect was present. We know from our previous discussion about power that it can be increased by increasing the sample size; that is, a weak or borderline effect can become statistically significant by increasing the size of our sample. The effect size, however, is not changed by increases in sample size, which gives meta-analysis a distinct edge as a technique for evaluating research.

The effect sizes themselves can be analyzed (averaged, for example) to draw a conclusion across many studies as to the *size* of the effect—not just whether it is statistically significant. Thus, meta-analysis is a synthesis technique for performing quantitative, rather than qualitative, research reviews. For more information on meta-analysis, see F. M. Wolf, 1986, *Meta-Analysis: Quantitative Methods for Research Synthesis*, Beverly Hills, CA: Sage.

Now that we have discussed and spelled out the hypothesis-testing procedure, we feel it is only fair to include a brief mention of a controversy that appears from time to time in the literature of psychology. Like many such controversies, this one often generates more heat than light. It concerns the value of the procedure we have just covered.

Should Hypothesis Testing Be Abandoned?

You can probably guess how we're going to answer this question, particularly after observing the lengths to which we have gone to teach you the method. However, some researchers and research statisticians have called for the very event indicated in the subheading—the abandonment of hypothesis testing. Although the debate on this topic is not new, it was recently rejuvenated in a series of articles in *Psychological Science*, which were introduced by P. E. Shrout in 1997. See "Should Significance Tests Be Banned? Introduction to a Special Section Exploring the Pros and Cons," *Psychological Science, 8*, pp. 1–2.

The debate has much to do with our previous discussion of Type I and Type II errors, power, and effect size. People who argue for abandoning hypothesis testing claim that such procedures often are misleading. Instead, they say, we should report confidence intervals and effect sizes. One of their points is that the error rate in psychological research is really much higher than most researchers realize.

Hypothesis testers assume that the error rate is .05, because they set the α level to this value by convention. However, there is still some chance for committing a Type II error—failing to reject a false null hypothesis—which doesn't get much attention. The anti-hypothesis testers claim that a large percentage of research studies don't have enough power to find what they are looking for—even when the effect is present—and consequently commit Type II errors at high rates, sometimes as high as 60%!

Although the point may be exaggerated, it is valuable if it makes us more attentive to having sufficient power in our research studies to find an effect when it is present. Because we know that power is affected by the α level, the sample size N, and the size of the effect ($\mu_0 - \mu_1$), what can we do to have enough power? We're "stuck" at .05 for the α level in most cases, so there's not much help on that front. However, we can try to avoid small sample sizes and to employ treatment effects that have as much impact as possible. Computations for required sample sizes for different effect sizes and desired power levels can be found in more advanced texts, such as J. Cohen, 1965, *Statistical Power Analysis for the Behavioral Sciences*, New York: McGraw-Hill.

The main benefit likely to come from the debate on significance testing is that more attention will be given to the size of an effect rather than only to the statistical significance of the effect—just as in meta-analysis—and more effect sizes will be reported. This could mean that the behavioral sciences would show greater advances, because more important effects would be investigated. Another benefit is that researchers may become more aware of the need for adequate power, achieved by adequate sample size. If we fail to learn the lessons of the debate, we may continue to make Type II "failure of detection" errors at a high rate.

SUMMARY

In this chapter, we introduced the sampling distribution of means. The sampling distribution of means was constructed from the means of successive random samples of a given size taken from some population. Here are its properties:

1. Its mean ($\mu_{\bar{X}}$) is equal to the mean of the population (μ).

2. It is symmetrical in shape and approaches normality with large samples, even if the population from which the samples are drawn is not normal. This is a simplified version of the central limit theorem.

3. Its standard deviation ($\sigma_{\bar{X}}$, called the standard error of the mean) becomes smaller as the size of the sample becomes larger.

The sample was used to estimate the population values μ, σ, and σ^2, as $\overline{X}$, s, and s^2 are unbiased estimates of the corresponding population values. Standard scores may be calculated using the estimated values, but the scores correspond to a t distribution, not to a z distribution. With large sample size, the t and z distributions become increasingly similar.

The sampling distribution of means was used to construct confidence intervals (defined as a range of values within which we have a certain degree of confidence that μ is contained) and to test hypotheses about the exact value of μ. The two confidence intervals discussed were the 95% CI and the 99% CI. The formula for the 95% CI is

$$95\% \text{ CI} = \pm t_{.05} s_{\overline{X}} + \overline{X},$$

where $t_{.05}$ is a value obtained from a table of t scores (Table B in Appendix 4) that cut off the deviant 5% and 1% of the sampling distribution of means. The critical value of t used depends on the degrees of freedom, defined as the number of values free to vary after certain restrictions are placed on the data. In the case of t with one sample, $df = N - 1$. The value $s_{\overline{X}}$ is an estimate of $\sigma_{\overline{X}}$ and is computed from the formula

$$s_{\overline{X}} = \frac{s}{\sqrt{N}}.$$

The formula for the 99% CI is

$$99\% \text{ CI} = \pm t_{.01} s_{\overline{X}} + \overline{X}.$$

Hypothesis testing involves making an assumption about whether a sample mean is representative of a population with a mean of μ; that is, if the $\overline{X}$ observed is very unlikely given the deviation between $\overline{X}$ and μ_0, the null hypothesis is rejected. Here are the actual steps:

1. State the null hypothesis H_0.
2. State the alternative hypothesis H_1. Both H_0 and H_1 should also be stated in words providing information about the problem.
3. Decide on a level for α, the level at which you will reject or fail to reject the null hypothesis. For most purposes, the 5% level ($\alpha = .05$) is satisfactory.
4. State the rejection rule for the t test. The rule says to reject H_0 if $|t_{comp}| \geq t_{crit}$ ($t_{.05}$ for $df = N - 1$). Thus, we compare the computed t score with the critical value of t from Table B with the appropriate df ($N - 1$). This rule is for a non-directional test.

    For a directional test, remember whether you expect t to be positive or negative. If you predict a negative t_{comp}, reject H_0 if $t_{comp} \leq t_{crit}$. If you predict a positive t_{comp}, reject H_0 if $t_{comp} \geq t_{crit}$. Otherwise, fail to reject H_0.
5. Compute the t-test statistic. This determines how far $\overline{X}$ deviates from the assumed value of μ (μ_0) in $s_{\overline{X}}$ units. We calculate a t score using the formula

$$t = \frac{\overline{X} - \mu_0}{s_{\overline{X}}}.$$

6. Make a decision to reject or fail to reject H_0 by applying the rejection rule in Step 4. If the absolute value of the computed t is equal to or greater than the table value, we reject H_0. Otherwise, we fail to reject H_0, for a nondirectional test.

7. Write a conclusion statement in the context of the problem. Include citation of the computed t, df, and p values in the style of a research report. If H_0 is rejected, $p < .05$ or $.01$; otherwise, $p > .05$.

Hypothesis testing is also known as testing for significance, and the values of t cutting off the deviant 5% and 1% of the distribution of t define the 5% and 1% levels of significance, respectively.

Two types of errors may be made when testing H_0. The Type I, or α, error is defined as rejection of a true null and has a probability equal to the α level. The Type II, or β, error is defined as failing to reject a false H_0. The probability of this type of error increases with decreases in α.

The power of a test is defined as the probability of detecting or rejecting a false H_0. Power is determined by the formula

$$\text{power} = 1 - \beta.$$

Three factors affecting power are the α level used, the size of N, and the distance between μ_0 and μ_1, a true alternative hypothesis.

Meta-analysis is a technique for evaluating and synthesizing a large number of research studies on a specific topic. Rather then relying solely on statistical significance, meta-analysis uses the size of the effect (the standardized distance between μ_0 and μ_1 in the case of the t test) to evaluate each study. This information is combined and synthesized to draw a conclusion across many studies. Meta-analysis is advantageous because it provides information on the *size* of the effect under investigation, not just whether the effect is statistically present.

The controversy about whether statistical tests should be abandoned was discussed briefly. Proponents of abandonment advocate reporting confidence intervals and effect sizes rather than tests of significance. It is unlikely that statistical tests will be banned, but recommendations for reporting effect size and attention to sufficient sample size for adequate power—and the avoidance of a high Type II error rate—should improve the quality of research in the behavioral sciences.

✴✴ *Troubleshooting Your Computations*

The computations covered in this chapter have been, for the most part, quite simple and require an understanding of what you are trying to find more than mathematical ability. However, there are some questions you should ask yourself after you have worked the problems in this chapter.

First of all, have you obtained a CI that seems reasonable in light of the sample information you have? For example, to be reasonable, the CI should contain the mean of the sample. When you found the t score to plug into the formula for the confidence interval, did you use df or N? You should have used df $(N - 1)$ rather than N.

When computing and reporting the t score, did you retain the appropriate sign throughout the computations? For example, if the mean of your sample is less than the value set for μ, your computed t score should be negative.

After making a decision to reject or not to reject the null hypothesis, go back and review the decision-making process. For nondirectional tests, consider whether or not your computed t score was larger in absolute value than the table value of t cutting off the deviant 5% of the distribution of t scores for samples with the df you observed. If so, you should have rejected H_0; if not, you should not have rejected H_0. For directional tests, t_{comp} must be less than or equal to a negative t_{crit} or greater than or equal to a positive t_{crit}.

EXERCISES

1. a. Given $\overline{X} = 100$, $s = 20$, and $N = 25$, find the 99% CI for μ.
   b. If $N = 147$, what is the 95% CI for μ? Note that 146 is closer to 120 than it is to ∞.

2. Find the 99% and 95% CIs for each of the following samples:
   a. $\overline{X} = 15$, $N = 17$, $s = 5$
   b. $\Sigma X = 240$, $N = 40$, $s_{\overline{X}} = 1.6$
   c. $N = 170$, $\Sigma X = 1{,}445$, $\Sigma X^2 = 12{,}343.25$

3. Find the 95% and 99% CIs for μ for the following scores:

X	f	X	f
42	1	22	2
30	2	21	1
26	6	19	2
25	1	18	4
24	1	17	2
23	3		

4. The ages of students in a night class on gerontology were collected with the following results:

X	f	X	f
37	1	29	3
36	1	27	2
34	3	26	1
32	1	25	1
31	5	20	1
30	4		

Find the 95% and 99% CIs for μ (average age).

5. The running time for 137 rats in a 6-foot runway is recorded. The data are $\Sigma X = 1{,}781$ seconds and $\Sigma X^2 = 25{,}345$. Assume that $\mu = 11.5$ seconds. Test H_0.

6. A company has developed a training procedure to improve scores on the SAT. Following the training, 100 high school students take the SAT. The average math score is 517, with $s = 90$. Assuming $\mu = 500$ for the math SAT, test the null hypothesis. Did the training significantly improve scores ($\alpha = .05$, directional)?

7. Briefly define the following terms:

   a. power of a test

   b. α error

   c. β error

   d. directional hypothesis

8. How was the sampling distribution of means derived, and what are its properties?

9. The human brain's delay in response to a sound has been found to be 5.68 milliseconds. A random sample of 10 participants is selected, and each subject is asked to go without sleep for 24 hours before a test for brain stem auditory response latency. The average latency is found to be 5.85 milliseconds, with $s = 0.14$. Test the hypothesis that lack of sleep has no effect on average latency.

10. A therapist treating clients for communication apprehension (fear of public speaking) assessed the effectiveness of the treatment by giving her clients a standard test at the beginning and at the end of treatment. The difference between the two scores was an indication of change. Here are the scores (a negative score indicates improvement):

X	X
-3	-3
-4	-1
2	4
-8	1
0	-5
-7	-6
6	

If the treatment produced no effect, the change score would be 0, so assume that $\mu = 0$. Test the null hypothesis ($\alpha = .05$, directional). Did the treatment significantly reduce communication apprehension?

11. In the chapter, we discussed the derivation of the sampling distribution of means. Suppose we have a finite population consisting of the scores 1, 3, 5, and 7. All possible samples of size $N = 2$ have been extracted from it and are as follows:

1, 1	5, 1	3, 5	5, 5
1, 3	1, 7	5, 3	5, 7
3, 1	7, 1	3, 7	7, 5
1, 5	3, 3	7, 3	7, 7

From these samples, construct the sampling distribution of means and show that the mean of the distribution is equal to μ. Demonstrate that $\sigma_{\bar{X}} = \sigma/\sqrt{N}$.

12. Over a period of several years in a sleep-therapy clinic, the average latency to fall asleep for adult males, age 20–30, has been found to be 335 seconds. In a study of the effectiveness of hypnotic therapy, 30 males of the appropriate age are given the treatment and then their latency to fall asleep is measured. The results are a mean latency of 283.7, with a variance of 5,756.26 seconds. Test the hypothesis that hypnotic therapy has no effect on sleep latency. Use an α level of .05 and a nondirectional test.

13. Using the sample information in Exercise 12, determine the 95% and 99% confidence intervals for μ.

14. Over a 20-year period, the average grade point average of applicants to our graduate program has been found to be 3.27. This year the mean grade point average of the 57 students applying to our graduate program is 3.53, with a standard deviation of 0.29. Test the hypothesis that the current sample came from a population in which $\mu = 3.27$. Use an α level of .05 and a nondirectional test.

15. Use the sample data from Exercise 14 to compute the 95% and 99% confidence intervals for μ. Is $\mu = 3.27$ in the 95% CI? Did you reject H_0 in Exercise 14? (If the null hypothesis value of μ is not in the 95% CI, then you will reject H_0 with $p < .05$.)

16. Return to the first example of the one-sample t test given in the chapter. Give the solution to the problem following the seven-step procedure.

17. A professor riding on a van to teach a night class in statistics for the behavioral sciences at a branch campus has a lively conversation with a statistics professor from the business college. A problem that has puzzled them both for years is whether coin use is declining in this era of credit cards. The business professor has been collecting data for years on the number of cents people carry in their pockets or purses and maintains that the population mean is 2.2 cents. Our professor polls his class that night and obtains the following data: 1, 2, 3, 0, 0, 19, 43, 2, 7, 9, 0, 0, 1, 0, 5. Had there been a change in the number of cents carried?

18. Explain the difference between a point estimate for μ ($\bar{X}$) and an interval estimate for μ (a 95% CI). What is the role of variability in each?

19. You may have seen the not-so-recent movie *WarGames* (1983) in which a young computer hacker accidentally breaks into the central nuclear defense computers at the North American Air Defense Command (NORAD). Once

in the systems, the hacker finds many computer games to play and chooses and starts to play one called Global Thermonuclear War. In the context of this game, the computer signals that a nuclear attack is being launched by the Soviets. The questions for NORAD are whether the attack is real and whether a counterstrike should be launched. Give a brief discussion of the situation in terms of Type I and Type II errors and the consequences of each.

20. Surprisingly, a study found that children under stress reported fewer symptoms of depression and anxiety but scored higher on a Lie Scale (a measure of tendency to give socially desirable responses). The population mean for the Lie Scale for nonstressed children is 3.8. A sample of 40 children under stress had a Lie Scale sample mean of 4.4, with a standard deviation of 2.5. Test the hypothesis that children under stress are more likely to give socially desirable answers. Write a complete conclusion in the context of the problem.

Significance of the Difference Between Two Sample Means

 Dr. Baxter tried a new approach to the treatment of panic disorder on a few clients, and they appeared to show more improvement than the clients with panic disorder she treated conventionally. When she spoke to her colleagues about the new technique, they seemed interested but unconvinced. Dr. Baxter knew that she and her colleagues needed better evidence to determine the worth of the new treatment.

Dr. Baxter had a large practice, with many panic disorder clients, so she decided that it would be possible to design an experiment to test the effectiveness of her new approach formally. It had been several years since her last statistics and research design course, but she thought she could devise a simple design with two independent groups that should serve the purpose.

Dr. Baxter collected the files of 25 clients with panic disorder who were all in the early stages of treatment, and by tossing a coin, she randomly assigned 13 clients to a "conventional" treatment group and 12 clients to an "experimental" treatment group. She then administered the appropriate treatment over a period of 8 weeks, which she thought was sufficient time for her patients to show some improvement.

At the end of this time, Dr. Baxter administered a standard assessment to the clients in both groups to determine their level of panic disorder. She listed the scores of the two groups, performed some calculations, and in a few minutes had her answer. The mean of the experimental group ($\overline{X} = 6.58$) was indeed lower than the mean of the conventional treatment group ($\overline{X} = 9.77$). Note that a lower score indicates less panic.

However, after all that time and effort, Dr. Baxter was still not satisfied. There was an average difference of 3.19 points, but it didn't seem very impressive. Would her colleagues be convinced by it? How could she clarify her findings? Was there a statistical procedure that could help her determine whether the groups differed significantly in their remaining symptoms?

Indeed, there is a statistical test that Dr. Baxter could use. It is called the independent t test, and it is one of the statistical procedures we will discuss in this chapter. The independent t test is used in situations such as the one created by Dr. Baxter, in which two separate, and independent, groups are compared.

Chapter 9 presented the one-sample t test as a means of evaluating the validity of a hypothesis about the population mean on the basis of a sample value. The material in this chapter is an extension of what was covered in Chapter 9. This time, rather than consider one sample extracted from a population at a time, we will consider two samples taken simultaneously.

In a one-sample t test, we test the hypothesis that $\mu = \mu_0$. We want to know the probability that a sample mean $\overline{X}$ came from a population with a mean equal to some known value μ_0. The sample mean is compared with a population mean $(\overline{X} - \mu_0)$ to determine the extent of the deviation. The population mean value is known at the outset, either because it is defined theoretically or because it has been established in previous research. Additionally, the population mean is a constant—it is a value that does not change. Thus, the one-sample t test compares a sample mean with a known constant (the assumed population mean).

In practice, one-sample t tests are rarely used because we usually don't know the population mean. When the population mean is unknown, we typically draw two samples. One sample receives the treatment, as in the one-sample t test. The second sample, often called the **control group,** is used to estimate the population mean. Instead of using the distance between a sample mean and a population mean $(\overline{X} - \mu_0)$ to test the significance of our treatment, we use the distance between two sample means $(\overline{X}_1 - \overline{X}_2)$. In so doing, we are testing the hypothesis that $\mu_1 = \mu_2$. The important difference is that both sample means can vary, because both are estimates. Therefore, we can no longer use the sampling distribution of means as our reference distribution. Instead, we must use a new distribution— the *sampling distribution of the mean differences.*

THE SAMPLING DISTRIBUTION OF THE DIFFERENCES BETWEEN SAMPLE MEANS

Research designs such as that employed by Dr. Baxter use a test of the difference between independent sample means. By **independent samples,** we mean samples in which the behavior of the members of one sample is not related to the behavior of the members of the other. Practically speaking, we will assume that conditions for independence have been satisfied as long as subjects are selected at random from a large group and are assigned randomly to the different treatment conditions.

In Chapter 9, to introduce the sampling distribution of means, we first considered a population. From this population we drew single random samples, all with the same size N, and computed a mean for each sample. The sampling distribution of means was constructed from the frequency distribution of the sample means.

Now, suppose that instead of drawing single samples from the population, we draw *pairs* of random samples. As before, we calculate the mean for some behavioral measure for each sample, but this time we take the *difference* between the pair of sample means. For any pair of samples drawn at random from the same population, it is unlikely, because of sampling error, that each would have the same mean.

What do we have at this point? We have a population from which we have drawn pairs of samples, we have the means that we have calculated for each sample of a pair, and we have the difference between the means for each pair of samples. We can now make a frequency distribution based on the differences between sample means and use the distribution to plot a frequency polygon. The shape of the resulting polygon will be symmetrical and, if the samples are large enough, approximately normal. The procedure outlined thus far is shown in Figure 10-1.

Step 1: Pairs of random samples are drawn from a population.

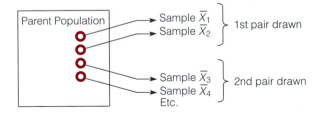

Step 2: The mean for some behavioral measure is found for each sample, and the difference is found for each pair of samples.

Step 3: The frequency polygon of the difference scores is plotted.

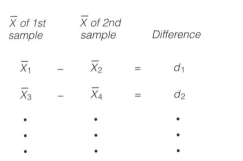

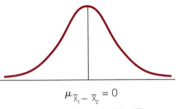

$$\mu_{\overline{X}_1 - \overline{X}_2} = 0$$

Difference scores $(\overline{X}_1 - \overline{X}_2)$

Figure 10-1   Development of the sampling distribution of mean differences.

The scores plotted along the X axis of the frequency polygon are differences between pairs of sample means ($\overline{X}_1 - \overline{X}_2$), so the distribution is called the **sampling distribution of the mean differences.** In Chapter 9, we talked about three important properties of the sampling distribution of means. The sampling distribution of differences also has three important properties; two of these are the same as corresponding properties of the sampling distribution of means. To begin, however, let's discuss the different property.

In the previous chapter, we saw that the mean of the sampling distribution of means was equal to the population mean, or μ. The mean of the sampling distribution of mean differences, on the other hand, is 0. Why is this true?

Remember that all samples are assumed to be drawn from the same population. Because of sampling error, we would expect that in some cases, the mean of the first sample of a pair chosen would be larger than the second mean, resulting in a positive difference. In other cases, the mean of the second sample would be the larger, resulting in a negative difference. Then, when the mean of all the differences was calculated, the positive differences would be canceled by the negative differences, resulting in a mean of 0.

However, what if the pairs of samples come from *different* parent populations, one with population mean μ_1 and the other with mean μ_2? In this case, the mean of the sampling distribution of mean differences would equal $\mu_1 - \mu_2$. We could write this in symbols as follows: $\mu_{\overline{X}_1 - \overline{X}_2} = \mu_1 - \mu_2$, where $\mu_{\overline{X}_1 - \overline{X}_2}$ is our notation for the population mean of the sampling distribution of mean differences. Thus, it is easy to see that if the different parent populations were the same—had the same mean ($\mu_1 = \mu_2$)—then $\mu_{\overline{X}_1 - \overline{X}_2}$ would equal 0.

The remaining properties of the sampling distribution of differences involve the shape of the distribution and are the same as corresponding properties of the sampling distribution of means. Specifically, the larger the size of the samples chosen from the population, the closer the sampling distribution of differences approximates the normal curve. Also, the larger the size of the samples drawn from the population, the smaller will be the standard deviation of the sampling distribution of differences. The standard deviation of the new distribution is called the **standard error of the difference between means** and is symbolized by $\sigma_{\overline{X}_1 - \overline{X}_2}$ (read "little sigma sub X-bar sub 1 minus X-bar sub 2"). The formula for the standard error of the difference between means is:

FORMULA 10-1 *Standard error of the difference between means*

$$\sigma_{\overline{X}_1 - \overline{X}_2} = \sqrt{\sigma_{\overline{X}_1}^2 + \sigma_{\overline{X}_2}^2},$$

where $\sigma_{\overline{X}}^2 = \sigma^2 / N$.

The last property—that the standard error of the difference between means decreases with increases in sample size—may be appreciated if you note that the larger the size of each sample, the closer the mean of the sample is likely to be to the population mean. In turn, the closer the mean of each sample of a pair is to the population value, the closer the sample means will be to each other. If the means of a pair of samples are close to each other, then the difference between their means will be small (i.e., close to 0). Finally, if the differences are close to 0, their variability around the mean of the sampling distribution of differences will be small.

To summarize, here are the properties of the sampling distribution of mean differences:

1. The mean of the sampling distribution of mean differences equals $\mu_1 - \mu_2$. If the pairs of samples come from the same population, then $\mu_1 - \mu_2 = 0$.

2. The larger the sample sizes, the more the sampling distribution of mean differences approximates the normal curve.

3. The larger the sample sizes, the smaller is the standard error of the difference $(\sigma_{\bar{X}_1 - \bar{X}_2})$.

Remember that only rarely do we know the population values of $\sigma_{\bar{X}_1}^2$ and $\sigma_{\bar{X}_2}^2$, so there aren't many occasions when we will be able to use Formula 10-1 to calculate the standard error of the differences. However, we can estimate it with $s_{\bar{X}_1 - \bar{X}_2}$, which we call the **estimated standard error of the mean differences.** Here is the definitional formula:

FORMULA 10-2   *Estimated standard error of the mean differences for independent samples (definitional formula)*

$$s_{\bar{X}_1 - \bar{X}_2} = \sqrt{s_{\bar{X}_1}^2 + s_{\bar{X}_2}^2}, \quad \text{where } s_{\bar{X}}^2 = \frac{s^2}{N}$$

Unfortunately, Formula 10-2 can be used only if the samples have equal N. For this reason, we now introduce a computational formula that can be used with equal or unequal N:

FORMULA 10-3   *Estimated standard error of the mean differences for independent samples (computational formula)*

$$s_{\bar{X}_1 - \bar{X}_2} = \sqrt{\left(\frac{(N_1 - 1)s_1^2 + (N_2 - 1)s_2^2}{N_1 + N_2 - 2}\right)\left(\frac{1}{N_1} + \frac{1}{N_2}\right)},$$

where N_1 and N_2 are the number of subjects in the first and second samples, respectively, and the variances of the samples are symbolized by s_1^2 and s_2^2.

You might wonder how we so quickly transformed (and expanded) Formula 10-2 into Formula 10-3. Actually, there's an interesting statistical story here. Take a look at Box 10-1 for the details. The box should help you better understand Formula 10-3 and serve as a foundation for the concept of estimating variance when we have two or more group samples, which will occur in later chapters.

We are now in a position to determine whether two samples differ significantly—that is, whether they come from different populations with different

Box 10-1   Two Statistics That Estimate the Same Variance

Let's take a closer look at Formula 10-1. $\sigma_{\overline{X}_1 - \overline{X}_2} = \sqrt{\sigma_{\overline{X}_1}^2 + \sigma_{\overline{X}_2}^2}$. Substituting $\sigma_{\overline{X}}^2 = \sigma^2/N$ and allowing for different sample sizes, we have $\sqrt{\sigma_1^2/N_1 + \sigma_2^2/N_2}$. Here we need to consider that our pairs of samples actually come from the same parent population, with population mean μ and population variance σ^2. If this is the case, then σ_1^2 and σ_2^2 are actually the same, and we can remove the subscripts from both, leaving

$$\sigma_{\overline{X}_1 - \overline{X}_2} = \sqrt{\frac{\sigma^2}{N_1} + \frac{\sigma^2}{N_2}} = \sqrt{\sigma^2 \left(\frac{1}{N_1} + \frac{1}{N_2} \right)}.$$

Now, here's the interesting part: We have two samples N_1 and N_2, and for each we can compute a sample mean ($\overline{X}_1$, $\overline{X}_2$) and a sample variance (s_1^2, s_2^2). Because these two samples come from the same parent population with variance σ^2, we have two estimates of σ^2: s_1^2 estimates σ^2 and s_2^2 estimates σ^2.

Which one should we use? Note that s_1^2 is based on N_1 scores and s_2^2 is based on N_2 scores. We want to use all of our data to get the best possible estimate of σ^2, so we need to combine s_1^2 and s_2^2. Although one way would be to average the two estimates, we want to combine them in such a way that we give more weight to the estimate based on *more* scores. This leads to a pooling procedure that is actually a *weighted* average. The sample variances are weighted by sample size minus 1, their degrees of freedom.

Thus, our best estimate for σ^2 is given by what we will call s_{pooled}^2:

$$s_{pooled}^2 = \frac{(N_1 - 1)s_1^2 + (N_2 - 1)s_2^2}{N_1 + N_2 - 2}$$

Take another look at Formula 10-3. You will recognize the first term in the denominator as s_{pooled}^2. We can now rewrite Formula 10-3 using our s_{pooled}^2 term:

$$s_{\overline{X}_1 - \overline{X}_2} = \sqrt{s_{pooled}^2 \left(\frac{1}{N_1} + \frac{1}{N_2} \right)}$$

We hope this exercise has given you a better understanding of the relationship between Formula 10-1 and Formula 10-3. Formula 10-3 ($s_{\overline{X}_1 - \overline{X}_2}$) is the estimate for Formula 10-1 ($\sigma_{\overline{X}_1 - \overline{X}_2}$): $\sqrt{s_{pooled}^2(1/N_1 + 1/N_2)}$ estimates $\sqrt{\sigma^2(1/N_1 + 1/N_2)}$, because s_{pooled}^2 estimates σ^2.

Here's something you might want to try. Go back to the preceding s_{pooled}^2 formula and assume that $N_1 = N_2 = N$; that is, remove all subscripts from the Ns and simplify the formula. You may be surprised at the result.

means. We can do this in the same way that we tested hypotheses about μ in Chapter 9. As you will recall, we first determined, in $s_{\bar{X}}$ units, how far our sample mean was from the hypothesized μ. In other words, we computed a t score and then compared our computed value with critical values of t from Table B in Appendix 4.

Hypothesis testing is the same whether we are considering pairs of samples or only one. Again, the first step is to determine how far, in $s_{\bar{X}_1 - \bar{X}_2}$ units, our observed difference in sample means deviates from the mean of the sampling distribution of differences. In other words, we will compute a t score just as we did in the last chapter. The formula for t is another variation on the basic formula for a standard score, or z score.

A z score was defined as the deviation of a raw score from the mean in standard deviation units, or

$$z \text{ score} = \frac{\text{score} - \text{mean}}{\text{standard deviation}}.$$

If we apply this formula to the sampling distribution of differences, the result is

FORMULA 10-4 z score for the sampling distribution of differences

$$z_{\bar{X}_1 - \bar{X}_2} = \frac{(\bar{X}_1 - \bar{X}_2) - (\mu_1 - \mu_2)}{\sigma_{\bar{X}_1 - \bar{X}_2}},$$

where $(\bar{X}_1 - \bar{X}_2)$ is a score in the distribution, $(\mu_1 - \mu_2)$ is the mean of the distribution, and $\sigma_{\bar{X}_1 - \bar{X}_2}$ is the standard deviation of the distribution.

Because we cannot determine $\sigma_{\bar{X}_1 - \bar{X}_2}$, we use $s_{\bar{X}_1 - \bar{X}_2}$ to estimate it. Substituting this value into the equation for z gives us:

FORMULA 10-5 t score for the sampling distribution of differences

$$t_{\bar{X}_1 - \bar{X}_2} = \frac{(\bar{X}_1 - \bar{X}_2) - (\mu_1 - \mu_2)}{s_{\bar{X}_1 - \bar{X}_2}}$$

Because $\mu_1 - \mu_2 = 0$ if the two samples come from the same population, the formula for t is usually written:

FORMULA 10-6   Two-sample t test for independent samples (definitional formula)

$$t_{\bar{X}_1 - \bar{X}_2} = \frac{\bar{X}_1 - \bar{X}_2}{s_{\bar{X}_1 - \bar{X}_2}}$$

After our raw score (difference between a pair of sample means) has been converted to a t score, the computed t is compared with t scores known to cut off the deviant 5% and 1% of the sampling distribution of differences. As in the previous chapter, sample size is converted to degrees of freedom, and the critical values of t are located in the same table as before, Table B.

Now that we have discussed how the t test is performed, let's consider an actual problem, compute t, and determine whether or not the samples were drawn from the same population.

COMPUTING t: INDEPENDENT SAMPLES

Tennis coach Tom Robson decided to try a new technique to help the members of his team improve their serves. He showed the entire team a videotape of the proper serving technique. Then Tom divided the team at random into two groups. One group would imagine the proper serving form for 10 minutes before each practice, and the other group would read a pamphlet on proper serving technique. After 1 week, Tom observed each team member's serving skills. On the basis of the difference between sample means that he observed, were the two groups drawn from the same population with the same mean, or did they come from different populations with different means? Let's see.

Tom found that the average number of good serves for the "imagining" group was 27.6 and the average number for the "reading" group was 22.1. There were 10 team members in each group. Assuming that the variance for the first group was 25.4 and the variance for the second group was 22.2, let's compute a t score using the $\alpha = .05$ level for the test.

If we combine Formulas 10-3 and 10-6, we have the following formula for t:

FORMULA 10-7 *Two-sample t test for independent samples (computational formula)*

$$t_{\overline{X}_1 - \overline{X}_2} = \frac{\overline{X}_1 - \overline{X}_2}{\sqrt{\left[\dfrac{(N_1 - 1)s_1^2 + (N_2 - 1)s_2^2}{N_1 + N_2 - 2}\right]\left(\dfrac{1}{N_1} + \dfrac{1}{N_2}\right)}}$$

Note and recall from Box 10-1 that the part of the formula

$$\frac{(N_1 - 1)s_1^2 + (N_2 - 1)s_2^2}{N_1 + N_2 - 2}$$

is also known as s_{pooled}^2, an estimate of the *common* variance of the populations from which our samples were drawn. Using this substitution, the t-test formula can also be written

$$t_{\overline{X}_1 - \overline{X}_2} = \frac{\overline{X}_1 - \overline{X}_2}{\sqrt{s^2_{pooled}\left(\dfrac{1}{N_1} + \dfrac{1}{N_2}\right)}}.$$

By evaluating s^2_{pooled} separately and substituting the result into the above formula, we can simplify the computation of the t test. However, when we compute portions of formulas separately from the main formula, we run the risk of forgetting that our answer is supposed to be substituted into a larger equation. Thus, we will use Formula 10-7 for our t-test examples.

Examining Formula 10-7, we see that we need values for each of the following: $\overline{X}_1$, $\overline{X}_2$, N_1, N_2, s^2_1, and s^2_2. Thus, the values we require are: $\overline{X}_1 = 27.6$, $\overline{X}_2 = 22.1$, $N_1 = N_2 = 10$, $s^2_1 = 25.4$, and $s^2_2 = 22.2$. It's time to compute t.

$$t = \frac{\overline{X}_1 - \overline{X}_2}{\sqrt{\left[\dfrac{(N_1 - 1)s^2_1 + (N_2 - 1)s^2_2}{N_1 + N_2 - 2}\right]\left(\dfrac{1}{N_1} + \dfrac{1}{N_2}\right)}}$$

$$= \frac{27.6 - 22.1}{\sqrt{\left[\dfrac{(10 - 1)25.4 + (10 - 1)22.2}{10 + 10 - 2}\right]\left(\dfrac{1}{10} + \dfrac{1}{10}\right)}}$$

$$= \frac{5.5}{\sqrt{\left(\dfrac{428.4}{18}\right)(.2)}} = \frac{5.5}{\sqrt{4.76}} = \frac{5.5}{2.18} = 2.52$$

What we have found is that a difference in sample means as large as we observed ($27.6 - 22.1 = 5.5$) is 2.52 estimated standard error units away from a mean of 0. Can we reject the null hypothesis or not?

The null hypothesis is that both samples were drawn from the same population and that the mean of the sampling distribution of differences is 0. This is often symbolized by

$$H_0\colon \mu_1 - \mu_2 = 0 \qquad \text{or} \qquad H_0\colon \mu_1 = \mu_2.$$

To use Table B, which contains critical values of t, we need to know a value for df. For the single samples we considered in the previous chapter, $df = N - 1$. For pairs of independent samples, $df = N - 1$ for each sample, which gives us

$$(N_1 - 1) + (N_2 - 1) = N_1 + N_2 - 2,$$

which is part of the denominator of the t ratio. For the example we have been considering, $df = 10 + 10 - 2 = 18$, and the critical values of t from Table B are 2.1009 at the 5% level and 2.8784 at the 1% level. Thus, for $df = 18$, t scores of ± 2.1009 cut off the deviant 5% of the sampling distribution, and t scores of ± 2.8784 cut off the deviant 1% for a two-tailed test.

The t ratio we observed was 2.52, which is larger than the table value required for significance (for rejection of H_0) at the 5% level but is less than the value required for rejection at the 1% level. We conclude, therefore, that the probability is less than .05 of obtaining a difference in sample means as large as we observed if the samples are both drawn from the same population. There is a significant difference between the groups, and, in this study at least, imagining the correct serve does improve performance relative to just reading about it. As mentioned earlier, the correct way to report this information in a research paper is $t(18) = 2.52$, $p < .05$. Box 10-2 presents a model solution for this example using the seven-step procedure.

Box 10-2 Model Solution for the Two-Sample t Test for Independent Samples

Problem Statement: A tennis coach conducted an experiment to determine which of two methods worked best for learning proper serving form. One group of 10 team members imagined proper serving before actually serving, whereas the other group of 10 read a pamphlet on the proper technique. In a test of serving after a week, the "imagining" group had an average of 27.6 good serves in 50 tries, and the "reading" group had an average of 22.1, with variances of 25.4 and 22.2, respectively. Which method is best?

Seven-Step Procedure

Let's assume that Group 1 is the "imagining" group, and Group 2 is the "reading" group.

1. $H_0: \mu_1 = \mu_2$ or $H_0: \mu_1 - \mu_2 = 0$. What this means is that there is *no difference* in the number of good serves by the imagining group and the reading group.

2. $H_1: \mu_1 \neq \mu_2$ or $H_0: \mu_1 - \mu_2 \neq 0$. This means that there is a difference in the number of good serves between the two groups.

3. Set $\alpha = .05$.

4. *Rejection Rule:* Reject H_0 if $|t_{comp}| \geq t_{crit}$ with $df = N_1 + N_2 - 2$, where $t_{.05}\ (df = 18) = 2.1009$ and $t_{.01}\ (df = 18) = 2.8784$.

5. *Computation and Test Statistic:*

Imagining Group	Reading Group
$\overline{X}_1 = 27.6$	$\overline{X}_2 = 22.1$
$s_1^2 = 25.4$	$s_2^2 = 22.2$
$N_1 = 10$	$N_2 = 10$

(continued)

Box 10-2 (*Continued*)

$$t_{comp} = \frac{(\overline{X}_1 - \overline{X}_2) - (\mu_1 - \mu_2)}{\sqrt{\left[\dfrac{(N_1 - 1)s_1^2 + (N_2 - 1)s_2^2}{N_1 + N_2 - 2}\right]\left(\dfrac{1}{N_1} + \dfrac{1}{N_2}\right)}}$$

(For H_0: $\mu_1 - \mu_2 = 0$)

$$= \frac{27.6 - 22.1}{\sqrt{\left[\dfrac{(10 - 1)25.4 + (10 - 1)22.2}{10 + 10 - 2}\right]\left(\dfrac{1}{10} + \dfrac{1}{10}\right)}}$$

$$= \frac{5.5}{\sqrt{\left(\dfrac{428.4}{18}\right)(0.2)}} = \frac{5.5}{\sqrt{4.76}} = \frac{5.5}{2.18} = 2.52.$$

6. *Decision:* Because $|t_{comp}| = 2.52 > 2.1009$, we reject H_0, $p < .05$.

7. *Conclusion:* The difference in the number of good serves between the imagining training group and the reading training group was statistically significant, $t(18) = 2.52$, $p < .05$. The imagining training method is better for learning to make good serves.

One-Tailed Versus Two-Tailed Tests

Although we mentioned one-tailed and two-tailed tests in Chapter 9 when we introduced Table B, we didn't go into much detail at that time. In fact, we suggested or implied that most tests of significance were two-tailed tests. This section should clarify the issue.

A **two-tailed test** is one that considers both ends of the distribution, whether it is the normal curve distribution, the sampling distribution of means, the sampling distribution of differences, or whatever. With a two-tailed test, we make no predictions about where our observed score will lie on the sampling distribution. With the two-tailed test, a negative value of t is just as meaningful for our test as a positive t, because we are looking at both ends of the sampling distribution. In summary, then, a two-tailed test is one in which we are interested in both tails of the distribution and in which we are not required to make any guesses about possible outcomes before beginning the experiment. In this case, we write a *nondirectional* alternative hypothesis, H_1: $\mu_1 \neq \mu_2$.

There are some situations, however, in which we can make a prediction about the possible outcome of an experiment before conducting it. For example, suppose a researcher wants to do a study to determine the effects of marijuana on time estimation. On the basis of anecdotal evidence and previous research, the experimenter decides he can predict the direction of the experiment's outcome, and he states at the outset that he expects to find that users overestimate the passage of time. Thus, if the marijuana group is the first group in the study and the control group is the second and time estimation is the dependent variable, the experimenter predicts that the first group will have a larger mean than the second. This outcome would result in a positive value for t, because the difference in sample means would be positive. Because of his prediction, the experimenter can focus on the upper half of the sampling distribution of differences, and ignore the lower half. For his significance test, the researcher can employ a one-tailed test and write a *directional* alternative hypothesis, $H_1: \mu_1 > \mu_2$ or $H_1: \mu_1 - \mu_2 > 0$.

The **one-tailed test** considers only one end of the sampling distribution—the end predicted by the experimenter. The researcher should have a good reason for his or her prediction, preferably a reason based on previous research, anecdotal evidence, or logic. Because only one end, or tail, of the distribution is considered, the one-tailed test is a more powerful test if the prediction comes true and the experimental result is in the desired direction. By more powerful, we mean that it will be easier for the experimenter to reject the null hypothesis; that is, the value required for significance in the table is lower for the one-tailed test than it is for the two-tailed test at the same level of significance. For example, with infinite degrees of freedom, the critical value of t at the 5% level for a two-tailed test is 1.9600. For a one-tailed test, the corresponding critical value is taken from the 10% column, following the instructions to halve the percentages for a one-tailed test. Thus, the critical value for a one-tailed test at the 5% level with infinite degrees of freedom is 1.6449.

There is a danger in using the one-tailed test, however. Remember, we must make a prediction about the outcome of the experiment *before* doing the study. What if our prediction is wrong and we observe a large difference in means in the direction *opposite* to our prediction? Because we are looking at the wrong tail with our one-tailed test, we will not be able to reject the null hypothesis; use of a two-tailed test would have permitted rejection. In other words, a one-tailed test is a more powerful test only if our prediction is accurate. For this reason and also because experimenters tend to acknowledge a rationale for the one-tailed test *after* the data are in, many statisticians argue against the use of the one-tailed test for any reason. Our position is that if we can reasonably predict the outcome's direction before data collection, then use of the more sensitive test is warranted. If we can legitimately apply a one-tailed test to our data, we halve the probability values in Table B to determine a critical value of t.

Another Example of the t Test for Independent Samples

Let's return to the example at the beginning of the chapter. Dr. Baxter was trying to demonstrate the effectiveness of a new form of therapy for panic disorder. Twelve clients with panic disorder received the experimental treatment and 13 received the conventional treatment. After 8 weeks, the clients' panic disorder was assessed using a standard scale of panic disorder. Using the seven-step procedure, (1) the null hypothesis is that the mean scores on the panic disorder scale *will not* be different for the experimental, compared to the conventional, treatment (H_0: $\mu_1 = \mu_2$ or H_0: $\mu_1 - \mu_2 = 0$); (2) the alternative hypothesis is that the mean panic scale scores *will* be different between the two groups (H_1: $\mu_1 \neq \mu_2$ or H_1: $\mu_1 - \mu_2 \neq 0$); (3) set $\alpha = .05$; and (4) reject H_0 if $|t_{comp}| \geq t_{crit}$, where $t_{.05}$ ($df = N_1 + N_2 - 2 = 23$) $= 2.0687$ and $t_{.01}$ (23) $= 2.8073$ from Table B. For step 5, computations and test statistic, here are the scores:

Experimental				Conventional			
X_1	f	fX_1	fX_1^2	X_2	f	fX_2	fX_2^2
10	1	10	100	14	1	14	196
9	2	18	162	13	3	39	507
8	1	8	64	12	2	24	288
7	3	21	147	10	1	10	100
6	2	12	72	8	2	16	128
5	1	5	25	7	2	14	98
3	1	3	9	5	2	10	50
2	1	2	4	$N_2 = 13$		$\Sigma fX_2 = 127$	$\Sigma fX_2^2 = 1{,}367$

$N_1 = 12$ $\Sigma fX_1 = 79$ $\Sigma fX_1^2 = 583$

As before, the first thing we should do is write Formula 10-7 and study it to see what we have to determine. We have

$$t = \frac{\overline{X}_1 - \overline{X}_2}{\sqrt{\left[\dfrac{(N_1 - 1)s_1^2 + (N_2 - 1)s_2^2}{N_1 + N_2 - 2}\right]\left(\dfrac{1}{N_1} + \dfrac{1}{N_2}\right)}}.$$

We need to know six things: N_1, N_2, $\overline{X}_1$, $\overline{X}_2$, s_1^2, and s_2^2. To find the means and variances, we will need to use ΣfX and ΣfX^2.

The means and variances are computed as follows.

• Experimental Therapy:

$$\overline{X}_1 = \frac{\Sigma fX_1}{N_1} = \frac{79}{12} = 6.58$$

$$s_1^2 = \frac{\Sigma fX_1^2 - \dfrac{(\Sigma fX_1)^2}{N_1}}{N_1 - 1} = \frac{583 - \dfrac{79^2}{12}}{12 - 1} = \frac{583 - 520.08}{11} = \frac{62.92}{11} = 5.72$$

• Conventional Therapy:

$$\overline{X}_2 = \frac{\Sigma fX_2}{N_2} = \frac{127}{13} = 9.77$$

$$s_2^2 = \frac{\Sigma fX_2^2 - \dfrac{(\Sigma fX_2)^2}{N_2}}{N_2 - 1} = \frac{1{,}367 - \dfrac{(127)^2}{13}}{13 - 1} = \frac{1{,}367 - 1{,}240.69}{12} = \frac{126.31}{12} = 10.53$$

We now have all the values we need to compute the t score:

$$t = \frac{6.58 - 9.77}{\sqrt{\left[\dfrac{(12 - 1)5.72 + (13 - 1)10.53}{12 + 13 - 2}\right]\left(\dfrac{1}{12} + \dfrac{1}{13}\right)}}$$

$$= \frac{-3.19}{\sqrt{\left(\dfrac{189.28}{23}\right)(.083 + .077)}} = \frac{-3.19}{\sqrt{8.23(.16)}}$$

$$= \frac{-3.19}{\sqrt{1.317}} = \frac{-3.19}{1.15} = -2.77,$$

with $df = N_1 + N_2 - 2 = 12 + 13 - 2 = 23$.

The negative value of t (-2.77) indicates that the mean of the first group (experimental treatment) is smaller than the mean of the second group (conventional treatment). Because we will apply a two-tailed test, we are interested in the absolute value of the t score in our comparison with critical table values. Remember that for the two-tailed test, it really doesn't matter whether the t score is positive or not; the sign simply tells us the direction of the difference in sample means.

If we had predicted at the beginning of the study that the experimentally treated clients would perform better than the conventionally treated clients, then for a one-tailed test the t score would have to be negative. Under these conditions, a positive t could never lead to rejection of H_0, no matter how large it was.

Looking in Table B for the critical values of t when $df = 23$, we have seen that 2.0687 is required for significance at the 5% level, and 2.8073 is required at the 1% level. Because our computed t of -2.77 is larger in absolute value than the 5% table value, our decision (step 6) is to reject the null hypothesis that the two samples were drawn from the same population at the 5% level but not at the 1% level. Another way to express this rejection of H_0 is to say that the difference in means that we observed has a probability less than .05. Alternatively, we can say that the two groups differ significantly at the 5% level. When we reject H_0 at the 5% level, we are in effect saying that the groups differ significantly, because the probability of their mean difference is less than .05 if both groups were really taken from the same population. Again, if you are reporting these results in a research paper, the correct format should include citation of the t and p values. We conclude from these results that the clients receiving the experimental treatment for panic disorders improved more than the clients treated conventionally, $t(23) = -2.77, p < .05$.

CHECKING YOUR PROGRESS

A group of researchers is studying the genetics of obesity. They have a group of 20 rats that are naturally obese because of the presence of two copies of a mutant gene referred to as the "obese gene." The researchers inject half of the rats (the experimental group) with a protein believed to reduce appetite and stimulate exercise (energy use). The other half receive an injection of saline solution (the control group). Both groups are allowed to eat as much as they want for 4 weeks. At the end of 4 weeks, all the rats are weighed. Their weights, in grams, are as follows:

Control Group	Experimental Group
437	383
455	355
483	313
392	410
455	289
469	344
513	418
452	400
444	344
410	310

Determine whether or not the protein injection had an effect on weight.

Answer: The experimental protein injections resulted in less weight gain than the saline injections, $t(18) = 5.28$, $p < .01$.

Assumptions of the Two-Sample t Test

To use the sampling distribution of differences for tests of significance between sample means, three assumptions must be made. First, we must assume *normal distribution* of the dependent variable in the populations from which we drew our samples. Second, we must assume **homogeneity of variance**—that is, that population variances are the same. We assume that $\sigma_1^2 = \sigma_2^2$, where σ_1^2 and σ_2^2 are the variances of the dependent variable in the populations from which we are sampling. Third, we assume that the two samples drawn are *independent*. That's why we have referred to the test as the t test for independent samples.

Fortunately, the first two assumptions apparently can be violated with little effect on the conclusions made from the t test. Of these two assumptions, normal distribution is considered less important than homogeneity of variance. As long as sample sizes are fairly large, even large deviations from normality seem to make little difference in the conclusions. Because of this, if we have reason to suspect that the population distributions are badly skewed, we should use large samples in our experiments.

The assumption of homogeneity of variance is considered more important. Although it may seem like the logical thing to do, a test for homogeneity of variance is rarely performed before t is computed, and most authorities agree that such a test is not worth the effort. In fact, it has been said that to "make the preliminary test testing this assumption on variances is rather like putting out to sea in a rowing boat to find out whether conditions are sufficiently calm for an ocean liner to leave port!" (G.E.P. Box, 1953, Non-Normality and Tests on Variances. *Biometrica, 40*, pp. 318–335.)

The property of a statistical test—in this case, the *t* test—to give valid conclusions even when assumptions of the test are violated is called **robustness.** We can say that the *t* test is *robust* to violations of its assumptions; that is, the *t* test (the ocean liner) can tolerate much violation of assumptions (rough water) and still give correct conclusions. The most troubling situation is violation of homogeneity of variance *and* very different sample sizes. This is the situation we want to avoid. However, as long as samples of equal size are used, a relatively great departure from homogeneity will have little effect on conclusions drawn from the *t* test. The moral is: If in doubt about homogeneity, use samples of equal size.

The third assumption is that the samples are *independent.* This says that how a particular person responds in one treatment condition has nothing to do with how another responds in a different condition. What if there were some relationship between these responses? Then our formula for the *t* test would not be correct. Therefore, we need to take a different approach when our samples are related.

COMPUTING *t*: DEPENDENT SAMPLES

In testing H_0, the most desired outcome is rejection of the null hypothesis. Although this seems odd to most students, the reason for it is that if we don't reject H_0, we can never be sure that it is true. Perhaps we just didn't do the experiment properly—our samples may have been too small, the variability within the groups may have obscured the difference in sample means, and so on. Thus, any procedure that increases the power of the test (makes rejection of H_0 more likely) is desirable. Using dependent samples is one such procedure.

Obtaining Dependent Samples

Dependent samples might be obtained in a number of ways. For example, we could form **matched pairs** of unrelated individuals; that is, subject pairs could be selected in which behavioral or physiological characteristics relevant to the dependent variable are as closely matched as possible. Then one member of each pair would be assigned to one treatment group, and the other member to the other group. Another way to obtain matched pairs is to use people who are related either by blood or by marriage. Thus, we might select wife–husband pairs or pairs of siblings from the population and then assign the members of each pair randomly to one or the other of our pair of samples. Yet another dependent-group experiment involves **within-subject comparisons.** In this situation, the same individuals are subjected to each of two treatments; that is, each subject is his or her own control. Because each subject is given both treatments, this type of experiment is sometimes called a **repeated measures design.**

How does the dependent-samples design help us to reject H_0 (increase the power of the test)? It helps by reducing the variability between the samples. The more similar we can make the groups before administering the independent variable, the more we reduce variability from individual differences. Using matched pairs or a repeated measures design reduces variability relative to randomly selecting subjects that we randomly assign to treatment conditions.

At the beginning of this chapter, we constructed the sampling distribution of differences by extracting pairs of random samples from a population. Further, we assumed that the pairs were independent of (unrelated to) each other. Let's look at how the sampling distribution of differences might be altered if, instead of having independent samples, we have samples that are dependent, or related to each other.

Earlier we found that the sampling distribution of differences was composed of difference scores between pairs of sample means. People who are related to each other (or are matched) are likely to be more similar to each other on a variety of measures than are unrelated individuals selected at random from the same population. Of course, the similarity is even greater when each subject appears in both samples (within-subject comparison). The result of this greater similarity between related samples is that the scores that make up the sampling distribution of differences for related samples are relatively small. They will be closer to the mean of the distribution, which is 0. Thus, the scores deviate less from the mean with related samples. The major difference in the sampling distribution of differences between related samples is that the standard deviation of the distribution (the standard error of the mean differences, $\sigma_{\bar{D}}$, estimated by $s_{\bar{D}}$) is smaller.

We won't be able to compute $\sigma_{\bar{D}}$, so let's go straight to the formula for $s_{\bar{D}}$:

$$s_{\bar{D}} = \sqrt{s_{\bar{X}_1}^2 + s_{\bar{X}_2}^2 - 2rs_{\bar{X}_1}s_{\bar{X}_2}}.$$

The formula is identical to the formula for $s_{\bar{X}_1 - \bar{X}_2}$, except for the expression $-2rs_{\bar{X}_1}s_{\bar{X}_2}$. The only term you haven't seen is r, which is the symbol for a correlation coefficient. The correlation coefficient r is a measure of the degree of relationship between pairs of scores in a pair of samples. What happens if the samples are independent and $r = 0$? In this case, the final expression drops out and

$$s_{\bar{D}} = \sqrt{s_{\bar{X}_1}^2 + s_{\bar{X}_2}^2} = s_{\bar{X}_1 - \bar{X}_2}.$$

However, with dependent samples, r is not 0, and $s_{\bar{X}_1 - \bar{X}_2}$ is reduced by the amount of $\sqrt{2rs_{\bar{X}_1}s_{\bar{X}_2}}$. Thus, $s_{\bar{D}}$ will be smaller than $s_{\bar{X}_1 - \bar{X}_2}$.

Again, the t ratio consists of the difference between sample means divided by the estimated standard error, which in this case is $s_{\bar{D}}$. The relatively small value of the denominator results in a relatively large value for t and makes rejection of the null hypothesis more likely. This, then, is one of the main reasons for using matched or related samples in an experiment; such samples decrease the estimated standard error and result in a larger t score.

The formula for the t test with related samples is

$$t = \frac{\overline{X}_1 - \overline{X}_2}{s_{\overline{D}}},$$

where $s_{\overline{D}} = \sqrt{s_{\overline{X}_1}^2 + s_{\overline{X}_2}^2 - 2rs_{\overline{X}_1} s_{\overline{X}_2}}$.

However, computation of the t ratio for dependent samples is quite tedious using this formula and for this reason, we turn now to a technique known as the direct difference method.

The Direct Difference Method

To discuss the direct difference method, let's consider a specific problem. A pharmaceutical company hires a psychologist to test the effectiveness of Painfree, a new painkiller they have manufactured. The experimenter decides to test the analgesic, or pain-reducing, effect of Painfree on a pain other than headache. Volunteer subjects are asked to immerse their hands in a pail of ice water. The response measure (the dependent variable) is the length of time each subject can tolerate the immersion.

Twelve persons are selected at random; half the group receives a dose of Painfree and the other half a placebo. After a delay of 10 minutes to allow the drug to take effect, each person is asked to place the preferred hand in the water and to keep it there until the pain becomes unbearable. The next day, the participants return to be tested again, but this time they receive a drug other than the one they were given for the first test. This procedure is called **counterbalancing** and is done to control for the possibility that order of drug presentation will affect the experimental result. A **double-blind** technique of drug presentation is employed; that is, neither the administrator nor the participant knows which drug is being given before a particular test.

The results of the experiment are as follows:

Participant	Painfree (Time in Seconds)	Placebo (Time in Seconds)
1	60	45
2	20	15
3	47	49
4	63	50
5	53	56
6	90	70
7	76	55
8	28	14
9	90	65
10	16	10
11	32	16
12	86	57

From this problem, we can see another advantage of the repeated measures, or within-subject, design. The number of participants required to do the study is halved. The same study employing a matched-pairs design would require 24 participants, 12 with each drug. Using each participant as his or her own control is obviously more efficient.

Let's take a look at the data we are saying represents *dependent* groups and examine more closely the data from individual participants. Because the same person participates in the experiment twice, we would expect her or his characteristics to be present under both conditions of measurement. For example, people differ in how well they tolerate pain. Look at the pairs of scores of the participants. Who is the "toughest," and withstood pain the longest? You would pick participants 6 and 9. Note that they withstood pain the longest in *both* conditions. As for the "tenderest," you would pick participant 10; note that this person had the shortest time in both conditions. The characteristics of each person— whether tough or tender—are with him or her in both conditions of the experiment. That is why we say that each participant acts as his or her own control in a repeated measures design.

The seven-step procedure for this test is quite similar to the one we presented in the previous example: (1) There is no difference in pain tolerance time between the Painfree and the placebo conditions (H_0: $\mu_1 = \mu_2$ or H_0: $\mu_1 - \mu_2 = 0$); (2) there is a difference between the two conditions (H_1: $\mu_1 \neq \mu_2$ or H_1: $\mu_1 - \mu_2 \neq 0$); (3) set $\alpha = .05$; (4) reject H_0 if $|t_{comp}| \geq t_{crit}$ ($df = N - 1$). Note that df for the direct difference method is the number of *pairs* of scores minus 1. For step 5, *computation and test statistic,* we have 12 pairs of scores. To use the direct difference method, we first subtract the second of the pair of scores from the first and call this the difference (D). All further calculations are based on the difference between each pair of scores rather than on the scores themselves.

The formulas for the t ratio for the direct difference method are as follows:

FORMULA 10-8   t test for dependent samples (computational formulas)

$$t = \frac{\overline{X}_D}{s_{\overline{X}_D}} \quad \text{or} \quad t = \frac{\overline{X}_D \sqrt{N}}{s_D}$$

because

$$s_{\overline{X}_D} = \frac{s_D}{\sqrt{N}} \quad \text{and} \quad t = \frac{\overline{X}_D}{\dfrac{s_D}{\sqrt{N}}} = \frac{\overline{X}_D \sqrt{N}}{s_D}$$

In essence, we divide the mean of the differences by the estimated standard error of the differences. The mean of the differences, or $\overline{X}_D$, is defined as the *algebraic* sum of the differences divided by the number of pairs of scores, or N. Because the sum of the differences is algebraic, we must remember to take the sign of the difference into account when summing. The estimated standard error of the differences is found by dividing the standard deviation of the differences by the square root of the sample size.

Remember that N is the number of differences, which is half the total number of scores. Also, $\overline{X}_D$ is equivalent to $\overline{X}_1 - \overline{X}_2$. Computing $\overline{X}_1 - \overline{X}_2$ can be used as a check to see whether $\overline{X}_D$ has been calculated correctly.

Let's examine the difference scores more closely. As you can see, $D =$ Painfree score $-$ placebo score. For any participant, a positive value for D suggests that Painfree helped the person to withstand pain longer—Painfree worked, in other words. On the other hand, a negative score suggests that Painfree didn't work and may even have sensitized the participant to pain. If you examine the following difference scores, you will see that all but two of the Ds are positive and some have rather large values. Thus, in thinking about the difference scores, a positive difference suggests that the drug worked, a 0 difference suggests it had no effect, and a negative difference suggests it had an effect the opposite of what was intended. You must always be aware of how the difference D is obtained. If D were calculated by subtracting the Painfree scores from the placebo scores, then the measuring of the positive and negative differences would be reversed. Paying attention to how the difference is calculated is the key to interpreting the results of the experiment.

Now that the formula for t has been described, you may recognize that it is the same formula as that for the one-sample t test from Chapter 9. In fact, as you will see, the dependent t test is the one-sample t test computed on the difference scores and testing the null hypothesis that $\mu_D = 0$. Because you have already worked such problems, you should find the dependent t test using the direct difference method easy to do.

Now, let's go back to the original problem, find the difference scores, and from them determine the mean and standard deviation of the differences. This has been done here:

Participant	Painfree (Time in Seconds)	Placebo (Time in Seconds)	Difference (D)	D^2
1	60	45	15	225
2	20	15	5	25
3	47	49	−2	4
4	63	50	13	169
5	53	56	−3	9
6	90	70	20	400
7	76	55	21	441
8	28	14	14	196
9	90	65	25	625
10	16	10	6	36
11	32	16	16	256
12	86	57	29	841
			$\Sigma D = 159$	$\Sigma D^2 = 3{,}227$

$$\overline{X}_D = \frac{\Sigma D}{N} = \frac{159}{12} = 13.25,$$

$$s_D = \sqrt{\frac{\Sigma D^2 - \frac{(\Sigma D)^2}{N}}{N - 1}} = \sqrt{\frac{3,227 - \frac{159^2}{12}}{12 - 1}},$$

$$= \sqrt{\frac{3,227 - 2,106.75}{11}} = \sqrt{\frac{1,120.25}{11}} = \sqrt{101.84}, = 10.09,$$

$$s_{\overline{X}_D} = \frac{s_D}{\sqrt{N}} = \frac{10.09}{\sqrt{12}} = \frac{10.09}{3.46} = 2.92,$$

and finally,

$$t = \frac{\overline{X}_D}{s_{\overline{X}_D}} = \frac{13.25}{2.92} = 4.54.$$

Alternatively,

$$t = \frac{\overline{X}_D\sqrt{N}}{s_D} = \frac{13.25\sqrt{12}}{10.09} = \frac{45.85}{10.09} = 4.54.$$

For degrees of freedom, we know that $df = N - 1$, where N is the number of pairs of scores. In this case, $df = 12 - 1 = 11$. With $df = 11$, the values of t that cut off the deviant 5% and 1% are 2.2010 and 3.1058, respectively. Our computed t score is 4.54, which is larger than either of the critical values from Table B. Therefore, our decision (step 6) is that we reject the null hypothesis that both groups come from the same population. Our conclusion (step 7) is that Painfree is significantly more effective than a placebo in the treatment of a pain other than headache, $t(11) = 4.54, p < .01$.

As you can see from the previous example, we have become and will continue to be less formal in our presentation of problem examples using the seven-step procedure. By this time, you should be familiar and comfortable with the steps and able to apply them on your own, without our continual reminders. In future examples, we may not list all the steps, but we will be sure to indicate when there needs to be a specific change in a particular step. We will also be sure to provide a model conclusion written in problem context, with citation of t and p values.

Let's look at another example. Ten pairs of individuals, matched as carefully as possible in terms of age, sex, education, and IQ, have been exposed either to a sedative or to a placebo in the form of a cookie. After 30 minutes, each participant is tested on a simple task requiring the crossing out of all the letters a on a sheet of paper containing a random assortment of letters. The number of errors (letters not crossed out) made by each subject in a 2-minute test is shown here, along with the computation of a dependent t score:

Pair	Sedative	Placebo	D	D^2
1	15	12	3	9
2	13	14	−1	1
3	16	13	3	9
4	22	16	6	36
5	8	7	1	1
6	13	10	3	9
7	12	14	−2	4
8	9	7	2	4
9	5	4	1	1
10	6	3	3	9
			$\Sigma D = 19$	$\Sigma D^2 = 83$

$$\overline{X}_D = \frac{\Sigma D}{N} = \frac{19}{10} = 1.9,$$

$$s_D = \sqrt{\frac{\Sigma D^2 - \frac{(\Sigma D)^2}{N}}{N - 1}} = \sqrt{\frac{83 - \frac{19^2}{10}}{10 - 1}} = 2.28,$$

$$t = \frac{\overline{X}_D \sqrt{N}}{s_D} = \frac{1.9\sqrt{10}}{2.28} = 2.64,$$

with $df = N - 1 = 10 - 1 = 9$. From Table B, the critical value of t at the 5% level for $df = 9$ is 2.2622. The computed t of 2.64 is larger than the critical t, so we reject the null hypothesis, $p < .05$. On the basis of this study, we can conclude that the ingestion of this sedative results in significantly more errors on the letter-crossing task, $t(9) = 2.64, p < .05$.

---

⑤ CHECKING YOUR PROGRESS

To fulfill the requirements for a class in experimental psychology, 10 students are given a 1-minute test on a mirror-tracing task in which the knowledge they receive about their efforts comes from their mirror reflection. A comparison is made of the average time spent in accurately tracing a star with the preferred and non-preferred hands. The results of the experiment are shown here. The experimental question is whether or not the hand used affects the accuracy of mirror tracing. Compute a t score by the direct difference method and test it for significance.

Student	Preferred Hand (Average Time in Seconds)	Nonpreferred Hand (Average Time in Seconds)
John	35	37
Vanessa	22	18
Doug	43	32
Bill	15	17
Robin	31	25
Laura	25	29
Moira	38	31
Mike	26	29
Jack	33	33
Susan	10	5

Answer: $t = 1.37$, which for $df = 9$ is not significant ($p > .05$). Using the preferred hand did not result in superior mirror tracing relative to using the nonpreferred hand, $t(9) = 1.37, p > .05$.

SUMMARY

This chapter has discussed a technique that allows us to make a comparison of the results from two independent samples and from two dependent samples. The technique is called the t test because we first convert our observed difference in sample means into a t score. The t score is an estimated version of a z score. In this chapter, the t score is a standard score on the X axis of the sampling distribution of the differences. The null hypothesis tested is that the two samples come from the same population. Thus, if the computed t score is very unlikely given the null hypothesis, we reject H_0 and conclude that the samples probably come from different populations with different means.

The computational formula for the t test based on independent (unrelated) samples is

$$t = \frac{\overline{X}_1 - \overline{X}_2}{\sqrt{\dfrac{(N_1 - 1)s_1^2 + (N_2 - 1)s_2^2}{N_1 + N_2 - 2}\left(\dfrac{1}{N_1} + \dfrac{1}{N_2}\right)}},$$

where N_1 and N_2 are the numbers of subjects in the first and second samples, $\overline{X}_1$ and $\overline{X}_2$ are the means of the first and second samples, and s_1^2 and s_2^2 are the variances of the first and second samples, respectively.

For the test of significance, the computed value of t is compared with the critical values in Table B using the appropriate degrees of freedom ($N_1 + N_2 - 2$). If

t_{comp} is equal to or larger in absolute value than the critical value at the 5% level, the null hypothesis is rejected for a nondirectional test. For a directional test, the sign of the predicted t must be considered. If the predicted t is positive, then H_0 is rejected when $t_{\text{comp}} \geq t_{\text{crit, one tail}}$. If the predicted t is negative, then H_0 is rejected when $t_{\text{comp}} \leq t_{\text{crit, one tail}}$.

Three assumptions for the two-sample independent t test are that the populations from which the samples are taken are normally distributed, the population variances are homogeneous, and the samples are independent. The first two assumptions may be violated with little effect on the conclusions drawn with the t test because of its robustness. It is often recommended that large and equal-sized samples be used if violation of the assumptions is suspected. In situations in which the samples are not independent, usually by design, the dependent t test should be performed.

Experiments are often performed in which matched, or related, samples are used, because such samples increase the power of the test. By reducing the size of the standard error, we increase t, which makes it more likely that the null hypothesis will be rejected. Dependent samples can be constructed by matching pairs of participants and then assigning each member of a pair to one or the other of the experimental treatments or by using each participant as her or his own control (within-subject comparison).

The direct difference method is used to compute a t score for dependent samples. The formula is

$$t = \frac{\overline{X}_D}{s_{\overline{X}_D}} \quad \text{or} \quad t = \frac{\overline{X}_D \sqrt{N}}{s_D},$$

where $\overline{X}_D$ is the mean of the differences, $s_{\overline{X}_D}$ is the estimated standard error $(s_D / \sqrt{N})$, and s_D is the standard deviation of the differences. The t score obtained by the direct difference method is compared with critical values in Table B, with $df = N - 1$. The H_0 and the rejection of H_0 for directional and nondirectional tests are determined in the same manner as for independent t tests.

We briefly discussed the difference between one-tailed and two-tailed tests of significance. If the direction of the difference in population means can be predicted before the data have been collected for an experiment, then the one-tailed test is appropriate. The one-tailed test is a more powerful test than the two-tailed test, because only one tail of the sampling distribution is considered. With the two-tailed test, both ends of the distribution are considered, and larger t values are required to reject H_0.

❋ *Troubleshooting Your Computations*

In this chapter, we considered two methods for comparing sample means. One method was used when the samples were independent of, or unrelated to, each other, and the other method was used with related, or dependent, samples. When choosing the form of the t test to apply, be careful to select the one appropriate to your data. If you have collected data on matched pairs or you are comparing two behaviors from the same individuals, the t test for dependent samples will be the correct choice. However, if your subjects have been selected at random from a population and randomly assigned to the two groups, you will need to apply the t test for independent samples.

Because of the complexity of the computational formula for the t test for independent samples, a number of errors can be made. For example, occasionally students compute $s_{\bar{X}_1 - \bar{X}_2}$ and report its value for t. Additionally, be sure that the value under the square root sign for $s_{\bar{X}_1 - \bar{X}_2}$ is positive; a negative value indicates a computational error.

Don't forget about the term

$$\frac{1}{N_1} + \frac{1}{N_2}$$

in the formula for $s_{\bar{X}_1 - \bar{X}_2}$. Some students omit it entirely by mistake. The easiest way to compute it is to first change the fractions to decimals and then add.

Be sure that the final t score you compute has the correct sign. It's easy to lose a negative sign in the last few steps, so be careful. Remember, if the mean of the first group is smaller than the mean of the second group, t will be negative.

In computing the t score for dependent samples, remember that all computations are performed on the difference scores rather than on the raw scores. Be careful as you add the difference scores algebraically; that is, remember to take the signs into account. One check on the accuracy of your computation of $\bar{X}_D$ is to compute $\bar{X}_1$ and $\bar{X}_2$ and find the difference between them. It should be $\bar{X}_D$.

Remember the decision rule: For a nondirectional test, if the absolute value of your computed t is equal to or larger than the critical value of t from Table B, reject H_0. Otherwise, fail to reject.

Also remember to consider the sign of the predicted t for a directional test. If the predicted t is positive, then H_0 is rejected when $t_{comp} \geq t_{crit, one\, tail}$. If the predicted t is negative, then H_0 is rejected when $t_{comp} \leq -t_{crit, one\, tail}$.

EXERCISES

1. An experiment was performed to measure the effect of sleep deprivation on cognitive performance. Twenty college juniors were randomly selected from a group of volunteers and arbitrarily assigned either to a sleep deprivation group or to a control group. The participants in the sleep deprivation group were kept awake for 24 hours; the members of the control group had a normal night's sleep. Participants were then asked to perform a simple mental arithmetic task, and the time it took each participant to complete the task was recorded. The results were as follows:

Sleep Deprivation Group (Time in Seconds)	Control Group (No Sleep Deprivation) (Time in Seconds)
10	13
15	8
13	14
5	11
27	8
7	7
16	2
20	2
21	17
13	5

Determine whether or not the groups differ significantly. If you reject the null hypothesis, tell what it means in the context of the problem. Give the table values required for significance.

2. The members of 13 pairs of identical twins were randomly assigned to one of two treatment conditions. One group learned a list of nonsense syllables while a tape of a speech by former President A was playing. The second group learned the same list of syllables while a tape of a speech by President B was playing. The number of presentations of the list before an errorless recital was as follows:

Twin Pair	President A	President B
1	26	23
2	13	16
3	10	6
4	24	19
5	24	25
6	25	21
7	23	25
8	20	17
9	16	17
10	13	5
11	15	10
12	19	15
13	22	20

Determine which president's speech was more distracting and whether or not the difference is significant. Tell what your result means in the context of the problem. Give table values required for significance.

3. Assume that the data in Exercise 2 were actually collected from independent samples: A randomly assigned group of 13 participants heard former President A, and a different group of 13 heard President B. Perform an independent *t* test on the data. Which president's speech was more distracting? Compare the results of the two *t* tests. What are the similarities and differences?

4. In a study of modeling, one group of 20 children saw an adult acting aggressively on videotape. Another group of 20 children saw the same adult acting aggressively in real life. Later, each child was placed in a room where he or she was given the opportunity to behave aggressively toward a Bobo doll (a humanlike dummy). The researchers recorded the number of aggressive acts toward the Bobo doll by each child in a 15-minute period. Here are the results:

Real-Life Model		Video Model	
X	f	X	f
37	1	25	1
35	2	23	3
34	3	22	2
30	2	21	5
27	4	19	4
22	3	18	2
19	2	17	2
18	3	10	1

Compare the two groups in terms of the aggressiveness displayed. If you reject the null hypothesis, tell what it means in the context of the problem.

5. A group of 10 navy pilots is first trained on a brightness discrimination task to a criterion of 9 correct responses in 10 trials. Following this, the same pilots are trained on a pattern discrimination task to the same criterion. Compare the results to see whether one task was easier to learn than the other. Scores shown are the number of errors made before achieving the criterion:

Pilot No.	Brightness Discrimination	Pattern Discrimination
1	22	14
2	16	8
3	10	5
4	15	7
5	25	13
6	33	15
7	8	10
8	26	15
9	18	11
10	13	14

Why do you think one task was easier to learn in this study?

6. Ten people learned two lists of nonsense syllables. Both lists were of equal difficulty. Test to see whether the order of learning had an effect on the number of trials to learn. If you reject the null hypothesis, tell what it means in the context of the problem.

Person No.	List A	List B
1	13	8
2	11	12
3	15	10
4	7	4
5	10	7
6	16	14
7	4	5
8	9	5
9	9	6
10	8	9

7. In a study of the relationship between violent pornography and aggression toward women, 18 male volunteers are selected and randomly assigned to one of two groups. One group views a violent, sexually explicit film, and the other group sees a nature film. A test to measure aggressive feelings toward women is then administered to all participants. The scores are shown here (high scores = high aggressiveness). Did viewing the film significantly increase aggressive feelings toward women? If you reject the null hypothesis, tell what it means in the context of the problem. Because we can predict the direction of the result—that the violent film will increase aggressiveness—a one-tailed test is appropriate.

Nature Film	Explicit Film
4	6
5	8
7	5
9	11
6	10
4	7
2	7
3	4
5	5

8. In another study of the effect of violent, sexually explicit material on aggression, the same researchers use a within-subject design rather than independent groups (as in Exercise 7). They test the aggressiveness of 9 volunteers, expose them to a violent, sexually explicit film, and then retest their aggressiveness. The data are shown here. Did viewing the film increase aggressiveness?

Subject #	Pretest	Posttest
1	4	6
2	5	8
3	7	5
4	9	11
5	6	10
6	4	7
7	2	7
8	3	4
9	5	5

Notice that the scores for Exercise 7 are identical to the scores in this exercise. Compare the *t* values and conclusions you would draw in each case.

9. What are the assumptions for the two-sample *t* test? Why is so little space devoted to their discussion?

10. Using the definition of a *z* score, demonstrate that the definitional formula for a two-sample *t* score is another variation on the basic formula for *z*.

11. A study is performed to determine how alcohol affects the brain's response to sound. Using appropriate control procedures, the researchers measure brain responses in 6 participants both before and after the participants drink an alcoholic beverage. The results are as follows:

Participant No.	Before	After
1	5.80	5.90
2	5.88	6.05
3	5.38	5.64
4	5.40	5.58
5	5.90	6.05
6	5.71	5.87

Determine whether or not alcohol ingestion affects brain response to sound.

12. Forty students are randomly assigned to two different groups. One group learns a list of scrambled letter sets with high association value (each set of letters elicits many associations), and the other group learns letter sets with low association value. The number of repetitions before an errorless recitation of the syllables is recorded for each student. The results are shown here. Compare the groups.

High Association Value		Low Association Value	
No. of Repetitions	*f*	No. of Repetitions	*f*
23	1	35	1
21	3	33	2
20	2	31	1

(*cont.*)

High Association Value		Low Association Value	
No. of Repetitions	f	No. of Repetitions	f
19	3	28	3
18	5	25	4
16	1	22	1
15	2	21	1
14	1	20	3
10	1	18	2
8	1	17	2

If you reject the null hypothesis, tell what it means in the context of the problem.

13. An experiment is designed to test the "bystander effect"—the tendency of a person to respond to an emergency more slowly if other people are present. Thirty students from a social psychology class are equally and randomly assigned to one of two treatment conditions. In condition A, a student is asked to fill out a questionnaire in a small room by him- or herself. After 5 minutes, artificial smoke is piped under the door of the room, and the student is timed to see how long it takes him or her to respond to the "emergency." In condition B, a student is asked to fill out a questionnaire in a room in which 3 other students (confederates of the experimenter) are seated. Again, artificial smoke is piped under the door and the participant's reaction time is recorded. From the following data, compute a t score and test it for significance:

   - Condition A: $N = 15, \Sigma X = 1{,}695, \Sigma X^2 = 250{,}685$
   - Condition B: $N = 15, \Sigma X = 3{,}645, \Sigma X^2 = 975{,}335$

If you reject the null hypothesis, tell what it means in the context of the problem.

14. The effects of alcohol intake on aggressive driving are studied in a group of students tested on a driving simulator. Thirty students are equally and randomly assigned either to a placebo group or to a group whose members receive an ounce of alcohol 30 minutes before the driving simulation test is given. The dependent variable is the number of crashes during the 5-minute driving simulation. Determine whether or not the alcohol increased aggressive driving. If you reject the null hypothesis, tell what it means in the context of the problem.

Alcohol	Placebo
10	7
15	7
12	5
8	8
5	10
21	13

(cont.)

Alcohol	Placebo
10	12
11	11
13	11
20	15
8	8
9	9
17	7
18	7
19	6

15. An observational study investigated the territorial behavior of drivers in a busy campus parking lot. Informal interviews indicated that most people would leave faster if a car were waiting for them to depart. To verify this, 30 drivers were observed and timed for how long it took each one to enter his or her car and leave the parking space. Fifteen were randomly selected to be intruded upon by having another car pull up near the parking space as if its driver were waiting to claim the vacated space. The other 15 were timed but not intruded upon. The data (in seconds) are given here. Does driver behavior confirm what the interviews indicated? Use the seven-step procedure to give a complete formal solution.

Intruded-Upon Drivers	Nonintruded-Upon Drivers
51	61
58	55
46	46
80	70
83	52
45	55
63	68
69	53
63	52
69	62
65	45
58	55
75	65
64	41
63	52

One-Way Analysis of Variance With Post Hoc Comparisons

Dr. Baxter was excited about the new treatment for panic disorder she had developed (remember Dr. Baxter from Chapter 10). She hoped that her new approach would revolutionize the treatment of this disabling condition. She felt that if she could convince her colleagues of the effectiveness of this new approach, she could make a real contribution to the field.

Knowing that the first step was to get her work published, Dr. Baxter submitted a paper detailing her work to the most prestigious journal in her area. The paper included the data and statistics from her comparison of patients treated conventionally and patients receiving her experimental treatment. Her numbers clearly supported the effectiveness of the new treatment.

To her disappointment, however, she received a rejection letter from the journal. The editor wrote that although the work was interesting and promising, there were fundamental flaws in the design used to evaluate the treatments. The editor encouraged Dr. Baxter to correct the problems and resubmit the paper.

In considering the problem, Dr. Baxter realized that she needed to include a group of untreated panic disorder patients to establish a baseline for comparison of the two treatment groups. As the editor pointed out, the observed difference between Dr. Baxter's two groups might have resulted from the conventional treatment making the clients worse. If the experimental treatment simply left the patients unaffected, there would still be a group difference. In this case, the difference would mean that the new treatment was superior to the old, but it would not demonstrate that the new treatment was better than no treatment at all.

237

The solution for Dr. Baxter was to collect more data, this time including patients who were not treated. She needed to measure the panic disorder levels of this untreated group during the same time period she was administering treatment to the other two groups.

Dr. Baxter once again collected data, but this time from three groups of 10 patients. When she was ready to analyze the data, she realized that using *t* tests to compare two groups at a time would require three separate analyses and unnecessary effort. She also realized that *t* tests wouldn't determine whether there was an overall difference, considering all the groups simultaneously. Leafing through her statistics book, she found that the test she needed now was one called analysis of variance.

In Chapter 10, we used the *t* test to compare the results from two samples to see if they differed significantly—that is, were drawn from different populations. As you probably realize, there are often occasions when we will want to compare more than two groups at a time. The most widely used test for this purpose in behavioral science is called **analysis of variance,** or **ANOVA** (ANalysis Of VARiance). The name of the test describes what we are actually going to do: develop a way to analyze the variance in our experimental groups.

One reason for preferring ANOVA over the independent *t* test is that computing multiple *t* tests is very tedious (unless you're using a computer). To analyze the results from a study with only three groups—A, B, and C—would require at least three separate *t*-score computations. We would have to compare groups A and B, groups A and C, and groups B and C. The addition of only one more group, D, would necessitate three more *t* scores: A and D, B and D, and C and D. However, there's a more important reason for not doing multiple *t* tests. The more tests you do on the same data, the more likely it is that you will get a spurious significant difference—that is, that you will reject a true null hypothesis (commit a Type I, or α, error). Using ANOVA helps prevent such errors.

There are numerous applications of ANOVA in the social sciences. It is a technique that transcends the limits of *t* tests. However, like the *t* test, it has two versions: a between-subjects ANOVA, which parallels an independent *t*, and a repeated measures ANOVA, sometimes referred to as within-subjects ANOVA, which is similar to a dependent *t* test. In terms of experimental design, one-way ANOVA is a simple extension of the *t* test in that it examines the effect of one independent variable—thus the name *one-way ANOVA*. (We examine two-way ANOVA, which analyzes the effect of two independent variables, in Chapter 12.) However, instead of comparing only two groups, ANOVA allows for the comparison of two, three, or more groups or the same group at different points in time. For example, an educational psychologist might be interested in evaluating the effectiveness of a new teaching method. Students might be tested before receiving a new form of instruction, immediately after the instruction, and at a 6-month follow-up. Similarly, a psychopharmacologist might be interested in the effect of a new drug on depression. The depression levels of a group of patients before and at several points during treatment could be compared, or a social psychologist might want to look at the effect of the number of witnesses on witness response in an emergency. To study the phenomenon, she could create groups consisting of one person, two people, four people, and so on, and expose each group to a simulated emergency. In all these cases, ANOVA is appropriate.

The between-subjects ANOVA, like the independent *t* test, assumes independent groups of participants. The repeated measures ANOVA, like the dependent *t* test, "repeatedly measures" the same group of participants. The same individuals receive all levels of the treatment. The same concepts of variability apply to both types of ANOVA, between-subjects and repeated measures. We begin this chapter with between-subjects ANOVA and discuss variability and other topics in this section. We will follow the discussion of between-subjects ANOVA with the presentation of techniques for post-ANOVA testing called the Fisher LSD test and the Tukey HSD test. Later in the chapter, we introduce repeated measures ANOVA, noting that much of the discussion under between-subjects ANOVA also applies to repeated measures ANOVA.

BETWEEN-SUBJECTS ANOVA

As already mentioned, analysis of variance is a simple extension of the *t* test. Remember that the *t* test is actually a measure of distance—the distance of a group mean from a population mean or of a group mean from another group mean in standard-score terms. Thus, a *t* score is basically a standard deviation, and a standard deviation is the square root of variance.

As we will show, one of the ways to compare more than two groups is to move from a statistic that is a measure of standard deviation to a statistic based on variance. Variance can be used to determine whether groups differ, but it is not limited to two groups. One of the reasons variance is not limited to two groups is that it has the property of additivity: The variance of a sum (or difference) of scores is equal to the sum of the variances of the parts, as long as the parts are independent of each other. The number of parts makes no difference. This property of **additivity** is expressed in Formula 11-1:

> **FORMULA 11-1**   *Variance of a sum of scores from independent groups*
>
> $$\sigma^2_{X_1+X_2} = \sigma^2_{X_1} + \sigma^2_{X_2}$$

Analysis of variance capitalizes on the property of additivity. We can take a set of scores and find a total variance in the entire set. Then, if we know that this total set of scores is composed of a number of subgroups corresponding to our treatment groups, we can divide this total variability into its component parts. One part would be the amount of variability in scores resulting from *differences among the groups*. Another part would be the inherent variability in the scores independent of the treatment—that is, *within-groups variability*. Finally, we can compare the relative sizes of the component parts to determine whether the variability stemming from differences among groups is large relative to the amount of inherent variability in the scores. Thus, ANOVA is a procedure that first finds a total variance, then breaks it down into its component parts and compares the parts. Before we present a computational example of the ANOVA, let's consider a graphically oriented way to conceptualize the technique.

Visualization of ANOVA Concepts

Let's assume that we have two different sets of data that could represent different possible results from Dr. Baxter's investigation of treatments for panic disorders. This time she includes three treatment groups. The first group consists of panic disorder patients who receive the new experimental treatment (ET). The next group of patients are untreated and will serve as a control group (C), and the third group receives the conventional or standard treatment (ST). To keep things simple, we will consider data from only three patients in each group; in an actual experiment, considerably more participants would be needed to provide adequate statistical power.

Outcome data sets I and II are shown graphically in Figures 11-1 and 11-2, respectively. As the name of this chapter indicates, we are analyzing variances or variability, and, as with the variance of a single sample (Chapter 6), *key deviations* are involved. The two components of variability in which we are interested are based on within-groups variability and between-groups variability. The *key deviations* for these components are $(X_g - \overline{X}_g)$ and $(\overline{X}_g - \overline{X}_{tot})$, respectively. The deviation $(X_g - \overline{X}_g)$ refers to the deviation of each score in a group (X_g) from the mean of that group $(\overline{X}_g)$. Looking at Figure 11-1 Outcome I scores, we see that the scores in each group deviate very little from the mean of each group. For example, in the ET group, the scores are 2, 3, and 4. The mean is 3, and scores 2 and 4 deviate at most only 1 point from the group mean. Similarly, scores in group ST deviate at most only 2 points from the mean of the ST group.

Now contrast these scores with Outcome II scores in Figure 11-2. Here we have much larger within-groups deviations. For group ET, the mean is 8 and the deviations are +1, +5, and −6 (don't worry about the algebraic sign right now). Also, for group ST, the mean is 7 and the deviations are 0, +4, and −4. It is evident that we have much smaller within-groups variability in Outcome I.

By showing the group means for each outcome, the lower graphs in Figures 11-1 and 11-2 focus on the between-groups variability. As previously stated, the key deviation here is $(\overline{X}_g - \overline{X}_{tot})$. Here, $\overline{X}_{tot}$ is simply the mean (average) of the three group means; therefore, $\overline{X}_{tot}$ is often called the *grand mean* (GM). The graphs of the means in each figure show the grand mean as a dashed line, and the key deviation is the extent that each group mean deviates from the grand mean line. For Outcome I means, the deviations are large (−4, +5, −1); for Outcome II means the deviations are small (+1, −1, 0). The graphs help us to see easily the within-groups variability for scores in each group and to see the between-groups variability for the group means relative to the grand mean.

Now, here's how we "analyze" these variances in ANOVA: We are interested in comparing the between-groups variability to the within-groups variability for a

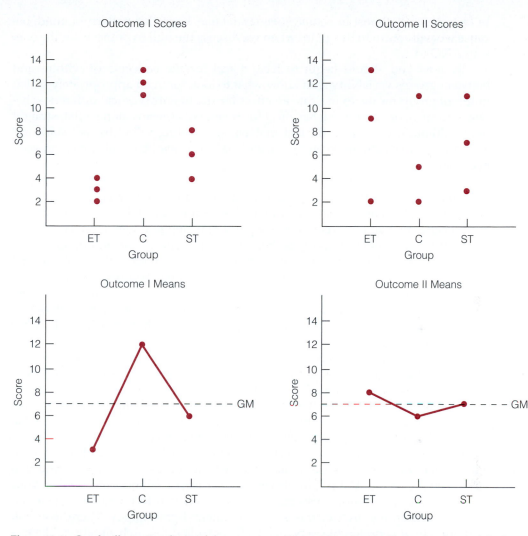

Figure 11-1 Graphs illustrating data with low within-groups variability and high between-groups variability. A treatment effect is present.

Figure 11-2 Graphs illustrating data with high within-groups variability and low between-groups variability. A treatment effect is absent.

given set of data. More specifically, we want the *ratio* of the average between-groups variability to the average within-groups variability. If between-groups variability is *large* relative to within-groups variability, as it is for Outcome I, we will probably conclude that the treatments had an effect, and the groups differ in the reduction of panic disorder symptoms. This effect is shown graphically for the Outcome I means by the large vertical differences between the group means.

If, on the other hand, between-groups variability is *not large* (or about the same) relative to within-groups variability, we will conclude that the treatments did not affect panic symptoms. This is the case in Outcome II. Note that the graph of Outcome II means does not show much difference between the group means.

In fact, they fall almost in a *straight horizontal line.* Keep this pattern in mind, because we will return to this point when we discuss the null hypothesis for the one-way ANOVA.

By now you should begin to have a feel for the concepts of within- and between-groups variability. You know what to look for in an appropriately scaled graph of group means to indicate an effect for treatments (vertical differences between means), or no appreciable effect for treatments (means along a flat, straight line). Although you may still feel that we are dealing with abstract statistical concepts, you've actually been practicing analysis of variance intuitively in your everyday life.

Everyday ANOVA   We encounter many situations in our everyday lives in which we are trying to detect something under adverse conditions. For example, you've almost certainly had the experience at a party of trying to understand a conversation and having difficulty doing so because of the loud music and other people talking. You may have experienced so much static on your cellular phone that you could not understand the person you were calling. You may even have experienced a pouring rain so loud that you couldn't hear the thunder. In these and similar situations, the background conditions can be considered "static" or "noise." This is analogous to *within-groups variability*—how participants differ within their groups.

Likewise, what you're trying to *detect*—a nearby conversation, a voice on the other end of the phone, or thunder in a rainstorm—can be considered the "message" or "signal." This is analogous to *between-groups variability*—group differences produced by some treatment effect. Thus, between-groups variability must exceed within-groups variability for a treatment effect to be detected, just as the "message" must be louder than the "static" for you to receive it.

For now, that's the main point we're trying to make about analysis of variance—that within-groups variability is statistical "background noise," and you have been practicing ANOVA intuitively in the form of "signal detection" in your everyday life. Our analogy also may be helpful for you to remember when you take a course in research methods or experimental psychology. There, you will find out why it is preferable to be in a well-controlled research situation, like trying to hear a pin drop over the phone (low statistical background noise), in contrast to a poorly controlled research situation, like trying to hear thunder in a rainstorm (high statistical background noise). We will now move to the computation of the analysis of variance.

Let's consider an example, and as we do so, we will present and discuss the basic concepts and logic of ANOVA on a more detailed level.

Suppose a psychiatrist suspects that certain psychoactive drugs (drugs known to have an effect on behavior) may be beneficial in the treatment of phobias. To test this idea, the psychiatrist designs an experiment in which consenting patients are given one of three different substances: (1) a placebo, (2) a mild tranquilizer, or (3) a mild stimulant.

The participants in the experiment have been selected on the basis of their fear of snakes, as determined by the distance they maintain between themselves and a live snake in an aquarium. Only patients who will not approach nearer than 10 feet in a preliminary test are used in the study.

In the experiment, each participant is given a capsule containing one of the three substances. Ten minutes later, each participant is tested a second time for approach to the feared object. The distance from the participant to the aquarium in the second test is the dependent variable. Here are the data:

Group 1 (Placebo)	Group 2 (Tranquilizer)	Group 3 (Stimulant)
10	6	11
8	5	12
9	4	10
7	2	10
5	1	9
3	0	8
$\Sigma X = 42$	$\Sigma X = 18$	$\Sigma X = 60$

The group means are as follows:

- Group 1 $\overline{X}_1 = \dfrac{\Sigma X}{N} = \dfrac{42}{6} = 7$

- Group 2 $\overline{X}_2 = \dfrac{18}{6} = 3$

- Group 3 $\overline{X}_3 = \dfrac{60}{6} = 10$

The total mean (or grand mean) is $(42 + 18 + 60)/18 = 120/18 = 6.67$.

Remember that we are interested in analyzing the variance in this chapter. What are the sources of variance in the data?

To begin, we can see that each of the 18 scores differs from the total, or overall, mean of 6.67. This source of variability is called the **total variability** and is related to the deviation of each score (X) from the total mean (X_{tot}), or

$$X - \overline{X}_{tot}.$$

An important thing to remember at this point is that you are already familiar with the variability of a group of scores and how to compute it (from Chaper 6). You merely need to think of all the data—all three groups—as forming one big (total) group with 18 scores.

Further, the total variability has two components. One component is the variability within each group, or the **within-groups variability.** For example, in Group 1, the mean is 7, but only one participant actually had this score; the rest of the group members deviated from the mean. We first encountered variability within a group in Chapter 6, where we learned that it is based on the deviation between each score in a group and the group's mean. As we have seen, this deviation is symbolized by

$$X_g - \overline{X}_g,$$

where X_g is a score within a group and $\overline{X}_g$ is the mean of the group.

What is the origin of the variability within groups? If each member of a group has the same treatment, why is there a difference between the scores? Basically, there are two sources of the variability: individual differences and experimental error.

Each of our experimental participants is a unique individual, with particular abilities, motives, background, and so forth. Thus, each individual is different from the others and is likely to act differently in response to the experimental treatment. This is what is meant by **individual differences.**

Experimental error may also contribute to the differences in scores within a group. By **experimental error,** we mean experimental control—such things as imprecise measuring equipment, momentary changes in experimenter and participant attention, and slight changes in background conditions during data collection (fluctuations in temperature, lighting, sound level, etc.). Because of individual differences and experimental error, it is highly unlikely that all participants within a treatment will have the same score.

In addition to the variability within each group, there is also variability between groups, or **between-groups variability.** Because the total mean ($\overline{X}_{tot}$) is 6.67, you can see that each of the group means (7, 3, 10) deviates from it. Again, as we have seen, the variability between groups is based on the deviation of each group mean from the total mean:

$$\overline{X}_g - \overline{X}_{tot}.$$

Why do the group means differ from the total mean? Why is there variability between groups? This time there are three potential sources of variability: individual differences, experimental error, and treatment effects.

Because our treatment groups contain different individuals, individual differences can be expected to play a role in the variability *between* groups as well as *within* them. Similarly, experimental error occurs across groups as well as within them to produce differing scores and differing group means. Individual differences and experimental error are tied together in obtaining scores for each participant and cannot be separated in this context. **Treatment effect** is the third potential source of variability between groups; that is, we have applied different treatments to each of our groups in the hope that the manipulations will produce behavioral changes. For example, if the mean of group 2 differs from the mean of group 1, it may be because the tranquilizer's active ingredient affects performance on the behavioral avoidance test.

In summary, the total variability contained in two or more groups is the sum of the variability between groups and the variability within each group. The test of significance based on the analysis of variance considers which of the two components of variability (between or within) contributes most to the total variability.

Suppose we have selected three large samples from the *same* population. The distribution of scores based on measurement of some behavioral characteristic might resemble the graph in Figure 11-3. From a study of the graph, note that the variability between groups based on the deviation of each group mean from the total mean is small relative to the variability within each group. There is a lot of spread of scores around each group mean, and the difference between each $\overline{X}_g$ and $\overline{X}_{tot}$ is small.

What about the situation in which one or more of the samples is taken from *different* populations? Assuming that the variability within each group is the same as before, the variability between groups will be large relative to the within-groups variability. A hypothetical situation is shown in Figure 11-4.

As we have discussed in a slightly different way, the significance test assesses the relative contribution of the two components of variability, assuming that the samples come from the same population. If this assumption is true, then the ratio of the variability between groups to the variability within groups (the F ratio) will be relatively small. Why is this? If we assume that the samples come from the same population, we are assuming that the different treatments are without effect; that is, there is no treatment effect. If this is the case, then the sources of variability within and between groups—individual differences and experimental error—are identical. Hence, the F ratio will have a value close to 1.00.

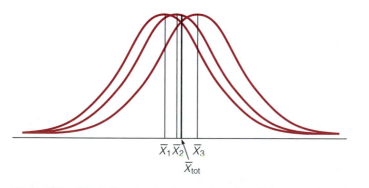

Figure 11-3 Graph showing the degree of overlap of three samples drawn from the same population.

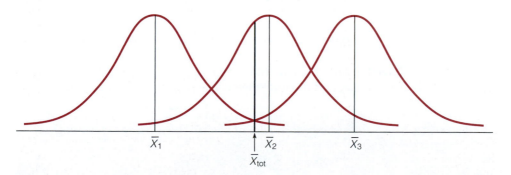

Figure 11-4 Graph illustrating the large amount of variability between groups when one or more of the groups come from different populations.

However, if the assumption is not true, then the F ratio will be relatively large because of the added source of variability (treatment effect) contributing to the between-groups differences. In this case, we will conclude that the samples come from different populations. The question at this point is, How do we measure the variability?

Measuring Variability: The Sum of Squares

The main component of the measure of variability is the *sum of squares,* which we introduced in Chapter 6. At that time, we said that the numerator of the formula for the sample variance was sometimes called the sum of squares, so you have already been exposed to this formula. We will need to compute three sums of squares: total, within groups, and between groups.

The **total sum of squares** (SS_{tot}) is the sum of the squared deviation of each score from the total mean, or:

FORMULA 11-2   *Total sum of squares (definitional formula)*

$$SS_{tot} = \Sigma(X - \overline{X}_{tot})^2$$

We also said that the variability within each group is based on the deviation between each score in a group and the mean of the group. Thus, the *sum of squares within each group* (SS_w) is the sum of the squared deviations of each score in a group from its group mean, and the deviations are summed across groups. The definitional formula is:

FORMULA 11-3   *Within-groups sum of squares (definitional formula)*

$$SS_w = \sum_{g} (X_g - \overline{X}_g)^2$$

The little g under the large sigma means that the deviations are summed across groups.

Finally, we have the *sum of squares between groups* (SS_b), based on the deviation between each group mean and the total mean. The definitional formula is:

FORMULA 11-4   *Between-groups sum of squares (definitional formula)*

$$SS_b = \sum_{g} N_g(\overline{X}_g - \overline{X}_{tot})^2$$

The definitional formula for SS_b says to square the deviation between each group mean and the total mean $[(\overline{X}_g - \overline{X}_{tot})^2]$, to multiply by the number of subjects in a particular group (N_g), and to sum over groups $(\sum_g)$.

As usual, we will not use the definitional formulas to compute the sums of squares. Instead, we will use computational, or raw-score, formulas. To begin, the equation for the total sum of squares is:

FORMULA 11-5   *Total sum of squares (computational formula)*

$$SS_{tot} = \sum X^2 - \frac{(\sum X)^2}{N}$$

If Formula 11-5 looks familiar, it is because it is the sum of squares, which we first saw in Chapter 6 as the numerator of sample variance. To compute the total sum of squares, we first square each score and then add all the squared scores together $(\sum X^2)$. Next we add all the scores, square the sum, and divide by N, or the total number of scores. Subtracting the last value from the first gives us SS_{tot}.

The computational formula for the within-groups sum of squares is:

FORMULA 11-6   *Within-groups sum of squares (computational formula)*

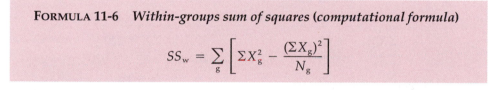

$$SS_w = \sum_g \left[\sum X_g^2 - \frac{(\sum X_g)^2}{N_g} \right]$$

Look carefully at Formula 11-6 and you will see that it is almost the same as the formula for the total sum of squares. The difference is that the computations are performed for each group separately and then summed across groups instead of being done on *all* the scores. The formula tells us to sum the squared scores within each group $(\sum X_g^2)$, to subtract from the total the sum of the scores within a group squared and divided by the number of subjects within the group $[(\sum X_g)^2 / N_g]$, and to sum the totals for each group.

The computational formula for the between-groups sum of squares is:

FORMULA 11-7   *Between-groups sum of squares (computational formula)*

$$SS_b = \sum_g \left[\frac{(\sum X_g)^2}{N_g} \right] - \frac{(\sum X)^2}{N}$$

The formula tells us first to sum the scores within a group, square the sum, and divide by the number within the group $[(\sum X_g)^2 / N_g]$. Next, we sum the totals across groups ($\sum_g$). From this total we subtract the sum of all the scores squared divided by the total number of scores [$(\Sigma X)^2/N$].

Computing the Sums of Squares

Even with the computational formulas, computing the sums of squares is a bit lengthy but not a difficult process if you are well organized. There is one thing we can do to simplify the task considerably. The secret is to compute the sum of the scores in each of the groups (ΣX_g), then compute the sum of the squared scores in each group (ΣX_g^2), and finally note the number of subjects in each group (N_g). From these values we can easily determine the sum of all the scores (ΣX), the sum of all the squared scores (ΣX^2), and the total N. Let's go back to our example about snake phobias and compute the sums of squares:

	Group 1	Group 2	Group 3	
	10	6	11	
	8	5	12	
	9	4	10	
	7	2	10	
	5	1	9	
	3	0	8	Totals
ΣX_g	42	18	60	$\Sigma X = 120$
ΣX_g^2	328	82	610	$\Sigma X^2 = 1{,}020$
N_g	6	6	6	$N = 18$
$\overline{X}_g$	7	3	10	$\overline{X}_{tot} = 6.67$

We have computed the sum of the scores for each group, and this is shown in the row labeled ΣX_g. For example, the sum of X_1 is found by adding $10 + 8 + \cdots + 3 = 42$. Similarly, $\Sigma X_2 = 18$ and $\Sigma X_3 = 60$.

To find the sum of the squared scores in each group, we square each of the scores in the group and add. For example, ΣX_1^2 is obtained by adding $10^2 + 8^2 + \cdots + 3^2 = 328$. Also, $\Sigma X_2^2 = 82$ and $\Sigma X_3^2 = 610$.

The totals are found by adding each row in the summary table; ΣX is found by summing $\Sigma X_1 + \Sigma X_2 + \Sigma X_3 = 42 + 18 + 60 = 120$. Similarly, ΣX^2 is found by adding the sums of the squared scores: $328 + 82 + 610 = 1{,}020$. The number of subjects in each group is 6, and the total N is 18. We are now ready to compute the sums of squares:

$$SS_{tot} = \Sigma X^2 - \frac{(\Sigma X)^2}{N}$$

$$= 1{,}020 - \frac{(120)^2}{18} = 1{,}200 - \frac{14{,}400}{18}$$

$$= 1{,}020 - 800 = 220,$$

$$SS_b = \sum_g \left[\frac{(\Sigma X_g)^2}{N_g} \right] - \frac{(\Sigma X)^2}{N} = \left[\frac{(\Sigma X_1)^2}{N_1} + \frac{(\Sigma X_2)^2}{N_2} + \frac{(\Sigma X_3)^2}{N_3} \right] - \frac{(\Sigma X)^2}{N}$$

$$= \left(\frac{42^2}{6} + \frac{18^2}{6} + \frac{60^2}{6} \right) - \frac{120^2}{18}$$

$$= \left(\frac{1,764}{6} + \frac{324}{6} + \frac{3,600}{6} \right) - \frac{14,400}{18}$$

$$= (294 + 54 + 600) - 800$$

$$= 948 - 800 = 148,$$

$$SS_w = \sum_g \left[\Sigma X_g^2 - \frac{(\Sigma X_g)^2}{N_g} \right]$$

$$= \left[\Sigma X_1^2 - \frac{(\Sigma X_1)^2}{N_1} \right] + \left[\Sigma X_2^2 - \frac{(\Sigma X_2)^2}{N_2} \right] + \left[\Sigma X_3^2 - \frac{(\Sigma X_3)^2}{N_3} \right]$$

$$= \left(328 - \frac{42^2}{6} \right) + \left(82 - \frac{18^2}{6} \right) + \left(610 - \frac{60^2}{6} \right)$$

$$= \left(328 - \frac{1,764}{6} \right) + \left(82 - \frac{324}{6} \right) + \left(610 - \frac{3,600}{6} \right)$$

$$= (328 - 294) + (82 - 54) + (610 - 600)$$

$$= 34 + 28 + 10 = 72.$$

We have now determined the total sum of squares (220), the between-groups sum of squares (148), and the within-groups sum of squares (72). To check our computations, we can see if the between-groups and within-groups sums total SS_{tot}. They do: $148 + 72 = 220$.

Although the sums of squares computations appear quite tedious, the amount of work is considerably lessened with the aid of the memory function on a pocket calculator. Try several of these computations for practice. You will find that they take less and less time the more you do them.

There is another approach to the computations that shortens the process. Remember additivity? In the one-way between-groups ANOVA we have been illustrating, there are two components in the total sum of squares: between-groups sum of squares and within-groups sum of squares. Once we have calculated the SS_{tot} and one of the components (SS_b or SS_w), we can find the other component by subtraction. Thus, $SS_w = SS_{tot} - SS_b$ and $SS_b = SS_{tot} - SS_w$. Although this procedure for determining one of the sums of squares if you know the other two is admittedly faster than computing each of the sums of squares separately, the downside is that there is no check on the accuracy of your computations. Hence, we don't recommend the shortcut.

A General Rule for Computing Sums of Squares

At this point you may be feeling overwhelmed with all the formulas for the sums of squares. Also, some of you may feel more comfortable operating at a verbal level rather than an algebraic formula level. For this reason, we will introduce the following rule for forming any sum of squares: *To form any SS, square the appropriate totals, divide by the number of scores on which each total is based, and sum. From this result, subtract $(\Sigma X)^2/N$.* If you can remember this rule and how to identify the "appropriate totals," you can compute any SS without the formula.

Let's try this rule for SS_b from the previous example. The first question is: What is the appropriate total for SS between groups? The answer is that it is the group total. Following the rule, we (1) square the appropriate totals and divide by the number of scores in each total

$$\frac{42^2}{6} \quad \frac{18^2}{6} \quad \frac{60^2}{6},$$

(2) sum the result

$$\frac{42^2}{6} + \frac{18^2}{6} + \frac{60^2}{6},$$

and (3) subtract $(\Sigma X)^2/N$. This gives us

$$SS_b = \frac{(42^2 + 18^2 + 60^2)}{6} - \frac{(120)^2}{18}.$$

Using the rule for SS_w, the appropriate totals are the scores *within* each group, and the rule must be repeated for each group. The first two steps are to square the appropriate totals, divide, and sum. This is just ΣX_g^2 for each group divided by 1, because each "sum" is one score. For group 1 only, this gives us $\Sigma X_1^2 = 328$. Then we subtract $(\Sigma X_g)^2/N_g = (42)^2/6$, because we are applying the rule *within* each group. The final result is

$$SS_w = \left(328 - \frac{42^2}{6}\right) + \left(82 - \frac{18^2}{6}\right) + \left(610 - \frac{60^2}{6}\right).$$

Using the rule for SS_{tot} is the easiest of all, because groups are ignored; thus, we proceed to compute SS for all scores as if there were one large group. This is just the way we computed SS in Chapter 6.

Now that we have the sums of squares, what do we do with them? The formulas for the sums of squares are very similar to the numerator of the formula for sample variance. We now need to define the denominator for each of the sums of squares so that we can compute a variance. It will simplify proceedings at this point if we introduce the analysis of variance *summary table.*

The Analysis of Variance Summary Table

The **ANOVA summary table** is a convenient place to summarize the values we have calculated and those we still need to determine. The table takes the following form:

ANOVA Summary Table

Source	SS	df	MS	F
Between groups				
Within groups				
Total				

Examination of the summary table reveals some items we have not yet discussed. First, note that there are places for the sums of squares (between groups, within groups, and total). Next, we see places for degrees of freedom, or *df*, which we have not identified for ANOVA. The *df* column is followed by a column labeled *MS*, the abbreviation for *mean square*, which will be discussed in the next paragraph. Finally, there is a heading at the end of the table labeled *F*. Under *F* we put the number indicating the relative contribution of the two sources of variability—the ratio we referred to earlier. The size of *F* determines whether or not we conclude that the samples were drawn from the same population.

The **mean square (MS)** is really the variance we want to analyze. You may recall from Chapter 6 that we defined the variance as the average (or mean) of the squared deviations. That's what we have here in the mean square, an average or mean of squared deviations; hence, the term mean square. It is determined by dividing the sums of squares by the appropriate degrees of freedom. All we need to do, then, is determine *df*, and *MS* will be easy to compute.

The between-groups *df* is equal to $K - 1$, where K is the number of groups we are comparing. For our specific example, $df_b = 2$, because we are comparing 3 groups and $K - 1 = 3 - 1 = 2$. The within-groups *df* equals $N - K$, which for our example is $18 - 3 = 15$. Finally, the total *df* equals $N - 1$, or $18 - 1 = 17$. Here again, the total is equal to the sum of the parts, just as it was for the sum of squares. Thus,

$$df_{tot} = df_b + df_w,$$

or

$$N - 1 = (K - 1) + (N - K),$$
$$N - 1 = N - 1 + K - K,$$
$$N - 1 = N - 1.$$

Summarizing the formulas for *df*, we have the following:

> **FORMULA 11-8   Between-groups degrees of freedom**
>
> $$df_b = K - 1$$

> **FORMULA 11-9   Within-groups degrees of freedom**
>
> $$df_w = N - K$$

> **FORMULA 11-10   Total degrees of freedom**
>
> $$df_{tot} = N - 1$$

As already noted, the mean squares are found by dividing the sums of squares by the appropriate degrees of freedom. Thus, we have the following formulas:

> **FORMULA 11-11   Between-groups mean square**
>
> $$MS_b = \frac{SS_b}{df_b}$$

> **FORMULA 11-12   Within-groups mean square**
>
> $$MS_w = \frac{SS_w}{df_w}$$

The final term we need for the summary table is F, which is the ratio of MS_b to MS_w (the **F ratio**):

> **FORMULA 11-13   F ratio**
>
> $$F = \frac{MS_b}{MS_w}$$

Here is the completed summary table for the problem we have been considering:

ANOVA Summary Table

Source	SS	df	MS	F
Between groups	148	$K - 1 = 2$	$\dfrac{SS_b}{df_b} = \dfrac{148}{2} = 74$	$F = \dfrac{MS_b}{MS_w}$
Within groups	72	$N - K = 15$	$\dfrac{SS_w}{df_w} = \dfrac{72}{15} = 4.8$	$= \dfrac{74}{4.8}$
Total	220	$N - 1 = 17$		$= 15.42$

At the end of the summary table, the F ratio has been computed; for our example, it is 15.42. What does this mean? Were the groups drawn from different populations or did they come from the same population? As noted earlier, if the groups are actually drawn from the same population, then there should not be very much difference between the group means; that is, there should be a small treatment effect, like the nearly flat line in Figure 11-2. With little treatment effect contributing to the variability between groups, the F ratio will be close to 1.00. However, our computed F ratio is obviously much larger than 1.00.

As in the two previous chapters, our significance test will require a comparison of the computed statistic with critical values found in a table. Table C in Appendix 4 contains critical values of F based on the F distribution. The F distribution is a family of curves whose shapes depend on both sample sizes and the number of samples being compared. Instead of being symmetrical, like t distributions, F distributions are positively skewed with a peak around 1.00. Note that, unlike the t test, the F test cannot be two-tailed. The reason is that F cannot be negative, because it's based on sums of squares. In fact, this observation is one of the main things for you to recall when you're troubleshooting your computations; if you obtain a negative value for one of the sums of squares, you have committed a major arithmetical error.

A portion of Table C is shown in Table 11-1. The critical values in the table are F ratios cutting off either the upper 5% or the upper 1% of a particular F distribution. If our computed F ratio equals or exceeds an appropriate critical value, we will reject the null hypothesis.

Under the table's title is the heading "df Associated With the Numerator (df_b)"; below this are the numbers 1 through 9 in a row. To the left is a column of numbers from 1 to 15 (in the appendix there are additional numbers, up to 120). The heading over this column is "df Associated With the Denominator (df_w)." The terms *numerator* and *denominator* refer to relevant portions of the F ratio. The numerator of the F ratio is MS_b, and its df is df_b. The denominator of the F ratio is MS_w, whose df is df_w.

For the problem we have been considering, $df = 2$ for the numerator and $df = 15$ for the denominator. Thus, to find the critical values for the test of our computed F ratio, we read down the row of numbers in the left margin of the table

TABLE 11-1

A Portion of Table C Showing Critical Values of F

df Associated With the Denominator (df_w)		df Associated With the Numerator (df_b)								
		1	2	3	4	5	6	7	8	9
1	5%	161	200	216	225	230	234	238	239	241
	1%	4052	5000	5403	5625	5764	5859	5928	5981	6022
2	5%	18.5	19.0	19.2	19.2	19.3	19.3	19.4	19.4	19.4
	1%	98.5	99.0	99.2	99.2	99.3	99.3	99.4	99.4	99.4
3	5%	10.1	9.55	9.28	9.12	9.01	8.97	8.89	8.85	8.81
	1%	34.1	30.8	29.5	28.7	28.2	27.9	27.7	27.5	27.3
4	5%	7.71	6.94	6.59	6.39	6.26	6.16	6.09	6.04	6.00
	1%	21.2	18.0	16.7	16.0	15.5	15.2	15.0	14.8	14.7
5	5%	6.61	5.79	5.41	5.19	5.05	4.95	4.88	4.82	4.77
	1%	16.3	13.3	12.1	11.4	11.0	10.7	10.5	10.3	10.2
6	5%	5.99	5.14	4.76	4.53	4.39	4.28	4.21	4.15	4.10
	1%	13.7	10.9	9.78	9.15	8.75	8.47	8.26	8.10	7.98
7	5%	5.59	4.74	4.35	4.12	3.97	3.87	3.79	3.73	3.68
	1%	12.2	9.55	8.45	7.85	7.46	7.19	6.99	6.84	6.72
8	5%	5.32	4.46	4.07	3.84	3.69	3.58	3.50	3.44	3.39
	1%	11.3	8.65	7.59	7.01	6.63	6.37	6.18	6.03	5.91
9	5%	5.12	4.26	3.86	3.63	3.48	3.37	3.29	3.23	3.18
	1%	10.6	8.02	6.99	6.42	6.06	5.80	5.61	5.47	5.35
10	5%	4.96	4.10	3.71	3.48	3.33	3.22	3.14	3.07	3.02
	1%	10.0	7.56	6.55	5.99	5.64	5.39	5.20	5.06	4.94
11	5%	4.84	3.98	3.59	3.36	3.20	3.09	3.01	2.95	2.90
	1%	9.65	7.21	6.22	5.67	5.32	5.07	4.89	4.74	4.63
12	5%	4.75	3.89	3.49	3.26	3.11	3.00	2.91	2.85	2.80
	1%	9.33	6.93	5.95	5.41	5.06	4.82	4.64	4.50	4.39
13	5%	4.67	3.81	3.41	3.18	3.03	2.92	2.83	2.77	2.71
	1%	9.07	6.70	5.74	5.21	4.86	4.62	4.44	4.30	4.19
14	5%	4.60	3.74	3.34	3.11	2.96	2.85	2.76	2.70	2.65
	1%	8.86	6.51	5.56	5.04	4.70	4.46	4.28	4.14	4.03
15	5%	4.54	3.68	3.29	3.06	2.90	2.79	2.71	2.64	2.59
	1%	8.68	6.36	5.42	4.89	4.56	4.32	4.14	4.00	3.89

Note. The entire table may be found in Appendix 4. From "Tables of Percentage Points of the Inverted Beta (*F*) Distribution," by M. Merrington and C. M. Thompson, 1943, *Biometrika, 33,* pp. 73–88. Reprinted with permission of the Biometrika Trustees.

until we come to 15, and then across the columns of numbers to the column headed by 2. The critical values are 3.68 at the 5% level and 6.36 at the 1% level.

We will now summarize the ANOVA procedure using the seven-step procedure:

1. H_0: $\mu_1 = \mu_2 = \mu_3$. There is no difference in fear approach among the three drug groups. This is equivalent to saying that the samples came from the same population. *Graphically,* this null hypothesis would be represented by the plot of a flat straight line of three identical *population* group means, a plot similar to the one shown in Figure 11-2.

2. The (population) fear approach distances among the three groups are *not* all the same.

3. Set $\alpha = .05$.

4. *Rejection Rule:* Reject H_0 if $F_{comp} \geq F_\alpha$ (df_b, df_w); $F_{.05}$ (2, 15) = 3.68 and $F_{.01}$ (2, 15) = 6.36.

5. *Computations and Test Statistic:* Already presented, these require getting the necessary sums of squares, completing the source table, and obtaining the computed value for the F ratio, $F(2, 15) = 15.42$.

6. *Decision:* Reject H_0, as $F(2, 15) = 15.42 > 6.36$, $p < .01$.

7. *Conclusion:* The fear approach distances for the three drug groups are not all the same, $F(2, 15) = 15.42$, $p < .01$. Based on this fictitious study, we conclude that the drugs tested had an effect on the behavioral avoidance test in the phobic patients. It would also be desirable to include a graph of the group means as shown in Figure 11-5.

The F test does not tell us which of the possible group comparisons is actually significant. All we know at this point is that there are significant differences

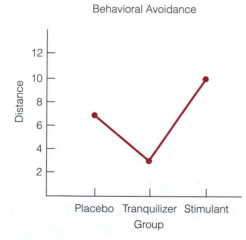

Figure 11-5 Line graph showing group means for the snake avoidance example.

somewhere in the data we have analyzed. In order to analyze our data fully, we want to know more than merely whether the groups are different; we want to know which group (or groups) is "best" or "worst" in the context of our research investigation. In our specific example, we want to know which drug treatment is best for reducing behavioral avoidance. We could perform t tests on the groups that we feel, from looking at the means, might be significantly different; however, by doing this we increase the risk of committing Type I errors (rejecting a true null hypothesis), and we want to avoid this problem. In fact, you will recall that we introduced the ANOVA as an alternative to performing multiple t tests. Fortunately, there are several **post-ANOVA tests**—tests that follow the analysis of variance—that we can use to analyze the data further. Some examples are the Scheffé test, the Tukey HSD test, the Fisher LSD test, the Newman–Keuls test, and the Duncan test. We will use the Fisher LSD and Tukey HSD tests to analyze the data further after we present another ANOVA example. Box 11-1 summarizes the procedure for computing F.

Another Between-Subjects ANOVA Example

Let's perform the ANOVA for the example about treatments for panic disorder at the beginning of the chapter. The data based on a standard assessment of panic disorder, in which a lower score represents less panic, are as follows:

Experimental	Conventional	Untreated
10	14	16
9	13	14
6	12	10
5	7	10
11	12	6
2	7	13
7	13	9
3	8	17
9	5	15
7	13	11

First, we need to determine the sum of the scores in each group, the sum of the squared scores in each group, the total sum of scores, and the total sum of squared scores. We will also note the number of subjects per group and total N. This has been done in the following chart, but check the computations:

	Experimental	Conventional	Untreated	Totals
ΣX_g	69	104	121	$\Sigma X = 294$
ΣX_g^2	555	1,178	1,573	$\Sigma X^2 = 3{,}306$
N_g	10	10	10	$N = 30$

Box 11-1   Summary of the Procedure for Calculating F

1. For each separate group, determine the number of subjects or observations in the group (N_g). Then add all the scores in the group (ΣX_g). Finally, square each of the scores and add the squared scores in the group (ΣX_g^2).

2. Use the values calculated in step 1 to determine N, the sum of all N_gs; ΣX, the sum of all ΣX_gs; and ΣX^2, the sum of all ΣX_g^2s.

3. Use Formula 11-5 to compute SS_{tot}.

4. Use Formula 11-6 to compute SS_w.

5. Use Formula 11-7 to compute SS_b; alternatively, SS_b or SS_w may be determined by subtraction once SS_{tot} and one or the other of the components has been computed; that is, $SS_b = SS_{tot} - SS_w$ and $SS_w = SS_{tot} - SS_b$.

6. After the sums of squares have been determined, construct and fill in the ANOVA summary table.

ANOVA Summary Table

Source	SS	df	MS	F
Between groups		$K - 1$	$\dfrac{SS_b}{df_b}$	$F = \dfrac{MS_b}{MS_w}$
Within groups		$N - K$	$\dfrac{SS_w}{df_w}$	
Total		$N - 1$		

7. Once the summary table is properly completed, compare the computed value of F, symbolized by F_{comp}, with critical values of F, symbolized by F_{crit}, from Table C for the appropriate degrees of freedom. The degrees of freedom for the F test are the degrees of freedom associated with the numerator of the F ratio (df_b) and the degrees of freedom associated with the denominator (df_w). If the computed F is larger than the critical value at the 5% level (1% if you need to be more conservative), reject the null hypothesis and conclude that the samples were drawn from different populations. A significant F ratio indicates that one or more of the groups came from different populations, but it doesn't tell you which. Further testing is needed to determine exactly where the significant differences lie.

It's time to compute the sums of squares:

$$SS_{tot} = \Sigma X^2 - \frac{(\Sigma X)^2}{N} = 3,306 - \frac{(294)^2}{30} = 3,306 - 2,881.2 = 424.8,$$

$$SS_w = \sum_g \left[\Sigma X_g^2 - \frac{(\Sigma X_g)^2}{N_g} \right]$$

$$= \left(555 - \frac{69^2}{10} \right) + \left(1,178 - \frac{104^2}{10} \right) + \left(1,573 - \frac{121^2}{10} \right)$$

$$= (555 - 476.1) + (1,178 - 1,081.6) + (1,573 - 1,464.1)$$

$$= 78.9 + 96.4 + 108.9 = 284.2,$$

$$SS_b = \sum_g \left[\frac{(\Sigma X_g)^2}{N_g} \right] - \frac{(\Sigma X)^2}{N} = \left(\frac{69^2}{10} + \frac{104^2}{10} + \frac{121^2}{10} \right) - \frac{294^2}{30}$$

$$= (476.1 + 1,081.6 + 1,464.1) - 2,881.2$$

$$= 3,021.8 - 2,881.2 = 140.6.$$

Now that the sums of squares have been computed, let's fill in the ANOVA summary table:

ANOVA Summary Table

Source	SS	df	MS	F
Between groups	140.6	2	70.3	6.68
Within groups	284.2	27	10.53	
Total	424.8	29		

Here are our computations:

$$df_b = K - 1 = 3 - 1 = 2,$$

$$df_w = N - K = 30 - 3 = 27,$$

$$df_{tot} = N - 1 = 30 - 1 = 29,$$

$$MS_b = \frac{SS_b}{df_b} = \frac{140.6}{2} = 70.3,$$

$$MS_w = \frac{SS_w}{df_w} = \frac{284.2}{27} = 10.53,$$

$$F = \frac{MS_b}{MS_w} = \frac{70.3}{10.53} = 6.68.$$

The final result is $F = 6.68$ with $df = 2, 27$. According to Table C, the critical values for 2 and 27 df are 3.35 at the 5% level and 5.49 at the 1% level. Because the computed F is larger than the critical value at the 5% and 1% levels, we reject the null hypothesis that the samples came from the same population and conclude that the panic disorder treatments varied in their effectiveness; $F(2, 27) = 6.68, p < .01$. Further analysis of these data must await the discussion in the next section.

⑤ CHECKING YOUR PROGRESS

Suppose we are interested in nonsense syllable learning. We select three groups of participants, each of which learns a list of nonsense syllables under different conditions. The first group learns the list in a normally lit room; the second group learns the list in a darkened room lit only by a small lamp placed near the memory drum (a rotating device with a small window where each nonsense syllable appears briefly); the third group learns the list in a room with flashing lights. We record the number of repetitions of the list each participant requires before he or she has an errorless repetition. We intended to have the same N in each group, but one of the participants was unable to complete training and her data were discarded. The data are as follows:

Group X_1 (Normal Room)	Group X_2 (Dark Room)	Group X_3 (Flashing Lights)
5	3	10
7	4	11
6	5	20
10	10	13
15	7	10
11	6	8
8	2	7
7	4	12
	5	12

Compute F and test it for significance.

Answer: $F = 9.02$, which for 2 and 23 df is significant ($p < .01$); $F(2, 23) = 9.02$, $p < .01$. Our conclusion is that the different lighting treatments affected the number of repetitions required to learn a list of nonsense syllables.

POST HOC COMPARISONS

The data analysis was complete, and Dr. Baxter was pleased. The one-way ANOVA comparing her treatment groups had yielded a significant F value. Now she could make the necessary changes to her paper and resubmit it to the journal. She had only to add some interpretation of her findings to the manuscript and she would be finished.

What did her results mean? Overall, Dr. Baxter could see that the mean of the group receiving the experimental treatment had reduced panic disorder symptoms. It was 3.5 (conventional group mean = 10.4; experimental group mean = 6.9; 10.4 − 6.9 = 3.5) points better than the mean of the group receiving the conventional treatment, which was 1.7 (untreated group mean = 12.1; 12.1 − 10.4 = 1.7) points below the untreated group. These findings meant that the experimental treatment group was 5.2 points better than the untreated group. However, the pattern wasn't as clear as Dr. Baxter expected. She realized that to make sense of the differences among the groups, she would have to use a different test—a post hoc comparison—to find out whether her experimental treatment was best.

Earlier we said that finding a significant F ratio is not sufficient to tell us which group or treatment comparisons might actually differ significantly. Suppose, for example, a one-way ANOVA includes four groups (A, B, C, D). A significant F value would not specify which groups or combination of groups is significantly different from which other group or groups. Group A might differ from groups B, C, and D, but B, C, and D might not differ from each other. Alternatively, group A might not differ from B, but might differ from C and D. Group B might differ from D but not C—and the possibilities go on. A significant F is only a first step. Further analysis is necessary to determine the exact pattern of differences involved and to find out which treatment is "best."

Remember that one of the main reasons for not doing multiple t tests initially was that there was an increased risk of committing a Type I, or alpha (α), error (rejecting a true null). Many **a posteriori** (after the fact) or **post hoc tests** avoid the problem of inflation of an α error by increasing the critical value needed to reject the null hypothesis. Here, we will consider two post hoc or multiple comparison tests: the Fisher LSD and the Tukey HSD. The tests could also be called post-ANOVA tests because they follow ANOVA. Many other useful post hoc tests can be found in higher level textbooks.

In addition to the post hoc or a posteriori tests, there are also **a priori tests,** or tests designed to look at specific hypotheses before the experiment is performed. A priori tests perform planned comparisons, in contrast to post hoc tests, which perform unplanned comparisons. The logic and computational procedures for a priori tests are beyond the scope of this text. Therefore, we restrict our discussion in this chapter to post hoc tests, which are conducted when the experimenter cannot predict the patterning of means before the research is performed.

THE FISHER LSD

The **Fisher LSD (least significant difference) test,** or simply **LSD test,** is easy to compute and is used to make all pairwise comparisons of group means. By pairwise comparisons, we mean that we make all possible comparisons between groups by looking at one pair of groups at a time. One advantage of the LSD for our purposes is that it doesn't require equal sample sizes. Another advantage is that it is a powerful test; that is, we are more likely to be able to reject the null hypothesis with it than with many other post hoc tests available, including the Tukey HSD test covered later. As experimenters, we would rather reject a few true nulls than fail to reject false hypotheses. In other words, the Type II (β) error ("failure of detection") is considered to be more serious than the α error ("false alarm").

The LSD test is sometimes called a **protected t test** because it follows a significant F test. If we used the t test to do all pairwise comparisons *before* the F test, the probability of committing an α error would be greater than α. However, by applying a form of the t test after the F test has revealed at least one significant comparison, the error rate (probability of α error) is protected.

The technique is simple. The difference between two sample means is significant if it is greater than LSD, which is found by the following formula:

FORMULA 11-14 *Least significant difference (LSD) between pairs of means (computational formula)*

$$\text{LSD}_\alpha = t_\alpha \sqrt{MS_w \left(\frac{1}{N_1} + \frac{1}{N_2} \right)}$$

As before, α is the level of significance—that is, either the 5% ($p = .05$) or 1% ($p = .01$) level. The value of t is obtained from Table B, the table of critical values of t, with $df = df_w(N - K)$. N_1 and N_2 are the sizes of the first and second samples being considered, respectively.

Using the Fisher LSD

Let's use the Fisher LSD to analyze Dr. Baxter's data further. From our earlier computations, we need the group means (experimental, 6.9; conventional, 10.4; untreated, 12.1), the MS_w (10.53), and the df_w (27). Further, the critical t scores from Table B are $t_{.05} = 2.0518$ and $t_{.01} = 2.7707$. With these values and Formula 11-14, we can compute the LSD$_{.05}$ and LSD$_{.01}$ as follows:

$$\text{LSD}_{.05} = t_{.05} \sqrt{MS_w \left(\frac{1}{N_1} + \frac{1}{N_2} \right)} = 2.0518 \sqrt{10.53 \left(\frac{1}{10} + \frac{1}{10} \right)}$$

$$= 2.0518 \sqrt{10.53(.2)} = 2.0518 \sqrt{2.106} = 2.98,$$

$$\text{LSD}_{.01} = t_{.01} \sqrt{MS_w \left(\frac{1}{N_1} + \frac{1}{N_2} \right)} = 2.7707 \sqrt{2.106} = 4.02.$$

Note that we only have to compute one value for each of the LSDs as long as the sample sizes are equal, but if we have unequal sample sizes, there will be slight differences in the values because of differences in $1/N_1$ and $1/N_2$.

Now, we have found that the least significant difference in means at the 5% level is 2.98, and it is 4.02 at the 1% level. In order to find which of Dr. Baxter's groups differ significantly, all we have to do is to subtract the smaller mean from the larger for each pairwise comparison. (Alternatively, we could always subtract in our usual order, $\overline{X}_1 - \overline{X}_2$, and use the absolute value of any negative differences obtained.) Thus, for the comparison of the experimental and conventional treatments, the difference is 3.5 (10.4 − 6.9 = 3.5), which is larger than 2.98 (LSD$_{.05}$) and is therefore significant. The difference between the experimental and the untreated groups is 5.2 (12.1 − 6.9 = 5.2), which is larger than 4.02, the LSD$_{.01}$ value. Finally, the difference between the conventional and the untreated groups is just 1.7 (12.1 − 10.4 = 1.7), which is not significant. We conclude that in Dr. Baxter's experiment, the experimental treatment was significantly better (produced lower mean panic scores) than both conventional treatment and no treatment. In addition, conventional treatment was not significantly better than no treatment.

Applying our seven-step procedure to this problem, we would have the following:

1. H_0: $\mu_1 = \mu_2$. (Test each pair of groups.)

2. H_1: $\mu_1 \neq \mu_2$. (Respective pairs of groups are significantly different.)

3. Set $\alpha = .05$.

4. *Rejection Rule:* If $|\overline{X}_1 - \overline{X}_2|$ (or subtract to get a positive difference) $\geq$ LSD$_{.05}$, then groups 1 and 2 (or the pair being tested) are significantly different by the LSD test, $p < .05$.

5. *Computation and Test Statistic:*

$$\text{LSD}_{.05} = t_{.05}\sqrt{MS_w\left(\frac{1}{N_1} + \frac{1}{N_2}\right)} = 2.0518\sqrt{10.53\left(\frac{1}{10} + \frac{1}{10}\right)}$$

$$= 2.98 \text{ (least significant difference)}.$$

6. *Making a Decision Using the Table of Differences.*

Table of Differences

		Experimental Group 6.9	Conventional Group 10.4	Untreated Group 12.1
Experimental	6.9		3.5*	5.2**
Conventional	10.4			1.7
Untreated	12.1			

Note. *$p < .05$; **$p < .01$.

Note that in constructing the table, we listed the means in ascending order. Also, each of the numbers in the body of the table represents the difference between a pair of means. For example, the number 3.5 in the block formed by comparing the conventional group with the experimental group is the difference between 10.4 and 6.9. By convention, we have used asterisks to depict the level at which we rejected H_0: One asterisk is for the 5% level and two are for the 1% level.

   7. *Conclusion:*   As we stated earlier, the experimental treatment was superior to either no treatment or conventional treatment, and conventional treatment was not significantly better than no treatment.

Another Fisher LSD Example

Let's use the Fisher LSD to complete the analysis of the data in the "Checking Your Progress" problem at the end of the between-subjects ANOVA section. As you will recall, the problem stated that three groups of participants learned a list of non-sense syllables under different conditions: One group learned the list in a normally lit room, one group learned in a darkened room, and the third group learned the list in a room with flashing lights. The data we need from the earlier analysis are the numbers of subjects in each group and the sums of scores in each group (in order to compute the group means), the MS_w, and the df_w. Those values are as follows:

	Normal Lighting	Dark Room	Flashing Lights
ΣX_g	69	46	103
N_g	8	9	9

$MS_w = 10.04, df_w = 23$

The group means are as follows: Normal Lighting, $69/8 = 8.63$; Dark Room, $46/9 = 5.11$; Flashing Lights, 11.44. Now, we need to compute LSD. Note that because we have unequal numbers of participants in each group, we will need to compute more than one LSD for the 5% level and more than one for the 1% level (if we decide we want to look at the lower probability). Specifically, we will need to compute an LSD for the comparison of groups 1 and 2 and 1 and 3 and then a separate LSD for the comparison of groups 2 and 3. The computations for the $LSD_{.05}$ are shown next.

$$LSD_{.05} \text{ for the comparison of 1 and 2 and 1 and 3} = t_{.05}\sqrt{MS_w\left(\frac{1}{N_1} + \frac{1}{N_2}\right)}$$

The $t_{.05}$ from Table B with $df = 23$ is 2.0687; $t_{.01} = 2.8073$.

$$= 2.0687\sqrt{10.04\left(\frac{1}{8} + \frac{1}{9}\right)}$$

$$= 2.0687\sqrt{10.04(.236)}$$

$$= 2.0687\sqrt{2.37}$$

$$LSD_{.05} = 3.18.$$

$$LSD_{.05} \text{ for the comparison of 2 and 3} = 2.0687\sqrt{10.04\left(\frac{1}{9} + \frac{1}{9}\right)} = 3.09.$$

As a separate exercise, you might want to compute the LSD values at the 1% level; the answers are 4.32 for the first two comparisons and 4.19 for the comparison of groups 2 and 3.

We can summarize our results in the Table of Differences we introduced in the previous problem.

Table of Differences

	Dark Room 5.11	Normal Lights 8.63	Flashing Lights 11.44
Dark 5.11		3.52*	6.33**
Normal 8.63			2.81
Flashing 11.44			

Note. *$p < .05$; **$p < .01$.

As you can tell from the table, nonsense syllable learning in the dark room required fewer repetitions of the list than learning in either of the other rooms. The difference between the number of repetitions in the room with normal lights and the room with flashing lights, although substantial, was not statistically significant.

ᔓ CHECKING YOUR PROGRESS

A study was performed to test the effect of attractiveness on perceived happiness. Three groups of participants were presented with photos of a very attractive person, a moderately attractive person, or an unattractive person. The participants then used a standardized scale to rate how happy they judged the person in the photo to be. The data are as follows:

Very Attractive	Moderately Attractive	Unattractive
6	5	4
8	6	3
8	8	3
10	9	6
7	7	2

The problem is to determine whether there is a significant overall result and, if there is, to determine which groups differ significantly. We won't go through all the computations resulting in F (treat this example as another review exercise); the summary table is as follows:

ANOVA Summary Table

Source	SS	df	MS	F
Between groups	49.73	2	24.87	$F = 10.67$, $df = 2, 12$, or
Within groups	28.00	12	2.33	$F(2, 12) = 10.67, p < .01$
Total	77.73	14		

Using the values from the summary table and from your computations on the raw scores, perform the Fisher LSD test.

Answer: The $\text{LSD}_{.05} = 2.10$, and $\text{LSD}_{.01} = 2.95$. For the comparison of groups Unattractive and Moderately Attractive, the mean difference is 3.4 ($p < .01$); comparing groups Unattractive and Very Attractive results in a mean difference of 4.2 ($p < .01$); the mean difference for the comparison of groups Moderately Attractive and Very Attractive is 0.8 ($p > .05$). Thus, both very attractive and moderately attractive people are perceived to be happier than unattractive people.

THE TUKEY HSD

Another popular post hoc test is the **Tukey HSD (honestly significantly difference) test,** or simply the **HSD test.** Although the HSD test can be used for more complex comparisons, we will use it when we have equal numbers per group for making all pairwise comparisons of the data. Actually, the HSD test can be done with unequal group sizes, but the computations are more complicated.

As for the Fisher LSD, the technique is simple. The difference between two sample means is significant if it is greater than HSD, which is found by the following equation:

FORMULA 11-15 *Honestly significant difference (HSD) between pairs of means (computational formula)*

$$\text{HSD}_\alpha = q_\alpha \sqrt{\frac{MS_w}{N_g}}$$

As before, α is the level of significance—that is, either the 5% ($p = .05$) or the 1% ($p = .01$) level. The value of q is obtained from the distribution of the studentized range statistic found in Table D. (The studentized range statistic is sometimes used instead of the F statistic for making group comparisons. It is generally a less powerful test than the F test.) To determine the value of q from the table, we need to know two things: the df_w (degrees of freedom within groups) and K (the number of groups, treatments, or means).

Using the Tukey HSD

Let's look at a specific example. Earlier in the chapter, we worked with some data from a hypothetical experiment in which snake avoidance was measured after one of three different treatments. The group means were these: group 1 (placebo), $\overline{X}_1 = 7$; group 2 (mild tranquilizer), $\overline{X}_2 = 3$; group 3 (mild stimulant), $\overline{X}_3 = 10$. The analysis of variance summary table is repeated here:

ANOVA Summary Table

Source	SS	df	MS	F
Between groups	148	2	74	$F = 15.42$
Within groups	72	15	4.8	
Total	220	17		

The first step is to define all the pairwise comparisons we are going to make and to find the difference in the means for each comparison. The possible pairwise comparisons are as follows: group 1 and group 2, group 1 and group 3, and group 2 and group 3. Subtracting the smaller mean from the larger for each comparison, we observe the following differences:

$$\overline{X}_1 - \overline{X}_2 = 7 - 3 = 4,$$
$$\overline{X}_3 - \overline{X}_1 = 10 - 7 = 3,$$
$$\overline{X}_3 - \overline{X}_2 = 10 - 3 = 7.$$

As we noted with the LSD test, we could have subtracted in the order originally specified and then used the absolute value of the differences in the comparison with HSD.

The next step is to determine HSD_α. Again, the formula for HSD_α is

$$HSD_\alpha = q_\alpha \sqrt{\frac{MS_w}{N_g}}.$$

With three groups and $df_w = 15$, the value of $q_{.05}$ from Table D is 3.67. The value of $q_{.01} = 4.84$. As $MS_w = 4.8$ from the summary table and $N_g = 6$,

$$HSD_{.05} = 3.67 \sqrt{\frac{4.8}{6}} = 3.67\sqrt{0.8} = 3.67(0.89) = 3.27,$$

$$HSD_{.01} = 4.84(0.89) = 4.31.$$

Now that the values for HSD have been computed, we can use the Table of Differences to summarize our results.

Table of Differences

	Tranquilizer 3	Placebo 7	Stimulant 10
Tranquilizer 3		4*	7**
Placebo 7			3
Stimulant 10			

Note. $*p < .05; **p < .01.$

In summary, the F test indicated that a significant difference(s) existed in the data. The Tukey HSD test revealed that the difference between the first and second groups (placebo and mild tranquilizer) was significant and that the difference between the second and third groups (tranquilizer and mild stimulant) was also significant. In other words, the tranquilizer was more effective than either the placebo or the mild stimulant in reducing the snake phobia. However, the stimulant was not significantly better (or worse) than the placebo.

At this point, we ordinarily would provide another solved example of the technique we have just covered—the Tukey HSD. However, because the HSD is so similar to the Fisher LSD—the only difference being the computation of HSD rather than LSD—we will proceed to an ANOVA technique analogous to the t test for dependent or related samples. (If you would like to practice the HSD further, use it to analyze the data sets for which we used the Fisher LSD, with the restriction that the samples employ equal numbers of subjects.) You will recall from Chapter 10 that one of the situations in which we used the dependent t involved repeated measures on the same sample of subjects. Thus, it should come as no surprise that our final technique in this chapter is the repeated measures ANOVA.

REPEATED MEASURES ANOVA

The analysis of variance situation discussed at the beginning of the chapter uses independent groups of participants at each level of the treatment; that is, the scores in each treatment group are based on different participants. This between-subjects ANOVA design extends the independent t test, which also uses independent groups.

As discussed in Chapter 10, there are also instances in which the same participants are tested repeatedly. If there are only two occasions for measurement, the appropriate analysis is the dependent t test. However, investigators often wish to measure the same participants on more than two occasions, most commonly in studies designed to examine the effectiveness of programs or interventions. These studies might, for example, include a pretest, a test administered after some period of treatment, another test administered at the end of treatment, and perhaps one or more follow-up tests. The advantage of a repeated measures (or within-subjects) design is that it allows us not only to follow the same people to determine whether a particular treatment is effective but also to see whether the treatment effect persists.

Recall from Chapter 10 that one of the main advantages of the dependent t test is that it reduces the error variability in the scores. Each participant is used as his or her own control (baseline). In other words, for the same scores, the denominator of a dependent t test is smaller than it is for an independent t test. However, the numerator is identical, so the reduction in the size of the denominator makes it more likely that the statistic will be significant. The same situation holds in one-way repeated measures ANOVA. By using each person as his or her own control, we are able to extract some of the variability from our scores.

Earlier in this chapter, we discussed the within-groups sum of squares (SS_w). We indicated that there are two sources of variability that contribute to SS_w: experimental error (SS_{error}) and the inherent variability in subjects (SS_{subj}). Thus, we can represent SS_w as being composed of SS_{subj} and SS_{error}:

> **FORMULA 11-16**   *Within-groups sum of squares in one-way repeated measures ANOVA (definitional formula)*
>
> $$SS_w = SS_{subj} + SS_{error}$$

The one-way repeated measures ANOVA allows us to remove the variance caused by variability in subjects; that is, we can estimate SS caused by individual differences and remove it from SS_w. We are left with SS caused by experimental error. It is this SS_{error} that we will use as the denominator in computing our F value.

Note that once again, the principle of additivity applies. We are simply breaking SS_{tot} into its component parts. For a one-way repeated measures ANOVA, this involves estimating one more component than we found in the one-way between-subjects ANOVA. The formula is:

> **FORMULA 11-17**   *Total sum of squares in one-way repeated measures ANOVA (definitional formula)*
>
> $$SS_{tot} = SS_b + SS_{subj} + SS_{error}$$

A sample problem will help illustrate the steps involved in the one-way repeated measures analysis of variance. Suppose we are interested in the effect of practice on the ability to solve algebra problems. First we test 6 participants in algebra performance before practice, recording the number of problems they solve correctly out of 10 problems. We then provide the participants with practice on algebra problems and retest their performance. We want to know whether the effects of practice persist, so we retest our participants after 1 day and again after 1 week following the practice session. Here are their scores:

	Pretest	Retest	1 Day After	1 Week After
Sarah	2	4	4	5
Marcus	4	7	6	6
Courtney	3	5	8	9
Ari	6	8	9	7
Joy	1	3	5	6
Margaret	5	6	7	3

In the first steps of the problem, we proceed exactly as in one-way between-subjects ANOVA. We calculate SS_{tot} and SS_b as before:

	Pretest (X_1)	Retest (X_2)	1 Day After (X_3)	1 Week After (X_4)	Totals
ΣX_g	21	33	39	36	$\Sigma X = 129$
ΣX_g^2	91	199	271	236	$\Sigma X^2 = 797$
N_g	6	6	6	6	$N = 24$
$\overline{X}_g$	3.5	5.5	6.5	6	

$$SS_{tot} = \Sigma X^2 - \frac{(\Sigma X)^2}{N} = 797 - \frac{(129)^2}{24} = 797 - 693.375 = 103.625$$

$$SS_b = \sum_g \left[\frac{(\Sigma X_g)^2}{N_g} \right] - \frac{(\Sigma X)^2}{N} = \left(\frac{21^2}{6} + \frac{33^2}{6} + \frac{39^2}{6} + \frac{36^2}{6} \right) - \frac{129^2}{24}$$

$$= 724.5 - 693.375 = 31.125$$

However, now we have an additional step: We must compute SS_{subj}. To do this, we first find a total for each subject. It is helpful to construct a table, such as the one for treatments. In a sense, subjects are dealt with as another treatment factor. Notice the similarity in the formulas for obtaining SS_{subj} and SS_b:

> **FORMULA 11-18** *Within-subjects sum of squares in one-way repeated measures ANOVA (computational formula)*
>
> $$SS_{subj} = \sum_s \left[\frac{(\Sigma X_m)^2}{K} \right] - \frac{(\Sigma X)^2}{N},$$

where K = number of treatments (groups of *scores*) and m refers to each subject. The $\sum_s$ means that we sum across subjects. Each subject's ΣX_m is the sum of that subject's scores across treatments. For example, Sarah's $\Sigma X_m = 2 + 4 + 4 + 5 = 15$. Here are our data and the computations:

	ΣX_m	K
Sarah	15	4
Marcus	23	4
Courtney	25	4
Ari	30	4
Joy	15	4
Margaret	21	4
Totals	$\Sigma X = 129$	$N = 24$

$$SS_{subj} = \sum_s \left[\frac{(\Sigma X_m)^2}{K}\right] - \frac{(\Sigma X)^2}{N} = \left(\frac{15^2}{4} + \frac{23^2}{4} + \frac{25^2}{4} + \frac{30^2}{4} + \frac{15^2}{4} + \frac{21^2}{4}\right) - \frac{129^2}{24}$$

$$= (56.25 + 132.25 + 156.25 + 225 + 56.25 + 110.25) - 693.375$$

$$= 736.25 - 693.375 = 42.875.$$

Once we have found SS_{subj}, we can determine SS_{error} by subtraction:

FORMULA 11-19   *Error sum of squares in one-way repeated measures ANOVA (computational formula)*

$$SS_{error} = SS_{tot} - SS_b - SS_{subj}$$

For our data, $SS_{error} = SS_{tot} - SS_b - SS_{subj} = 103.625 - 31.125 - 42.875 = 29.625$.

The last step is to construct a summary table. It is similar to the summary table for the one-way between-subjects ANOVA except that our SS_{tot} is composed of three parts instead of two. First we fill in the appropriate SS for each of the sources:

ANOVA Summary Table

Source	SS	df	MS	F
Between groups	31.125	$K - 1 = 3$	$\dfrac{SS_b}{df_b} = \dfrac{31.125}{3} = 10.375$	$F = \dfrac{MS_b}{MS_{error}}$
Subjects	42.875	$S - 1 = 5$		$= \dfrac{10.375}{1.975}$
Error	29.625	$(K-1)(S-1) = 3 \times 5 = 15$	$\dfrac{SS_{error}}{df_{error}} = \dfrac{29.625}{15} = 1.975$	$= 5.253$
Total	103.625	$N - 1 = 23$		

Our next step is to find *df* for each source. Note that df_b corresponds to the number of levels of the treatment minus 1 ($K - 1$), just as in one-way between-subjects ANOVA. For subjects, degrees of freedom are found by subtracting 1 from the number of subjects $(S - 1)$. Degrees of freedom for error is the product of df_b and df_{subj}, as shown in Formula 11-20:

FORMULA 11-20   *Error degrees of freedom*

$$df_{error} = (K - 1)(S - 1)$$

Alternatively, df_{error} can be found by subtracting df_b and df_{subj} from df_{tot}:

$$df_{error} = df_{tot} - df_b - df_{subj}.$$

Next, we find MS_b as in one-way between-subjects ANOVA and MS_{error} using Formula 11-21:

FORMULA 11-21   *Mean square error in one-way repeated measures ANOVA (computational formula)*

$$MS_{error} = \frac{SS_{error}}{df_{error}}$$

Finally, the F ratio for our treatment is found by dividing MS_b by MS_{error}, as indicated in Formula 11-22:

FORMULA 11-22   **F *ratio in one-way repeated measures ANOVA (computational formula)***

$$F = \frac{MS_b}{MS_{error}}$$

Once we have computed the F value, we use Table C to find the critical value for F. Remember to use the correct degrees of freedom—df corresponding to the numerator and denominator used in calculating F (df_b and df_{error}, respectively). In this example, $F_{comp} = 5.253$ and $F_{crit} = 3.29$ at the 5% level; $F(3, 15) = 5.253$, $p < .05$. Thus, we reject the null hypothesis. We can conclude that practice did affect algebra performance.

Normally, an F value for subjects is not computed, although it could be. The reason for this is that an F value for subjects doesn't tell us anything useful in our research. We know that people differ on the dimension employed. Our primary purpose is to remove statistically the contribution of individual differences to the variability in our scores.

Finally, it's possible to perform the post hoc tests we covered on the repeated measures ANOVA. For the Fisher LSD test, substitute MS_{error} for MS_w in the formula and use df_{error} rather than df_w when you obtain your t_{crit} from Table B. Otherwise, the procedure is the same. For the Tukey HSD test, again substitute MS_{error}

for MS_w in the formula and use df_{error} rather than df_w when you obtain your q value from Table D.

⑤ CHECKING YOUR PROGRESS

Suppose we are interested in the effect of practice on public speaking anxiety. We recruit eight volunteers and pretest them on public speaking anxiety on a standardized test. We then provide the volunteers with several practice sessions in giving speeches and test them again. To see if the practice causes a lasting change in their anxiety, we administer a follow-up test 6 months later. Here are the data (higher scores indicate higher anxiety):

	Pretest	Posttest	Follow-Up
Volunteer 1	8	6	7
Volunteer 2	6	4	5
Volunteer 3	5	5	7
Volunteer 4	7	7	2
Volunteer 5	7	4	5
Volunteer 6	3	1	2
Volunteer 7	10	6	4
Volunteer 8	10	7	8

Compute F and test it for significance. If F is significant, use the LSD to do all pairwise comparisons.

Answer: $F = 4.67$, which for 2 and 14 df is significant ($p < .05$); $F(2, 14) = 4.67$, $p < .05$. One or more of the groups (testing situations) came from different populations. We can conclude that practice reduced public speaking anxiety, at least for these volunteers. For the post hoc test, $LSD_{.05} = 1.62$, and the differences in means for the pairwise comparisons were 2, 2, and 0 for Pretest–Posttest, Pretest–Follow-Up, and Posttest–Follow-Up, respectively. Thus, the first two comparisons were significant (public speaking anxiety was lower at the posttest and the follow-up than it was at the pretest), and the comparison of public speaking anxiety at the posttest and the follow-up indicated that there was no difference between them.

SUMMARY

In this chapter, we covered a technique that allows us to perform a significance test on the results of comparing two or more levels of an independent variable. The test is called the one-way analysis of variance, or ANOVA. There are two types of one-way ANOVA. Between-subjects ANOVA is used when independent groups receive each level of the treatment; repeated measures ANOVA is used when the same individuals receive all levels of the treatment. ANOVA is analogous to detecting a "message" (treatment) over "static" (error variance). The analysis of variance results in computation of an F ratio, which is compared with critical values from Table C.

The determination of F begins with the calculation of the sums of squares. We first compute the total sum of squares using the formula

$$SS_{tot} = \Sigma X^2 - \frac{(\Sigma X)^2}{N}.$$

The total sum of squares is divided into the between-groups sum of squares and the within-groups sum of squares, which are computed from the formulas

$$SS_b = \sum_g \left[\frac{(\Sigma X_g)^2}{N_g} \right] - \frac{(\Sigma X)^2}{N}$$

and

$$SS_w = \sum_g \left[\Sigma X_g^2 - \frac{(\Sigma X_g)^2}{N_g} \right].$$

The mean square (MS) is found by dividing each sum of squares by the appropriate degrees of freedom. In the case of SS_b, $df_b = K - 1$, where K is the number of groups being compared. The df for SS_w is $N - K$, where N is the total number of subjects. The total degrees of freedom is $df_{tot} = N - 1$.

The F ratio is calculated by dividing MS_b by MS_w. Using the degrees of freedom associated with the numerator of the ratio (df_b) and the degrees of freedom associated with the denominator (df_w), we can locate critical values of F in Table C. If the computed value is equal to or larger than the critical value at the 5% level, we reject the null hypothesis (that all groups came from the same population).

One-way repeated measures ANOVA is identical to one-way between-subjects ANOVA in the computation of SS_{tot} and SS_b. However, SS_w is divided into SS_{subj} and SS_{error} using the following formulas:

$$SS_{subj} = \sum_s \left[\frac{(\Sigma X_m)^2}{K} \right] - \frac{(\Sigma X)^2}{N},$$

where K is the number of treatments, m refers to each subject, and $\underset{s}{\Sigma}$ means that you sum across subjects. Then

$$SS_{error} = SS_{tot} - SS_b - SS_{subj}.$$

As in one-way between-subjects ANOVA, mean squares are found by dividing each SS by the appropriate df. Degrees of freedom for subjects is $S - 1$, where S is the number of subjects. Degrees of freedom for error is $(K - 1)(S - 1)$. The F value is found by dividing MS_b by MS_{error}. The critical value for F is found in

Table C using df_b and df_{error}. If the computed F is greater than or equal to the 5% critical value, we reject the null hypothesis. Ordinarily, an F value for subjects is not computed.

For either type of ANOVA, if the F ratio is significant, further analysis of the data may be performed with post hoc tests such as the Fisher LSD and the Tukey HSD. For the Fisher test after a significant between-groups (independent) ANOVA, any difference between a pair of means is significant if it is equal to or larger than LSD, which is computed from the following formula:

$$\text{LSD}_\alpha = t_\alpha \sqrt{MS_w \left(\frac{1}{N_1} + \frac{1}{N_2} \right)},$$

where α is the level of significance, either 5% or 1%. The value of t is obtained from Table B, with $df = df_w$. Following a significant within-subjects (dependent) ANOVA, the formula for LSD is the same as the above except that MS_{error} is used instead of MS_w and df_{error} is used instead of df_w to obtain the appropriate t value from Table B.

For the Tukey HSD test, any difference between a pair of means is significant if it is equal to or larger than HSD, which is computed from the following formula:

$$\text{HSD}_\alpha = q_\alpha \sqrt{\frac{MS_w}{N_g}},$$

where q is obtained from Table D. The same substitutions used for the LSD test are applied to the HSD test following a significant within-subjects ANOVA. For both tests, the smaller mean is always subtracted from the larger, or absolute values of the differences are used in the comparison with either LSD or HSD.

❈ *Troubleshooting Your Computations*

Using formulas as complex as the ones discussed in this chapter increases the possibility of computational error. Two obvious signs of trouble when computing the sums of squares are a negative value for any sum of squares and the failure of $SS_b + SS_w$ or $SS_b + SS_{subj} + SS_{error}$ to total SS_{tot}. If either of these occurs, 99% of the time the error will be in the original computations—a failure to compute correctly one or more of the sums of scores or the sums of squared scores. Prevention is always preferable to treatment, and we suggest you check all your original computations twice as you do them to be sure you aren't making a mistake that will haunt you later.

If your mistake is not in the original summing of the scores and of the squared scores, check your formulas to see that they have been copied correctly. Then be sure that you substituted the correct number for the appropriate symbol in the equations. If you have unequal N_g values, be sure you noted this in substituting in the SS_b and SS_w equations.

The most common error in filling in the summary table is to determine df incorrectly. Remember that $df_b = K - 1$, where K is the number of groups you are comparing; that $df_w = N - K$; that $df_{subj} = S - 1$, where S is the number of subjects; and that df_{error} is $(K - 1)(S - 1)$. Also, $df_{tot} = df_b + df_w = df_b + df_{error} + df_{subj} = N - 1$.

The most common computational error made in calculating either LSD or HSD is to use N instead of N_g in the expression under the radical sign. Another error that is made with some regularity is to use a value from the F table (Table C) rather than the critical t (Table B) in the formula for LSD or instead of the q value (Table D) in the HSD formula. Also, be sure to subtract to obtain positive differences or to use the absolute values of your differences in the significance tests. As in all the significance tests we have done to this point, if your computed value is equal to or *larger* than the critical value, then you reject the null hypothesis for that test.

EXERCISES

1. We know that some people are more susceptible to hypnosis than others and that people who are highly suggestible have a vivid imagination and fantasy life. This leads us to hypothesize that the ability to recall dreams will also be affected by hypnotic susceptibility (HS). Using the Stanford Scale of Hypnotic Susceptibility, we create low, medium, and high susceptibility groups by selecting from volunteers who took the scale. We then ask the volunteers to keep a dream diary for 1 month. At the end of the month, we collect the diaries and count the number of dreams recalled for each person:

Low HS	Medium HS	High HS
4	14	22
9	12	26
6	3	13
8	26	20
14	15	27
16	19	19
8	17	16
10	5	14

Compare the groups on dream recall. If you obtain a significant F, use the LSD and HSD tests to make all pairwise comparisons.

2. An experiment is performed to determine the effects of taking a statistics class on the ability to perform simple algebra problems. Ten statistics students are given a 20-item algebra test at the beginning of a statistics course, after completing the course, and 6 months after the course. Here are the data, which represent the number of problems completed correctly:

Student	Before	After	6 Months After
1	10	11	10
2	12	14	14
3	14	20	15
4	6	10	11
5	15	16	14
6	12	14	16
7	12	15	13
8	2	7	7
9	9	10	10
10	8	18	15

Did experience with a statistics course affect algebra performance? Use the chapter's post hoc tests to make all pairwise comparisons after a significant F.

3. An investigator in child development research is studying the development of object permanence—the understanding that an object still exists even if it is out of sight. She tests three groups of infants—ten 9-month-olds, ten 12-month-olds, and ten 15-month-olds. She presents each of the 30 infants with 10 trials. On each trial, a toy is first shown to the child and then covered with a piece of cloth. The infant demonstrates object permanence if he or she looks for the object or shows signs of distress when it is covered. Each infant is given a score for the number of trials (out of 10) on which he or she shows object permanence. Here are the scores:

9 Months	12 Months	15 Months
8	10	10
3	5	8
4	6	9
6	7	9
5	6	8
4	5	7
9	10	9
2	3	6
0	3	6
1	3	8

Determine whether there were group differences in object permanence, and do all pairwise comparisons with the LSD if your F is significant.

4. Trauma victims frequently suffer from intrusive memories and images of the traumatic event. We are interested in the effectiveness of a new therapeutic technique that uses structured recall of the traumatic event in conjunction

with a cognitive restructuring of the experience. We have seven trauma patients record their intrusive thoughts for a 1-week period before receiving the therapy (0 months), after 2 months of therapy (2 months), at termination (4 months), and again 2 months after completing therapy (6 months). Here are the data:

Patient #	0 Months	2 Months	4 Months	6 Months
1	14	10	9	10
2	10	8	5	6
3	8	7	5	2
4	16	12	8	10
5	12	11	10	9
6	9	8	5	5
7	8	7	7	7

Did the new therapy significantly affect intrusive memories in these patients?

5. In a study of the effect of fatigue on performance of simple tasks, volunteers were instructed to perform a data entry task as rapidly and as accurately as possible. The number of errors committed during four 15-minute time periods was recorded:

Person	First 15 Minutes	Second 15 Minutes	Third 15 Minutes	Fourth 15 Minutes
1	4	2	8	10
2	5	5	12	10
3	11	11	14	20
4	16	18	15	23
5	4	4	11	17

Did fatigue influence performance? Use the HSD test to make all pairwise comparisons after a significant F ratio.

6. Several student volunteers were deprived of sleep for varying periods, and their performance on a pursuit rotor task was measured. The object of the pursuit rotor task is to keep a stylus in contact with a spot on a rotating turntable. It is primarily a measure of hand–eye coordination and should be sensitive to the effects of sleep deprivation. The length of the deprivation and the amount of time during a 1-minute test each student could keep the stylus in contact with the target are shown here. Determine whether lack of sleep affected performance on the task. People scoring 0 often fell asleep at the start of a session. Use the LSD test to make all pairwise comparisons if your F ratio is significant.

| | Sleep Deprivation | | |
0 Hr.	24 Hr.	48 Hr.	72 Hr.
30	10	5	5
45	10	10	3
15	5	5	5
20	15	5	0
30	20	0	0
35	10	20	6

7. Assume that the data shown in Exercise 3 have been collected from the same 10 infants on three different occasions—at 9 months, 12 months, and 15 months. Perform the appropriate analysis to determine whether object permanence changed over time. Compare the summary table to that obtained in Exercise 3.

8. An experiment has been done to investigate the effect of alcohol on the reaction time of adult males. Reaction time was measured in a simulated driver's seat from the moment a picture of a stop sign appeared until the subject applied force to a brake. Forty subjects were selected and randomly assigned to one of four treatment groups: group 1, placebo; group 2, 0.5 ounce of alcohol; group 3, 1.0 ounce; group 4, 2.0 ounces. Testing was conducted 30 minutes after alcohol ingestion. Here are the data:

| | Reaction Time in Seconds | | |
0.0 Oz.	0.5 Oz.	1.0 Oz.	2.0 Oz.
0.8	1.1	1.5	2.0
1.2	1.5	1.3	1.8
0.7	0.9	1.2	1.7
0.9	1.6	1.4	1.5
1.1	1.4	1.6	1.8
1.5	1.3	0.9	1.7
0.6	1.4	1.1	1.6
0.8	0.9	1.8	1.7
1.0	1.1	1.5	1.5
1.1	1.2	1.4	2.1

Determine whether there were group differences, and if there were, use the LSD and HSD tests to make all pairwise comparisons.

9. In Exercise 4, the same 7 patients were asked to report their intrusive thoughts at four different times. What if the data had been collected from four different groups of patients? Reanalyze the data in Exercise 4, assuming that the data have been collected from 28 trauma patients assigned to one of four groups based on their position in the therapy process. Compare your results to those obtained in Exercise 4. What are the similarities and differences in the summary tables?

10. Sixteen guinea pigs have been randomly assigned to four groups. Within each group, each guinea pig is given 10 trials with a particular type of food. The response measure is the number of pieces of food eaten by each subject. The scores are shown here.

Lettuce Pieces	Carrot Pieces	Alfalfa Pellets	Strawberry Pieces
10	8	5	1
9	8	5	1
9	9	4	2
10	7	6	1

Perform an overall test of significance. If the test is significant, make all pairwise comparisons.

11. We know that the presence of others often interferes with an individual's complex problem solving. Two-digit multiplication problems with answers are presented to participants on a computer screen. Their task is to respond "correct" or "incorrect" as quickly as possible. Response latencies (time taken to respond) are recorded by the computer. Participants perform the task alone (1-person group), in the presence of another person (2-person group), or in the presence of three other people (4-person group). In the 4-person group, a computer failure led to the loss of one participant's data. Perform an overall test of significance. If the test is significant, do all pairwise comparisons.

1-Person Group	2-Person Group	4-Person Group
0.55	1.55	3.28
1.23	2.69	2.15
0.25	1.10	5.63
0.36	0.85	1.18
1.16	0.75	4.75
0.15	1.25	2.65
0.80	3.16	

12. In a study of the influence of environment factors on small group interaction, four groups of five people each discussed the use of music in films. The people in the groups were either seated close together or far apart, and the group discussions took place either in a brightly or dimly lit room. Each participant in the study was asked to rate the intimacy level of the discussion, with higher numbers representing greater intimacy. Determine if the environmental factors affected perceived intimacy. If so, use the LSD test to make all pairwise comparisons. Write a complete conclusion in the context of the problem.

Far Bright	Far-Dim	Close-Bright	Close-Dim
2	4	1	5
1	3	2	6
3	2	1	4
2	4	1	5
1	5	2	7

Two-Way Analysis of Variance

 Dr. Baxter (remember Dr. Baxter from Chapters 10 and 11) was attending a convention of psychotherapists. She was pleased with the interest of her colleagues in the development of her new approach to the treatment of panic disorder.

While having coffee in the lobby of the convention hotel one morning, she was approached by Dr. Salinger, a representative of a well-known and respected drug company. Dr. Salinger informed Dr. Baxter that he had a proposal to make that might be mutually beneficial. He asked if she had ever considered including psychoactive drugs in her work. His company, he told her, had recently developed a new drug (Panic-EA) specifically for sufferers of panic attack. Based on what he had read about Dr. Baxter's work, he felt that the new drug would be particularly effective when used in conjunction with a psychotherapeutic approach like that developed by Dr. Baxter. Dr. Salinger's proposal was that if Dr. Baxter included Panic-EA in her next treatment study, his company would fund the research.

The drug company was interested in the same basic research design used by Dr. Baxter in the first study but wanted to add a second factor: Panic-EA. Thus, Dr. Baxter would once again collect data on panic attack patients receiving no treatment, conventional treatment, or experimental treatment. However, half of each treatment group would receive a placebo and the other half would receive Panic-EA. Dr. Salinger drew a diagram of the research design he had in mind.

Drug

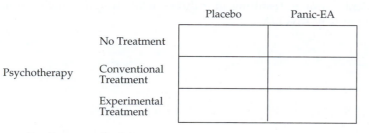

Dr. Baxter asked for some time to consider the proposal. Later that night she thought about the research design and realized that a one-way ANOVA would not be suitable to analyze data she might collect. She needed a statistical test that could accommodate more complex data. She needed a different kind of ANOVA.

In Chapter 11, the one-way analysis of variance, or ANOVA, was introduced as a method for analyzing data that result from the administration of two or more levels of an independent variable. In this chapter, we look at an additional complication: the introduction of another independent variable. When we have more than one independent variable, we use a test called the **two-way analysis of variance,** or **two-way ANOVA.** The variables in this type of test are called **factors.** In Dr. Baxter's new study, the two factors are type of treatment and drug. Let's look at some additional examples of experiments with two-factor ANOVA designs.

Suppose an experimenter wants to examine the effects of task difficulty and anxiety level on problem-solving behavior. She decides to have three levels of task difficulty (easy, moderate, hard) and three levels of anxiety as determined by scores on the Taylor Manifest Anxiety Scale (low, medium, high). The dependent variable is the average time to solve 10 word problems. Because there are three levels of each of her two independent variables (task difficulty, anxiety level), the resulting experiment is called a 3 × 3 **factorial design.** Nine groups are required: Subjects with low anxiety are given easy, moderate, or hard problems to solve; subjects with medium anxiety are given easy, moderate, or hard problems; and subjects with high anxiety are given easy, moderate, or hard problems. That is why the design is called *factorial*—each level of one factor occurs with each level of the second factor.

In another example, a personality psychologist might be interested in the effects of subjects' thrill-seeking tendency and alcohol intake on their performance on a simulated driving task. He first administers a test that measures a tendency for thrill seeking and divides his subject pool into two categories: low and high. Volunteers from each category are given no alcohol, a low dose of alcohol, or a high dose, and their performance is scored on the driving task. This illustrates a 2 × 3 factorial design, because there are two levels of thrill seeking and three levels of alcohol.

Of course, each of the studies we've described has exemplified a two-factor ANOVA design. Theoretically, there's nothing to prevent us from adding other independent variables. In each of the studies outlined, gender could be an additional independent variable, resulting in a three-factor design, which would be analyzed by a three-way ANOVA.

MAIN EFFECTS AND EFFECTS OF INTERACTION

In a two-factor experiment, the effect of *each* independent variable, considered by itself, is called a **main effect.** Returning to Dr. Baxter's study, let's call type of treatment factor A (row variable) and type of drug factor B (column variable). If we looked at the effect of the treatment while ignoring the type of drug received, we would be looking at the main effect of factor A. Similarly, an examination of the effect of type of drug without considering the treatment would be an examination of the main effect of factor B. Thus, it is possible to look at the data from a two-factor experiment as though we had two separate single-factor studies.

What is special about a factorial design is that in addition to the main effects in a two-factor experiment, there is the possibility of interaction. **Interaction** is related to the joint effect of the two independent variables. An interaction occurs when two factors work together to produce an effect that is more than the effect the factors by themselves produce. If an interaction effect exists, the effect of one factor *depends* on the levels of the second factor. In a sense a factorial design gives us *three* results for the price of two. We could conduct two single-factor studies (two one-way ANOVAs)—one testing Dr. Salinger's drug and another testing Dr. Baxter's therapy treatment. However, if we combine the two studies in a factorial design, we can also measure the interaction effect of the two factors. We will address this issue in more detail later.

Consider the prediction made by Dr. Salinger for the effect of Panic-EA. He thought the drug would be especially effective for patients receiving the experimental treatment. In other words, the effects of the drug were not expected to be uniform across all levels of the treatment. Thus, if asked what the predicted effects of Panic-EA were, Dr. Salinger would say, "It depends." It depends on whether you are talking about the untreated, conventionally treated, or experimentally treated patients. Panic-EA was expected to reduce panic in all patients, but the reduction should be most marked in the patients receiving Dr. Baxter's experimental treatment.

One way to look at interaction or lack of it in a factorial study is to graph the results. A typical graph shows the mean dependent variable scores for factor B plotted over levels of factor A. The observed data for Salinger's predictions and some hypothetical alternative results are graphed in Figure 12-1.

If there is no interaction between factors, the graph of the data will show essentially parallel lines or lines that are approximately equidistant at each data point. An example of this is shown in the middle graph of the figure. Here, the placebo patients have a higher mean than patients receiving Panic-EA at each level of factor A.

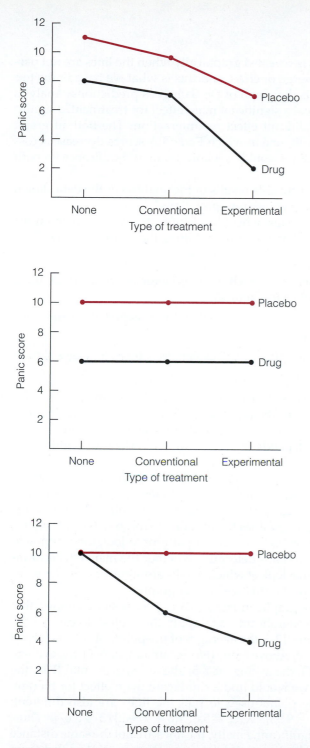

Figure 12-1 Graphs of Dr. Salinger's predictions and alternative results. [Note: These figures use line graphs to represent levels of panic scores for separate groups (treatment conditions). You may recognize the inconsistency of this use with the guidelines for using line graphs we presented in Chapter 4. In fact, there is a growing trend for researchers (and journals) to prefer bar graphs for this type of data, because the levels of the therapy treatment are separate, discrete groups. However, there is a long tradition for patterns of effects and interactions to be shown with line graphs, as we have done here.]

Interaction between factors is revealed graphically when the lines are not parallel, especially when they converge or cross, and this is what we have in the top and bottom graphs. At the top is the graph of Dr. Salinger's predictions. Analysis of the data would probably reveal a significant main effect for treatment, a significant effect for drug, and a significant effect for interaction. The bottom graph shows another hypothetical result, one in which Panic-EA scores decrease across levels of factor A. Again, an analysis would probably result in significance for both main effects and the interaction.

Note that we're given some probable results of the analysis of the data shown in the graphs. How did we arrive at these interpretations?

To interpret a graph of cell means, where levels of factor A are shown on the X-axis and levels of factor B are plotted as different lines, the following "rules" are beneficial:

1. If the averages of the points above each level of factor A are unequal, there may be a significant main effect for factor A.

2. If the averages of the points used to plot the lines are unequal, there may be a significant main effect for factor B.

3. If the lines converge or cross—that is, are *not parallel*—there may be a significant interaction.

Note that for each of the "rules," there *may* be a significant main effect or a significant interaction; that is, as in the one-way ANOVA, the two-way ANOVA involves the computation of F ratios. Whether an F ratio is large enough to allow us to reject a null hypothesis depends in large part on variability within each group (MS_w). Although there may be a great deal of separation between treatment means on the graph, if there is a lot of variability *within* each treatment condition, the appropriate F ratio will be small. Thus, we should view graphs of our means as painted in "broad brush strokes" rather than as precise points. For the same reason, it is quite possible for plotted lines to cross or converge without a significant interaction occurring. The "rules" are clues or patterns to look for in trying to interpret results; the computed F ratios determine whether the main effects or interactions are significant. We must look at which results are significant in our summary table to determine what we should "see" in our graphs.

Assume that for each of the graphs in Figure 12-1, MS_w is small enough that any apparent difference will be significant. Let's apply the "rules" to each of the graphs. In the top graph of Figure 12-1, the averages of the points above each level of therapy (factor A) are different. Above None (No Treatment, or NT), the average is 9.5; above Conventional (CT), the average is 8.5; above Experimental (ET), the average is 4.5. In other words, we would find a significant main effect for therapy treatment. The averages of the points used to plot the lines are also different: $\overline{X}_{placebo} = 9.33$ [$(11 + 10 + 7)/3 = 9.33$]; $\overline{X}_{drug} = 5.67$ [$(8 + 7 + 2)/3 = 5.67$]. Thus, the main effect for the drug is significant. Finally, the lines are not the same distance apart at all treatment levels, indicating a significant interaction. Notice that there is a 5.5-point difference for the experimental treatment, but only a 3-point difference at the other two treatment levels. To summarize, the top graph shows both drug conditions decreasing from NT to CT to ET, indicating a main effect for therapy treatment. It shows the drug groups consistently lower than the placebo groups, indicating a main effect for drug. The lines are not parallel—the greatest decrease for drug occurs for the experimental treatment—indicating interaction.

In the middle graph, the averages of the points above each level of factor A are the same—8 at each treatment level—leading us to conclude that there is not a significant treatment effect. However, there is a drug effect, because the points used to plot the lines average 10 for the placebo and 6 for the drug. The lines are parallel, so the interaction would not be significant.

In the bottom graph, there are different averages of the points above each treatment. For NT, $\overline{X} = 10.0$; for CT, $\overline{X} = 8.0$; and for ET, $\overline{X} = 7.0$. Thus, the effect of treatment may be significant. Similarly, the averages of the points used to plot the line are different ($\overline{X}_{placebo} = 10.0$, $\overline{X}_{drug} = 6.7$), suggesting a significant drug effect. The lines are not parallel, so there is also a significant interaction effect.

ADVANTAGES OF THE TWO-FACTOR DESIGN

Are there advantages to incorporating both independent variables in the same study? What does the two-factor ANOVA design add that could not be learned with two separate one-factor ANOVA experiments?

The main advantage of the two-factor design is that we can test for the presence of an *interaction* between the factors. If we did Dr. Baxter's study first with a placebo and then later with Panic-EA, we could test to see whether the treatment was effective without the drug, and we could test to see whether the treatment was effective with the drug, but there would be no way to do a significance test on the interaction of the drug and the treatment.

A second advantage of the two-factor design is that it allows a *savings in the number of subjects* we need for our study. Suppose Dr. Baxter had decided to do her study without Panic-EA and wanted to have 20 patients at each treatment level. With three levels of treatment, she would need 60 patients. Repeating the study with Panic-EA would require another 60 patients. Thus, doing the study as two one-factor ANOVAs requires 120 subjects.

However, suppose Dr. Baxter actually does the study as a two-factor design with 20 subjects tested under each treatment. In this case, she will need only 60 subjects—30 receiving the placebo and 30 receiving Panic-EA, with 10 of each receiving each type of treatment. Exactly half the number of subjects is needed for the two-factor design as is needed for two one-factor designs.

A third advantage of the two-factor design is an *increase in power* of the statistical tests on the main effects, power defined as the likelihood of rejecting a false null. The two-factor ANOVA design usually has greater power than two separate one-factor designs, because we are separating the total variance into more parts. In doing so, we are removing variance from MS_w. This makes it more likely that we will find a significant effect, because the obtained F value will be larger.

Yet another advantage of the two-factor design is *greater generalizability.* For example, in Dr. Baxter's study we know the effects of one factor for either two or three levels of the other factor. This information is not available with two separate one-way ANOVAs. We know how different treatments affect both patients given the placebo and patients given Panic-EA. We can generalize to more conditions than we could if we had done two one-way ANOVAs.

LOGIC OF THE TWO-WAY ANOVA

Although the equations and the computations are more complicated with the two-way ANOVA than with the one-way ANOVA, the underlying rationale for the tests is the same as that encountered in Chapter 11. The two-factor ANOVA results in three hypothesis tests rather than only one as before. The three tests are as follows:

1. A test of the main effect of factor A. The null hypothesis for the test is that there are no population mean differences among the different levels of factor A.
2. A test of the main effect of factor B. The null hypothesis for the test is that there are no population mean differences among the different levels of factor B.
3. A test of the interaction of factors A and B. The null hypothesis is that there is no interaction (parallel lines in the plot of means).

Analysis of the data results in three F ratios, each having the same general form we encountered in Chapter 11. Each consists of the variance between treatments (for factor A, for factor B, or for the A × B interaction) divided by the variance within treatments. The same error term, variance within treatments, or MS_w, is used for each of the F ratios.

As before, the variance between treatments is assumed to be caused by individual differences, experimental error, and a treatment effect, and the variance within treatments is caused by individual differences and experimental error. Thus, a value of the F ratio close to 1.00 indicates the lack of a treatment effect, and a value much larger than 1.00 suggests a valid treatment effect.

INTERPRETATION OF RESULTS

Basically, interpretation of the two-way ANOVA depends on whether the interaction is significant. If the interaction is not significant, a significant main effect can be analyzed with post hoc tests such as the ones discussed in Chapter 11. For example, suppose Dr. Baxter found that the effect of treatment was significant but the drug and the treatment by drug interaction were not. She could then do pairwise comparisons of the different treatments with either the Tukey HSD or the Fisher LSD or with some other test not discussed in this text.

Unfortunately, the main advantage of the two-factor ANOVA, the ability to test an interaction effect, is a mixed blessing. Although such a test provides important additional information about a study, a positive result—that is, a significant interaction—may complicate the study's interpretation considerably. If Dr. Baxter found a significant interaction between the drug and the type of treatment, her interpretation of a main effect for the drug would be more complicated. The interaction would mean that the effect of the drug would differ from treatment to treatment. Remember that Dr. Baxter and Dr. Salinger predicted that Panic-EA would have a stronger effect when paired with the experimental psychotherapy.

The first step in interpreting a significant interaction is to plot the group means. The resulting graph will indicate by its crossing or converging lines where the interaction is occurring. Further interpretation involves individual group comparisons. For example, we might investigate the interaction by testing to see whether there was a significant effect for the drug for *each* type of therapy. In the bottom graph of Figure 12-1, we might find no significant effect for the drug when there was no treatment, no effect for the drug with conventional treatment, but a significant effect of the drug with the experimental treatment.

The main point here is that a significant interaction effect indicates that interpretation may not be completely straightforward; that is, the action of one factor is not uniform across all levels of the other factor.

A LOOK AT TWO-WAY ANOVA COMPUTATIONS

Although the main goal of this chapter is to offer a basic overview of two-way ANOVA, in this section we present a greatly simplified look at the computations required by the analysis. Let's analyze Dr. Baxter's data, assuming the scores in each treatment condition or group are as shown next. The sums of scores and squared scores are shown in each group, along with row and column totals.

		Placebo	Drug	Row Totals
No Treatment	ΣX ΣX	12, 10, 14, 8, 15, 10, 9, 7, 12, 13 110 1,272	7, 8, 12, 10, 10, 10, 8, 7, 5, 13 90 864	$\Sigma X = 200$ $\Sigma X^2 = 2{,}136$
Conventional Treatment	ΣX ΣX^2	9, 10, 12, 8, 12, 10, 9, 10, 12, 8 100 1,022	8, 9, 4, 3, 10, 4, 6, 5, 8, 3 60 420	$\Sigma X = 160$ $\Sigma X^2 = 1{,}442$
Experimental Treatment	ΣX ΣX^2	10, 12, 10, 12, 9, 8, 7, 6, 8, 8 90 846	0, 4, 3, 2, 6, 1, 2, 4, 5, 3 30 120	$\Sigma X = 120$ $\Sigma X^2 = 966$
Column Totals	ΣX ΣX^2	300 3,140	180 1,404	$\Sigma X = 480$ $\Sigma X^2 = 4{,}544$

a = levels of factor A (treatment) = 3
b = levels of factor B (drug) = 2
N_g = number of patients per group = 10

(cont.)

N = total number of subjects = 60
ΣX^2 = sum of *all* squared scores
ΣX = sum of *all* scores
ΣX_R^2 = sum of squared scores in a given row; row variable is factor A, or treatment
ΣX_R = sum of scores in a given row
ΣX_C^2 = sum of squared scores in a column; column variable is factor B, or drug
ΣX_C = sum of scores in a column

There are six sums of squares to compute for the analysis, but two can be found by subtraction. The following are the simplified equations for the SS that we need:

$$SS_{tot} = \Sigma X^2 - \frac{(\Sigma X)^2}{N}$$

$$SS_{cells} = \sum_g \left[\frac{(\Sigma X_g)^2}{N_g} \right] - \frac{(\Sigma X)^2}{N} \qquad SS_{cells} \ (SS \text{ between all groups})$$

$$SS_A = \sum_R \left[\frac{(\Sigma X_R)^2}{(N_g)(b)} \right] - \frac{(\Sigma X)^2}{N} \qquad SS \text{ for factor A}$$

$$SS_B = \sum_C \left[\frac{(\Sigma X_C)^2}{(N_g)(a)} \right] - \frac{(\Sigma X)^2}{N} \qquad SS \text{ for factor B}$$

$$SS_{AB} = SS_{cells} - SS_A - SS_B \qquad \text{interaction } SS$$

$$SS_w = SS_{tot} - SS_{cells} \qquad \text{within-groups } SS, \text{ or the error term}$$

SS_w can be computed directly from the following equation:

$$SS_w = \sum_g \left[\sum X_g^2 - \frac{(\Sigma X_g)^2}{N_g} \right]$$

Now let's compute the sums of squares:

$$SS_{tot} = 4{,}544 - \frac{(480)^2}{60} = 4{,}544 - 3{,}840 = 704,$$

$$SS_{cells} = \left[\frac{(110)^2}{10} + \frac{(100)^2}{10} + \frac{(90)^2}{10} + \frac{(90)^2}{10} + \frac{(60)^2}{10} + \frac{(30)^2}{10} \right] - \frac{(480)^2}{60}$$
$$= (1{,}210 + 1{,}000 + 810 + 810 + 360 + 90) - 3{,}840 = 4{,}280 - 3{,}840 = 440,$$

$$SS_A = \left[\frac{(200)^2}{20} + \frac{(160)^2}{20} + \frac{(120)^2}{20} \right] - \frac{(480)^2}{60} = (2{,}000 + 1{,}280 + 720) - 3{,}840$$
$$= 4{,}000 - 3{,}840 = 160,$$

$$SS_B = \left[\frac{(300)^2}{30} + \frac{(180)^2}{30} \right] - \frac{(480)^2}{60} = (3{,}000 + 1{,}080) - 3{,}840$$
$$= 4{,}080 - 3{,}840 = 240,$$

$$SS_{AB} = SS_{cells} - SS_A - SS_B = 440 - 160 - 240 = 40,$$

$$SS_w = SS_{tot} - SS_{cells} = 704 - 440 = 264.$$

Alternatively, we could compute SS_w directly, as follows:

$$SS_w = \left[1{,}272 - \frac{(110)^2}{10}\right] + \left[864 - \frac{(90)^2}{10}\right] + \left[1{,}022 - \frac{(100)^2}{10}\right] +$$

$$\left[420 - \frac{(60)^2}{10}\right] + \left[846 - \frac{(90)^2}{10}\right] + \left[120 - \frac{(30)^2}{10}\right] = 264.$$

As with the one-way ANOVA, computing the sums of squares is only the first step in analyzing the variance. We must now determine degrees of freedom for each SS and use df to compute the mean squares.

$$df_{tot} = N - 1 = 60 - 1 = 59,$$
$$df_{cells} = (a \times b) - 1 = (3 \times 2) - 1 = 5,$$
$$df_A = a - 1 = 3 - 1 = 2,$$
$$df_B = b - 1 = 2 - 1 = 1,$$
$$df_{AB} = df_{cells} - df_A - df_B = 5 - 2 - 1 = 2, \text{ or}$$
$$df_{AB} = df_A \times df_B = 2 \times 1 = 2,$$
$$df_w = df_{tot} - df_{cells} = 59 - 5 = 54,$$
$$MS_A = \frac{SS_A}{df_A} = \frac{160}{2} = 80,$$
$$MS_B = \frac{SS_B}{df_B} = \frac{240}{1} = 240,$$
$$MS_{AB} = \frac{SS_{AB}}{df_{AB}} = \frac{40}{2} = 20,$$
$$MS_w = \frac{SS_w}{df_w} = \frac{264}{54} = 4.89.$$

There are also three F ratios to compute, as shown here.

$$F_A = \frac{MS_A}{MS_w} = \frac{80}{4.89} = 16.36,$$
$$F_B = \frac{MS_B}{MS_w} = \frac{240}{4.89} = 49.08,$$
$$F_{AB} = \frac{MS_{AB}}{MS_w} = \frac{20}{4.89} = 4.09.$$

As before, we can summarize our results in a table.

Two-Way ANOVA Summary Table

Source	SS	df	MS	F	p
Between groups (cells)	440	5	88		
A (treatment)	160	2	80	16.36 $(df = 2, 54)$	< .01
B (drug)	240	1	240	49.08 $(df = 1, 54)$	< .01
A × B (treatment × drug)	40	2	20	4.09 $(df = 2, 54)$	< .05
Within groups	264	54	4.89		
Total	704	59			

For $df = 2, 60$, the critical values from Table C in Appendix 4 are 3.15 at the 5% level and 4.98 at the 1% level. These df, $df = 2, 60$, are the closest df in the table to the df we had in the study for the treatment comparison and for the test of the interaction (treatment by drug). For more conservative tests, we could use the critical F values for $df = 2, 40$. Either way, the result would be the same: We reject the null hypothesis at the 1% level ($p < .01$) for the treatment and drug main effects and at the 5% level ($p < .05$) for the interaction.

Our conclusion: All effects were significant, indicating that both the type of treatment and the drug reduced panic. The significant interaction confirmed the prediction that the combination of Panic-EA and experimental treatment was especially effective. Post hoc comparisons would be needed to confirm the statistical significance of each of these *cell* differences.

SUMMARY

This chapter presented the simplest of the factorial designs: the two-factor or two-way analysis of variance. The two-factor design differs from the one-way ANOVA discussed in Chapter 11 by having different levels of two independent variables rather than only one. In a factorial design, each level of one factor occurs with each level of the second factor.

A test of the effect of each of the independent variables, considered in isolation, is called a main effect. The row variable is called factor A, and the column variable is called factor B. The joint effect of the two variables or factors is called interaction.

A typical graph of data from a two-factor study shows the mean dependent variable scores for factor B plotted over levels of factor A. Unequal averages of the points (*not* a flat, straight line) above each level of factor A indicate a significant main effect for factor A. If the averages of the points used to plot the lines are unequal, there is probably a significant factor B main effect. A significant interaction between factors is shown by converging or crossing lines (nonparallel lines) on the graph.

The two-factor ANOVA results in three hypothesis tests or *F* ratios: one for the main effect of factor A, one for the main effect of factor B, and one for the interaction of A and B. As in Chapter 11, if an *F* ratio has a value much above 1.00, the null hypothesis for the test will probably be rejected.

The main advantage of the two-factor ANOVA design is the test for an interaction between the factors. A significant interaction makes interpretation of the results more challenging but provides more information. Other advantages include a savings in the number of subjects required, greater generalizability, and an increase in the power of the tests on the main effects. If there is no interaction, interpretation of a significant main effect is the same as it was in Chapter 11.

EXERCISES

1. For each of the following graphs, tell the probable outcome of each of the significance tests:

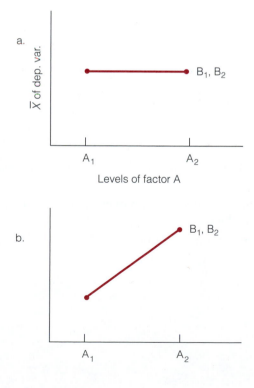

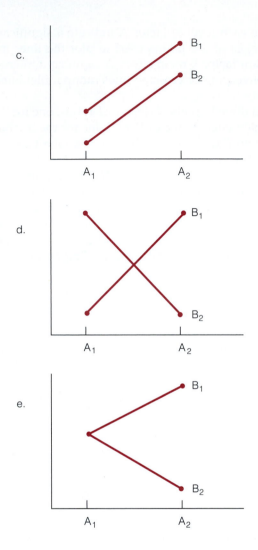

2. In what way is a two-way ANOVA more economical than two one-way ANOVAs on the same variables?

3. What is the main advantage of the two-factor design over the one-factor design? Why is the advantage a mixed blessing?

4. What is the first step in interpreting a significant interaction?

5. How is a significant interaction revealed graphically?

13

Correlation and Regression

Joe Galvan was 5 feet 2 inches tall. He was also the president of Galvan's Nuts and Bolts, a large and prosperous company. Joe picked up that day's *Wall Street Journal* and almost fell out of his chair. There, on the front page, was a story about something he had always suspected: "Tall Workers Earn More Money."

According to the writer, a variety of studies revealed that height is related to salary, with short individuals earning less money than their taller counterparts. The author even speculated that the salary–height relationship explained the lower salaries paid to women.

Joe considered the implications of the article. Then he decided to see whether he could corroborate the article's theory by looking at his own company managers' heights and salaries. He had the human resources manager collect the information and give it to him that afternoon. The 14 managers were listed from tallest to shortest as follows:

Name	Height (in inches)	Salary (in thousands of dollars)
Bill Robertson	77	47.1
Sam Kline	74	45.5
Al Krieger	73	46.2
Sue Milanovich	72	46.1
Mort Fein	70	42.8
Doug Johnson	70	38.3

(cont.)

293

Name	Height (in inches)	Salary (in thousands of dollars)
Sarah Chu	69	45.4
Tom Garibaldi	68	36.5
Amelia Gonzalez	67	42.1
Ann Margulies	67	37.2
Lisa McMillen	66	34.1
Petra Dahl	64	35.1
Tashia Stone	63	33.1
Fiona Lowery	60	33.0

Joe surveyed the list in disbelief. The *Wall Street Journal* was right. There was a relationship between height and salary, and the evidence for it was right here in his own company.

In this example the relationship, spurious or not, is apparent. However, there are situations in which the relationship is less obvious, such as when we have much more data or when the scores are not strongly related. In these and many other instances, it is helpful to be able to quantify the degree of relationship. In this chapter, we will look at techniques to quantify the relationship between variables and will discover a method for prediction based on correlation.

LINEAR CORRELATION

Correlation, a term used by most of us, is defined as the degree of relationship between two or more variables. Correlation literally refers to the *co-relationship* between variables. In this chapter, we will discuss **linear correlation,** or the degree to which a straight line best describes the relationship between two variables. Of course, not all relationships are linear. Many take complex, curvilinear forms. However, the linear relationship is the simplest and most common case. The idea of a straight line, or linear relationship, between two variables will become more apparent when we look at graphs in the next section.

To illustrate what is meant by correlation, consider the variables height and weight. In general, the taller you are, the more you weigh, and we say that the two variables are highly correlated. In other words, the variables go together and are related to each other. No doubt, many of us know an exception to the rule that height and weight are related. We may know someone who is only 5 feet tall and weighs 237 pounds or someone who is 6 feet tall and weighs 135 pounds. When we said that there is a correlation between height and weight, we didn't say it is perfect! As long as the relationship between two variables is not perfect, there will be exceptions.

Classes of Correlation

The degree of relationship between two variables may assume an infinite number of values ranging from −1 to +1. It is customary to speak of three different classes of correlation: positive, negative, and zero. Correlations between 0 and +1 are called positive, and correlations between 0 and −1 are called negative.

Positive Correlation   One example of positive correlation is the relationship that Joe Galvan explored, the correlation between height and salary. A **positive correlation** between variables exists when a high score on one variable is associated with a high score on the other or when a low score on one variable is associated with a low score on the other. In other words, positive correlation implies a direct relationship between the variables.

Other examples of positive correlation include height and weight, brain size and body size, and time spent studying for an exam and the score earned on the exam. Thus, we would expect taller people to weigh more, bigger animals to have larger brains, and people who spend more time studying to earn higher scores. Suppose we have actually collected some data on time spent studying and exam performance. It might resemble the following:

Student	Number of Hours Spent Studying	Exam Score
A	28	95
B	25	95
C	3	58
D	10	75
E	0	44
F	15	83
G	20	91
H	24	87
I	7	65
J	8	70

One way to study the relationship between the two variables is to look at the scatterplot of the data. The **scatterplot** is a graph that plots pairs of scores, with the scores on one of the variables plotted on the X axis and the scores on the other variable plotted on the Y axis. A scatterplot of the students' exam scores as a function of time spent studying is shown in Figure 13-1.

In general, if the pattern of points on the scatterplot of some data falls pretty closely around a straight line slanting upward to the right, we are dealing with a positive correlation. Figure 13-1 reveals a strong linear relationship between the two variables, because most of the points are close to the straight line. It is the line that best fits the data. (We will discuss how to compute such lines later in the

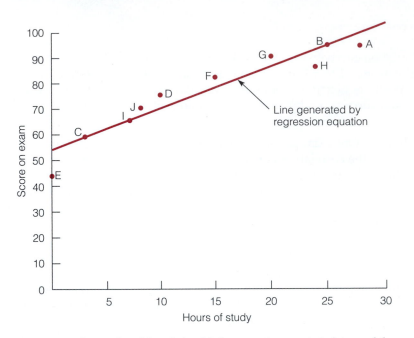

Figure 13-1   Scatterplot of the relationship between time spent studying and the score on an exam. The line best fitting the data is shown.

chapter using the linear regression equation.) Because the line slants upward to the right, the correlation is positive; that is, a high score on one variable (study time) is related to a high score on the other variable (exam score). Later we will study how to compute statistics to represent the degree of linear relationship, but for now let's consider other types of correlation.

Negative Correlation   A **negative correlation** is one in which a high score on one variable is associated with a low score on the other. In other words, there is an inverse relationship between the two variables. One example of negative correlation is the relationship between speed over 55 miles per hour and fuel economy; that is, the faster you drive over 55, the fewer miles per gallon you get. Another example is the relationship between family size and IQ; correlational research has revealed that larger family sizes are associated with lower IQ scores. (Note that the relationship is correlational and tells us nothing about causality.) Over 100 years ago, a famous psychologist named Hermann Ebbinghaus found a negative correlation between the number of times he rehearsed a list of nonsense syllables and the amount of time it took him to relearn it 24 hours later. Specifically, frequent repetitions of a list resulted in less time to relearn.

As another example of negative correlation, suppose we have noticed that students who live off campus seem less involved in campus activities and organizations than students who live on campus. To investigate this observation, we survey students in 10 classes. We record the percentage of students in each class who live off campus and the percentage who are involved in at least one activity or group. The data are given here:

Class	% Off Campus	% Involved
A	100	0
B	40	95
C	95	5
D	90	20
E	92	30
F	85	40
G	55	50
H	60	70
I	98	0
J	20	100

As can be seen from the scatterplot in Figure 13-2, the points form a reasonably close approximation to a straight line that slopes downward to the right. (The line best fitting the data has been drawn.) The slope downward to the right indicates a negative correlation. Thus, our observation was correct: Living off campus is associated with less involvement in campus activities and organizations.

Zero Correlation   The final category of correlation is **zero correlation.** Here there is no relationship between the variables; a high score on one variable is just as likely to be associated with a low score as it is with a high score or even with a

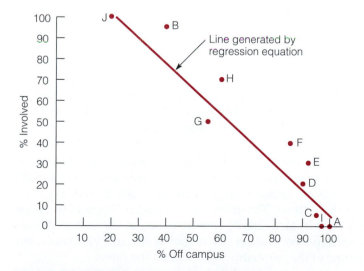

Figure 13-2   Scatterplot of the negative correlation between percentage of students living off campus and percentage of students involved in campus activities. The line best fitting the data is shown.

medium score on the other variable. In other words, knowing a value for one variable provides no information that will help predict a corresponding value on the other variable. A classic example of zero correlation is the relationship between the number and location of bumps on the skull and the intelligence or special abilities of a person. Despite the lack of such a relationship, phrenology was *the* science of the mind for a number of years and big business for many more. Another example of zero correlation is the relationship between the length of the lines in the palm of your hand and your life span.

To illustrate a scatterplot of zero correlation, suppose a professor wants to see whether there is a relationship between the order in which students turn in test papers and their scores on the exam. As the students turn in their papers, the instructor adds a number to the top of the test, indicating the order of completion. After the tests have been graded, the following data are noted:

Order of Completion	Score
1	95
2	57
3	90
4	70
5	75
6	65
7	60
8	85
9	87
10	75
11	76
12	72
13	93
14	85

The scatterplot of the data, shown in Figure 13-3, reveals essentially a random pattern of points; that is, the scores seem to be "scattered" and don't seem to be well described by a straight line (or any other manner of line).

Strength of the Correlation   Before leaving the classes of correlation, we should note that negative correlation is just as meaningful as positive correlation. Knowing that a correlation is negative rather than positive just tells us that the relationship is inverse rather than direct. *The strength of the relationship is given by the absolute value of the correlation.* In fact, simply reversing one of the scales of measurement will convert a positive correlation to a negative one and vice versa, but the strength (absolute value) of the correlation will remain the same.

To illustrate, we earlier considered the direct relationship between amount of study time and an exam score. Suppose that instead of recording the score on the exam as the *Y* variable, we noted the number of errors made by each student. Now

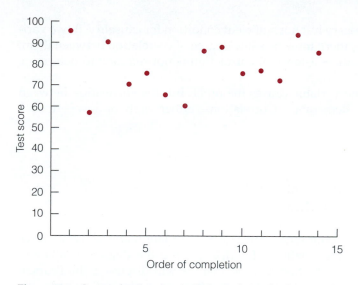

Figure 13-3 Scatterplot showing the lack of relationship between the order of completion of a test paper and the test score.

we would find that the more time a student spent studying, the fewer mistakes he or she would make, and vice versa. In other words, we would now have an inverse relationship instead of a direct one. Thus, a negative correlation is just as much of a relationship—and is just as meaningful—as a positive one.

Correlation and Causation

A final point about correlation that is often ignored or overlooked is that correlation does not *necessarily* mean one variable *causes* the other. For example, there is a positive correlation between the amount of television that children watch and their aggressiveness. Many people conclude from this that TV watching causes aggressiveness, although it is possible that highly aggressive children prefer to watch television over other activities, such as reading books. It is also possible that some other factor is responsible for both TV watching *and* aggressiveness. For example, it may be that children whose parents are more aggressive tend to watch more TV and are more aggressive. Clearly, it is not as simple as "TV causes aggression."

Similarly, many studies have reported a significant positive correlation between the level of cholesterol (a fatty substance) in the blood and heart disease. Does this mean that high cholesterol *causes* coronary artery disease? Again, the answer is not necessarily. It is possible that some other factor, such as low blood levels of vitamin B6, is responsible for atherosclerosis (clogged arteries). Foods high in cholesterol may be deficient in vitamin B6, with the result that a diet high in cholesterol leads to heart disease. As you can see, however, coronary artery disease may result from the vitamin deficiency rather than from an excess of cholesterol.

Correlation is a necessary but not sufficient condition for causality. If two variables are causally linked, there must be some degree of correlation between them; it is *necessary*. However, the existence of correlation is not *sufficient* to determine causality.

It is possible that one variable causes the other, but the correlation between them doesn't prove it. Remember: Correlation—either high or low—doesn't prove causation.

THE PEARSON PRODUCT-MOMENT CORRELATION COEFFICIENT

Now that we have talked about what is meant by correlation and about its three classes, it is time to consider methods for determining the degree of relationship between the variables. The first method that we will discuss is the **Pearson product-moment correlation coefficient,** or the **Pearson r.** Formally stated, the Pearson *r* is the mean of the *z*-score products for *X* and *Y* pairs, where *X* stands for one variable and *Y* stands for the other. The term *product-moment* is used because the value of *r* is a function of the *moment*, or potency, of the *z*-score products. The formula for *r* based on the definition is:

FORMULA 13-1   *Pearson* **r** *(definitional formula)*

$$\text{Pearson } r = \frac{\Sigma z_X z_Y}{N}$$

where z_X and z_Y are the *z* scores for the *X* and *Y* variables, respectively, and *N* is the number of pairs of scores.

To compute *r* with the definitional formula, we must first compute the *z* score for each *X* and for each *Y*. Then we multiply the *z* scores for each *X-Y* pair, sum the products, and divide by *N*. As you can imagine, computing *r* with the definitional formula is quite tedious, particularly if *N* is large. For this reason, we will introduce a computational, or raw-score, formula to compute *r*. However, before we leave the definitional formula, let's use it to get an intuitive feel for why a direct relationship between variables results in a positive value for *r* and why an inverse relationship results in a negative value.

Understanding the Pearson *r* Definitional Formula

Suppose we have a sample of *X-Y* pairs in which there is a direct relationship between the variables; that is, high scores are associated with high scores and low scores with low scores. What does a *z* score tell us? It tells us the location of a particular score in a distribution relative to the distribution's mean. If a score is above the mean, the sign of the corresponding z score is positive; if a score is below the mean, it converts to a negative z score. Thus, with a direct relationship, a z score on the X variable is likely to be paired with a z score on the Y variable having the same sign, either positive or negative. When the products are found before summing, the majority will be positive, resulting in a positive value for r.

Similarly, for an inverse relationship, high scores on one variable will tend to be paired with low scores on the other variable, with the result that paired z scores will have opposite signs. The products will tend to be negative, resulting in a negative value for r.

In the case of no relationship, or zero correlation, there won't be any pattern to the signs of paired z scores; that is, a positive z score is just as likely to be paired with a negative z score as it is to be paired with a positive z score. The result is that the cross products will be a mixture of positive and negative values that tend to cancel each other out, resulting in a low value for r.

One final note before the computational formula is introduced: *The range of the Pearson r is from +1 to −1.* A positive value for r indicates a direct relationship between the variables; a negative value indicates an inverse relationship. The closer the value of r is to 1, the greater is the correlation. If the value of r is close to 0, in either a positive or a negative direction, we are probably dealing with an example of zero correlation.

Correlation, Variance, and Covariance

Another approach to understanding the Pearson correlation is based on the familiar concept of the variance, which we first introduced in Chapter 6. We have used the variance (or standard deviation) in the formulas for the one-sample t test, the two-sample t test (remember s^2_{pooled}), and in computing MS_w to calculate the F ratio in ANOVA. We will now use the variance and its close "relative," the covariance, to help understand the correlation formula and to introduce the computational formula for r.

Scores Varying With Themselves and With Other Scores: The Variance and the Covariance   In Chapter 6, the following defining formula was introduced for the sample variance:

$$s^2 = \frac{\Sigma(X - \overline{X})^2}{N - 1}.$$

If we rewrite the squared term in the numerator, we have

$$s^2 = \frac{\Sigma(X - \overline{X})(X - \overline{X})}{N - 1}.$$

We can think of this formula as describing how scores vary *with themselves*. For each value of X—whether high or low—that score varies perfectly with itself. We could also say that each X *covaries* perfectly with itself.

However, what if one of the X measures is something else? Suppose that instead of measuring weight (X) and how these measures of weight vary "with themselves," instead we measure height (Y) and want to consider how X varies with Y, or how weight and height vary together. Remember that for each person we measure a pair of scores, a weight (X) and a height (Y). These scores can vary (or deviate) from their overall means. Thus, we can express this covariation by the product of the deviations ($X - \overline{X}$) and ($Y - \overline{Y}$), which will give us the defining formula for a new statistic called the covariance:

$$\text{cov}_{XY} = \frac{\Sigma(X - \overline{X})(Y - \overline{Y})}{N - 1}.$$

We now define the **covariance** as the extent to which two variables vary together. Notice the similarity between this formula and the previous one for s^2. Actually, you can now see that the covariance is the more general formula that can express the covariation of *any* two variables, X and Y. The variance, then, is a *special case* of the covariance of X and X—the variance of a variable with itself. By "special case" we mean that one formula can be mathematically derived from the other formula. In this case, the formula for the variance can be obtained easily by substituting ($X - \overline{X}$) for ($Y - \overline{Y}$) in the covariance formula.

We now must consider standardization. Remember that in Chapter 6, in which we defined a z score, we took the deviation of a score (X) from its mean ($\overline{X}$) and *standardized* it by dividing by s. This gave us the following:

$$z = \frac{X - \overline{X}}{s}.$$

Consider the variance, s^2. If we similarly standardize the variance by dividing it by s, we simply have the *standard* deviation:

$$\frac{s^2}{s} = s.$$

Now we want to standardize the covariance. However, the covariance involves two variables, X and Y, so to get the standardized covariance, we must divide by s_X and s_Y. When we do so, we have a very simple formula for the Pearson correlation:

$$r = \frac{\text{cov}_{XY}}{s_X s_Y}.$$

Now that we know what the covariance is, we can think of r simply as a standardized covariance between X and Y. The advantage to thinking of r in terms of this formula is that it consists of *familiar terms*—standard deviations of X and Y in the denominator and the "variance" between X and Y (covariance) in the numerator.

To derive the computational formula, we substitute the computational formulas for the standard deviations of X and Y, substitute the computational formula for the covariance, a modified version of the computational formula for s^2 in which ΣX^2 is replaced with ΣXY and $(\Sigma X)^2$ is replaced with $(\Sigma X)(\Sigma Y)$, and do some canceling.

Now we can consider the computational formula that is derived from either of the definitional formulas and has been reduced to its simplest computational form:

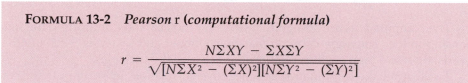

FORMULA 13-2 *Pearson r (computational formula)*

$$r = \frac{N\Sigma XY - \Sigma X \Sigma Y}{\sqrt{[N\Sigma X^2 - (\Sigma X)^2][N\Sigma Y^2 - (\Sigma Y)^2]}}$$

When confronted with a formula as involved as Formula 13-2, the first thing we need to do is look at it to see exactly what we are asked to compute. Taking the components individually, we see that there is almost nothing here that we have not seen before. Specifically, we need to determine the values of the following terms: N, ΣXY, ΣX, ΣY, ΣX^2, and ΣY^2. The only new term is ΣXY, which is found by multiplying each X by each Y and summing the result. Let's use Formula 13-2 to compute the correlation between height and salary in Joe Galvan's company. Here are the data:

Employee	Height (X)	X^2	Salary (Y)	Y^2	XY
A	77	5,929	47.1	2,218.41	3,626.7
B	74	5,476	45.5	2,070.25	3,367.0
C	73	5,329	46.2	2,134.44	3,372.6
D	72	5,184	46.1	2,125.21	3,319.2
E	70	4,900	42.8	1,831.84	2,996.0
F	70	4,900	38.3	1,466.89	2,681.0
G	69	4,761	45.4	2,061.16	3,132.6
H	68	4,624	36.5	1,332.25	2,482.0
I	67	4,489	42.1	1,772.41	2,820.7
J	67	4,489	37.2	1,383.84	2,492.4
K	66	4,356	34.1	1,162.81	2,250.6
L	64	4,096	35.1	1,232.01	2,246.4
M	63	3,969	33.1	1,095.61	2,085.3
N	60	3,600	33.0	1,089.00	1,980.0
	$\Sigma X = 960$	$\Sigma X^2 = 66,102$	$\Sigma Y = 562.5$	$\Sigma Y^2 = 22,976.13$	$\Sigma XY = 38,852.5$

Computing for r, we get

$$r = \frac{N\Sigma XY - \Sigma X\Sigma Y}{\sqrt{[N\Sigma X^2 - (\Sigma X)^2][N\Sigma Y^2 - (\Sigma Y)^2]}}$$

$$= \frac{(14)(38,852.5) - (960)(562.5)}{\sqrt{[(14)(66,102) - 960^2][(14)(22,976.13) - 562.5^2]}}$$

$$= \frac{543,935 - 540,000}{\sqrt{(3,828)(5,259.57)}} = \frac{3,935}{4,487.05} = .88.$$

The computations are straightforward, and the Pearson r, indicating the relationship in Joe's company between managers' height and salary, is $+.88$. In other words, there is a high positive relationship between the variables.

To illustrate the computation of a negative correlation, let's compute the correlation coefficient for the data on off-campus living and student involvement. The data and computations are as follows:

Class	% Off Campus (X)	X^2	% Involved (Y)	Y^2	XY
A	100	10,000	0	0	0
B	40	1,600	95	9,025	3,800
C	95	9,025	5	25	475
D	90	8,100	20	400	1,800
E	92	8,464	30	900	2,760
F	85	7,225	40	1,600	3,400
G	55	3,025	50	2,500	2,750
H	60	3,600	70	4,900	4,200
I	98	9,604	0	0	0
J	20	400	100	10,000	2,000
	$\Sigma X = 735$	$\Sigma X^2 = 61,043$	$\Sigma Y = 410$	$\Sigma Y^2 = 29,350$	$\Sigma XY = 21,185$

$$r = \frac{N\Sigma XY - \Sigma X\Sigma Y}{\sqrt{[N\Sigma X^2 - (\Sigma X)^2][N\Sigma Y^2 - (\Sigma Y)^2]}}$$

$$= \frac{(10)(21,185) - (735)(410)}{\sqrt{[(10)(61,043) - 735^2][(10)(29,350) - 410^2]}}$$

$$= \frac{211,850 - 301,350}{\sqrt{(70,205)(125,400)}} = \frac{-89,500}{93,828.07} = -.95.$$

It may help you to evaluate a correlation coefficient of $-.95$ to recall that the range of r is from $+1$ to -1. Thus, the value of r that expresses a perfect direct relationship between two variables is $+1$, whereas -1 expresses a perfect inverse relationship. Anything close to $r = 0$ indicates no relationship between the variables. However, when we say close to 0, how close do we mean? To answer this question, let's look at how to test r for significance.

Testing r for Significance

To test r for significance, we first assume there is no relationship in the population between the two variables. In other words, we make the assumption that in the population from which our sample was drawn the two variables are not related. We assume that the underlying population correlation coefficient, ρ or rho, is zero. This assumption of no relationship in the population is yet another version of the null hypothesis.

If it is true that the underlying population correlation coefficient is zero, what is the likelihood or probability of obtaining a sample correlation coefficient as deviant as the one we obtained? At this point, it may be helpful to consider an actual correlation coefficient based on a sample.

In the problem we just solved, the correlation between off-campus living and student involvement was $-.95$. What is the probability of obtaining a sample of size 10 with a correlation coefficient as deviant as .95 from a population in which off-campus living and student involvement are not related? Most of the samples of size 10 from a population with a zero coefficient would have coefficients fairly close to zero and only a few samples would have values as extreme as the one we obtained. To actually determine the probability of our sample value, we would need to know the standard deviation of the distribution of sample coefficients or we would have to estimate it. However, as with the t test, the determination of the actual probability is unnecessary.

Instead, we can refer to a table containing correlation coefficients so deviant that they occur less than 5% or 1% of the time in samples of a given size drawn from a population with a zero coefficient. The table is Table E, and its title indicates that it contains values of r at the 5% and 1% levels of significance. In other words, if our sample value exceeds the values in the table for the appropriate degrees of freedom, we reject the null hypothesis and conclude that the sample was *not* drawn from a population with a zero correlation coefficient. If the null hypothesis is rejected, we say that a significant relationship exists between the variables in question.

Looking at the table, we see that the left column is labeled "Degrees of Freedom" or df. In the case of r, $df = N - 2$, where N is the number of pairs of scores. The two restrictions placed on r have to do with the fact that r measures the degree of linear relationship between X and Y. Both restrictions are required in fitting a straight line to a sample of score pairs.

In the example we've been considering, $N = 10$ and $df = N - 2 = 10 - 2 = 8$. For $df = 8$, the coefficient required for significance at the 5% level is .632. Because $-.95$ is larger in absolute value than .632, we can reject the null hypothesis at the 5% level and conclude that a relationship probably exists between the two variables. We can also reject the null hypothesis at the 1% level as $-.95$ is larger in absolute value than .765, the critical table value. In summary, we have found, by referring to a table of critical values for r, that the probability of obtaining a correlation coefficient as large as the one we obtained from a population for which $\rho = 0$ is less than .01.

Thus, we decide that, because the probability of our obtained sample value is so small given that the population correlation coefficient is really zero, it is only reasonable to conclude that the population coefficient is *not* zero. It is likely that a relationship exists between the variables "off-campus living" and "student involvement." Because we rejected the null hypothesis at the 5% (or 1%) level, does this mean that the population coefficient is not zero? Unfortunately, the answer is not an unequivocal yes. Rejecting the null hypothesis means that it is very unlikely that a coefficient as large as we got would be found in a sample drawn from a population with a zero correlation: very unlikely but not impossible. We could obtain a sample with a high correlation coefficient from a population in which $\rho = 0$, but in our example the probability was less than .01.

Let's apply our seven-step procedure to test the null hypothesis for the Pearson r.

1. $H_0: \rho = 0$; that is, our sample came from a population in which there is no linear relationship between off-campus living and student involvement.

2. $H_1: \rho \neq 0$. This means there is a relationship between off-campus living and student involvement in the population we've sampled.

3. Set $\alpha = .05$.

4. *Rejection Rule:* Reject H_0 if $|r_{comp}| \geq r_{crit}$ with $df = N - 2$, where $r_{.05}$ $(df = 8) = .632$ and $r_{.01}$ $(df = 8) = .765$.

5. *Computation:* We've already computed r and found it to be $-.95$.

6. *Decision:* Because $|r_{comp}| = .95 > .765$, we reject H_0, $p < .01$.

7. *Conclusion:* There is a significant inverse relationship between off-campus living and student involvement; students who live off campus are less likely to be involved in campus activities than students who live on campus. We can write our result as follows: $r(8) = -.95, p < .01$.

The Effect of Range on Correlation

To properly determine the relationship between two variables, we must use a full range of scores on both variables. Restricting the range of either the X or the Y variable lowers the correlation. To illustrate, suppose there is a high positive correlation between SAT scores and freshman academic performance measured by grade point average. A scatterplot of data based on a large number of students is shown in Figure 13-4.

As you can see, the scatterplot of *all* the points indicates a high correlation that would be well summarized by a line sloping upward to the right. However, what if we look at the restricted portion of the plot shown between the vertical lines on the graph? Within this restricted range on the X variable, the correlation may be

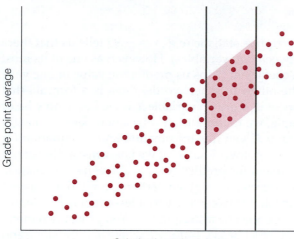

Figure 13-4 Scatterplot showing the effect of restricting the range on correlation.

quite low. Thus, low correlation may reflect a restricted range on either variable rather than a lack of relationship in the population.

ᑐ CHECKING YOUR PROGRESS

A psychologist has developed a new intelligence test based on brain wave activity. She wants to determine its reliability; that is, she wants to see the degree to which the test yields the same score each time it is administered to a person. To measure its reliability, she gives the test to 12 selected persons on two separate occasions, with an intertest interval of 3 weeks. Scores on the test range from 1 to 25, and the data from the 12 individuals are shown here. Compute the correlation coefficient and test it for significance.

Subject #	Score 1	Score 2	Subject #	Score 1	Score 2
1	3	5	7	11	12
2	22	17	8	13	15
3	19	21	9	7	9
4	18	16	10	6	4
5	15	17	11	20	22
6	10	8	12	18	10

Answer: $r = .85$. The correlation coefficient is .85, which is significant ($p < .01$). The conclusion is that the intelligence test has good reliability.

The Linear Regression Equation

So far, we've looked at r as a descriptive statistic (e.g., $r = -.95$ tells us that there is a high inverse relationship between two variables). However, as one of its most useful functions, the correlation coefficient helps us predict the value of one variable if we know the value of the other. In other words, there is a formula that allows us to predict how someone will score on variable Y if we know how he or she did on variable X. For example, we found a high correlation between height and salary in Joe Galvan's company. Given this information and an equation for prediction, we could predict a new employee's salary if we knew his or her height.

The development of an instrument for prediction, called a *regression equation*, is based on the definition of linear correlation given earlier. Correlation was defined as the degree of *linear* relationship between the variables—that is, the degree to which the relationship can be described by a straight line. You probably remember from algebra that the equation for a line is $y = mx + b$ where m is the slope and b is the y-intercept. The same *form* of the equation for a line is used in the linear regression equation. One difference here is that the slope and intercept are indicated by different symbols. The general equation for the regression equation is

$$Y = a + bX \quad \text{or} \quad Y = bX + a,$$

where b is the slope of the line and a is the point at which the line intercepts the Y axis. The slope of the line, b, is sometimes called the **regression coefficient.**

The **regression equation** is the equation for the straight line that best describes the relationship between the variables. The question is, How do we decide which of many possible straight lines best fits the data? Also, in what sense do we mean best fit?

Figure 13-5 is the scatterplot of Joe Galvan's data, and the best-fitting line has been added to it. Look at the vertical distance (the deviation) between each data point and the line. This is the *key deviation* in regression. The regression line is the line that makes the squared deviations around it as small as possible, and it is found by using basic calculus (often taught today in high school) to find a solution that gives the minimum value. This is the sense in which the regression line is the best fit: It minimizes the squared deviations. Because it minimizes the squared deviations, the regression line is also called the **least squares line.** The word *regression* refers to regression toward the mean; that is, the regression line for Y given X yields an approximation of the mean value of Y for any given value of X.

We may think of the regression line as a "moving average"; that is, the regression line gives us the average Y value that we can expect from any value of X. As X changes, so does our predicted (or average) Y. The term *moving average* also helps us understand the concept of least squares. Think of the Y value on the regression line as the estimate of the mean of the Y values in a scatterplot corresponding to a particular X value. However, we have many X values, and where the least squares method "places" the regression line corresponds to the mean of these scatterplots at each value of X in the best manner possible. Thus, the regression line can be considered a series of means (moving average); it also constitutes a line that gives

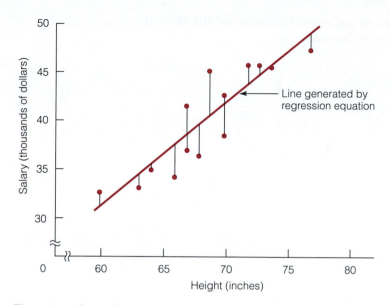

Figure 13-5   Scatterplot showing the relationship between height and salary in Joe Galvan's company. The line generated by the regression equation is shown.

us the least (minimum) squared deviations—the best "fit" to the data. The formulas we use guarantee this.

The equation for the regression line is:

FORMULA 13-3   Y *predicted from* **X**

$$\hat{Y} = \left(\frac{rs_Y}{s_X}\right)X + \left[\overline{Y} - \left(\frac{rs_Y}{s_X}\right)\overline{X}\right]$$

Note that the form of the regression prediction equation is

$$\hat{Y} = bX + a,$$

where

$$b(\text{slope}) = \left(\frac{rs_Y}{s_X}\right) \quad \text{and} \quad a(\text{intercept}) = \left[\overline{Y} - \left(\frac{rs_Y}{s_X}\right)\overline{X}\right].$$

$\hat{Y}$ ("Y-caret") is the symbol for our estimated or predicted value of Y. Note that the caret over a letter always indicates an estimated value. All the terms in the regression equation are familiar ones. To solve the equation, we will need to know $r, s_X, s_Y, \overline{X},$ and $\overline{Y}$.

Let's determine the regression equation for the height–salary example. Earlier, we found that $r = .88$, $\Sigma X = 960$, $\Sigma X^2 = 66{,}102$, $\Sigma Y = 562.5$, $\Sigma Y^2 = 22{,}976.13$, and

$N = 14$. From these values we can calculate all the other information needed to compute the regression equation:

$$\overline{X} = \frac{\Sigma X}{N} = \frac{960}{14} = 68.57,$$

$$s_X = \sqrt{\frac{\Sigma X^2 - \frac{(\Sigma X)^2}{N}}{N - 1}} = \sqrt{\frac{66{,}102 - \frac{960^2}{14}}{14 - 1}} = \sqrt{\frac{273.43}{13}} = \sqrt{21.03} = 4.59,$$

$$\overline{Y} = \frac{562.5}{14} = 40.18,$$

$$s_Y = \sqrt{\frac{\Sigma Y^2 - \frac{(\Sigma Y)^2}{N}}{N - 1}} = \sqrt{\frac{22{,}976.13 - \frac{562.5^2}{14}}{14 - 1}} = \sqrt{\frac{375.68}{13}} = \sqrt{28.9} = 5.38,$$

$$\hat{Y} = \left(\frac{rs_Y}{s_X}\right)X + \left[\overline{Y} - \left(\frac{rs_Y}{s_X}\right)\overline{X}\right]$$

$$= \left[\frac{(.88)(5.38)}{4.59}\right]X + \left\{40.18 - \left[\frac{(.88)(5.38)}{4.59}\right](68.57)\right\}$$

$$= 1.03X + [40.18 - (1.03)(68.57)] = 1.03X + (40.18 - 70.63)$$

$$\hat{Y} = 1.03X - 30.45.$$

As you can see, our regression equation is the equation for a straight line whose slope is 1.03 and whose Y intercept is -30.45.

Although the computations are fairly straightforward, there is one particular point at which many students go awry. In the step immediately before the final answer, the last two terms are $+40.18$ and -70.63. Written in this fashion, it should be obvious that the algebraic sum of the two is -30.45. However, there is a tendency to not treat the last two terms as though they should be combined algebraically. Keep the parentheses around these numbers until they are simplified to one signed number. Be careful on this step.

Using the Regression Equation for Prediction   Based on Joe's data, the equation relating height (the X variable) to salary (the Y variable) is

$$\hat{Y} = 1.03X - 30.45 \quad \text{or} \quad \hat{Y} = -30.45 + 1.03X.$$

We can use this equation to predict the salary of a new employee in Joe's company, assuming Joe doesn't change the rules. For example, if a 65-inch female is hired, what would we predict for her salary? Substituting 65 for X would give us

$$\hat{Y} = 1.03(65) - 30.45 = 66.95 - 30.45 = 36.5.$$

Thus, we would predict that a person 65 inches tall would make $36,500 in Joe's company. Notice that this equation is similar to the general equation for a straight line ($\hat{Y} = a + bX$) given earlier. The preceding equation is in the form, $\hat{Y} = bX + a$, but remember that order makes no difference in addition. Thus, this equation is equivalent to $\hat{Y} = -30.45 + 1.03X$ ($\hat{Y} = a + bX$).

Let's take another look at Figure 13-5. To find the points for the regression line, all we have to do is solve the regression equation for a few X values (any two will do). We've already calculated one: For $X = 65$, $\hat{Y} = 36.5$. Another is $\hat{Y} = 41.7$ for $X = 70$. Why is there a discrepancy between the regression line and the actual data points? The answer is that the correlation, high though it is, is not perfect.

Let's look at an example that will illustrate the usefulness of the regression equation. Suppose we have given a 10-point quiz in statistics class during the fourth week of the term and another during the eighth week. Twelve students have taken the quizzes. The scores are as follows:

| Quiz 1 | | Quiz 2 | | |
X	X^2	Y	Y^2	XY
8	64	7	49	56
6	36	7	49	42
7	49	8	64	56
0	0	0	0	0
9	81	9	81	81
4	16	2	4	8
2	4	2	4	4
0	0	1	1	0
4	16	5	25	20
3	9	3	9	9
7	49	5	25	35
10	100	9	81	90
$\Sigma X = 60$	$\Sigma X^2 = 424$	$\Sigma Y = 58$	$\Sigma Y^2 = 392$	$\Sigma XY = 401$

We can use the calculated relationship between the quizzes to predict Quiz 2 scores from Quiz 1 scores. For example, if a student's score on the first quiz was 8, what score would we predict for this student on the second quiz? The first step is to find r:

$$r = \frac{N\Sigma XY - \Sigma X \Sigma Y}{\sqrt{[N\Sigma X^2 - (\Sigma X)^2][N\Sigma Y^2 - (\Sigma Y)^2]}} = \frac{(12)(401) - (60)(58)}{\sqrt{[(12)(424) - 60^2][(12)(392) - 58^2]}}$$

$$= \frac{1,332}{\sqrt{(1,488)(1,340)}} = \frac{1,332}{1,412.06} = .94$$

As you can see, there is a strong correlation between the scores obtained on Quiz 1 and the scores obtained on Quiz 2. For practice, test it for significance.

The next step is to compute the regression equation.

$$\hat{Y} = \left(\frac{rs_Y}{s_X}\right)X + \left[\overline{Y} - \left(\frac{rs_Y}{s_X}\right)\overline{X}\right]$$

$$\overline{X} = \frac{\Sigma X}{N} = \frac{60}{12} = 5$$

$$s_X = \sqrt{\frac{\Sigma X^2 - \frac{(\Sigma X)^2}{N}}{N - 1}} = \sqrt{\frac{424 - \frac{60^2}{12}}{12 - 1}} = 3.36$$

$$\overline{Y} = \frac{\Sigma Y}{N} = \frac{58}{12} = 4.83$$

$$s_Y = \sqrt{\frac{\Sigma Y^2 - \frac{(\Sigma Y)^2}{N}}{N - 1}} = \sqrt{\frac{392 - \frac{58^2}{12}}{12 - 1}} = 3.19$$

$$\hat{Y} = \left[\frac{(.94)(3.19)}{3.36}\right]X + \left\{4.83 - \left[\frac{(.94)(3.19)}{3.36}\right]5\right\}$$

$$\hat{Y} = .89X + [4.83 - (.89)(5)] = .89X + (4.83 - 4.45)$$

$$\hat{Y} = .89X + .38$$

Finally, we can use the equation for our regression line to find the Quiz 2 score we would predict from a Quiz 1 score of 8:

$$\hat{Y} = bX + a = .89X + .38 = .89(8) + .38 = 7.12 + .38 = 7.50.$$

In other words, given a Quiz 1 score of 8, we would predict that the student would obtain a Quiz 2 score of 7.5. We could also use the regression equation to predict other Quiz 2 scores from the scores on Quiz 1. We need only to substitute the Quiz 1 score (X) into our regression equation $\hat{Y} = .89X + .38$.

What if we wanted to predict X scores from Y? Can we use the equation we've computed for predicting Y from X to also predict X from Y? Unfortunately, the answer is no. Instead, we have to interchange the Xs and Ys in the equation for r in Formula 13-3 (the regression equation). The equations for predicting X and Y are equivalent only when $r = 1.00$.

More Than One Predictor   There's one final point we need to make about our prediction tool—the regression equation: The concept and formulas for regression can be extended to include more than one "predictor." For example, we could predict freshman grade point average more accurately using the high school average, the SAT score, and a self-efficacy measure of personality than we can using only the SAT score. This extension of regression is called *multiple regression* and is covered in more advanced texts.

⟲ CHECKING YOUR PROGRESS

In a study of alcoholics, a significant correlation has been found between blood alcohol concentration (BAC) and the score on a 50-item test of recent memory. The average BAC in the persons studied was 0.01% with $s = 0.004$, and the average number of items correctly answered on the recent memory test was 35, $s = 6$. Assuming a correlation of $-.83$, find the regression equation and predict the score of a person with a BAC of 0.015%.

Answer: $\hat{Y} = -1{,}245X + 47.45$ for the regression equation, and $\hat{Y} = 28.78$ or about 29 for the number of correct responses on the recent memory test.

The Coefficient of Determination

If we compare scatterplots such as the one in Figure 13-1 with the one in Figure 13-4, we notice that the higher the correlation between two variables, the narrower the range of Y values for any value of X. The points "hug" the regression line more closely in Figure 13-1 than in Figure 13-4 (if it had a regression line), because Figure 13-1 shows a higher correlation than Figure 13-4. In a sense, as r increases, the range of Y values decreases for a given X. We refer to this phenomenon of restricting the range of possible scores on one variable by knowing values on another variable as "explaining variance." In this case we are talking about a decrease in the range of the observed Y scores about the regression line $(Y - \hat{Y})$. Remember that this is our *key deviation* for regression. This deviation is *error* of prediction, and we are reducing it when more variance is explained. Thus, the higher the correlation between X and Y, the more our knowledge of X restricts the range of Y (helping us more accurately predict Y). The more variance in Y we can "explain," the less error we have.

An index called the **coefficient of determination** has been developed to express the amount of explained variability. The coefficient of determination is equal to the square of r:

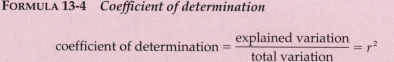

FORMULA 13-4 *Coefficient of determination*

$$\text{coefficient of determination} = \frac{\text{explained variation}}{\text{total variation}} = r^2$$

To illustrate, if $r = .9$, the coefficient of determination, r^2, is .81; if $r = .8$, $r^2 = .64$; and so forth. Note that if $r = \pm1.0$, 100% ($r^2 = 1.00$) of the variance is explained, and if $r = .0$ none ($r^2 = .00$) of the variance is explained. The coefficient of determination is important, because we are often interested in knowing the percentage variance in a variable that is explained by another variable. In fact, once we have a significant r, the size of r and the size of the coefficient of determination (r^2) are the most important things to know about a correlation relationship. They tell us *how big* the relationship is, and r^2 allows us to express this handily as a percentage.

What is a "good" (meaningful, important) value for r^2? The answer depends on the research situation. Before we comment on this, think back to our discussion of ANOVA in which we said that within-groups variability is analogous to "statistical static." Likewise, it has been said of psychology that everything is related to everything else—at least a little. This too can be considered statistical background noise, and *with a large enough sample size, you can find a significant correlation* between two variables that are *not* related in any meaningful way. To prove this to yourself, look in the table of critical values of r (Table E). For a sample size of about 400, $r_{.05} = .098$, which is approximately equal to .1. Here, $r^2 = .0096$ or .1%, 1/10th of 1% variance explained. Yet a correlation of this magnitude would be statistically significant with $N = 400$, and this is why we focus on r^2 rather than the significance level (p) for a correlation.

Now we return to the question of how large r^2 should be to be meaningful. In the social sciences, explaining 5% or 10% of the variance may be considered "good," and we would be extremely happy to be able to explain more variance than this. Once again, there is the matter of practical versus statistical significance. Although 2% may not sound like an effect of any practical significance, if we had devised a way to reduce traffic fatalities nationwide by 2%, most of us would agree that this reduction would be meaningful.

To summarize our discussion, r^2, the coefficient of determination, gives us a way to assess how large the relationship is between X and Y in terms of the percentage of explained variance. This is much more important than our significance level (p), which can always be reduced by taking larger samples. Values of r^2—percentage of explained variance—must be evaluated in the context of a research situation to determine their practical significance.

THE SPEARMAN RANK ORDER CORRELATION COEFFICIENT

The **Spearman rank order correlation coefficient, r_s,** was originally derived in the precomputer era as an easy-to-compute special case of the Pearson r. In addition to being computationally simpler, it is useful when the data are ranks at the outset, or the researcher believes the data must be reduced to ranks.

The Pearson r applies to linearly-related variables measured with at least interval scales, whereas the Spearman coefficient assumes only ordinal scale measurement. Remember that with interval or ratio scale measurement, we can precisely identify the length of the interval between measurements. Sometimes, however, the crudeness of our measurement prevents us from being able to specify precisely the length of the interval between measurements.

For example, suppose one student in the class is designated a "judge" and is given the assignment of rating the tastes of five different types of coffee. On a scale from 1 to 10, the "judge" gives one cup a score of 8, another a score of 6, and a third a score of 4. Again, we cannot assume that the intervals between the scores are equal or that the coffee with a score of 8 tastes twice as good as the coffee with a score of 4. In other words, there's no reason for assuming either interval or ratio scaling. All we can say with any certainty is that the coffee with the score of 8 ranks higher than the coffee with the score of 6, which ranks higher than the coffee with the score of 4.

Even though numbers may be used, rating psychological variables, such as authoritativeness, confidence, or compulsiveness, is a relatively crude measure of the variable in question. Depending on the situation, some investigators may believe that such ratings should be used only to determine a ranking of the individual relative to other individuals; that is, the level of measurement is at best ordinal scale.

When we have (or assume) either interval or ratio scale measurement, we should use the Pearson r to compute a correlation coefficient. In general, using the Pearson r with data that are not reduced to ranks is preferred. Reducing data to ranks discards information, which is usually *not* a good thing to do because it reduces power. However, when we have ordinal scale measurement, we can use the Spearman r_S or the Pearson r because they are equivalent in this situation. This should be good news, because you already know how to compute the Pearson r. However, we will present an example of computing the Spearman r_S for illustration and because it demonstrates the process of converting data to ranks. Although this ranking process could be performed separately, it is typically performed before computation of r_S, because r_S assumes (and is correct when) the data are ranked.

Let's consider a problem in which the Spearman r_S would be appropriate. An experimenter wants to see whether anxiety level is related to perception of noise level. Ten people are first given a rating scale instrument to determine their levels of anxiety. Based on their responses to the items on the scale, each person is given a number from 0 to 10 as a summary rating of anxiety level. Later, each person is exposed to a noise at a particular level and asked to rate its loudness on a scale from 0 to 10. The investigator is unwilling to assume that the ratings are interval-level measurement and wants to convert them to ranks. The paired scores are as follows.

Participant	Anxiety Rating (X)	Noise Rating (Y)
1	10	8
2	5	5
3	9	10
4	4	3
5	6	7
6	9	9
7	8	6
8	3	5
9	5	2
10	1	0

The formula for r_S is:

FORMULA 13-5   *Spearman rank order correlation coefficient*

$$r_S = 1 - \frac{6\Sigma d^2}{N(N^2 - 1)},$$

---

where d is the difference between the ranks of individuals on the two variables and N is the number of *pairs* of observations, as it was for *r*.

Looking at the formula, we can see that the only thing we have to determine before calculating r_S is the value of Σd^2. To do this, we *rank* the scores on each of the variables from highest to lowest, take the difference between the ranks, square it, and then sum the squared differences. Let's compute r_S for the preceding example. Here are our data:

Number	X	Rank of X	Y	Rank of Y	d	d^2
1	10	1	8	3	−2	4
2	5	6.5	5	6.5	0	0
3	9	2.5	10	1	1.5	2.25
4	4	8	3	8	0	0
5	6	5	7	4	1	1
6	9	2.5	9	2	0.5	0.25
7	8	4	6	5	−1	1
8	3	9	5	6.5	2.5	6.25
9	5	6.5	2	9	−2.5	6.25
10	1	10	0	10	0	0
					$\Sigma d^2 =$	21

As you can see, each participant was assigned a rank on each of the two variables; for each pair of ranks, the rank on the *Y* variable was subtracted from the rank on the *X* variable; each of the differences was squared; and the squared differences were summed to give Σd^2. Let's take a closer look at the assigning of the ranks.

Consider the *ordered* anxiety ratings:

10   9   9   8   6   5   5   4   3   1

The ranks would be

1   2.5   2.5   4   5   6.5   6.5   8   9   10

We start with the highest score (10 on the X variable) and give that score the rank of 1. Two participants had the next highest score of 9, so we give each participant the average of the tied ranks (the average of 2 and 3 is 2.5). The procedure is continued until all the scores on the X variable are ranked; then the scores on the Y variable are similarly ranked.

Now we can compute r_S:

$$r_S = 1 - \frac{6\Sigma d^2}{N(N^2 - 1)} = 1 - \frac{6(21)}{10(10^2 - 1)} = 1 - \frac{126}{990}$$

$$= 1 - 0.13 = .87.$$

The value of r_S that we obtain (.87) indicates a sizable relationship between a person's rating on an anxiety scale and the same person's perception of noise level.

However, is the value of r_S large enough for us to conclude that there is a significant relationship between the *ranks* of the variables in the population?

The null hypothesis for the significance test of r_S is that no relationship exists between the ranks of the two variables in the population from which the sample was drawn. To test r_S, we merely have to compare its value with critical values in Table F for the appropriate sample size. For our example, the sample size is 10. From Table F we find that the values of r_S at the 5% and 1% levels of significance for samples of size 10 are .648 and .794, respectively. Our obtained r_S of .87 is larger than the value required for rejection of the null hypothesis at the 1% level. Therefore, we reject H_0 and conclude that anxiety level is related to the perception of noise level; higher anxiety is associated with a perception of increased noise level, $p < .01$.

⑤ CHECKING YOUR PROGRESS

Two "judges" have been asked to rate independently the pictures of eight individuals in terms of attractiveness on a scale of 1 to 10. Interval-level measurement is not assumed. Here are the ratings:

Picture	Judge A	Judge B
1	4	4
2	2	2
3	4	2
4	1	2
5	7	5
6	5	6
7	6	7
8	8	8

Find the correlation between the ratings and test it for significance.

Answer: $r_S = .89$, which indicates a high positive relationship between the attractiveness ratings. The correlation is significant at the .05 level (critical $r_S = .738$).

Other Correlation Coefficients

In this section, we will discuss two correlation coefficients that are, like the Spearman r_S, just special cases of the Pearson r. For further details about them, consult M. J. Allen and W. M. Yen, 1979, *Introduction to Measurement Theory*, Monterey, CA: Brooks/Cole. In both cases, we will indicate how to use the now-familiar Pearson r formula to compute them.

The **point biserial correlation (r_{pbis})** is used when one variable is *dichotomous* (has only two values) and the other variable is continuous or interval level of measurement. For example, we might be interested in the correlation between gender and a measure of spatial reasoning ability, or the correlation between a true–false item on a test with the overall test score. If gender is our X variable, we can assign a 1 for females and a 0 for males (1/0 coding is preferred, although any two numbers will do). The Y variable is simply spatial reasoning scores. Compute the Pearson r, and the result will be the point biserial correlation coefficient, r_{pbis}.

The **phi coefficient (ϕ)** is used when both variables are dichotomous. For example, we might be interested in the relationship between gender and success in psychotherapy. To compute phi, we first code each variable with two numbers. We might code gender, the X variable, as 1 = female and 2 = male; for therapy success, the Y variable, we use 1 = success and 0 = no success. Again, it makes no difference which two code values are used in either case. Now, compute the Pearson r on the paired scores, and the result will be the phi coefficient, ϕ.

Now that we have finished our discussion of correlation, regression, and special correlation coefficients, let's take a moment to consider more broadly what we have done in inferential statistics.

A BROADER VIEW OF INFERENTIAL TECHNIQUES— THE *GENERAL LINEAR MODEL*

Our presentation in Chapter 13 has shown that correlation techniques and linear regression are closely related. Earlier, we indicated that correlation can be viewed as the way two measures X and Y vary together or *covary*, which is standardized by dividing the covariance by the standard deviations of X and Y. Further, although correlation was needed in our formulas to get the regression equation, there is a way to compute the regression equation without computing r first. In fact, if the regression equation is available, r can be computed from it. However, *neither* can be computed without knowing the *covariance*—the "heart" of both techniques.

We also noted that the concept of regression employing one predictor, as introduced in this chapter, can be extended to several predictors and is called *multiple regression*. In essence, the multiple regression technique is the *most general* technique of all the ones we have studied. In its general form, multiple regression *is* what we call the *general linear model* (GLM). It is called linear because it deals with "straight-line" relationships between variables, under usual conditions. Under the

GLM, we can include t tests, ANOVA, two-variable correlation and regression, prediction using more than one predictor (multiple regression), and other more advanced techniques. In fact, t tests and ANOVA are only special cases in which formulas have been developed specifically for particular situations. The inclusion of all these techniques under the GLM is accomplished by special coding strategies applied to the predictors (the Xs) in multiple regression.

All this is to say that the most general way of looking at data has to do with *relationships* between variables or measures. We can see clearly that regression and correlation provide us with direct information about the statistical significance of a relationship (determined by testing r for significance) and most importantly, about the *strength* of a relationship (r^2, the coefficient of determination). The other tests—t tests and ANOVA F tests—were constructed to investigate *group differences*, which is the other way to investigate *relationships*.

Of course, it may also be true that tests of group differences were developed because the results from them are relatively easy to explain and understand. Suppose we are interested in the relationship between gender and spatial reasoning. One way we could approach this research issue is by determining the size and direction of the correlation between gender and scores on a test of spatial reasoning. Another way we could investigate the relationship is by examining *differences* (who did better) between males and females on the spatial reasoning test.

Psychology and other behavioral/experimental sciences, with their grand traditions of experimentalism, have more frequently designed their investigations as experiments with treatment and control groups in their desire to establish cause–effect relationships. As a result, they have frequently (and proudly) used *group difference methods* to investigate any relationships of interest. It is also probably true that results are easier to explain and understand when presented as group differences than when presented as correlations. For example, it may be clearer to say that males scored significantly higher than females on a test of spatial reasoning than to say that there is a moderate positive correlation (e.g., $r = .4$) between gender (being male) and spatial reasoning. In the same vein, a bar graph showing group differences may be easier to comprehend than a scatterplot showing the relationship.

Without realizing it, you've been using the general linear model to analyze your data since we discussed the one-sample t test in Chapter 9. You have learned various methods for investigating relationships—either *group difference methods* or *relationship methods*—that were all under the GLM umbrella.

SUMMARY

Linear correlation is the degree of linear relationship between two variables; the classes of correlation are positive, negative, and zero. Two different techniques for determining the degree of relationship were discussed. The first was the Pearson product-moment correlation coefficient, or the Pearson r. The Pearson r is defined as the mean of the z score products for the X and Y variables. The Pearson r can also be defined as the covariance of X and Y divided by the standard deviations of X and Y. The computational, or raw-score, formula for the Pearson r is

$$r = \frac{N\Sigma XY - \Sigma X\Sigma Y}{\sqrt{[N\Sigma X^2 - (\Sigma X)^2][N\Sigma Y^2 - (\Sigma Y)^2]}}.$$

The obtained coefficient can be compared to values given in Table E to determine whether there is a significant relationship between the two variables. The test of significance assumes no relationship between the variables in the population ($H_0: \rho = 0$). The null hypothesis is rejected at either the 5% or the 1% level if the sample coefficient is equal to or larger in absolute value than the appropriate values in Table E. The degrees of freedom for the test of r are $N - 2$, where N is the number of pairs of scores.

After r is obtained, it can be used to compute the linear regression equation, which is the equation for the straight line that best fits the data from the sample. This equation is used to make predictions about a score on one variable if we know a score on the other. The formula for predicting Y from X is

$$\hat{Y} = \left(\frac{rs_Y}{s_X}\right)X + \left[\overline{Y} - \left(\frac{rs_Y}{s_X}\right)\overline{X}\right]$$

which can be reported as either

$$\hat{Y} = a + bX \quad \text{or} \quad \hat{Y} = bX + a.$$

The coefficient of determination, r^2, tells the amount of variability in one variable accounted for by the variability in the other variable and is critical for interpreting the importance of the correlation.

The second type of correlation coefficient introduced in this chapter was the Spearman rank order correlation coefficient, or r_S. The Spearman coefficient, a special case of the Pearson r, is based on the difference in the ranks of the two variables and is useful when the level of measurement of one or both variables is ordinal or when ease of computation is desired. The formula for r_S is

$$r_S = 1 - \frac{6\Sigma d^2}{N(N^2 - 1)}.$$

After computing r_S, it can be tested for significance by comparing it to values in Table F for the observed sample size.

Two additional coefficients that are special cases of the Pearson correlation and can be calculated with the Pearson formula and appropriately coded data are the point biserial correlation (r_{pbis}) and the phi coefficient (ϕ). The point biserial correlation is used when one variable is dichotomous and the other is interval level, whereas the phi coefficient is used with two dichotomous variables.

Finally, we briefly discussed how all of the inferential statistical techniques covered to this point can be tied together: Techniques testing group differences (e.g., the t test) and techniques measuring relationships (e.g., correlation) are part of a general, relationship-oriented multiple predictor approach called the general linear model (GLM).

Troubleshooting Your Computations

When computing either of the correlation coefficients discussed, there is a built-in check on the accuracy of your computations: Always remember that the range of r and r_S is from $+1$ to -1. An answer outside this range is incorrect, and you need to reexamine both your formula and *all* calculations. Arithmetical errors are usually made in the *initial* calculations.

A frequently made error in computing r_S is forgetting to rank the scores on the X and Y variables. Remember the name of the statistic: the Spearman *rank order* correlation coefficient. In other words, it is the coefficient based on the relationship between the ranks, and you must obtain the ranks before any computations can be made.

Another mistake in computing r_S involves the application of the equation. You must remember that the first term in the equation, 1, is separate from the fraction

$$\frac{6\Sigma d^2}{N(N^2 - 1)}$$

and that the fraction is subtracted from it. If you're not careful, the 1 may inadvertently become part of the fraction's numerator. Also, don't become so involved in computing the fraction that you report *it* as r_S.

One major problem area in computing the regression equation is in the handling of the last two terms in the equation,

$$\overline{Y} - \left(\frac{rs_Y}{s_X}\right)(\overline{X}).$$

If your r is positive, simplifying the terms will result in something in the form $B - A$. These two numbers must be added algebraically.

Remember that r_S should be used when you can assume only ordinal scale data; that is, the precise intervals between the scores cannot be specified, and ranking, or ordering, of the scores is appropriate. When the data have been collected using either an interval or ratio scale, then the use of r is preferable.

EXERCISES

1. Consider the following data: $\Sigma X^2 = 285$, $\Sigma Y^2 = 253$, $\Sigma XY = 259$, $\Sigma X = 45$, $\Sigma Y = 43$, $N = 9$.

   a. Calculate r and test it for significance.
   b. Calculate the regression equation for $\hat{Y}$.
   c. Find $\hat{Y}$ when $X = 6$.

2. Consider the following data: $\Sigma XY = 1{,}555.2$, $\Sigma X^2 = 1{,}308$, $\Sigma Y^2 = 1{,}920$, $\Sigma X = 120$, $\Sigma Y = 144$, $N = 12$.

   a. Calculate r.
   b. Calculate the regression equation for $\hat{Y}$.
   c. Find $\hat{Y}$ when $X = 13$.

3. We are interested in the relationship between test scores on two quizzes given 2 weeks apart. Here are the scores:

Student	Quiz 1	Quiz 2	Student	Quiz 1	Quiz 2
1	10	9	6	6	2
2	9	7	7	3	1
3	7	6	8	4	1
4	8	4	9	7	5
5	8	7	10	2	6

   a. Calculate r and test it for significance. Tell what your decision means in the context of the exercise.
   b. Compute the regression equation.
   c. What Quiz 2 score would you predict from a Quiz 1 score of 5?

4. For what purpose is the regression equation used? Why is the prediction usually not perfect? What is the coefficient of determination?

5. Rank the following correlation coefficients on degree of linear relationship: $+.08$, $+.95$, $+.57$, $-.98$, $-.37$, $+.85$.

6. A professor has devised a new personality test and wants to test its reliability. To do this she divides the test items in half and administers one half to 12 people. A week later she administers the other half to the same people. Determine the correlation between the two halves of the test, and test it for significance. Tell what your decision means in the context of the exercise.

Person	First Half	Second Half
1	34	37
2	25	22
3	15	15
4	17	16
5	20	19
6	23	25
7	24	22
8	31	30
9	18	14
10	10	8
11	7	10
12	16	20

7. IQ scores are determined for eight pairs of identical twins. From the following data, what is the correlation between the scores? Is it significant? Tell what your decision means in the context of the exercise.

Pair	Twin A	Twin B
1	106	115
2	127	117
3	85	89
4	73	61
5	102	98
6	85	100
7	97	98
8	110	108

8. IQ scores are determined for eight pairs of fraternal twins. From the following data, what is the correlation between the scores? Test it for significance. Tell what your decision means in the context of the exercise.

Pair	Twin A	Twin B
1	101	110
2	153	110
3	115	107
4	97	105
5	75	68
6	120	126
7	110	112
8	105	100

9. Compute a coefficient to show the relationship between order of completion and exam score. Test it for significance, and tell what your decision means in the context of the exercise.

Order of Completion	Score	Order of Completion	Score
1	95	8	85
2	57	9	87
3	90	10	75
4	70	11	76
5	75	12	72
6	65	13	93
7	60	14	85

10. Two friends attend a wine tasting party at which they taste and rate nine wines. Each wine is rated on a scale of 1 (undrinkable) to 20 (wine of the

century). At the end of the tasting the two friends compare their ratings to see how much they agree. Their ratings are below. Assume the ratings are no better than rankings. Calculate the appropriate correlation coefficient, and test it for significance. Tell what your decision means in the context of the exercise.

Wine	Friend A	Friend B
1	14	12
2	7	6
3	3	4
4	12	12
5	18	18
6	10	12
7	14	19
8	9	10
9	7	8

11. In the process of selecting students for a graduate program, two faculty members read the letters of recommendation in each student's file. Each faculty member rates the letters on a scale of 1 (poor) to 10 (outstanding). The ratings for 12 applicants follow. Assume the ratings are ordinal-level measurement at best. What is the correlation between the judges' ratings? Is it significant? What does your decision mean in the context of the exercise?

Applicant	Judge A	Judge B
1	6	8
2	9	8
3	4	2
4	2	4
5	4	5
6	7	6
7	10	9
8	8	10
9	6	4
10	9	9
11	9	8
12	1	2

12. Twelve students were rated on the extent of their class participation, with a value of 0 assigned to someone who never talks in class and a value of 7 to a student who frequently participates in class discussions. The same people also were rated on an extravert–introvert (E-I) scale, with a score of 0 for a person who is quiet and shy (introvert) up to a score of 5 for a person who is outgoing (extravert). Determine whether there is any relationship between extraversion–introversion and class participation. Compute the correlation three ways:

a. Assume the ratings on participation and extraversion are interval-level data.

b. Assume the ratings are only valid as ordinal-level measurement.

c. Compute the Pearson correlation on the rankings of the data and compare all three results. Test your answers for significance, and tell what your decisions mean in the context of the exercise.

Student	Participation Rating (X)	E-I Rating (Y)
A	6	4
B	7	4
C	6	4
D	1	1
E	3	5
F	3	3
G	2	2
H	5	4
I	2	3
J	2	2
K	6	1
L	7	5

13. Convert the data from the previous exercise on class participation to a dichotomous variable by assigning a 1 to ratings of 3 or lower and assigning a 2 to ratings of 4 and above. Leaving the E-I ratings unchanged, calculate the point biserial correlation and compare your result with that of the previous exercise.

14. Using the data from Exercise 13, convert the E-I ratings to a dichotomous variable by assigning a 0 to ratings of 3 or lower and assigning a 1 to ratings of 4 and above. You should now have two columns of dichotomous data, in which participation scores are coded 1 or 2 and E-I scores are coded 0 or 1. Compute the phi coefficient, and compare your results to those of the previous two exercises. What happens to the correlation as our coding of the data removes information?

Chi Square

 Jackie worked at the admissions desk of a health clinic. Part of her job was to screen patients as they came in for treatment. This included taking a health history, checking insurance forms, and completing all paperwork. As the latest patient described his symptoms, Jackie was struck by the realization that he was yet another person who lived near the industrial park and was reporting respiratory symptoms. The clinic was always busy, and only a small portion of patients sought treatment for respiratory problems, but it still seemed to Jackie that of the patients reporting respiratory symptoms, an unusually large proportion lived near the industrial park.

Part of Jackie's job was to be alert to trends in admissions so that staffing and resources at the clinic could be properly distributed. However, Jackie wasn't certain her observation was correct. Was there an unusual number of patients with respiratory symptoms from the industrial park area, or was she imagining this relationship?

She decided to see what the record showed. She examined the files of patients seen at the clinic in the past week and classified them by neighborhood (industrial park vs. nonindustrial park) and type of symptoms (respiratory vs. nonrespiratory). She found that 120 patients had been seen. Eighty patients had nonrespiratory symptoms and 40 had respiratory symptoms. Twelve of the patients were from the industrial park area and 108 were from other neighborhoods. Jackie tabulated her data as shown here.

	Industrial Park	Nonindustrial Park	Row Totals
Nonrespiratory Symptoms	4	76	80
Respiratory Symptoms	8	32	40
Column Totals	12	108	$N = 120$

Jackie knew that 10% of the clinic patients typically came from the industrial park area and 90% came from elsewhere. She also knew that 33% of the clinic patients had respiratory symptoms and 67% didn't. Thus, she would expect that 12 of the 120 patients (10%) would come from the industrial park. Of these 12, 4 (33%) would be expected to have respiratory symptoms and 8 (67%) would be expected to have nonrespiratory symptoms. (This could be continued to get expected values for the patients who were not from the industrial park.) She used these proportions to determine the number of patients with respiratory symptoms who should come from each residential area. She found that 4 patients from the industrial park area and 36 patients from other areas could be expected to have respiratory problems. Eight residents of the industrial park area and 72 patients from other residential areas could be expected to report nonrespiratory symptoms. Jackie added this information to her table.

	Industrial Park	Nonindustrial Park	Row Totals
Nonrespiratory Symptoms	4 (8)	76 (72)	80
Respiratory Symptoms	8 (4)	32 (36)	40
Column Totals	12	108	$N = 120$

Note. Expected values are in parentheses.

The trends seemed clear enough to Jackie, but what would a statistician say about these data?

Jackie's problem is a common one in the social sciences. She has a set of observed frequencies of an outcome and a set of expected frequencies. However, her data are nominal (frequencies in categories) rather than interval or ratio (measurements along some continuum). Therefore, she is reluctant to perform statistical procedures that involve certain arithmetic operations, such as averaging scores, and that *make assumptions about the underlying distribution* of scores. In this chapter, we discuss a statistic for testing data of the sort collected by Jackie.

NONPARAMETRIC TESTS

In previous chapters, we considered two powerful inferential tests: the *t* test and the *F* test. The *t* test and the *F* test are examples of **parametric tests**—tests designed to test hypotheses about population parameters. For example, when we used the one-sample *t* test, the null hypothesis was that our sample was drawn from a population in which the mean had a particular value. We assumed a certain value for a population parameter, the mean (or μ). Another assumption we made in using the *t* test and the *F* test was that there was a normal distribution of the variable we measured in the population from which our sample(s) was obtained. These tests also require measurement level (usually interval or ratio) data, which we often don't have.

In this chapter and the next, we study tests that don't make inferences about population parameters and that don't test hypotheses about such parameters. Because population parameters are not considered, the tests are sometimes called **nonparametric tests.** Because the tests don't assume any particular distribution, they are also called **distribution-free tests.** Before discussing the first of the nonparametric tests, chi square, let's review a topic encountered in Chapter 2: scaling.

In Chapter 2, we defined four different measurement scales: nominal, ordinal, interval, and ratio. The nominal scale (frequency data) is used for labeling only; we cannot specify the interval between values or the ranking or ordering of the values. We can only record frequencies of occurrence—the number of subjects falling under a particular label or name. However, that's exactly the kind of data generated by Jackie. She counted the number of clinic patients with and without respiratory symptoms who came from the industrial park area and from other areas.

How can we analyze Jackie's data? The inferential tests (*t* and *F*) that we studied previously assume at least interval scale data, and the data analyzed with *t* and *F* were scores (measurements), not frequencies of occurrence. Now we need a new test, something appropriate with categorical data: the **chi-square test,** symbolized by χ^2 (read "ki-square," with a long *i*).

THE CHI-SQUARE GOODNESS-OF-FIT TEST

Actually, there are two different chi-square tests: one in which we have different levels of a *single* categorical variable and one in which we have different levels of *two* categorical variables. A chi-square test on a single categorical variable is called a **chi-square goodness-of-fit test.** Let's look at an example of data involving a single categorical variable.

A professional test constructor is interested in whether the true–false items on a recently constructed 20-item ability test are uniformly difficult throughout the test. She doesn't want difficult or easy items concentrated in any one area of the test. As a check, she has 20 people take the test; she then plots their errors for each five-item segment of the test. She finds that 39 errors occur in the first segment, 15 in the second, 28 in the third, and 18 in the fourth. A total of 100 errors were made. The data can be summarized as follows:

	1–5	6–10	11–15	16–20	Total
Item #					
Frequency Within Segment	39	15	28	18	$N = 100$

If the errors were no more likely to occur in one segment than another, she should have observed 25 errors in each segment; that is, there were 100 errors, and there were four different segments: 100/4 = 25. How well do the observed data fit what was expected? How good is the fit? It's time to apply the chi-square goodness-of-fit test.

The formula for the test is very simple:

FORMULA 14-1 *Chi square*

$$\chi^2 = \Sigma \frac{(O - E)^2}{E},$$

where O stands for the *observed* frequency and E stands for the *expected* frequency.

The observed frequencies—39, 15, 28, and 18—are what the test constructor actually saw in her study. As noted, assuming an equal distribution of frequencies in the test segments, each of the expected frequencies is 25. Computation of χ^2 then is as follows:

$$\chi^2 = \Sigma \frac{(O - E)^2}{E} = \frac{(39 - 25)^2}{25} + \frac{(15 - 25)^2}{25} + \frac{(28 - 25)^2}{25} + \frac{(18 - 25)^2}{25}$$

$$= \frac{196}{25} + \frac{100}{25} + \frac{9}{25} + \frac{49}{25}$$

$$= 7.84 + 4.00 + 0.36 + 1.96 = 14.16.$$

For the goodness-of-fit test, the degrees of freedom are determined by $K - 1$, where K is the number of categories. Thus, for this problem, $df = 3$, because there are four segments and the sum of the frequencies is fixed. Three values are free to vary, because the values in the first three segments could have been any numbers less than 100, and the value of the fourth segment would be determined by the frequencies in the first three segments.

As before, to determine whether to reject the null hypothesis—that there are no differences in error distribution across the segments—we consult a table of critical values of the test statistic, in this case Table G. For $df = 3$, the critical values are 7.82 at the 5% level and 11.34 at the 1% level. Because 14.16 is larger than the table value at the 1% level, we reject the null hypothesis and conclude that errors are not evenly distributed across the segments.

In this example, the expected frequencies were found by dividing the total number of observations by the number of segments. In other words, we assumed equal distribution of observations across categories.

The goodness-of-fit test can also be used when the expected frequencies are not assumed to be equally distributed. In one study, a personality test called the Myers–Briggs Type Indicator (MBTI) was administered to a sample of 93 people with diagnosed and treated heart disease. The rationale for the study was to learn whether heart patients differ in personality characteristic(s) as measured by the MBTI from comparable persons without heart disease. If personality types are associated with heart disease, it might be possible to modify the personality characteristics that place a person most at risk. The MBTI assigns a score on each of four paired dimensions: extraversion–introversion, or E–I; sensing–intuition, or S–N; thinking–feeling, or T–F; judging–perceiving, or J–P. A given individual may be classified as ISTJ or ENFP or as any other of 16 different types based on the four-letter combinations.

Let's look at the results from just the E–I scale. For the sample of 93 heart patients, there were 38 extraverts and 55 introverts. However, what would the researchers have expected to observe in normal people, people without diagnosed heart disease?

Based on data gathered by the Center for Applied Psychological Type (CAPT) in Florida, 55% of the people of ages similar to the ages of the sample are introverts and 45% are extraverts. Thus, in a sample of 93 normal people, there should be 51 introverts (93 × 55%) and 42 extraverts (93 × 45%). The data are summarized here with expected values in parentheses:

	MBTI Designation		
	Extravert (E)	Introvert (I)	Total
Frequency Within Category	38 (42)	55 (51)	$N = 93$

Chi square is computed as before.

$$\chi^2 = \Sigma \frac{(O - E)^2}{E} = \frac{(38 - 42)^2}{42} + \frac{(55 - 51)^2}{51}$$

$$= 0.38 + 0.31 = 0.69.$$

With $df = K - 1 = 2 - 1 = 1$, the critical value of chi square at the 5% level (from Table G) is 3.84, or $\chi^2(1, N = 93) = 0.69$, $p > .05$. Thus, the null hypothesis is not rejected; there's no reason to believe from this sample that people with known heart disease differ on the E–I scale of the MBTI from what would be predicted based on data from CAPT.

Confirming Hypotheses With Chi Square

It should be noted that the χ^2 goodness-of-fit test *null hypothesis* is occasionally the *research hypothesis* that the investigator seeks to confirm. This represents a variation on the usual logical arrangement in hypothesis testing in which the research or experimental hypothesis is the alternative hypothesis, H_1. To illustrate, in the example we have just considered, it may have been that MBTI theory predicted a 45% to 55% Extraversion–Introversion ratio for heart disease patients. In this case, failure to reject such a specific null hypothesis may provide some confirmation of the theory. The degree of confirmation depends on whether the investigator has a large enough sample to give adequate statistical power to detect deviation from the expected frequency ratio among groups. The degree of confirmation also depends on whether replication (repeating the study) leads to the same conclusion.

⑤ CHECKING YOUR PROGRESS

Let's look at performance by the heart disease sample on another MBTI scale. On the S–N scale, 79 heart disease patients were classified as S and 14 as N. The prediction from the CAPT data is that there will be 60% Ss and 40% Ns. Use the chi-square goodness-of-fit test to test the null hypothesis.

Answer: $\chi^2(1, N = 93) = 24.11$, $p < .01$. Heart patients were more likely to be Ss (and less likely to be Ns) than would be expected from the 60% to 40% proportion of Ss and Ns in the population.

THE CHI-SQUARE TEST OF INDEPENDENCE

The chi-square test based on two categorical variables is called variously the **chi-square test of independence,** the *two-sample chi-square test,* and the *chi-square test of significance.* With this test, we want to determine whether the two categorical variables are independent (i.e., are not related in any way). We want to see whether the distribution of frequencies across the levels of one variable is the same for all levels of the other variable. We assume the categorical variables are independent (the null hypothesis) and reject the null hypothesis if the test shows they probably are not.

Let's look at some examples. First, the problem introduced in the story at the beginning of the chapter was a two-variable problem. The two categorical variables (respiratory symptoms, neighborhood) form a frequency table called a **contingency table,** which is repeated here.

	Industrial Park	Nonindustrial Park	Row Totals
Nonrespiratory Symptoms	4 (8)	76 (72)	80
Respiratory Symptoms	8 (4)	32 (36)	40
Column Totals	12	108	$N = 120$

Note. Expected values are in parentheses.

The table is called a 2 × 2 contingency table because there are two rows and two columns (the totals don't count as rows and columns). If there were no difference in the proportion of patients with respiratory and nonrespiratory symptoms from the two different neighborhoods, we would expect to see similar percentages of the total frequency of respiratory symptoms in patients from each neighborhood. Obviously, this is not the case; a greater than expected proportion of patients with respiratory symptoms are from the industrial park area, and a smaller than expected proportion of patients with nonrespiratory symptoms are from the industrial park area. Is the difference great enough for us to conclude that there is a lack of independence in the groups, that the likelihood of having respiratory symptoms is contingent on where a person lives?

The formula for the chi-square test of independence is the same as the one introduced for the goodness-of-fit test—that is, Formula 14-1. The formula is repeated here:

$$\chi^2 = \Sigma \frac{(O - E)^2}{E}.$$

To get chi square, we have to determine the expected frequency for each cell in the 2 × 2 table, subtract it from the observed frequency in the cell, square the result and divide it by the expected frequency, and add together the results from each cell. Remember that Jackie calculated the expected frequencies in each cell by using the proportion of patients who came from each neighborhood and the proportions of respiratory and nonrespiratory patients examined at the clinic. These values are in parentheses in the table. We are now ready to use Formula 14-1 to calculate chi square.

$$\chi^2 = \Sigma \frac{(O - E)^2}{E} = \frac{(4 - 8)^2}{8} + \frac{(76 - 72)^2}{72} + \frac{(8 - 4)^2}{4} + \frac{(32 - 36)^2}{36}$$

$$= \frac{-4^2}{8} + \frac{4^2}{72} + \frac{4^2}{4} + \frac{-4^2}{36} = 2 + 0.22 + 4 + 0.44$$

$$= 6.66.$$

With $df = 1$, the value required for significance at the 5% level is 3.84 and at the 1% level is 6.64. Let's use the seven-step procedure to summarize our chi-square test of independence results.

1. H_0: The two categorical variables—respiratory symptoms, neighborhood— are independent. Whether or not someone reports respiratory symptoms is unrelated to whether that person lives in the industrial park area or away from the area.

2. H_1: The two categorical variables are dependent on or related to each other. The presence or absence of respiratory symptoms depends on whether a person lives in the industrial park area or away from the area.

3. Set $\alpha = .05$.

4. *Rejection Rule:* Reject H_0 if $\chi^2_{comp} \geq \chi^2_{crit}$ [$df = (R - 1)(C - 1)$], where R = the number of rows and C = the number of columns. With two rows and two columns, $df = (2 - 1)(2 - 1) = (1)(1) = 1$, and the critical values from Table G are 3.84 at the 5% level and 6.64 at the 1% level.

5. *Computations and Test Statistic:* As presented, we found $\chi^2_{comp} = 6.66$.

6. *Decision:* Reject H_0, as $\chi^2(1, N = 120) = 6.66 > 6.64$, $p < .01$.

7. *Conclusion:* Respiratory symptoms and neighborhood are related, $\chi^2(1, N = 120) = 6.66$, $p < .01$. People who report respiratory symptoms are more likely to live near the industrial park.

An Alternative Method for Finding Expected Values

Most of the time we do not have information from previous research or theory that allows us to establish expected values a priori. In these instances, we can calculate expected values by multiplying the marginal totals for a particular cell and dividing the result by the overall total. Doing this gives us Formula 14-2:

FORMULA 14-2 *Expected frequencies for the chi-square test of independence*

$$E = \frac{RT \times CT}{N},$$

where RT stands for row total and CT stands for column total. N is the total number of observations.

Using our original example, let's assume that we don't know proportions of patients from each neighborhood. In that case, we would have to use the formula to find the expected frequency of patients with *nonrespiratory symptoms from the industrial park area*. The row total for the cell of interest is 80, and the column total is 12. We compute E as follows:

$$E = \frac{(80)(12)}{120} = \frac{960}{120} = 8.$$

The expected frequencies for a given row or column must sum to the row or column total, so for a 2 × 2 table we have to calculate only one of the Es; we can determine the rest by subtraction. Thus, the expected number of patients with non-respiratory symptoms from neighborhoods other than the industrial park area is $80 - 8 = 72$; E for patients for respiratory symptoms from the industrial park area is $12 - 8 = 4$; and E for patients with respiratory symptoms from neighborhoods other than the industrial park area is $40 - 4 = 36$. Note that our new method for determining expected frequencies results in precisely the same values as before. Box 14-1 presents the logic behind the determination of E for the two-sample chi square.

Let's consider another example to illustrate the use of Formula 14-2 for computing expected frequencies.

Box 14-1   Logic of Determining Expected Frequencies

Let's look at the logic behind the determination of the expected frequencies for the two-sample chi-square test. Let's again use the example of the patients with respiratory and nonrespiratory symptoms.

First, what is the probability that a person coming to the clinic will have symptoms of something other than a respiratory problem? In Chapter 7, we said that the probability of an event was the ratio of the number of times the event occurred to the total number of events. Jackie screened 80 patients with nonrespiratory symptoms out of a total sample of 120. The probability is $80/120 = .67$.

Now, what is the probability that a patient will be from the industrial park area? There were 12 such patients in the 120 total, giving a probability of $12/120 = .10$.

Finally, what is the probability that a patient will have nonrespiratory symptoms *and* be from the industrial park area? Here we need to refer to the multiplication rule from Chapter 7. The rule is that the probability both events A and B will occur is the product of their individual probabilities. In other words, the probability of a patient's having nonrespiratory symptoms and being from the industrial park area is

$$(.67)(.10) = .067.$$

We would expect about 6.7% of the 120 patients—8.04—to have both characteristics. This number is quite close to the 8 we obtained with Formula 14-2. However, the number obtained with Formula 14-2 is more accurate, because there is no rounding.

A medical researcher is interested in the effect of a new drug treatment for Parkinson's disease, a progressively debilitating motor disorder. Seventy-five patients with early symptoms of Parkinson's receive either the new drug treatment or a placebo, and the dependent variable is whether or not the disease progressed to debility (e.g., need for a wheelchair) before the end of the study's 2-year time period. A contingency table of the results is shown here.

| | | Treatment | | Row Totals |
		Drug	Placebo	
Disease Course	**Progressed to Debility**	10	20	30
	Didn't Progress to Debility	28	17	45
	Column Totals	38	37	$N = 75$

Using Formula 14-2, we can compute the expected frequency for the first cell in the table, the one showing the number of patients who progressed to debility while taking the new drug. The row total for the cell is 30 and the column total is 38. E is computed as follows:

$$E = \frac{(30)(38)}{75} = \frac{1,140}{75} = 15.2.$$

Because the expected frequencies for a given row or column must sum to the row or column total, we can determine the rest of the Es by subtraction. Thus, E for the number of placebo patients who progressed to debility is the row total (30) minus the E we just computed, or 14.8. The expected value for the number of drug patients who didn't progress is $38 - 15.2 = 22.8$; E for the number of placebo patients who didn't progress is $45 - 22.8 = 22.2$. The E values are shown in parentheses in the following contingency table:

| | | Treatment | | Row Totals |
		Drug	Placebo	
Disease Course	**Progressed to Debility**	10 (15.2)	20 (14.8)	30
	Didn't Progress to Debility	28 (22.8)	17 (22.2)	45
	Column Totals	38	37	$N = 75$

We are now ready to compute chi square.

$$\chi^2 = \Sigma \frac{(O - E)^2}{E}$$

$$= \frac{(10 - 15.2)^2}{15.2} + \frac{(20 - 14.8)^2}{14.8} + \frac{(28 - 22.8)^2}{22.8} + \frac{(17 - 22.2)^2}{22.2}$$

$$= \frac{(-5.2)^2}{15.2} + \frac{(5.2)^2}{14.8} + \frac{(5.2)^2}{22.8} + \frac{(-5.2)^2}{22.2}$$

$$= 1.78 + 1.83 + 1.19 + 1.22 = 6.02.$$

Again, we need to know degrees of freedom in order to use Table G for our test of significance. Recall that degrees of freedom was defined as the number of values free to vary after certain restrictions are placed on the data. For the chi-square test of independence, the restriction on the data is that the row and column totals are fixed.

Now, how many expected frequencies did we actually have to compute? The answer is 1, because the others were obtained by subtraction. Thus, degrees of freedom for a 2×2 contingency table will always be 1, as this is the number of values free to vary with the row and column totals fixed. A formula to determine the degrees of freedom was introduced in the seven-step summary of our previous example and will be formalized here as follows:

FORMULA 14-3   *Degrees of freedom for the chi-square test of independence*

$$df = (R - 1)(C - 1),$$

where R is the number of rows and C is the number of columns.

In our example, both R and C were 2, and $df = (2 - 1)(2 - 1) = (1)(1) = 1$. With $df = 1$, the value required for significance at the 5% level is 3.84 and at the 1% level is 6.64, or $\chi^2(1, N = 75) = 6.02, p < .05$. The new drug appears to offer early Parkinson's patients some protection against progression to a debilitating state.

Another Chi-Square Test of Independence Example

Another example of the chi-square test of independence may be instructive. A social psychologist was interested in learning whether the presence of others influenced people's helping behavior. He approached people on a city street who were either walking alone or walking with one or two others. He showed the person (the potential helper) his camera and asked if he or she would be willing to take his (the investigator's) photo. The number of people in each condition who complied with the request are summarized in the following 2×2 contingency table.

	Complied	Refused	Row Totals
In a Group	6	74	80
Alone	25	55	80
Column Totals	31	129	$N = 160$

The first step is to determine the expected frequencies, and we can use Formula 14-2 to do this. How many helpers should we have observed in the group condition if the presence of others is independent of helping behavior?

$$E = \frac{RT \times CT}{N} = \frac{(80)(31)}{160} = \frac{2,480}{160} = 15.5$$

The remaining expected frequencies can be found by subtraction and are shown in parentheses in the completed contingency table.

	Complied	Refused	Row Totals
In a Group	6 (15.5)	74 (64.5)	80
Alone	25 (15.5)	55 (64.5)	80
Column Totals	31	129	$N = 160$

Having determined the expected frequencies, let's now compute chi square.

$$\chi^2 = \Sigma \frac{(O - E)^2}{E} = \frac{(6 - 15.5)^2}{15.5} + \frac{(74 - 64.5)^2}{64.5} + \frac{(25 - 15.5)^2}{15.5} + \frac{(55 - 64.5)^2}{64.5}$$

$$= \frac{(-9.5)^2}{15.5} + \frac{(9.5)^2}{64.5} + \frac{(9.5)^2}{15.5} + \frac{(-9.5)^2}{64.5}$$

$$= \frac{90.25}{15.5} + \frac{90.25}{64.5} + \frac{90.25}{15.5} + \frac{90.25}{64.5}$$

$$= 5.82 + 1.40 + 5.82 + 1.40 = 14.44.$$

For $df = 1$, the critical values from Table G are 3.84 at the 5% level and 6.64 at the 1% level, or $\chi^2(1, N = 160) = 14.44$, $p < .01$. As 14.44 is larger than the critical value at the 1% level, we reject the null hypothesis of independence between the variables and conclude that people are more likely to comply with a request for assistance when they are alone than when they are with one or two others.

⑤ CHECKING YOUR PROGRESS

Based on teacher assessments, an experimenter has divided 100 students into two groups, one judged to have high self-esteem and one judged to have low self-esteem. The experimenter administers a survey of common fears to the two groups of students. She arbitrarily decides that a score of 1 to 10 on the scale indicates a low number of fears, 11 to 20 a moderate number of fears, and 21 to 30 a high number of fears. For the low self-esteem group, she finds that 10 fall into the low category, 15 fall into the moderate category, and 25 fall into the high category. The results for the high self-esteem group are just the opposite: 25 students are in the low category, 15 in the moderate category, and 10 in the high category. Perform a chi-square test of independence to see whether high and low self-esteem students differ on the fear survey.

Answer: $\chi^2(2, N = 100) = 12.86$, $p < .01$, indicating that self-esteem and fears are related. Students in the low self-esteem group have more fears than students in the high self-esteem group.

RESTRICTIONS ON CHI SQUARE

A number of conditions must be met for chi square to be applied. First, *chi square can be used only with frequency data.* In practice, this is no problem as it is possible to convert whatever data we have into frequency data by selecting different categories and counting the number of scores that fall into each one. This is exactly what was done in the example about test-item difficulty. The 20-item test was divided into four segments, and the number of errors was determined for each segment. The primary danger in converting measurement data into frequency data is that chi square is a less sensitive test than others we might apply.

A second restriction that must be placed on chi square is that *the individual events or observations that constitute the data must be independent of each other.* This would not be true, for example, if we asked each subject multiple questions and then treated each of the responses as though it were independent of the others. Similarly, if we were dealing with wife–husband pairs, we should not expect their responses to be independent of each other.

The third restriction is that *we must have in the data both the frequency of occurrence and the frequency of nonoccurrence if we are recording whether or not an event occurs.* This restriction is necessary for the sums of the observed and expected frequencies to be the same.

The fourth restriction placed on chi square is that *no expected frequencies should be less than 5.* If any expected frequencies are less than 5, the distribution of chi square may have different values from those shown in Table G. There are ways to circumvent this rule, however. First, the rule may be relaxed if there are more than four cells and only a few of them have expected frequencies less than 5. Second, if we have a 2 × 2 table and expected frequencies less than 5, an alternative to chi square is the *Fisher exact probability test*. One source for this test is S. Siegel and N. J. Castellan, Jr., 1988, *Nonparametric Statistics for the Behavioral Sciences*, New York: McGraw-Hill. Finally, we can always test more subjects so that the expected frequencies are larger.

SUMMARY

A nonparametric test is a test that doesn't examine hypotheses about population parameters and doesn't require normality assumptions. Nonparametric tests are sometimes called distribution-free tests. This chapter considered one nonparametric test: the chi-square test.

The chi-square test is applied when the measurement scale is nominal and the data consist of frequency counts. A chi-square test on a single categorical variable is called a goodness-of-fit test; a test on two categorical variables is called a chi-square test of independence, a two-sample chi-square test, or a chi-square test of significance.

The formula for chi square is

$$\chi^2 = \Sigma \frac{(O - E)^2}{E},$$

where O is the observed frequency and E is the expected frequency. For the goodness-of-fit test, the expected frequencies are determined either by equally distributing the total number of observations across categories or by assigning the frequencies on the basis of percentages obtained from previous research. For the chi-square test of independence, the expected frequencies for a given cell in a contingency table may be found by solving the following equation:

$$E = \frac{RT \times CT}{N},$$

where RT stands for row total, CT stands for column total, and N is the total number of observations. Because the expected frequencies for a given row or column must sum to the row or column total, most of the expected frequencies may be obtained by subtraction. Another way to determine the expected frequencies is to base them on known proportions when these are available.

The computed value of chi square is compared with the values in Table G with the appropriate degrees of freedom. For the goodness-of-fit test, $df = K - 1$, where K is the number of categories; for the chi-square test of independence, $df = (R - 1)(C - 1)$, where R is the number of rows and C is the number of columns. If the computed chi square is equal to or larger than the appropriate table value at the 5% level, we reject the null hypothesis.

There are certain restrictions on the use of chi square that must always be considered:

1. Chi square can be used only with frequency data.
2. The individual events or observations that constitute the data must be independent of each other.
3. The data on which chi square is computed must contain both the frequency of occurrence and the frequency of nonoccurrence if both have been recorded.
4. No expected frequencies should be less than 5. This rule may be relaxed if there are more than four cells and only a few have expected frequencies less than 5. An alternative to chi square with a 2 × 2 table and small expected frequencies is the *Fisher exact probability test*. As a last alternative, more observations can be made to increase the expected frequencies.

Troubleshooting Your Computations

The computations for chi square usually cause little trouble, but there are a few things to remember. First, practice computing *E* for the test of significance and watch your subtraction if you're using this approach to determine *E* for a particular cell. Both the expected frequencies and the observed frequencies must sum to give you a row or column total. Also, because you are squaring each of the differences between *O* and *E* for a cell before you divide by *E*, be sure no negative signs creep in for a cell total. Finally, be careful in computing degrees of freedom for the test of significance; it would be unfortunate if you computed chi square correctly only to make the wrong decision because of incorrect degrees of freedom.

EXERCISES

1. As voters leave a polling place, they are asked whether they consider themselves conservative, moderate, or liberal. They are then asked whether they voted for or against a tax to fund an experimental program in the schools. The frequencies are given in the table.

	Conservative	Moderate	Liberal
For	36	63	81
Against	45	27	18

Determine whether political orientation is related to support for the tax.

2. A professor wants to determine whether college algebra should be kept as a prerequisite for the course entitled Introductory Psychological Statistics. Ac-

cordingly, some students are allowed to register for the course on a pass—fail basis regardless of whether they have had the prerequisite. Of the 70 students in the class, 40 have had algebra and 30 have not. At the end of the semester, the professor compares the number of students passing or failing the course with whether they had algebra. The results are summarized in the table.

	Pass	Fail
Algebra	34	6
No Algebra	12	18

Determine whether having studied algebra is related to student success in the statistics course.

3. In a social psychology experiment, 56 students are asked to wait individually outside a closed door. While they are sitting outside the room waiting their turn, a person who is either well dressed or shabbily dressed walks toward them carrying a large notebook filled with loose papers. Under the pretext of stumbling, the person drops the notebook, spilling a large number of papers onto the floor. The experiment is designed to find whether there is a difference in willingness to aid a stranger as a function of whether the stranger is well or shabbily dressed.

    Of the 26 participants exposed to the well-dressed clumsy person, 20 helped and 6 continued to wait their turn in the experiment. Of the 30 partici-pants exposed to the shabbily dressed clumsy person, 10 helped. Construct the appropriate 2 × 2 table and apply the chi-square test.

4. There is some evidence for asymmetry in the size of the left and right hemi-spheres of the human brain. In a study of 100 brains, the left hemisphere was found to be larger in 60, the right hemisphere in 15, and 25 had left and right hemispheres equal in size. Perform a chi-square goodness-of-fit test on the data to see whether there is evidence for asymmetry. Assume there is none and that the expected frequencies are evenly distributed.

5. A test of need for affiliation has been given to 50 first-born and 40 later-born students. The results, put into three categories of need for affiliation—high, medium, and low—are shown in the table.

	High	Medium	Low
First Born	10	24	16
Later Born	26	8	6

Perform a test of significance to see whether need for affiliation is related to birth order.

6. The student population of a local college is approximately one-third blond and two-thirds other hair color. Over a 2-day period, the hair color of each student entering the student union building is tallied, with the following results: blonds, 452; others, 1,548. Determine whether blonds and others are as likely to enter the union as would be predicted on the basis of their percentage in the student population.

7. A researcher administers a survey to 25 randomly selected persons from a rural community and finds that 16 of them demonstrate conservative political preferences. In a randomly selected group of 25 persons from an urban region, he finds that 7 demonstrate conservative political preferences. Do the two groups differ significantly?

8. In a study of intraspecific aggression (aggression directed toward other members of the same species), an experimenter finds that 16 of 23 animals tested in Species A exhibit aggression, but only 6 of 25 are aggressive in Species B. Do the two species differ significantly in terms of intraspecific aggression?

9. In a voter survey, people of different religious affiliations were asked whether they had voted for a Republican or a Democrat in the last presidential election. The results are shown in the table.

	Baptist	Catholic	Methodist	Episcopal
Republican	27	24	10	2
Democrat	9	15	33	14

Determine whether religious affiliation had anything to do with the way people voted.

10. A chimpanzee was trained to make same–different judgments about pairs of stimuli. For pictures of objects, the animal's score was 23/24 correct. As each question had two choices (same–different), the expected value was 12/24. Perform a chi-square goodness-of-fit test on the animal's correct–incorrect responses.

11. In a study of the effectiveness of an antipsychotic drug, patients treated with the drug were compared to patients receiving a placebo. In terms of the number relapsing, 698 of 1,068 patients relapsed after taking the placebo, whereas 639 of 2,127 patients relapsed after taking the antipsychotic drug. Was the antipsychotic drug effective in preventing relapse?

12. A new drug has been developed that may have some protective benefits against the development of Alzheimer's disease (AD) by women at genetic risk for developing the disorder. In a 20-year study, a large group of at-risk women receive either the new drug or a placebo, and at the end of the study, whether or not they have been diagnosed with Alzheimer's is determined. Of the 253 women receiving the drug, 10 have AD by the end of the study;

of the 228 women receiving the placebo, 23 are diagnosed with AD. Is the new drug beneficial?

13. A clinical psychologist interested in alcohol abuse and a rural sociologist team up to conduct a field study of alcohol consumption in country-and-western bars. They are both interested in whether music tempo in these establishments increases drinking rate. In the bar being studied, each researcher selects four persons at random to observe during the playing of different country songs. A tape recorder is used unobtrusively to record songs and data. At 30-second intervals during each song, observations are taken. At the time of observation, each of the investigators taps his table if the targets have sipped a drink during the observation interval. The data were tabulated over 45 minutes, and music tempos were divided into three beats-per-minute (bpm) ranges. For below 60 bpm, there were 66 sips; for 60 to 84 bpm, 55 sips; and for 85 bpm and above, 37 sips. Determine whether the consumption rate is the same for the different tempo categories.

14. Our researchers in the previous exercise suspect that type of lyrics ("tear-jerker" vs. "other") may be related to tempo in the determination of consumption rate. In relation to the lyrics and the tempo, the sip frequencies were as follows:

	Slow	Moderate	Fast
Other	18	34	16
Tearjerker	48	21	21

Analyze the data to investigate the researchers' hypothesis.

CHAPTER

Alternatives to *t* and *F*

 Brad was working on his honors dissertation in psychology. He wanted to study the effect of different schedules of reinforcement on the rate of extinction of a response. He hypothesized that a more complex reinforcement schedule would result in slower extinction than a simpler reinforcement schedule.

Brad randomly assigned 20 rats to one of two groups. In both groups, the rats were rewarded with a food pellet on a variable-interval (VI) schedule for barpressing behavior. In one group, the rats received a reward approximately every 30 seconds; this was the Simple VI schedule. In the other group, the range of intervals was much greater, although the average was still about 30 seconds; this was the Complex VI schedule.

Brad trained the rats until their responding stabilized. He then switched to extinction: The rats no longer received a reward pellet for pressing the bar. However, before he got to this phase of his experiment, Brad had to eliminate four rats from the study (three from the Simple group and one from the Complex group) because they developed respiratory infections.

Brad kept track of the number of days it took for the rats to stop responding. Two rats from the Complex group, however, continued to respond, and it looked as though they might go on forever. After consulting with his advisor, Brad decided to cut off the study at some arbitrary point. He chose twice the number of sessions it took the longest responding rat in the Simple group to stop responding. After 24 days, he terminated the experiment, with two of the animals in the Complex group still barpressing for no reward.

Brad's results were as follows:

Days to Extinction

Group Simple	Group Complex
12	24*
12	24*
11	16
8	15
7	14
6	12
6	11
	10
	9

*Arbitrary cut-off score; animal still responding.

Brad had planned to analyze his data with a *t* test, but he realized now that his samples were too small and uneven. Additionally, two of the rats never achieved the criterion, and he'd had to cut them off arbitrarily; he really didn't know what their scores would have been if they had been allowed to continue. To compute the means and variances and to generate estimated population parameters, he needed *all* the scores.

Brad knew there were several nonparametric alternatives to the *t* and *F* tests; now he had to decide which one would be most suitable for his data.

In the last chapter, we studied chi square, an example of a nonparametric or distribution-free test. A nonparametric test is one in which population parameters such as μ and σ are not involved; such a test is distribution free because no particular distribution is assumed. In this chapter, we examine three more nonparametric methods: the Mann–Whitney *U* test, the Wilcoxon test, and the Kruskal–Wallis test.

When should nonparametric alternatives to *t* and *F* be used? It is often suggested that part of the answer to this question involves scaling, the topic discussed in Chapter 2; parametric statistics assume measurement data, usually at least interval-scale measurement. If our level of measurement is nominal scale—that is, if we have frequency data—we use chi square for a test of significance, as we saw in Chapter 14. It is frequently recommended that with scores on an ordinal scale—measures that are rank ordered, although intervals between them may not be equal—nonparametric techniques should be used. However, it is not the level of measurement per se but rather the nature of the data that most contributes to the decision to use nonparametric tests. If the data suggest that we cannot make the usual assumptions of a normal population, homogeneous variances, and use of the mean as a good measure of central tendency, then nonparametric procedures are appropriate. These conditions often arise when we have small, unequal-sized samples containing extreme scores.

The question of when to use parametric tests has been argued in statistics for many years. People who favor parametric tests feel that the *cited* assumptions of these tests are overly restrictive in practice and that the robustness of the tests means that they are little affected by violations of distributional assumptions. By contrast, proponents of nonparametric tests consider that their *main advantage* is they do not make restrictive assumptions about the shape of populations sampled. Another advantage of nonparametric tests is that they are more concerned with medians than with means. Thus, if your data are best described using medians—such as when cut-off scores are substituted, or you have a small sample with a few extreme scores (outliers)—then nonparametric tests are preferable.

Power is another issue. An experimenter may elect to use a nonparametric test even when the parametric method is also appropriate. However, when both parametric and nonparametric tests are appropriate, the parametric test is recommended because the power of parametric tests is generally greater. All things being equal, we will be more likely to reject the null hypothesis with a parametric than with a nonparametric test.

Nonparametric tests are considered to have low power—to be less likely to detect an effect—relative to the corresponding parametric test, when the assumptions for the parametric test are met and, arguably, even when the assumptions are moderately violated. However, nonparametric tests have a power advantage when the data have outliers or extreme cut-off scores. Such extreme scores increase error variance and reduce the power of parametric tests. Many of the nonparametric tests begin by ranking data and operate on ranks, with the result that the tests of central tendency they provide are not influenced by extreme data points.

In summary, remember that the parametric tests assume normality in the population from which we take our sample(s). If our sample is badly skewed and our sample sizes are small, we may feel uncomfortable with this assumption of normality. In this case, the nonparametric test may be preferable. Also, from our experience as researchers, we have found nonparametric tests to be most useful when a study involves small samples with unequal numbers of subjects. Small samples often have a few extreme scores that contribute a disproportionate amount to the sample's variability. In test statistics such as t and F, the denominator is a measure of variability; hence, the greater the variability, the smaller is the test statistic and the less likely we are to be able to reject the null hypothesis. Because it avoids the measure of variability, the nonparametric alternative may have greater power and result in detection of an effect, which would not occur with t or F.

THE MANN–WHITNEY U TEST

The **Mann–Whitney (M–W) U test** is a powerful alternative to the t test for independent samples. It is used in two major instances:

1. When the level of measurement is ordinal scale and the best we can do with the numbers is to rank them from highest to lowest, and

2. When the assumption of normality in the population from which the samples were drawn cannot be made.

The Mann–Whitney test can also be applied when the level of measurement is interval scale and when other assumptions of the *t* test are met. However, the *t* test is preferable in situations for which both tests are appropriate, as mentioned earlier.

The assumptions required by the Mann–Whitney test are that the samples are independent, that there is an underlying continuous scale of measurement, and that the measurement scale is at least ordinal. The hypothesis tested is that the population distributions from which the samples are drawn are identical in form.

The rationale for the test is based on the null hypothesis being tested. Assuming that the populations being sampled are identical, if we rank the combined observations from our two samples, we would expect to find the scores from the two samples rather evenly mixed in our combined ranking. If the scores are not evenly mixed in the combined ranking (that is, most of the scores from one sample have lower ranks than most of the scores in the other sample), then they probably come from different populations. The test is based on a determination of how evenly mixed the scores are from the two samples.

Let's consider a type of problem for which the Mann–Whitney test is appropriate: Brad's response extinction study. The data are repeated here.

Group Simple	Group Complex
12	24
12	24
11	16
8	15
7	14
6	12
6	11
	10
	9

There are at least two reasons for not applying the *t* test to Brad's data. First, a parametric test is inappropriate—we should not compute the mean of the samples because some of the animals were eliminated from the study before achieving the criterion of extinction. In Chapter 5, we said that $\overline{X}$ should not be calculated when there are arbitrary cut-off points in the data.

Second, the sample sizes are small and the samples are oddly distributed. They are so oddly distributed, in fact, that it would be difficult to justify the assumption of normality in the population from which they came. Let's apply the Mann–Whitney U test, for which the formula is:

FORMULA 15-1   *Mann–Whitney U test (computational formula)*

$$U = N_1 N_2 + \frac{N_1(N_1 + 1)}{2} - R_1,$$

where R_1 is the sum of the ranks of the scores in the first group, N_1 is the number of subjects in the first group, and N_2 is the number of subjects in the second group. The Mann–Whitney U test involves computing both U and U' (pronounced "you-prime").

The procedure for computing and testing U for significance is as follows:

1. Rank the scores from both groups combined from the lowest to the highest, with the smallest score receiving the rank of 1. Give tied scores the average of the tied ranks.

2. Sum the ranks for the first sample and call the result R_1.

3. Once you obtain R_1, compute U using Formula 15-1.

4. After computing U, calculate U' from the following equation:

FORMULA 15-2 U'

$$U' = N_1 N_2 - U$$

The *lower* value, either U or U', is used for the significance test.

5. The null hypothesis is that the two samples are drawn from populations identical in shape. The alternative to this is that the two populations are different.

6. Compare the smaller of U or U' to values in Table H. Use of Table H depends on the size of the samples and will be explained when we have a U (or U') to test.

Let's compute U for Brad's experiment and test it for significance. The first step is to rank the combined sets of scores; the result of this ranking is as follows:

Group Simple	Rank	Group Complex	Rank
12	10	24	15.5
12	10	24	15.5
11	7.5	16	14
8	4	15	13
7	3	14	12
6	1.5	12	10
6	1.5	11	7.5
		10	6
		9	5
	$R_1 = 37.5$		$R_2 = 98.5$

As you can see, the scores have been ranked, with the smallest score receiving the lowest rank. In this case, there were two scores of 6, so each 6 received the average of the tied ranks (1 and 2: average = 1.5). The next lowest score, 7, received the next rank, or 3, the 8 received a rank of 4, and so on until the highest scores, 24, received the average of their tied ranks, or 15.5.

After the combined scores in the two groups were ranked, the sum of the ranks for the first group was found and called R_1. We are now ready to compute U, using the values $N_1 = 7$, $N_2 = 9$, and $R_1 = 37.5$.

$$U = N_1 N_2 + \frac{N_1(N_1 + 1)}{2} - R_1$$

$$= (7)(9) + \frac{7(7 + 1)}{2} - 37.5$$

$$= 63 + 28 - 37.5 = 53.5,$$

$$U' = N_1 N_2 - U = (7)(9) - 53.5 = 63 - 53.5 = 9.5.$$

U' (the smaller of U and U') is compared with critical values in Table H. With $N_1 = 7$ and $N_2 = 9$, the critical value for a two-tailed test at the 5% level is 12. Let's use the seven-step procedure to summarize our Mann–Whitney U test results.

1. H_0: The populations sampled (rats undergoing extinction after being trained on either a Simple VI schedule or a Complex VI schedule) are identical in shape. There's no difference in barpressing during extinction for rats trained on the two different schedules of reinforcement.

2. H_1: The populations sampled are not identical; there is a difference in barpressing during extinction for rats trained on the different schedules.

3. Set $\alpha = .05$.

4. *Rejection Rule:* Reject H_0 if the smaller of U or U' is equal to or *less than* the critical value from Table H.

5. *Computations and Test Statistic:* According to the preceding computations, we found that $U' = 9.5$.

6. *Decision:* From Table H, with $N_1 = 7$ and $N_2 = 9$, the critical value for a two-tailed test at the 5% level is 12. Therefore, we reject H_0 at the 5% level because our computed value (9.5) is *less* than the critical value (12) at that level.

7. *Conclusion:* Rats trained on the Complex VI schedule of reinforcement require more time to extinguish a response than rats trained on the Simple VI schedule. Note we have emphasized that we reject the null hypothesis when our computed test statistic is *less* than the critical table value, not more than the critical value, as in the parametric tests we have studied.

Let's look at another example. An investigator is interested in the effect of "speed" instructions on memory. Fifteen students are asked to memorize a list of 4-digit numbers. Seven of the students are told to memorize as quickly as possible. The other 8 are told to work at their own pace. One week later, the 15 students are retrained on the list, this time without instructions to hurry. A percentage savings score is computed for each student. Any student requiring more than twice as many trials to relearn the list as were needed to learn it originally is assigned a score of −100% and testing is discontinued. The savings scores are as follows:

Speed Instructions	Own Pace Instructions
40	70
35	68
10	65
−20	55
−50	50
−100	−10
−100	−30
	−100

We have arbitrary cut-off scores and uneven groups with a lot of variability, so the M–W test is indicated. As before, we need to rank the scores from the combined groups, sum the ranks for each sample, and compute U and U'. The ranked scores and the summed ranks are as follows:

Speed	Rank	Own Pace	Rank
40	10	70	15
35	9	68	14
10	8	65	13
−20	6	55	12
−50	4	50	11
−100	2	−10	7
−100	2	−30	5
		−100	2
	$R_1 = 41$		$R_2 = 79$

As you can see, the scores have been ranked algebraically, with the largest negative score having the lowest rank. At the bottom are three scores of −100, which are tied for the ranks of 1, 2, and 3. Each of the three is assigned the average of the tied ranks:

$$\frac{1 + 2 + 3}{3} = \frac{6}{3} = 2.$$

Next lowest is a score of −50, which is assigned the rank of 4 (1, 2, and 3 have already been used); next is −30, with the rank of 5; and so on until the highest score is ranked. After the scores are ranked, we sum the ranks and find $R_1 = 41$ and $R_2 = 79$. We are now ready to compute U, using the values $N_1 = 7$, $N_2 = 8$, and $R_1 = 41$:

$$U = N_1 N_2 + \frac{N_1(N_1 + 1)}{2} - R_1$$

$$= (7)(8) + \frac{7(7 + 1)}{2} - 41$$

$$= 56 + 28 - 41 = 43,$$

$$U' = N_1 N_2 - U = (7)(8) - 43$$

$$= 56 - 43$$

$$= 13 \text{ (the smaller of } U \text{ and } U').$$

U' is compared with critical values in Table H. With $N_1 = 7$ and $N_2 = 8$, the critical value for a one-tailed test at the 5% level is 13. Our computed value is equal to the table value, so we reject the null hypothesis and conclude that the two groups differ significantly. In terms of this study, we conclude that students who learned the list at their own pace had better memory of the 4-digit numbers than students who learned under speed conditions.

It is also possible to compute U' directly, with a slight change in the equation for U. The equation for U' is:

FORMULA 15-3   U′

$$U' = N_1 N_2 + \frac{N_2(N_2 + 1)}{2} - R_2$$

Applying this equation to the previous problem, we have

$$U' = (7)(8) + \frac{8(8 + 1)}{2} - 79 = 56 + 36 - 79$$

$$= 92 - 79 = 13.$$

As you can see, solving Formula 15-3 is a useful check on the accuracy of the original computations.

The Mann–Whitney U test may also be used for comparing groups larger than $N = 20$. The procedure is the same except that after U (or U') has been computed, it is converted to a z score using the following equation:

FORMULA 15-4   *z score for large-sample* U

$$z = \frac{U - \dfrac{N_1 N_2}{2}}{\sqrt{\dfrac{(N_1)(N_2)(N_1 + N_2 + 1)}{12}}}$$

If the z score obtained is equal to or larger than 1.96 (two-tailed test, 5% level) or 1.64 (one-tailed test, 5% level), the null hypothesis is rejected. You may recall from Chapter 8 that z scores of ± 1.96 and ± 1.64 cut off the deviant 5% and 10% of the normal curve, respectively. As the M–W test is most useful for small samples, further examples illustrating its use with large samples will not be shown in this text. One final note: Either U or U' will result in the same absolute value for z. Only the sign will differ.

⑤ CHECKING YOUR PROGRESS

An experimenter predicted that extraverted children would display more social motivation than introverted children. To test this idea, she had a teacher divide the 22 children in her class into two groups, introverts and extraverts. Each child was shown five pictures of people engaged in various activities and was asked to make up a story about each picture. The stories were then read by a trained judge who rated each story for affiliative images as an indication of social motivation. Each story received a score from 0 (no affiliative imagery) to 20 (consistent, high affiliative imagery). The total scores for the five stories are as follows:

Introverts	Extraverts	Introverts	Extraverts
21	63	7	48
15	57	6	45
10	55	5	43
9	54	4	42
8	49	4	20
			14
			11

Using the M–W U test, compare the two groups.

Answer: $U' = 5$, $p < .01$, two-tailed test, indicating that extraverts showed significantly more social motivation than introverts.

THE WILCOXON MATCHED-PAIRS SIGNED-RANKS TEST

In Chapter 10, we discussed the t tests for both independent and dependent samples. In this chapter we have so far examined the Mann–Whitney test, which is a nonparametric alternative to the t test for independent samples. Now let's look at the **Wilcoxon matched-pairs signed-ranks test,** which is an alternative to the *t* test for dependent or related samples.

As an example, suppose we want to test the effectiveness of an analgesic agent (Painfree) on a pain other than headache. We conduct the experiment as described in Chapter 10 except that, instead of measuring the length of time each volunteer participant can tolerate the immersion of his or her hand in ice water, we have each participant rate the subjective quality of his or her pain on a scale of 0 to 20 after the hand has been immersed in ice water for a set period of time. The results are as follows:

Participant	Placebo	Painfree
A	15	10
B	17	15
C	10	11
D	8	8
E	14	13
F	13	7
G	10	5
H	8	5

As you can see, we have eight participants, and each has been tested with both Painfree and the placebo, resulting in eight pairs of scores. Our level of measurement is no better than ordinal because of the subjectivity of the ratings, and so we will use the Wilcoxon test.

The assumptions of the test are that the participants must be randomly and independently selected, that the scale of measurement must be at least ordinal, and that we must be able to rank-order the difference scores. The null hypothesis is that the distributions of the populations under each condition are identical.

Computation of the test is simple. We first find the difference (d) between each pair of scores, discarding pairs with 0 differences. Next, we rank-order the difference scores by absolute magnitude, retaining the appropriate sign. Finally, we sum the ranks with the less frequently occurring sign and compare this value with table values in a test of significance.

If the distributions of the populations under each condition are identical, there will usually be about the same number of positive and negative differences, and the sums of the ranks for the positive and negative differences will not vary to any great extent. However, if the population distributions are not the same, then we could expect to see many more differences of one sign than of the other. Thus, the smaller the sum of the less frequently occurring ranks, the more likely it is that the population distributions under each condition are different.

Let's go back to the problem and solve it.

Participant	Placebo	Painfree	d	Rank of d	Rank With Less Frequent Sign
A	15	10	5	5.5	
B	17	15	2	3	
C	10	11	−1	−1.5	1.5
D	8	8	0		
E	14	13	1	1.5	
F	13	7	6	7	
G	10	5	5	5.5	
H	8	5	3	4	
					$T = \overline{1.5}$

The differences (d) have been found and the absolute values ranked. Ranking is performed as before, with the smallest difference having the first rank and so on until all the differences have been ranked. Tied scores are given the average rank; for example, in absolute value, two differences had a magnitude of 1 and each received the average of ranks 1 and 2, or 1.5. In the last column, the ranks with the less frequent sign are entered. In our example, only one negative difference occurred and the rank of this difference, 1.5, appears. Finally, the ranks (rank in this case) with the less frequent sign are summed and called T. Thus, our obtained $T = 1.5$. For comparative purposes, the sum of the positive ranks is 26.5. Remember that if the population distributions are really identical, the sums of the positive and negative ranks will not be very different.

The obtained T of 1.5 is compared with the appropriate values in Table I. The table's title tells us that it contains critical values of T. Thus, for $N = 7$, a T of 2 or *less* is required for rejection of the null hypothesis at the 5% level, two-tailed test. Incidentally, although we had eight pairs of scores originally, differences were found between only seven of them, and the pair having no difference was discarded. Our obtained T was 1.5, so we reject the null hypothesis. The participants' subjective rating of pain following use of Painfree was lower than after the administration of a placebo.

Let's look at another example of the use of the Wilcoxon test. A teacher was interested in the effect of public speaking training on the quality of speeches given by her students. Ten students gave speeches, and their quality was rated on a 30-point scale. The students then received training in public speaking and were asked to give another speech, which was also rated on a 30-point scale. The before and after training scores are as follows:

Student	Before	After	d	Rank of d	Rank With Less Frequent Sign
A	27	29	−2	−3	3
B	22	14	8	8	
C	5	5	0		

Student	Before	After	d	Rank of d	Rank With Less Frequent Sign
D	9	7	2	3	
E	17	18	−1	−1	1
F	30	21	9	9	
G	14	7	7	7	
H	3	5	−2	−3	3
I	8	5	3	5	
J	7	3	4	6	

$$T = \overline{7}$$

The difference is found for each pair of scores, and then the differences are ranked without regard to sign. Student C did not change and her data are discarded. Finally, the ranks with the less frequent sign are summed, giving a T of 7. In Table I, with $N = 9$, we see that a T of 6 or less is required for rejection at the 5% level of significance with a two-tailed test. We conclude that our observed result is not different enough from chance to enable us to reject the null hypothesis. In this study, training did not cause a statistically significant change in speech quality.

Table I cannot be used with samples greater than 25. However, as we've discovered with a number of other test statistics, with large samples the distribution of T is approximately normal. Thus, we can convert our T score to a z score using the formula:

FORMULA 15-5 *z score for large-sample* T

$$z = \frac{T - \dfrac{N(N + 1)}{4}}{\sqrt{\dfrac{N(N + 1)(2N + 1)}{24}}}$$

If the value computed for z is 1.96 or larger (1.64 for a one-tailed test), the null hypothesis is rejected at the 5% level, two-tailed test.

↻ CHECKING YOUR PROGRESS

An experiment is performed to study the effects of movie depiction of altruism on expressed attitudes toward helping. Each member of 12 pairs of identical twins is randomly assigned to one of two treatment conditions. One member of each pair watches scenes from a movie showing altruistic behavior and self-sacrifice. The other member watches neutral scenes from the same movie. Each participant is then given a self-rating scale designed to elicit attitudes about helping behavior. High scores represent a low threshold for the expression of helping. The results are as follows:

Twin Pair Number	Group Altruism	Group Neutral
1	23	15
2	13	15
3	15	12
4	17	17
5	19	15
6	23	19
7	25	19
8	10	10
9	16	17
10	8	5
11	7	2
12	12	11

Test the null hypothesis.

Answer: $T = 4.5$, which has a $p < .02$ for a two-tailed test. Exposure to the movie scenes of altruism and self-sacrifice produced significantly lower thresholds for the expression of helping than did exposure to the neutral scenes.

THE KRUSKAL–WALLIS ONE-WAY ANOVA

The **Kruskal–Wallis (K–W) one-way analysis of variance by ranks test** is a useful technique for comparing more than two groups when we have at least ordinal scale measurement and the assumptions of the one-way analysis of variance test cannot be met. In other words, it is used in situations similar to those we discussed favoring the M–W U test except that more than two independent groups are compared.

The K–W test is actually an extension of the M–W test and again requires that we rank the scores from the combined groups. The null hypothesis tested is that the samples have identically shaped population distributions. If the distributions from which we draw our samples are identical, the sums of the ranks of each sample should be similar. Very different sums suggest that the samples come from different populations and result in rejection of the null hypothesis. Let's consider a problem for which the K–W test is appropriate.

The head of the anthropology department at a local college has three candidates in his department for an excellence in teaching award, and he wants to select the candidate with the best teaching skills. Each candidate currently teaches a section of Anthropology 101. The department head develops an evaluation form and asks five students from each of the three sections to fill it out. On the form, students are asked to rate their current instructor on a scale of 1–30 for such qualities as command of the material, ability to explain difficult concepts, and availability to students outside of class. The ratings are as follows:

Instructor A	Instructor B	Instructor C
26	17	30
23	15	25
19	14	20
17	12	18
15	10	16

Obviously there are some differences in the ratings given to the three instructors, but are the differences great enough for us to conclude that the samples come from different populations? The K–W test is appropriate here because of the level of measurement used; that is, the ratings of the instructors are considered to constitute an ordinal level of measurement. The formula for the test is:

FORMULA 15-6 *Kruskal–Wallis test (computational formula)*

$$H = \frac{12}{N(N + 1)} \sum \frac{R_i^2}{N_i} - 3(N + 1),$$

---

where N_i = the number of observations in a particular sample,
N = the total number of observations in all samples combined, and
R_i = the sum of the ranks for a particular sample.

The large summation sign tells us to sum the squared ranks divided by the N in a group over all groups. With three groups and at least five participants in each group, H is distributed approximately as chi square, and we can use Table G with $df = K - 1$ (K is the number of samples) to evaluate H. However, with three groups and fewer than five participants in any group, H is sufficiently deviant from chi square that Table G cannot be used. An appropriate table may be found in S. Siegel and N. J. Castellan, Jr., 1988, *Nonparametric Statistics for the Behavioral Sciences*, 2d ed., New York: McGraw-Hill.

Let's find H. As with the M–W test, the first step is to rank the combined scores from the lowest to the highest and then to sum the ranks for each sample.

Instructor A	Rank	Instructor B	Rank	Instructor C	Rank
26	14	17	7.5	30	15
23	12	15	4.5	25	13
19	10	14	3	20	11
17	7.5	12	2	18	9
15	4.5	10	1	16	6
	$R_1 = 48$		$R_2 = 18$		$R_3 = 54$

The lowest rating in the combined groups is 10, and this is assigned a rank of 1. The same instructor also receives a rating of 12, which is given the rank of 2. The ranking is continued until the highest score, 30, is reached, and this receives a rank of 15. As before, tied scores receive the average of the tied ranks. Finally, the sum of the ranks for each instructor is found: R_1 (the sum of the ranks of Instructor A) is 48, $R_2 = 18$, and $R_3 = 54$. We're now ready to compute H.

$$H = \frac{12}{N(N + 1)} \sum \frac{R_i^2}{N_i} - 3(N + 1)$$

$$= \frac{12}{15(15 + 1)} \left(\frac{48^2}{5} + \frac{18^2}{5} + \frac{54^2}{5} \right) - 3(15 + 1)$$

$$= \frac{12}{(15)(16)} \left(\frac{2{,}304}{5} + \frac{324}{5} + \frac{2{,}916}{5} \right) - 3(16)$$

$$= \frac{12}{240} (460.8 + 64.8 + 583.2) - 48$$

$$= 0.05(1{,}108.8) - 48 = 55.44 - 48 = 7.44$$

With $df = K - 1 = 3 - 1 = 2$, the critical value at the 5% level from Table G is 5.99. As our observed $H = 7.44$, we reject the null hypothesis and conclude that the samples come from different populations. Note that, unlike our previous tests of significance in this chapter, we rejected H_0 because our computed H was *larger* than the critical table value; the reason is that we are testing our computed H as though it were really χ^2. In other words, the three instructors differ in their ratings. Looking at the scores, it appears that Instructors A and C received higher ratings than Instructor B. Further testing will be needed to determine which differences are significant.

Let's consider another example. Recruiters from a national hotel chain interviewed college seniors majoring in psychology, history, business, and sociology for management training positions. Two interviewers evaluated each candidate on a scale of acceptability from 0 (unacceptable) to 7 (highly desirable). The ratings of the two interviewers were summed to give an overall rating. The interviewers were interested in whether students from some majors received higher ratings than students from other majors. To answer the question, they analyzed the data using a Kruskal–Wallis one-way ANOVA.

Psychology	History	Business	Sociology
13	14	12	10
12	7	11	8
11	7	10	8
10	7	8	6
7	6	6	6
6	5	5	5
6	5	5	5
4	2	4	1

As before, the first step is to rank the combined scores. Once this has been done, we can sum the ranks for each sample and compute H. The computations are as follows:

Psychology	Rank	History	Rank	Business	Rank	Sociology	Rank
13	31	14	32	12	29.5	10	25
12	29.5	7	18.5	11	27.5	8	22
11	27.5	7	18.5	10	25	8	22
10	25	7	18.5	8	22	6	13.5
7	18.5	6	13.5	6	13.5	6	13.5
6	13.5	5	7.5	5	7.5	5	7.5
6	13.5	5	7.5	5	7.5	5	7.5
4	3.5	2	2	4	3.5	1	1
	$R_1 = 162$		$R_2 = 118$		$R_3 = 136$		$R_4 = 112$

$$H = \frac{12}{N(N+1)} \sum \frac{R_i^2}{N_i} - 3(N+1)$$

$$= \frac{12}{32(32+1)} \left(\frac{162^2}{8} + \frac{118^2}{8} + \frac{136^2}{8} + \frac{112^2}{8} \right) - 3(32+1)$$

$$= \frac{12}{1,056} (3,280.5 + 1,740.5 + 2,312 + 1,568) - 99$$

$$= 0.01136(8,901) - 99 = 101.12 - 99 = 2.12.$$

Note that the fraction 12/1,056 has been carried out to five decimal places rather than being rounded to hundredths. If we use 0.01, the final answer will have a negative value (-9.99), which is impossible. It would be slightly more accurate to multiply the numerator of the fraction by 8,901 [(12)(8,901) = 106,812] and divide the result by 1,056 (106,812/1,056 = 101.15). Then the final answer would be $H = 2.15$.

Do you notice that there are quite a few tied scores? Actually, the value of H is affected by ties; for this reason, there is a procedure to correct for them. However, the correction is minor, and it would be worth applying only in a situation in which the H value computed was slightly below that required for significance. For this problem, the H value corrected for ties is 2.16 even though there were eight sets of tied scores including almost all of the 32 scores in the four samples. Because the difference is negligible, the correction procedure will not be presented. (For further details of the procedure, consult *Nonparametric Statistics for the Behavioral Sciences*, 2d ed., by Siegel and Castellan.)

From Table G we find that the critical values for chi square with $df = 3$ ($K - 1 = 4 - 1 = 3$) are 7.82 and 11.34 at the 5% and 1% levels, respectively. Our H value, corrected or uncorrected, is much less than the value at the 5% level, and we cannot reject the null hypothesis. Thus, there is no reason to believe that students from some majors received higher ratings than students from other majors.

---

⑤ CHECKING YOUR PROGRESS

Research has suggested that birth order influences people's social competence. To verify this finding, 21 students were categorized as first born, second born, or later born, and then rated by their classmates on the amount of their class participation. The score for each student is the sum of the student's ratings. The scores are shown here:

First born	Second born	Later born
25	28	14
24	27	12
23	26	10
20	18	7
19	15	5
18	15	5
15	14	
	12	

Compute H and test it for significance.

Answer: $H = 11.41$, $p < .01$, suggesting that birth order has a significant effect on class participation. Further testing (e.g., of pairs of groups with the Mann–Whitney U test) is needed to determine specific group differences, as we will discuss next.

FURTHER TESTING AFTER A SIGNIFICANT H

What happens when a significant H value is obtained? Does this tell us which group comparisons are significant? The answer is no, just as it was with the F test. In this case, individual comparisons can be made with a test we've already discussed in this chapter, the Mann–Whitney U test. Recall that the K–W is an extension of the M–W.

To illustrate, let's reconsider the first example of the K–W we solved—the ratings of the three anthropology instructors. Suppose that, after finding differences among the instructors, the department head wanted to compare the ratings obtained by Instructors A and B. Computation of the M–W test is as follows:

Instructor A	Rank	Instructor B	Rank
26	10	17	6.5
23	9	15	4.5
19	8	14	3
17	6.5	12	2
15	4.5	10	1
	$R_1 = 38$		$R_2 = 17$

$$U = N_1 N_2 + \frac{N_1(N_1 + 1)}{2} - R_1$$

$$= (5)(5) + \frac{5(5 + 1)}{2} - 38$$

$$= 25 + 15 - 38 = 40 - 38 = 2,$$

$$U' = N_1 N_2 - U = (5)(5) - 2 = 25 - 2 = 23.$$

The smaller of U and U' is $U = 2$, and this is the value we will test for significance. From Table H we find that 2 is the critical value for a two-tailed test at the .05 level (for a one-tailed test at the .025 level). Thus, we reject the null hypothesis for the comparison between Instructors A and B. Instructor A received higher ratings than Instructor B.

---

⑤ CHECKING YOUR PROGRESS

To check your progress, compare Instructors A and C and Instructors B and C.

Answer: $U' = 10, p > .05$ for the comparison between Instructors A and C; $U' = 1$, $p = .02$, two-tailed test, for the comparison between Instructors B and C. Instructor C received higher ratings than Instructor B but did not differ from Instructor A.

SUMMARY

The techniques studied in this chapter—the Mann–Whitney U test, the Wilcoxon matched-pairs signed-ranks test, and the Kruskal–Wallis H test—are valuable alternatives to the t test and the one-way ANOVA. Instead of being based on a comparison of the means of independent samples or on a comparison of the variances, the M–W and the K–W tests compare the ranks of the sample scores. The Wilcoxon test studies the ranks of the difference scores. The tests are nonparametric and are used primarily for comparing data generated by an ordinal scale—that is, rank-ordered data.

The M–W test is used to compare two independent samples. The procedure is as follows:

1. Rank the scores from the combined samples from the lowest to the highest, giving the lowest score the rank of 1. Give tied scores the average of the tied ranks.

2. Find the sum of the ranks for each sample.

3. Compute the statistic U using the formula

$$U = N_1 N_2 + \frac{N_1(N_1 + 1)}{2} - R_1,$$

where N_1 is the number of observations in the first sample, N_2 is the number of observations in the second sample, and R_1 is the sum of the ranks in the first sample.

4.   Compute U' from the equation

$$U' = N_1 N_2 - U.$$

Use the smaller of U or U' in the significance test.

5.   Compare the smaller of U or U' with table values from Table H for the appropriate sample sizes. If U or U' is *smaller* than the critical table value, reject the null hypothesis.

6.   For samples larger than $N = 20$, convert U or U' to a z score using the formula

$$z = \frac{U - \dfrac{N_1 N_2}{2}}{\sqrt{\dfrac{(N_1)(N_2)(N_1 + N_2 + 1)}{12}}}.$$

If the absolute value of the z score is equal to or larger than 1.96, reject the null hypothesis at the 5% level.

The Wilcoxon test is useful as an alternative to the t test for dependent samples when the assumptions for t cannot be met. The difference between pairs of scores is found and ranked without regard to sign. The sum of the ranks with the less frequently occurring sign is found, and if N is 25 or less, the resulting T is compared with values in Table I. If T is equal to or *less* than critical values in the table, the null hypothesis is rejected. For samples larger than 25, the distribution of T is approximately normal and z is computed from the equation

$$z = \frac{T - \dfrac{N(N + 1)}{4}}{\sqrt{\dfrac{N(N + 1)(2N + 1)}{24}}}.$$

If the z score is 1.96 or larger, the null hypothesis is rejected at the 5% level.

The K–W test is an extension of the M–W test for situations in which three or more samples are to be compared. As with the M–W test, the combined scores from the groups are first ranked and then the sum of the ranks for each sample is found. A statistic H is computed from the formula

$$H = \frac{12}{N(N + 1)} \sum \frac{R_i^2}{N_i} - 3(N + 1),$$

where N_i is the number of observations for a particular sample, N is the total number of observations for the combined groups, and R_i is the sum of the ranks for a particular sample.

With sample sizes of at least 5 and at least 3 samples, H is distributed approximately as chi square; Table G is used to evaluate H, with $df = K - 1$, where K is the number of samples.

✻ *Troubleshooting Your Computations*

Although the techniques discussed in this chapter are fairly simple to apply, there are some possible problem areas and warnings that something has gone awry in your proceedings. For example, both the K–W test and the M–W test require ranking of the *combined* scores in the groups from the lowest to the highest. The rank of the highest score should be equal to N unless the highest scores are tied. If the highest score doesn't receive a rank of N, you should go back to the beginning of the ranking procedure and be sure you haven't skipped a rank somewhere along the way.

The value you obtain for either U or H should be a positive number. If it is not, check the sum of the ranks to be sure you haven't made an error there.

If you are using the M–W U test, be sure to compute U' as well as U, and be sure to use the smaller of the two values in the significance test. Also, when using Table H, be sure to remember that the value of U or U' is significant if it is *less* than the appropriate table value, not greater, as in the other tests we have considered.

When using the Wilcoxon test be sure to discard all zero differences. Also, the difference scores are ranked in terms of absolute value—that is, without regard to sign. To be significant, the obtained T must be equal to or *less* than the table value.

EXERCISES

1. Ten monkeys, five reared with a surrogate (artificial) mother and five reared normally, have been observed over a 10-day period in a group play area. The number of self-directed behaviors has been scored for each animal during a 20-minute daily test session. The summed scores for each animal are as follows:

Reared With Surrogate Mother	Normally Reared
255	173
241	150
213	142
185	131
151	75

Compute the M–W *U* and test it for significance. What does your decision mean in the context of the exercise?

2. The Myers–Briggs Type Indicator (MBTI) has been administered to a large number of people to determine their personality types. On the basis of this test, a number of persons have been designated as either thinking or feeling types and have been given a questionnaire concerning their attitudes toward extrasensory perception. Each person has received a score on the questionnaire reflecting the degree of his or her belief in ESP, with higher scores reflecting more positive attitudes about ESP. The scores are as follows:

Group Thinking	Group Feeling
8	20
7	18
7	15
5	15
3	14
1	12
0	6
0	5
	4
	1

Compare the groups, and tell what your decision means in the context of the exercise.

3. In situations in which both parametric and nonparametric tests could be used, why is the parametric test usually preferable?

4. The quality of articles from the most recent issue of four different professional sociology journals has been rated, with higher numbers representing higher ratings. The results are as follows:

Journal A	Journal B	Journal C	Journal D
12	45	20	37
10	43	13	35
9	42	11	28
9	41	8	27
8	36	6	20
7	25	5	13
3	23	4	10
2	15	1	
	10		

Determine whether the differences are significant. Note: Carry the division of $12/[N(N + 1)]$ to at least 5 decimal places.

5. Perform all pairwise comparisons for Exercise 4, and tell what each result means in the context of the exercise.

6. What does it mean to call a test nonparametric?

7. Using the MBTI mentioned in Exercise 2, researchers have identified a large number of students classified as feeling types. From this group, 14 persons expressing strong belief in ESP on a questionnaire have been shown a film presenting a very negative view of ESP's validity. Before and after scores on the ESP questionnaire are listed here:

Student	Before the Film	After the Film	Student	Before the Film	After the Film
1	20	22	8	25	28
2	18	13	9	10	10
3	15	15	10	12	13
4	15	18	11	17	23
5	17	16	12	15	11
6	16	14	13	13	17
7	14	10	14	10	10

Test the null hypothesis, and tell what your result means in the exercise context.

8. An identical procedure to that followed in Exercise 7 has been performed, except that 13 thinking types have been selected for low belief in ESP. The students have been shown a biased film presenting ESP in a favorable light. Before and after scores on the ESP questionnaire are as follows:

Student	Before the Film	After the Film
1	7	7
2	5	8
3	0	5
4	3	7
5	2	4
6	1	3
7	4	10
8	4	12
9	5	4
10	7	4
11	8	8
12	5	15
13	2	11

Test the null hypothesis, and tell what your results mean in the context of the exercise.

9. An investigator wants to learn whether there are occupational differences in self-ratings on a scale of sociability. Eight salespeople, 10 delivery persons, and 7 of the office staff rate themselves on a 20-item scale of sociability. The ratings are as follows:

Sales	Delivery	Office
17	18	18
15	16	13
14	15	10
13	14	9
12	11	8
10	10	8
5	10	5
4	9	
	5	
	3	

Compare the groups on the sociability ratings, and tell what your result means in the context of the exercise.

10. In a study of Alzheimer's disease, biochemical assays of the brains of nine people with the disorder are compared with similar assays performed on the brains of nine persons who died of nonneurological causes. The aluminum content of the brains, expressed as $\mu g/100g$, dry weight, are as follows:

Persons With AD	Controls
65	12
24	10
52	31
86	6
120	5
82	5
399	29
87	9
139	12

Compare the groups, and tell what your result means in the context of the exercise.

REVIEW OF INFERENTIAL STATISTICS

We have now completed our survey of the basic inferential techniques, and it's time to take a look back because it's easy to lose sight of the forest when you're traveling through the trees. Chapters 7–15 covered techniques designed to allow conclusions (inferences) to be made about a population(s) based on a sample(s) taken from it.

Chapter 7 covered some of the fundamental information from probability theory on which inferential statistics is based. Some elementary rules of probability theory were presented, and the chapter closed with a look at a simple theoretical probability distribution—the binomial. With increases in sample size, the binomial distribution more closely approximates the normal probability distribution, which was covered in detail in Chapter 8.

Chapter 9 began with a discussion of the *sampling distribution of means,* which becomes increasingly similar to the normal curve as sample sizes increase. The sampling distribution was used to work problems of the two types discussed in Chapter 8: finding scores when you know areas and finding areas when you know scores. Determining the *confidence interval*—a range of score values around the sample mean in which we have a certain degree of assurance the population mean is contained—is analogous to finding scores when we know areas. The sampling distribution of means also was used to test hypotheses about an exact value for μ, the population mean; this is analogous to finding areas when we know scores. The method we developed to test hypotheses in Chapter 9 was the *one-sample* t *test.*

In Chapter 10, the *sampling distribution of the mean differences* was constructed by drawing pairs of samples from a population and taking the differences between the sample means. From the distribution, the *two-sample* t *test* was developed; this was an extension of the one-sample test from Chapter 9 to two samples. The two-sample *t* test was used to test the difference between means for pairs of *independent* samples and for pairs of *dependent* samples.

Chapter 11 introduced and discussed the *one-way analysis of variance* or *ANOVA,* a powerful tool designed to compare two or more groups drawn from a population. If the groups are independent, then the between-subjects ANOVA is used for the analysis, whereas dependent groups are analyzed with the repeated measures ANOVA. Two methods for paired-group comparisons following a significant ANOVA were also developed in the chapter—the *Fisher LSD* and the *Tukey HSD*. The Tukey test is quite conservative, whereas the Fisher test is less conservative (and more powerful).

Chapter 12 presented an intuitive, nonquantitative look at the *two-way ANOVA*, a technique designed to make inferences from data based on two independent variables. Chapter 13 covered linear correlation and regression, which have both inferential and descriptive applications. Correlation refers to the co-relationship between two variables, and the specific correlation coefficients discussed included the *Pearson product-moment correlation coefficient* (used when both variables are at least interval level), the *Spearman rank order correlation coefficient* (useful when the data are ordinal level), the *point biserial correlation coefficient* (used when one variable is interval level and the other is dichotomous—can take only two values), and the *phi coefficient*, which is used when both variables are dichotomous. Chapter 13 brought to a close the discussion of *parametric* inferential tests, which are tools designed to examine hypotheses about population parameters such as μ and σ.

Chapters 14 and 15 examined several popular *nonparametric* or relatively *distribution-free* tests. Nonparametric tests do not test hypotheses about population parameters and do not require assumptions of normality in the populations from which the samples are taken.

In Chapter 14, two chi-square tests were presented—the *chi-square goodness-of-fit* test and the *chi-square test of independence*. Both tests are performed when the measurement level is nominal and the data consist of frequency counts on categorical variables. The goodness-of-fit test is used with one categorical variable, and the test of independence is performed with two categorical variables.

Chapter 15 examined some nonparametric alternatives to the *t* test and the *F* test. With ordinal scale data and possible violation of the normality assumption, the *Mann–Whitney U* test, the *Wilcoxon* test, and the *Kruskal–Wallis* test are preferable to the *t* test for independent samples, the *t* test for dependent samples, and the *F* test, respectively. A table summarizing the main inferential tests covered in this text is shown next.

Summary of Inferential Techniques

Name of Test	Test Statistic	Measurement Level	Purpose of Test	Nonparametric (N) or Parametric (P) Alternative
Chi-Square Goodness-of-Fit	χ^2	Nominal	To determine whether frequency distribution across levels of a categorical variable matches expected distribution	
Chi-Square Test of Independence	χ^2	Nominal	To determine whether two categorical variables are independent	
Mann–Whitney	U	Ordinal	To compare two independent samples	t test for independent samples (P)
Wilcoxon	T	Ordinal	To compare two dependent samples	t test for dependent samples (P)
Kruskal–Wallis	H	Ordinal	To compare two or more independent samples	F test (P)
One-Sample t Test	t	Interval or ratio	To test an assumed value for μ	
Two-Sample t Test, Independent Samples	t	Interval or ratio	To compare two independent samples	Mann–Whitney (N)
Two-Sample t Test, Dependent Samples	t	Interval or ratio	To compare two dependent samples	Wilcoxon T (N)
One-Way Between-Subjects ANOVA	F	Interval or ratio	To compare two or more independent samples	Kruskal–Wallis (N)
One-Way Repeated Measures ANOVA	F	Interval or ratio	To compare two or more dependent samples	
Fisher Least Significant Difference Test	LSD	Interval or ratio	Post-ANOVA testing after a significant F test	Mann–Whitney (N) after a significant Kruskal–Wallis H (independent samples)
Tukey Honestly Significant Difference Test	HSD	Interval or ratio	Post-ANOVA testing after a significant F test	M–W (N) after K–W H
Two-Way ANOVA	F	Interval or ratio	To analyze data from the administration of two independent variables	

Review of Inferential Statistics

CHOOSING THE CORRECT INFERENTIAL TEST

One of the most common questions asked by beginning statistics' students is, "How do I know when to use which test?" The following diagram is designed to answer that question—to help you choose the appropriate statistical test to apply in different research situations (at least the ones described in this book). To use

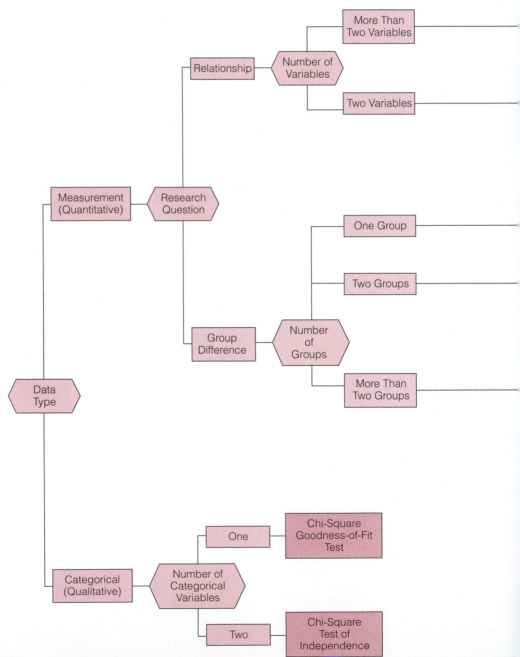

the chart, you will need to think about your data. What level of measurement is involved? Proceed through the chart carefully, considering the research question you want to ask. The diagram should lead you to the appropriate statistical procedure for your situation.

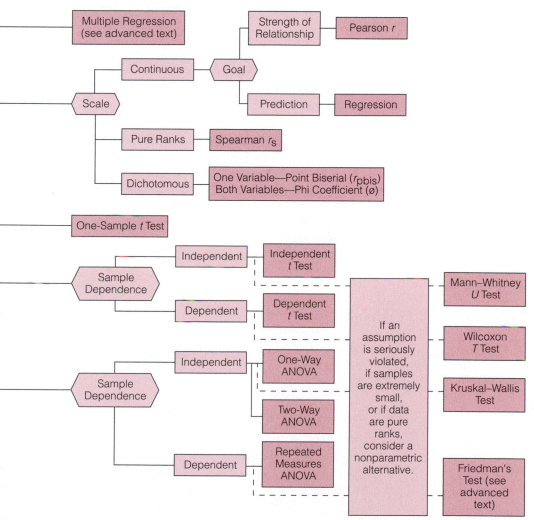

Brief Math–Algebra Review

Let's face it: There's a lot of variability in the mathematical sophistication under-graduates bring to their first statistics courses. From our experience, preparation ranges from avoidance of any college math to completion of an advanced college calculus course. If your background qualifies you for the calculus end of the range, read no further; this appendix is not for you. On the other hand, if you've avoided college math before this, read on. The material in this appendix is designed to refresh your memory of topics long forgotten and to prepare you for the very basic mathematics presented elsewhere in this text.

SYMBOLS

Symbol	Read	Example
$=$	equals	$7 = 7$
$\neq$	is not equal to	$6 \neq 37$
$>$	greater than	$5 > 2$
$<$	less than	$2 < 5$
$\geq$	greater than or equal to	$p \geq .05$
$\leq$	less than or equal to	$p \leq .01$
$+$	plus	$3 + 3 = 6$
$-$	minus	$3 - 3 = 0$
$\times$ or ( )( ) or $\cdot$	times	$3 \times 3 = 9$
		$(3)(3) = 9$
		$3 \cdot 3 = 9$
$\div$ or /	divided by	$6 \div 3 = 2$
		$6/3 = 2$

Symbol	Read	Example
$(\ )^2$	square	$(3)^2 = 3^2 = 9$
$\sqrt{\ }$	square root	$\sqrt{4} = 2$
$|\ |$	absolute value of	$|-5| = 5$
	(the number without	$|5| = 5$
	regard to sign)	
$\pm$	plus or minus	6 ± 5 is
		$6 + 5 = 11$
		and
		$6 - 5 = 1$

ARITHMETIC OPERATIONS

Addition

Numbers may be added in any order or combination.

Example:

$$8 + 4 + 3 = 3 + 4 + 8 = (3 + 4) + 8 = 15$$

Addition of Negative Numbers

Add as though the numbers were positive; then put a negative sign before the result.

Example:

$$(-1) + (-3) + (-5) + (-7) = -(1 + 3 + 5 + 7) = -16$$

Subtraction

Subtraction is equivalent to the addition of a negative number.

Example:

$$12 - 3 = 12 + (-3) = 9$$

As with addition, numbers may be subtracted in any order or combination.

Example:

$$27 - 4 - 12 = 27 + (-4) + (-12)$$
$$= 27 + [(-4) + (-12)]$$
$$= -4 + (-12) + 27 = 11$$

Adding a Combination of Positive and Negative Numbers

Sum the positive and negative numbers separately; take the difference between the sums; then put the sign of the larger sum on the result.

Examples:

$$(+5) + (+3) + (+6) + (-2) + (-5) + (-15)$$
$$= +14 + (-22) = -8 \qquad \text{(The difference between 22 and 14 is 8,}$$
$$\text{and the sign of the larger difference is } -.)$$
$$(+5) + (+10) + (-3) + (-5) = +15 + (-8) = 7$$

Subtracting Negative Numbers

Change the sign of the negative number to be subtracted and add.

Examples:

$$10 - (-5) = 10 + 5 = 15$$
$$-15 - (-6) = -15 + 6 = -9$$

MULTIPLICATION AND DIVISION

In multiplication and division, the result is positive if all of the terms are positive or if there is an even number of negative terms. The result is negative if there is an odd number of negative terms.

Examples:

$$(6)(3) = +18$$
$$(-6)(-3) = +18$$
$$(-6)(3) = -18 \qquad \text{or} \qquad (6)(-3) = -18$$
$$\frac{-6}{-3} = +2$$
$$\frac{6}{3} = +2$$
$$\frac{6}{-3} = -2$$
$$\frac{-6}{3} = -2$$

As with addition and subtraction, order of computation makes no difference.

Example:

$$(6)(-3)(-4) = (-4)(-3)(6) = 72$$

ORDER OF OPERATIONS

Work from the inside out; that is, do everything inside parentheses or brackets first. Within an expression, follow the order of operations summarized in the mnemonic "Follow My Dear Aunt Sally."

1. Follow = Functional operations such as square or square root
2. My Dear = Multiplication and Division
3. Aunt Sally = Addition and Subtraction

Example 1:

$$6(5 - 2^2) + \frac{13\sqrt{25}}{8} = 6(5 - 4) + \frac{(13)(5)}{8} = 6(1) + \frac{65}{8} = 6 + 8.13 = 14.13$$

Example 2:

$$\left[\frac{(.9)(5)}{4}\right]X + \left[20 - \left(\frac{(.9)(5)}{4}\right)(12)\right]$$

Do everything inside parentheses or brackets first. Multiply, then divide:

$$\left(\frac{4.5}{4}\right)X + \left[20 - \left(\frac{4.5}{4}\right)(12)\right]$$

$$1.13X + [20 - (1.13)(12)]$$

Multiply before adding:

$$1.13X + (20 - 13.56)$$

$$1.13X + 6.44$$

In adding -13.56 and $+20$, take the difference between the numbers and give the sign of the larger number to the result.

WORKING WITH FRACTIONS

In these days of the pocket calculator, the simplest way to work with fractions is to convert them to decimals and carry out the operations specified by the equation. To convert a fraction to a decimal, divide the numerator (top part of the fraction) by the denominator (bottom part of the fraction).

Examples:

$$\frac{1}{15} + \frac{1}{17} = 0.07 + 0.06 = 0.13$$

$$\left(\frac{3}{19}\right)\left(\frac{7}{16}\right) = (0.16)(0.44) = 0.07$$

Nevertheless, there are times when it is more convenient or it is necessary (such as when your calculator breaks) to work with fractions. In these situations, there are several rules, specific to fractions, that must be followed.

Addition or Subtraction of Fractions

In adding or subtracting fractions, first express each fraction in terms of the least common denominator. Then add (or subtract) the numerators and place the result over the common denominator.

Examples:

$$\frac{1}{8} + \frac{1}{2} + \frac{1}{4} = \frac{1}{8} + \frac{4}{8} + \frac{2}{8} = \frac{7}{8}$$

$$\frac{11}{12} - \frac{1}{6} - \frac{1}{3} = \frac{11}{12} - \frac{2}{12} - \frac{4}{12} = \frac{5}{12}$$

Multiplication of Fractions

In multiplying fractions, find the product of the numerators and divide by the product of the denominators.

Examples:

$$\frac{2}{3} \times \frac{3}{5} = \frac{2 \times 3}{3 \times 5} = \frac{6}{15}$$

$$\frac{1}{2} \times \frac{3}{7} \times \frac{3}{5} = \frac{1 \times 3 \times 3}{2 \times 7 \times 5} = \frac{9}{70}$$

Multiplying a Whole Number by a Fraction

In multiplying fractions and whole numbers, multiply the numerator of the fraction(s) by the whole number(s) and divide by the denominator.

Examples:

$$\left(\frac{1}{9}\right)(5) = \frac{(1)(5)}{9} = \frac{5}{9}$$

$$\left(\frac{1}{7}\right)(4)(3) = \frac{(1)(4)(3)}{7} = \frac{12}{7}$$

$$\left(\frac{4}{5}\right)\left(\frac{1}{3}\right)(7) = \frac{(4)(1)(7)}{(5)(3)} = \frac{28}{15}$$

SOLVING EQUATIONS WITH ONE UNKNOWN

You frequently will be required to solve equations with one unknown. These are quite simple and usually involve performing arithmetic steps to isolate the unknown on one side of the equation and then to simplify the other side of the equation. The specific steps required are different for each problem. The principle to remember is that whatever you do on one side of the equation must also be done on the other side. Examples of the basic types of problems you may encounter will illustrate the procedures involved.

Solving for X by addition:

$$X - 7 = 4$$
$$X - 7 + 7 = 4 + 7 \quad \text{(add 7 to both sides)}$$
$$X = 11$$

Solving for X by subtraction:

$$X + 6 = 10$$
$$X + 6 - 6 = 10 - 6 \quad \text{(subtract 6 from both sides)}$$
$$X = 4$$

Solving for X by division:

$$3X = 15$$
$$\frac{3X}{3} = \frac{15}{3} \quad \text{(divide both sides by 3)}$$
$$X = 5$$

Solving for X by multiplication:

$$\frac{X}{7} = 4$$

$$(7)\frac{X}{7} = (4)7 \qquad \text{(multiply both sides by 7)}$$

$$X = 28$$

Solving for X by a combination of procedures:

$$X + 2 = 18$$

$$4X + 2 - 2 = 18 - 2 \qquad \text{(subtract 2 from both sides)}$$

$$4X = 16$$

$$\frac{4X}{4} = \frac{16}{4} \qquad \text{(divide both sides by 4)}$$

$$X = 4$$

$$\frac{X - 10}{3} = 2$$

$$(3)\left(\frac{X - 10}{3}\right) = 2(3) \qquad \text{(multiply both sides by 3)}$$

$$X - 10 = 6$$

$$X - 10 + 10 = 6 + 10 \qquad \text{(add 10 to both sides)}$$

$$X = 16$$

EXERCISES

1. $\dfrac{3 + (13 - 3^2)}{(4)(6 - 3)(5 + 2^2)} = \,?$

2. $\dfrac{1}{10} + \dfrac{5}{17} + \left(\dfrac{6}{23}\right)\left(\dfrac{5}{11}\right) = \,?$

3. $\left(\dfrac{15}{27}\right)\left(\dfrac{3^2}{13^2}\right) = \,?$

4. $13 + (-7) + 14 + (-3^2) = \,?$

5. $15 - (-10) = \,?$

6. $|-27| = \,?$

7. $(-11)^2 = \,?$

8. $(-10)(13) = \,?$

9. $\dfrac{10\sqrt{5}}{\sqrt{\dfrac{275}{12} - 4^2}} = ?$

10. $\dfrac{(8)(7^2) + 1/3(7 + 6^2)}{(10 + 11 - 2)(6 - 3)} = ?$

11. $\dfrac{17}{10 - 15} = ?$

12. $\dfrac{3X + 14}{5} = 10 \qquad X = ?$

13. $\dfrac{2}{3}X - 3 = 11 \qquad X = ?$

14. $\dfrac{3(X + 2)}{7} = 6 \qquad X = ?$

15. $7X - 15 = -1 \qquad X = ?$

Glossary of Statistical Terms

abscissa   the horizontal axis, or X axis, on a graph

absolute value   value of a number without regard to sign

addition rule of probability   for mutually exclusive random events, the probability that either one event or another event occurs equals the sum of the probabilities of the individual events

additivity   the property of variance that, for individual samples, the variance of a sum of parts is equal to the sum of the variances of the parts

alternative hypothesis (H_1)   in hypothesis testing, the hypothesis that the value of a population parameter is something other than what we have assumed it to be

analysis of variance (ANOVA)   parametric inferential technique designed to test for significant differences among two or more different groups

ANOVA summary table   table used to summarize the results of the analysis of variance; contains values for SS, df, MS, and the F ratio

a posteriori tests   unplanned comparisons following a significant F ratio; also called post-ANOVA or post hoc tests

apparent limits   limits of class intervals with gaps between them

a priori tests   tests designed to look at specific hypotheses before the experiment is done

average deviation (AD)   average amount that each score in a distribution deviates from the distribution's mean

bar graph   type of histogram used to graph nominal scale or categorical data; each bar is separated from its neighbors

Bayesian statistics   statistics involving the use of prior and conditional probabilities based on the work of Thomas Bayes, who initiated the use of probability to establish a mathematical basis for statistical inference

between-groups variability   part of the ANOVA test based on the deviation between each group mean and the total mean; variability between the groups

biased sample   sample that is not representative of the population of interest

bimodal   referring to a distribution with two modes

binomial distribution   probability distribution based on events for which there are only two possible outcomes on each occurrence

central limit theorem   a simplified version is that as sample size increases, the resulting sampling distribution of means more closely approximates the normal distribution

central tendency   tendency for a distribution's scores to be concentrated near the middle of the distribution

chi-square goodness-of-fit test   chi-square test on different levels of a single categorical variable

chi-square test   nonparametric test for nominal scale data

chi-square test of independence   chi-square test on different levels of two categorical variables; also called the chi-square test of significance and the two-sample chi-square test

coefficient of determination (r^2)   amount of variability in one variable explained by variability in another

conditional probability   probability of an event given that another event has already occurred

confidence interval (CI)   range of values within which we are reasonably confident the population mean lies

contingency table   tabular presentation of frequencies by category

continuous variable   variable whose measurement can assume an infinite number of values

control group   group of subjects not subjected to experimental treatment, but like the experimental group(s) in all other ways; the purpose of the control group is to provide a base against which to measure any change in the experimental group(s)

correlation   degree of relationship between two or more variables

counterbalancing   method to control for order effects in a repeated measures design by including all orders of treatment presentation

covariance   extent to which two variables vary together

cumulative frequency curve, or **cumulative frequency polygon**   polygon created from a cumulative frequency distribution

cumulative frequency distribution   frequency distribution in which the frequencies are accumulated from the lowest score to the highest score

cumulative percentage distribution   frequency distribution in which the percentage frequencies are accumulated from the lowest score to the highest score

cumulative percentage polygon   curve plotted from a cumulative percentage distribution

data   numbers; the results of measurement

degree of certainty   how sure we are

degrees of freedom (*df*)   number of values free to vary after certain restrictions are placed on the data

dependent variable   in behavioral science, the measurement of behavior

descriptive statistics   statistical techniques used to illustrate or describe data

deviations   differences of scores from a standard or reference value; usually refers to differences between a score and the mean

directional hypothesis   alternative hypothesis that states the direction of the difference between a population parameter and the value assumed by H_0

discrete variables   variables capable of assuming only specific values such as integers

dispersion   spread of scores around the mean

distribution-free tests   see *nonparametric tests*

double-blind   referring to an experimental design in which neither the participant nor the treatment administrator knows the participant's group designation

effect size   difference between the null and alternative hypotheses in standardized units

estimated standard error of the mean differences ($s_{\bar{X}_1 - \bar{X}_2}$)   estimated standard deviation of the sampling distribution of the differences

estimated standard error of the mean ($s_{\bar{X}}$)   estimated standard deviation of the sampling distribution of means

estimation   process for defining a value for a population parameter based on a sample value

experimental error   source of variability in data caused by such things as imprecise measuring equipment, momentary changes in experimenter and subject attention, and slight changes in background conditions during data collection

factorial design   experimental design in which there are two or more independent variables

factors   designation for variables when there are two or more

Fisher LSD (least significant difference) test   powerful post-ANOVA test that compares pairwise differences in means with a computed least significant difference; also called the protected *t* test

_F_ ratio   ratio of the variability between groups to the variability within groups; test statistic for the ANOVA test

frequency   number of times a score occurs

frequency distribution   listing of scores from highest to lowest with each score's frequency beside it

frequency polygon   graphic representation of a frequency distribution, in which scores are plotted on the X axis and frequencies are plotted on the Y axis

grouped frequency distribution   frequency distribution in which the range of scores is divided into a number of mutually exclusive intervals

histogram   graph of a frequency distribution in which a rectangular bar is drawn over each score value on the X axis

homogeneity of variance   condition in which population variances are the same

HSD test   see *Tukey HSD (honestly significant difference) test*

independent events   events for which occurrence of one event doesn't alter the probability of any other event

independent samples   samples in which the behavior of the members of one sample is not related to the behavior of the members of the other sample

independent sampling   sampling such that the selection of one person or object has no effect on the probability of another person or object being selected; see also *random sampling*

independent *t* test   test for situations in which two separate and independent groups are compared

independent variable   variable controlled or manipulated by the experimenter

indices   the summary numbers that result from an analysis of data

individual differences   differences between participants in an experiment because of different participant backgrounds, experiences, abilities, motives, and so on

inferential statistics   statistical techniques that allow you to make conclusions about a larger group based on results from some portion of it

interaction   joint effect of two independent variables on behavior

interpolation method   procedure for finding the median from a grouped frequency distribution

interval scale   measurement scale with equal intervals between the scores in addition to the properties of naming and ranking of objects or events

Kruskal–Wallis (K–W) one-way analysis of variance by ranks test   nonparametric alternative to the one-way ANOVA

least squares line   line generated by the regression equation

linear correlation   degree to which a straight line best describes the relationship between two variables

line graph   type of graph in which an independent variable is plotted on the X axis and some measure of the dependent variable is plotted on the Y axis

LSD test   see *Fisher LSD (least significant difference) test*

main effect   in a factorial experiment, the effect of each independent variable, considered by itself

Mann–Whitney (M–W) *U* test   nonparametric alternative to the *t* test for independent samples

matched pairs   dependent samples in which subject pairs are as closely matched as possible on some characteristic(s) relevant to the dependent variable

mean ($\overline{X}, \mu$)   the sum of the scores divided by the number of scores; the arithmetic average

mean square (*MS*)   the analyzed variance in the ANOVA test, found by dividing each sum of squares by the appropriate *df*

median (*Md*)   point on the score scale separating the top 50% of the scores from the bottom 50%; the score at the 50th percentile

meta-analysis   procedure for analyzing research results from large numbers of studies using effect sizes

midpoint   score value in the center of a class interval

mode (*Mo*)   most frequently occurring score(s) in a distribution

multimodal   refers to a distribution with two or more modes

multiplication rule of probability   the probability of two or more independent events occurring on separate occasions is the product of their individual probabilities

negative correlation   inverse relationship between two variables; high scores on one variable are associated with low scores on the other variable

negatively skewed curve   skewed curve whose tail is to the left end of the X axis

nominal scale   measurement scale assigning a name, or label, to different objects or events

nondirectional hypothesis   an alternative to H_0 that states that the population parameter is not equal to the value specified by the null hypothesis

nonindependent events   events for which the occurrence of one event alters the probability of any other event

nonparametric, or **distribution-free, tests**   tests that do not test hypotheses about population parameters and do not assume any particular distribution; examples are the chi-square test, the Mann–Whitney test, the Wilcoxon test, and the Kruskal–Wallis test

normal curve   symmetrical, bell-shaped curve whose tails never reach the X axis and whose measures of central tendency are identical

normal distribution   distribution of the normal curve

null hypothesis (H_0)   in hypothesis testing, the hypothesis that assumes a particular value for a population parameter

one-tailed test   significance test that considers only one end of the distribution, the end predicted by the experimenter

ordinal scale   measurement scale in which numbers both name objects or events and allow the objects or events to be ranked

ordinate   the vertical axis, or Y axis, on a graph

parameters   numerical summary characteristics of populations

parametric tests   statistical tests designed to test hypotheses about population parameters

Pearson product-moment correlation coefficient, or **Pearson r**   mean of the z-score products of the X and Y variables

percentage frequencies   frequencies of occurrence presented as percentages of the total sample

percentile   score at or below which a given percentage of the scores lie

percentile rank   percentage of cases up to, and including, the one in which we're interested; total percentage of the distribution below a score

phi coefficient (ϕ)   correlation used when both variables are dichotomous (have only two values)

point biserial correlation (r_{pbis})   correlation useful when one variable is dichotomous (has only two values) and the other is continuous

population   complete collection of something

positive correlation   direct relationship between two variables; high scores are associated with high scores, and low scores with low scores

positively skewed curve   skewed curve whose tail is to the right end of the X axis

post-ANOVA tests   see *a posteriori tests*

post hoc tests   see *a posteriori tests*

power   probability that the inferential test will detect a false null hypothesis

probability   the proportion of times an event would occur if the chances for occurrence were infinite

probability distribution   the probabilities associated with scores in addition to the scores themselves

protected *t* test   see *Fisher LSD test*

random sampling, or **random and independent sampling**   sampling method in which each population member has an equal chance of being selected

range   difference between the highest score and the lowest score in a distribution

ranking, or **rank ordering**   placing objects or events in order, from highest to lowest

ratio scale   interval scale with a true zero

real limits   limits of scores without gaps between them

real world, or **empirical, probability**   probability based on experiential data

regression coefficient   the slope of the regression line

regression equation   equation for the straight line that best describes the linear relationship between two variables

repeated measures design   experimental design in which each subject experiences all levels of the independent variable; also known as a within-subjects design

robustness   property of a statistical test to give valid conclusions even when assumptions of the test are violated

sample   portion or subset of the population

sampling   the process of selecting a sample from a population

sampling distribution   distribution whose scores are sample statistics computed from an infinite number of samples drawn from some population

sampling distribution of means   distribution whose scores are means of samples drawn from some population

sampling distribution of the mean differences   distribution whose scores are differences between pairs of sample means

sampling without replacement   sampling in which each chosen individual is not returned to the population before the next selection

sampling with replacement   sampling in which each selected individual is returned to the population before the next selection

scales, or **scales of measurement**   rules used for assigning numbers to objects or events

scatterplot   graphical representation of correlation in which pairs of scores are plotted, with the scores on one variable plotted on the X axis and the scores on the other variable plotted on the Y axis

score   data point, symbolized by X

significant   in statistics, a term indicating rejection of the null hypothesis

skewed curve   curve in which a large number of scores are piled at one end or the other with a tail at the opposite end

Spearman rank order correlation coefficient (r_s)   nonparametric alternative to the Pearson r

standard deviation (s, σ)   square root of the average squared deviation; square root of the variance

standard error of the difference between means ($\sigma_{\bar{X}_1 - \bar{X}_2}$)   standard deviation of the sampling distribution of the mean differences

standard error of the mean ($\sigma_{\bar{X}}$)   standard deviation of the sampling distribution of the means

standard normal curve   normal, or bell-shaped, curve with a mean of 0 and a standard deviation of 1

standard score   deviation of a raw score from the mean in standard deviation units; also known as a z score

statistic   numerical summary characteristic of a sample

statistical hypotheses   predictions about a population based on sample results

statistics   set of tools and procedures concerned with the collection, organization, and analysis of data

stem-and-leaf plot   data display created by splitting each score into a stem and a leaf, listing the different stems from lowest to highest, and putting each leaf beside its stem

stratified random sampling   sampling in which the population is divided into relevant groups (strata) and random samples are taken from each group

subjective, or **personal, probability**   probabilities based on an individual's experience

sum of squares (SS)   sum of the squared deviations of the scores from the mean; one of the main components of the analysis of variance

t distribution   probability distribution of t scores, which are estimated z scores

theoretical probability   the way things are supposed to work in terms of probability theory

total sum of squares (SS_{tot})   sum of the squared deviation of each score from the total mean in the analysis of variance

total variability   variability in data based on the deviation between each score and the overall, or total, mean

treatment effect   variability in data caused by administration of the independent variable

Tukey HSD (honestly significant difference) test   post-ANOVA test that compares each mean difference with a computed HSD or honestly significant difference

two-tailed test   significance test that considers both ends of the distribution

two-way analysis of variance, or **two-way ANOVA**   ANOVA technique used for analyzing data resulting from the administration of two or more levels of two independent variables

Type I, or α**, error**   rejecting a true null hypothesis

Type II, or β**, error**   failing to reject a false null hypothesis

unbiased estimate   statistic that shows no systematic tendencies in relation to the estimated parameter

unbiased sample   sample that accurately reflects the population from which it was drawn

variable   anything that may take on different values or amounts

variance (s^2, σ^2)   average squared deviation

Wilcoxon matched-pairs signed-ranks test   nonparametric alternative to the *t* test for dependent samples

within-groups variability   part of the ANOVA test based on the deviation between each score in a group and the group mean; variability within a group

within-subjects comparisons   the same individuals are subjected to each of two treatment conditions; each subject is his or her own control

zero correlation   no relationship between two variables

z score   deviation of a raw score from the mean in standard deviation units; also called a standard score

Symbol Glossary and Glossary of Computational Formulas

CHAPTER 3: THE FREQUENCY DISTRIBUTION

Symbols

Symbol	Stands For
X	a score
f	frequency of a score
i	width of a class interval
R	range of scores
N	sum of the frequencies, or total sample size; number of observations
Cum f	cumulative frequency

Formulas

Formula 3-1. Percentage from frequency

$$\%age \text{ (percentage)} = \frac{f}{N}(100)$$

Formula 3-2. Cumulative percentage from cumulative frequency

$$\text{Cum } \%age \text{ (cumulative percentage)} = \frac{\text{Cum } f}{N}(100)$$

CHAPTER 4: GRAPHING DATA

Symbols

Symbol	Stands For
MP	midpoint of a class interval

CHAPTER 5: MEASURES OF CENTRAL TENDENCY

Symbols

Symbol	Stands For
Mo	mode
Md	median
LRL	lower real limit of an interval
$\overline{X}$	sample mean
Σ	capital sigma, denotes sum of what follows
$X - \overline{X}$	deviation of a score from the mean
μ	population mean, read "mu"

Formulas

Formula 5-1. Mean

$$\overline{X} = \frac{\Sigma X}{N}$$

Formula 5-2. Mean for a frequency distribution

$$\overline{X} = \frac{\Sigma f X}{N}$$

CHAPTER 6: MEASURES OF DISPERSION AND STANDARD SCORES

Symbols

Symbol	Stands For
R	range of a set of scores
AD	average deviation

(continued)

Symbol	Stands For
σ^2	population variance
s^2	sample variance
σ	population standard deviation
s	sample standard deviation
s_{approx}	approximation of the sample standard deviation
SS	sum of squares
z	standard score, or z score

Formulas

Formulas 6-2 and 6-3. Average deviation

$$AD = \frac{\Sigma|X - \overline{X}|}{N} \quad \text{or} \quad AD = \frac{\Sigma f|X - \overline{X}|}{N}$$

Formulas 6-8 and 6-9. Sample variance

$$s^2 = \frac{\Sigma X^2 - \frac{(\Sigma X)^2}{N}}{N - 1} \quad \text{or} \quad \frac{\Sigma fX^2 - \frac{(\Sigma fX)^2}{N}}{N - 1}$$

Formula 6-14. Sample standard deviation

$$s = \sqrt{\frac{\Sigma X^2 - \frac{(\Sigma X)^2}{N}}{N - 1}}$$

Formula 6-15. Sample standard deviation for a frequency distribution

$$s = \sqrt{\frac{\Sigma fX^2 - \frac{(\Sigma fX)^2}{N}}{N - 1}}$$

Formula 6-17. z score from a raw score using sample statistics

$$z = \frac{X - \overline{X}}{s}$$

Formula 6-19. Raw score from a z score using sample statistics

$$X = zs + \overline{X}$$

CHAPTER 7: PROBABILITY

Symbols

Symbol	Stands For
p	probability
$p(A)$	probability of event A
$p(A \text{ or } B)$	probability of event A or event B
$p(A, B)$	probability of both A and B
$p(A \mid B)$	probability of event A given that event B has occurred

Formulas

Formula 7-1. Addition rule of probability

$$p(A \text{ or } B) = p(A) + p(B)$$

Formula 7-2. Multiplication rule of probability

$$p(A, B) = p(A) \times p(B)$$

Formula 7-3. Probability of a sequence of nonindependent events

$$p(A, B) = p(A) \times p(B \mid A)$$

CHAPTER 8: THE NORMAL DISTRIBUTION

Formula

Formula 8-1. Probability from percentage area

$$p(\text{probability}) = \frac{\% \text{ area}}{100}$$

CHAPTER 9: CONFIDENCE INTERVALS AND HYPOTHESIS TESTING

Symbols

Symbol	Stands For
$\sigma_{\overline{X}}$	standard error of the mean
$\mu_{\overline{X}}$	mean of the sampling distribution of means

(continued)

Symbol	Stands For
$z_{\overline{X}}$	z score for a sample mean
$s_{\overline{X}}$	estimated standard error of the mean
$t_{\overline{X}}$ or t	t score, which is an estimate of a z score
df	degrees of freedom
CI	confidence interval
$t_{.05}$ or $t_{.01}$	t scores from Table B cutting off deviant 5% or 1% of the distribution [occur with probability of .05 (.01) or less]
μ_0	specific value that represents the untreated population mean
H_0	null hypothesis
H_1	alternative hypothesis
α	alpha level, level at which we test H_0
t_{comp}	computed t score
t_{crit}	critical t score from Table B
Type I or α error	rejecting true H_0
Type II or β error	failing to reject false H_0

Formulas

Formula 9-3. Sample mean from population values

$$\overline{X} = z(\sigma_{\overline{X}}) + \mu$$

Formula 9-4. Estimated standard error of the mean

$$s_{\overline{X}} = \frac{s}{\sqrt{N}}$$

Formula 9-5. t score

$$t_{\overline{X}} = \frac{\overline{X} - \mu}{s_{\overline{X}}}$$

Formulas 9-6 and 9-7. Confidence intervals for the population mean

$$95\% \text{ CI} = \pm t_{.05} s_{\overline{X}} + \overline{X} \qquad 99\% \text{ CI} = \pm t_{.01} s_{\overline{X}} + \overline{X}$$

CHAPTER 10: SIGNIFICANCE OF THE DIFFERENCE BETWEEN TWO SAMPLE MEANS

Symbols

Symbol	Stands For
$\sigma_{\overline{X}_1 - \overline{X}_2}$	standard error of the difference between means
$\mu_{\overline{X}_1 - \overline{X}_2}$	population mean of the sampling distribution of mean differences; also symbolized as $\mu_1 - \mu_2$
$s_{\overline{X}_1 - \overline{X}_2}$	estimated standard error of the differences
$\overline{X}_1 - \overline{X}_2$	score in the sampling distribution of the differences
$z_{\overline{X}_1 - \overline{X}_2}$	z score based on the sampling distribution of the differences
$t_{\overline{X}_1 - \overline{X}_2}$	t score based on the sampling distribution of the differences
s^2_{pooled}	pooled variance; an estimate of the common variance of the populations from which the samples were drawn
$\sigma_{\overline{D}}$	standard error of the mean differences
$s_{\overline{D}}$	estimated standard error of the mean differences
r	correlation coefficient
$\overline{X}_D$	mean of the differences
$s_{\overline{X}_D}$	estimated standard error of the differences
s_D	standard deviation of the differences
D	difference between a pair of scores

Formulas

Formula 10-3. Estimated standard error of mean differences for independent samples

$$s_{\overline{X}_1 - \overline{X}_2} = \sqrt{\left(\frac{(N_1 - 1)s_1^2 + (N_2 - 1)s_2^2}{N_1 + N_2 - 2} \right)\left(\frac{1}{N_1} + \frac{1}{N_2} \right)}$$

Formulas 10-6 and 10-7. Two-sample t test for independent samples

$$t_{\overline{X}_1 - \overline{X}_2} = \frac{\overline{X}_1 - \overline{X}_2}{s_{\overline{X}_1 - \overline{X}_2}} \quad \text{or} \quad \frac{\overline{X}_1 - \overline{X}_2}{\sqrt{\left(\frac{(N_1 - 1)s_1^2 + (N_2 - 1)s_2^2}{N_1 + N_2 - 2} \right)\left(\frac{1}{N_1} + \frac{1}{N_2} \right)}}$$

Formula 10-8. t test for dependent samples

$$t = \frac{\overline{X}_D}{s_{\overline{X}_D}} \quad \text{or} \quad \frac{\overline{X}_D \sqrt{N}}{s_D}$$

CHAPTER 11: ONE-WAY ANALYSIS OF VARIANCE

Symbols

Symbol	Stands For
$\overline{X}_{tot}$	total mean or grand mean (GM)
X_g	score within a group
$\overline{X}_g$	mean of a group
SS_{tot}	total sum of squares
SS_w	sum of squares within a group
SS_b	sum of squares between groups
N_g	number of subjects within a group
N	total number of subjects
$\sum_g$	sum over or across groups
MS_b	mean square between groups
MS_w	mean square within groups
df_b	degrees of freedom between groups
K	number of groups
df_w	degrees of freedom within groups
df_{tot}	total degrees of freedom
F	F ratio, ANOVA test
F_{comp}	computed F ratio
$F_{.05}, F_{.01}$	critical value of F at the 5% and 1% levels, respectively
LSD	least significant difference
HSD	honestly significant difference
q	studentized range statistic
SS_{subj}	measure of inherent variability in subjects
SS_{error}	measure of inherent error
X_m	a subject's scores across treatments
S	subjects

Formulas

Formula 11-5. Total sum of squares

$$SS_{tot} = \Sigma X^2 - \frac{(\Sigma X)^2}{N}$$

Formula 11-6. Within-groups sum of squares

$$SS_w = \sum_g \left[\Sigma X_g^2 - \frac{(\Sigma X_g)^2}{N_g} \right]$$

Formula 11-7. Between-groups sum of squares

$$SS_b = \sum_g \left[\frac{(\Sigma X_g)^2}{N_g} \right] - \frac{(\Sigma X)^2}{N}$$

Formulas 11-8, 11-9, and 11-10. Between-groups degrees of freedom, within groups degrees of freedom, and total degrees of freedom, respectively

$$df_b = K - 1 \qquad df_w = N - K \qquad df_{tot} = N - 1$$

Formula 11-11. Between-groups mean square

$$MS_b = \frac{SS_b}{df_b}$$

Formula 11-12. Within-groups mean square

$$MS_w = \frac{SS_w}{df_w}$$

Formula 11-13. F ratio

$$F = \frac{MS_b}{MS_w}$$

Formula 11-14. Least significant difference (LSD) between pairs of means

$$LSD_\alpha = t_\alpha \sqrt{MS_w \left(\frac{1}{N_1} + \frac{1}{N_2} \right)}$$

Formula 11-15. Honestly significant difference (HSD) between pairs of means

$$HSD_\alpha = q_\alpha \sqrt{\frac{MS_w}{N_g}}$$

Formula 11-16. Within-groups sum of squares in one-way repeated measures ANOVA

$$SS_w = SS_{subj} + SS_{error}$$

Formula 11-17. Total sum of squares in one-way repeated measures ANOVA

$$SS_{tot} = SS_b + SS_{subj} + SS_{error}$$

Formula 11-18. Within-subjects sum of squares in one-way repeated measures ANOVA

$$SS_{subj} = \sum_s \left[\frac{(\Sigma X_m)^2}{K} \right] - \frac{(\Sigma X)^2}{N}$$

Formula 11-19. Error sum of squares in one-way repeated measures ANOVA

$$SS_{error} = SS_{tot} - SS_b - SS_{subj}$$

Formula 11-20. Error degrees of freedom

$$df_{error} = (K - 1)(S - 1)$$

Formula 11-21. Mean square error in one-way repeated measures ANOVA

$$MS_{error} = \frac{SS_{error}}{df_{error}}$$

Formula 11-22. F ratio in one-way repeated measures ANOVA

$$F = \frac{MS_b}{MS_{error}}$$

CHAPTER 12: TWO-WAY ANALYSIS OF VARIANCE

Many new symbols and formulas were introduced in an example in this chapter. Because the goal of the chapter was to provide an intuitive look at two-way ANOVA, this material may be bypassed.

CHAPTER 13: CORRELATION AND REGRESSION

Symbols

Symbol	Stands For
r	Pearson r, Pearson product-moment correlation coefficient
z_X, z_Y	z scores for the X and Y variables, respectively
cov_{XY}	covariance of X and Y; the extent to which X and Y vary together
ρ	rho, the population correlation coefficient
$\hat{Y}$ or $\hat{X}$	Y caret or X caret: predicted values for Y or X based on the regression equation
s_Y, s_X	standard deviation of the Y and X variables, respectively
b	regression coefficient; the slope of the regression line
a	Y intercept of the regression line

Symbol	Stands For
r^2	coefficient of determination
r_S	Spearman rank order correlation coefficient
d	difference between the ranks
r_{pbis}	point biserial correlation
ϕ	phi coefficient

Formulas

Formula 13-2. Pearson r

$$r = \frac{N\Sigma XY - \Sigma X\Sigma Y}{\sqrt{[N\Sigma X^2 - (\Sigma X)^2][N\Sigma Y^2 - (\Sigma Y)^2]}}$$

Formula 13-3. Y predicted from X

$$\hat{Y} = \left(\frac{rs_Y}{s_X}\right)X + \left[\overline{Y} - \left(\frac{rs_Y}{s_X}\right)\overline{X}\right]$$

Formula 13-4. Coefficient of determination

$$\text{coefficient of determination} = \frac{\text{explained variation}}{\text{total variation}} = r^2$$

Formula 13-5. Spearman rank order correlation coefficient

$$r_S = 1 - \frac{6\Sigma d^2}{N(N^2 - 1)}$$

CHAPTER 14: CHI SQUARE

Symbols

Symbol	Stands For
χ^2	chi square
O	observed frequency
E	expected frequency
K	number of categories
RT	row total
CT	column total

(continued)

Symbol	Stands For
R	number of rows
C	number of columns
χ^2_{comp}	computed chi square
χ^2_{crit}	critical value of chi square from Table G

Formulas

Formula 14-1. Chi square

$$\chi^2 = \Sigma \frac{(O - E)^2}{E}$$

Formula 14-2. Expected frequencies for the chi-square test of independence

$$E = \frac{RT \times CT}{N}$$

Formula 14-3. Degrees of freedom for the chi-square test of independence

$$df = (R - 1)(C - 1)$$

CHAPTER 15: ALTERNATIVES TO t AND F

Symbols

Symbol	Stands For
U or M–W U or U'	statistic computed for the Mann–Whitney (M–W) test of significance
N_1, N_2	number of subjects in the first and second groups, respectively
R_1, R_2	sum of the ranks of the scores in the first and second groups, respectively
d	differences between pairs of scores in the Wilcoxon test
T	sum of the ranks of the scores with the less frequent sign (Wilcoxon test)
H or K–W H	statistic computed for the Kruskal–Wallis (K–W) test
N_i	number of observations in a particular sample
R_i	sum of the ranks for a particular sample
K	number of samples

Formulas

Formula 15-1. Mann–Whitney U test

$$U = N_1 N_2 + \frac{N_1(N_1 + 1)}{2} - R_1$$

Formula 15-2. U'

$$U' = N_1 N_2 - U$$

Formula 15-4. z score for large-sample U

$$z = \frac{U - \dfrac{N_1 N_2}{2}}{\sqrt{\dfrac{(N_1)(N_2)(N_1 + N_2 + 1)}{12}}}$$

Formula 15-5. z score for large-sample T

$$z = \frac{T - \dfrac{N(N + 1)}{4}}{\sqrt{\dfrac{N(N + 1)(2N + 1)}{24}}}$$

Formula 15-6. Kruskal–Wallis test

$$H = \frac{12}{N(N + 1)} \sum \frac{R_i^2}{N_i} - 3(N + 1)$$

APPENDIX **4**

Tables for Inferential Tests

TABLE A

Areas under the right half (positive z scores) of the standard normal curve ($\mu = 0$, $\sigma = 1$)

(A) z	(B) area between mean and z	(C) area beyond z	(A) z	(B) area between mean and z	(C) area beyond z	(A) z	(B) area between mean and z	(C) area beyond z
0.00	00.00	50.00	0.40	15.54	34.46	0.80	28.81	21.19
0.01	00.40	49.60	0.41	15.91	34.09	0.81	29.10	20.90
0.02	00.80	49.20	0.42	16.28	33.72	0.82	29.39	20.61
0.03	01.20	48.80	0.43	16.64	33.36	0.83	29.67	20.33
0.04	01.60	48.40	0.44	17.00	33.00	0.84	29.95	20.05
0.05	01.99	48.01	0.45	17.36	32.64	0.85	30.23	19.77
0.06	02.39	47.61	0.46	17.72	32.28	0.86	30.51	19.49
0.07	02.79	47.21	0.47	18.08	31.92	0.87	30.78	19.22
0.08	03.19	46.81	0.48	18.44	31.56	0.88	31.06	18.94
0.09	03.59	46.41	0.49	18.79	31.21	0.89	31.33	18.67
0.10	03.98	46.02	0.50	19.15	30.85	0.90	31.59	18.41
0.11	04.38	45.62	0.51	19.50	30.50	0.91	31.86	18.14
0.12	04.78	45.22	0.52	19.85	30.15	0.92	32.12	17.88
0.13	05.17	44.83	0.53	20.19	29.81	0.93	32.38	17.62
0.14	05.57	44.43	0.54	20.54	29.46	0.94	32.64	17.36
0.15	05.96	44.04	0.55	20.88	29.12	0.95	32.89	17.11
0.16	06.36	43.64	0.56	21.23	28.77	0.96	33.15	16.85
0.17	06.75	43.25	0.57	21.57	28.43	0.97	33.40	16.60
0.18	07.14	42.86	0.58	21.90	28.10	0.98	33.65	16.35
0.19	07.53	42.47	0.59	22.24	27.76	0.99	33.89	16.11
0.20	07.93	42.07	0.60	22.57	27.43	1.00	34.13	15.87
0.21	08.32	41.68	0.61	22.91	27.09	1.01	34.38	15.62
0.22	08.71	41.29	0.62	23.24	26.76	1.02	34.61	15.39
0.23	09.10	40.90	0.63	23.57	26.43	1.03	34.85	15.15
0.24	09.48	40.52	0.64	23.89	26.11	1.04	35.08	14.92
0.25	09.87	40.13	0.65	24.22	25.78	1.05	35.31	14.69
0.26	10.26	39.74	0.66	24.54	25.46	1.06	35.54	14.46
0.27	10.64	39.36	0.67	24.86	25.14	1.07	35.77	14.23
0.28	11.03	38.97	0.68	25.17	24.83	1.08	35.99	14.01
0.29	11.41	38.59	0.69	25.49	24.51	1.09	36.21	13.79
0.30	11.79	38.21	0.70	25.80	24.20	1.10	36.43	13.57
0.31	12.17	37.83	0.71	26.11	23.89	1.11	36.65	13.35
0.32	12.55	37.45	0.72	26.42	23.58	1.12	36.86	13.14
0.33	12.93	37.07	0.73	26.73	23.27	1.13	37.08	12.92
0.34	13.31	36.69	0.74	27.04	22.96	1.14	37.29	12.71
0.35	13.68	36.32	0.75	27.34	22.66	1.15	37.49	12.51
0.36	14.06	35.94	0.76	27.64	22.36	1.16	37.70	12.30
0.37	14.43	35.57	0.77	27.94	22.06	1.17	37.90	12.10
0.38	14.80	35.20	0.78	28.23	21.77	1.18	38.10	11.90
0.39	15.17	34.83	0.79	28.52	21.48	1.19	38.30	11.70

(continued)

TABLE A

continued

(A)	(B)	(C)	(A)	(B)	(C)	(A)	(B)	(C)
z	area between mean and z	area beyond z	z	area between mean and z	area beyond z	z	area between mean and z	area beyond z
1.20	38.49	11.51	1.60	44.52	05.48	2.00	47.72	02.28
1.21	38.69	11.31	1.61	44.63	05.37	2.01	47.78	02.22
1.22	38.88	11.12	1.62	44.74	05.26	2.02	47.83	02.17
1.23	39.07	10.93	1.63	44.84	05.16	2.03	47.88	02.12
1.24	39.25	10.75	1.64	44.95	05.05	2.04	47.93	02.07
1.25	39.44	10.56	1.65	45.05	04.95	2.05	47.98	02.02
1.26	39.62	10.38	1.66	45.15	04.85	2.06	48.03	01.97
1.27	39.80	10.20	1.67	45.25	04.75	2.07	48.08	01.92
1.28	39.97	10.03	1.68	45.35	04.65	2.08	48.12	01.88
1.29	40.15	09.85	1.69	45.45	04.55	2.09	48.17	01.83
1.30	40.32	09.68	1.70	45.54	04.46	2.10	48.21	01.79
1.31	40.49	09.51	1.71	45.64	04.36	2.11	48.26	01.74
1.32	40.66	09.34	1.72	45.73	04.27	2.12	48.30	01.70
1.33	40.82	09.18	1.73	45.82	04.18	2.13	48.34	01.66
1.34	40.99	09.01	1.74	45.91	04.09	2.14	48.38	01.62
1.35	41.15	08.85	1.75	45.99	04.01	2.15	48.42	01.58
1.36	41.31	08.69	1.76	46.08	03.92	2.16	48.46	01.54
1.37	41.47	08.53	1.77	46.16	03.84	2.17	48.50	01.50
1.38	41.62	08.38	1.78	46.25	03.75	2.18	48.54	01.46
1.39	41.77	08.23	1.79	46.33	03.67	2.19	48.57	01.43
1.40	41.92	08.08	1.80	46.41	03.59	2.20	48.61	01.39
1.41	42.07	07.93	1.81	46.49	03.51	2.21	48.64	01.36
1.42	42.22	07.78	1.82	46.56	03.44	2.22	48.68	01.32
1.43	42.36	07.64	1.83	46.64	03.36	2.23	48.71	01.29
1.44	42.51	07.49	1.84	46.71	03.29	2.24	48.75	01.25
1.45	42.65	07.35	1.85	46.78	03.22	2.25	48.78	01.22
1.46	42.79	07.21	1.86	46.86	03.14	2.26	48.81	01.19
1.47	42.92	07.08	1.87	46.93	03.07	2.27	48.84	01.16
1.48	43.06	06.94	1.88	46.99	03.01	2.28	48.87	01.13
1.49	43.19	06.81	1.89	47.06	02.94	2.29	48.90	01.10
1.50	43.32	06.68	1.90	47.13	02.87	2.30	48.93	01.07
1.51	43.45	06.55	1.91	47.19	02.81	2.31	48.96	01.04
1.52	43.57	06.43	1.92	47.26	02.74	2.32	48.98	01.02
1.53	43.70	06.30	1.93	47.32	02.68	2.33	49.01	00.99
1.54	43.82	06.18	1.94	47.38	02.62	2.34	49.04	00.96
1.55	43.94	06.06	1.95	47.44	02.56	2.35	49.06	00.94
1.56	44.06	05.94	1.96	47.50	02.50	2.36	49.09	00.91
1.57	44.18	05.82	1.97	47.56	02.44	2.37	49.11	00.89
1.58	44.29	05.71	1.98	47.61	02.39	2.38	49.13	00.87
1.59	44.41	05.59	1.99	47.67	02.33	2.39	49.16	00.84

(continued)

TABLE A

continued

(A)	(B)	(C)	(A)	(B)	(C)	(A)	(B)	(C)
z	area between mean and z	area beyond z	z	area between mean and z	area beyond z	z	area between mean and z	area beyond z
2.40	49.18	00.82	2.80	49.74	00.26	3.20	49.93	00.07
2.41	49.20	00.80	2.81	49.75	00.25	3.21	49.93	00.07
2.42	49.22	00.78	2.82	49.76	00.24	3.22	49.94	00.06
2.43	49.25	00.75	2.83	49.77	00.23	3.23	49.94	00.06
2.44	49.27	00.73	2.84	49.77	00.23	3.24	49.94	00.06
2.45	49.29	00.71	2.85	49.78	00.22	3.25	49.94	00.06
2.46	49.31	00.69	2.86	49.79	00.21	3.30	49.95	00.05
2.47	49.32	00.68	2.87	49.79	00.21	3.35	49.96	00.04
2.48	49.34	00.66	2.88	49.80	00.20	3.40	49.97	00.03
2.49	49.36	00.64	2.89	49.81	00.19	3.45	49.97	00.03
2.50	49.38	00.62	2.90	49.81	00.19	3.50	49.98	00.02
2.51	49.40	00.60	2.91	49.82	00.18	3.60	49.98	00.02
2.52	49.41	00.59	2.92	49.82	00.18	3.70	49.99	00.01
2.53	49.43	00.57	2.93	49.83	00.17	3.80	49.99	00.01
2.54	49.45	00.55	2.94	49.84	00.16	3.90	49.995	00.005
2.55	49.46	00.54	2.95	49.84	00.16	4.00	49.997	00.003
2.56	49.48	00.52	2.96	49.85	00.15			
2.57	49.49	00.51	2.97	49.85	00.15			
2.58	49.51	00.49	2.98	49.86	00.14			
2.59	49.52	00.48	2.99	49.86	00.14			
2.60	49.53	00.47	3.00	49.87	00.13			
2.61	49.55	00.45	3.01	49.87	00.13			
2.62	49.56	00.44	3.02	49.87	00.13			
2.63	49.57	00.43	3.03	49.88	00.12			
2.64	49.59	00.41	3.04	49.88	00.12			
2.65	49.60	00.40	3.05	49.89	00.11			
2.66	49.61	00.39	3.06	49.89	00.11			
2.67	49.62	00.38	3.07	49.89	00.11			
2.68	49.63	00.37	3.08	49.90	00.10			
2.69	49.64	00.36	3.09	49.90	00.10			
2.70	49.65	00.35	3.10	49.90	00.10			
2.71	49.66	00.34	3.11	49.91	00.09			
2.72	49.67	00.33	3.12	49.91	00.09			
2.73	49.68	00.32	3.13	49.91	00.09			
2.74	49.69	00.31	3.14	49.92	00.08			
2.75	49.70	00.30	3.15	49.92	00.08			
2.76	49.71	00.29	3.16	49.92	00.08			
2.77	49.72	00.28	3.17	49.92	00.08			
2.78	49.73	00.27	3.18	49.93	00.07			
2.79	49.74	00.26	3.19	49.93	00.07			

Source: This table is from R. P. Runyon and A. Haber, *Fundamentals of Behavioral Statistics,* 3d ed., 1976, Reading, MA: Addison-Wesley, pp. 377–379. Copyright © 1976 by Addison-Wesley. Reprinted with permission of The McGraw-Hill Companies.

TABLE B

Critical Values of t
df = N − 1 *for one-sample* t *test, confidence intervals, and for the* t *test for dependent samples*
df = N₁ + N₂ − 2 *for two-sample* t *test for independent samples*

	Level of Significance for Two-Tailed Test			
	(For One-Tailed Test, Halve the Following Percentages)			
	10%	**5%**	**2%**	**1%**
df	**(*p* = .10)**	**(*p* = .05)**	**(*p* = .02)**	**(*p* = .01)**
1	6.3138	12.7062	31.8207	63.6574
2	2.9200	4.3027	6.9646	9.9248
3	2.3534	3.1824	4.5407	5.8409
4	2.1318	2.7764	3.7469	4.6041
5	2.0150	2.5706	3.3649	4.0322
6	1.9432	2.4469	3.1427	3.7074
7	1.8946	2.3646	2.9980	3.4995
8	1.8595	2.3060	2.8965	3.3554
9	1.8331	2.2622	2.8214	3.2498
10	1.8125	2.2281	2.7638	3.1693
11	1.7959	2.2010	2.7181	3.1058
12	1.7823	2.1788	2.6810	3.0545
13	1.7709	2.1604	2.6503	3.0123
14	1.7613	2.1448	2.6245	2.9768
15	1.7531	2.1315	2.6025	2.9467
16	1.7459	2.1199	2.5835	2.9208
17	1.7396	2.1098	2.5669	2.8982
18	1.7341	2.1009	2.5524	2.8784
19	1.7291	2.0930	2.5395	2.8609
20	1.7247	2.0860	2.5280	2.8453
21	1.7207	2.0796	2.5177	2.8314
22	1.7171	2.0739	2.5083	2.8188
23	1.7139	2.0687	2.4999	2.8073
24	1.7109	2.0639	2.4922	2.7969
25	1.7081	2.0595	2.4851	2.7874
26	1.7056	2.0555	2.4786	2.7787
27	1.7033	2.0518	2.4727	2.7707
28	1.7011	2.0484	2.4671	2.7633
29	1.6991	2.0452	2.4620	2.7564
30	1.6973	2.0423	2.4573	2.7500
35	1.6869	2.0301	2.4377	2.7238
40	1.6839	2.0211	2.4233	2.7045
45	1.6794	2.0141	2.4121	2.6896
50	1.6759	2.0086	2.4033	2.6778
60	1.6706	2.0003	2.3901	2.6603
70	1.6669	1.9944	2.3808	2.6479
80	1.6641	1.9901	2.3739	2.6387
90	1.6620	1.9867	2.3685	2.6316
100	1.6602	1.9840	2.3642	2.6259
110	1.6588	1.9818	2.3607	2.6213
120	1.6577	1.9799	2.3598	2.6174
∞	1.6449	1.9600	2.3263	2.5758

Source: This table is from D. B. Owen, *Handbook of Statistical Tables,* 1962, Reading, MA: Addison-Wesley, pp. 28–30. Copyright © 1962 by Addison-Wesley Publishing Company, Inc. Reprinted with permission of Addison-Wesley Longman.

TABLE C

Critical Values of F

df Associated With the Denominator (df_w)		*df* Associated With the Numerator (df_b)								
		1	2	3	4	5	6	7	8	9
1	5%	161	200	216	225	230	234	238	239	241
	1%	4052	5000	5403	5625	5764	5859	5928	5982	6022
2	5%	18.5	19.0	19.2	19.2	19.3	19.3	19.4	19.4	19.4
	1%	98.5	99.0	99.2	99.2	99.3	99.3	99.4	99.4	99.4
3	5%	10.1	9.55	9.28	9.12	9.01	8.97	8.89	8.85	8.81
	1%	34.1	30.8	29.5	28.7	28.2	27.9	27.7	27.5	27.3
4	5%	7.71	6.94	6.59	6.39	6.26	6.16	6.09	6.04	6.00
	1%	21.2	18.0	16.7	16.0	15.5	15.2	15.0	14.8	14.7
5	5%	6.61	5.79	5.41	5.19	5.05	4.95	4.88	4.82	4.77
	1%	16.3	13.3	12.1	11.4	11.0	10.7	10.5	10.3	10.2
6	5%	5.99	5.14	4.76	4.53	4.39	4.28	4.21	4.15	4.10
	1%	13.7	10.9	9.78	9.15	8.75	8.47	8.26	8.10	7.98
7	5%	5.59	4.74	4.35	4.12	3.97	3.87	3.79	3.73	3.68
	1%	12.2	9.55	8.45	7.85	7.46	7.19	6.99	6.84	6.72
8	5%	5.32	4.46	4.07	3.84	3.69	3.58	3.50	3.44	3.39
	1%	11.3	8.65	7.59	7.01	6.63	6.37	6.18	6.03	5.91
9	5%	5.12	4.26	3.86	3.63	3.48	3.37	3.29	3.23	3.18
	1%	10.6	8.02	6.99	6.42	6.06	5.80	5.61	5.47	5.35
10	5%	4.96	4.10	3.71	3.48	3.33	3.22	3.14	3.07	3.02
	1%	10.0	7.56	6.55	5.99	5.64	5.39	5.20	5.06	4.94
11	5%	4.84	3.98	3.59	3.36	3.20	3.09	3.01	2.95	2.90
	1%	9.65	7.21	6.22	5.67	5.32	5.07	4.89	4.74	4.63
12	5%	4.75	3.89	3.49	3.26	3.11	3.00	2.91	2.85	2.80
	1%	9.33	6.93	5.95	5.41	5.06	4.82	4.64	4.50	4.39
13	5%	4.67	3.81	3.41	3.18	3.03	2.92	2.83	2.77	2.71
	1%	9.07	6.70	5.74	5.21	4.86	4.62	4.44	4.30	4.19
14	5%	4.60	3.74	3.34	3.11	2.96	2.85	2.76	2.70	2.65
	1%	8.86	6.51	5.56	5.04	4.70	4.46	4.28	4.14	4.03
15	5%	4.54	3.68	3.29	3.06	2.90	2.79	2.71	2.64	2.59
	1%	8.68	6.36	5.42	4.89	4.56	4.32	4.14	4.00	3.89
16	5%	4.49	3.63	3.24	3.01	2.85	2.74	2.66	2.59	2.54
	1%	8.53	6.23	5.29	4.77	4.44	4.20	4.03	3.89	3.78
17	5%	4.45	3.59	3.20	2.96	2.81	2.70	2.61	2.55	2.49
	1%	8.40	6.11	5.18	4.67	4.34	4.10	3.93	3.79	3.68

(continued)

TABLE C

continued

df Associated With the Denominator (df_w)		df Associated With the Numerator (df_b)								
		1	2	3	4	5	6	7	8	9
18	5%	4.41	3.55	3.16	2.93	2.77	2.66	2.58	2.51	2.46
	1%	8.29	6.01	5.09	4.58	4.25	4.01	3.84	3.71	3.60
19	5%	4.38	3.52	3.13	2.90	2.74	2.63	2.54	2.48	2.42
	1%	8.18	5.93	5.01	4.50	4.17	3.94	3.77	3.63	3.52
20	5%	4.35	3.49	3.10	2.87	2.71	2.60	2.51	2.45	2.39
	1%	8.10	5.85	4.94	4.43	4.10	3.87	3.70	3.56	3.46
21	5%	4.32	3.47	3.07	2.84	2.68	2.57	2.49	2.42	2.37
	1%	8.02	5.78	4.87	4.37	4.04	3.81	3.64	3.51	3.40
22	5%	4.30	3.44	3.05	2.82	2.66	2.55	2.46	2.40	2.34
	1%	7.95	5.72	4.82	4.31	3.99	3.76	3.59	3.45	3.35
23	5%	4.28	3.42	3.03	2.80	2.64	2.54	2.44	2.37	2.32
	1%	7.88	5.66	4.76	4.26	3.94	3.71	3.54	3.41	3.30
24	5%	4.26	3.40	3.01	2.78	2.62	2.51	2.42	2.36	2.30
	1%	7.82	5.61	4.72	4.22	3.90	3.67	3.50	3.36	3.26
25	5%	4.24	3.39	2.29	2.76	2.60	2.49	2.40	2.34	2.28
	1%	7.77	5.57	4.68	4.18	3.86	3.63	3.46	3.32	3.22
26	5%	4.23	3.37	2.98	2.74	2.59	2.47	2.39	2.32	2.27
	1%	7.72	5.53	4.64	4.14	3.82	3.59	3.42	3.29	3.18
27	5%	4.21	3.35	2.96	2.73	2.57	2.46	2.37	2.31	2.25
	1%	7.68	5.49	4.60	4.11	3.78	3.56	3.39	3.26	3.15
28	5%	4.20	3.34	2.95	2.71	2.56	2.45	2.36	2.29	2.24
	1%	7.64	5.45	4.57	4.07	3.75	3.53	3.36	3.23	3.12
29	5%	4.18	3.33	2.93	2.70	2.55	2.43	2.35	2.28	2.22
	1%	7.60	5.42	4.54	4.04	3.73	3.50	3.33	3.20	3.09
30	5%	4.17	3.32	2.92	2.69	2.53	2.42	2.33	2.27	2.21
	1%	7.56	5.39	4.51	4.02	3.70	3.47	3.30	3.17	3.07
40	5%	4.08	3.23	2.84	2.61	2.45	2.34	2.25	2.18	2.12
	1%	7.31	5.18	4.31	3.83	3.51	3.29	3.12	2.99	2.89
60	5%	4.00	3.15	2.76	2.53	2.37	2.25	2.17	2.10	2.04
	1%	7.08	4.98	4.13	3.65	3.34	3.12	2.95	2.82	2.72
120	5%	3.92	3.07	2.68	2.45	2.29	2.18	2.09	2.02	1.96
	1%	6.85	4.79	3.95	3.48	3.17	2.96	2.79	2.66	2.56

Source: This table is adapted from M. Merrington and C. M. Thompson, Tables of percentage points of the inverted beta (F) distribution, *Biometrika, 33,* 1943, 73–88. Reprinted with permission of the Biometrika Trustees.

TABLE D

Critical Values of q_α

(df_w)	α	\multicolumn{9}{c}{K = Number of Groups (Means)}
		2	3	4	5	6	7	8	9	10
1	.05	17.97	26.98	32.82	37.08	40.41	43.12	45.40	47.36	49.07
	.01	90.03	135.00	164.30	185.60	202.20	215.80	227.20	237.00	245.60
2	.05	6.08	8.33	9.80	10.88	11.74	12.44	13.03	13.54	13.99
	.01	14.04	19.02	22.29	24.72	26.63	28.20	29.53	30.68	31.69
3	.05	4.50	5.91	6.82	7.50	8.04	8.48	8.85	9.18	9.46
	.01	8.26	10.62	12.17	13.33	14.24	15.00	15.64	16.20	16.69
4	.05	3.93	5.04	5.76	6.29	6.71	7.05	7.35	7.60	7.83
	.01	6.51	8.12	9.17	9.96	10.58	11.10	11.55	11.93	12.27
5	.05	3.64	4.60	5.22	5.67	6.03	6.33	6.58	6.80	6.99
	.01	5.70	6.98	7.80	8.42	8.91	9.32	9.67	9.97	10.24
6	.05	3.46	4.34	4.90	5.30	5.63	5.90	6.12	6.32	6.49
	.01	5.24	6.33	7.03	7.56	7.97	8.32	8.61	8.87	9.10
7	.05	3.34	4.16	4.68	5.06	5.36	5.61	5.82	6.00	6.16
	.01	4.95	5.92	6.54	7.01	7.37	7.68	7.94	8.17	8.37
8	.05	3.26	4.04	4.53	4.89	5.17	5.40	5.60	5.77	5.92
	.01	4.75	5.64	6.20	6.62	6.96	7.24	7.47	7.68	7.86
9	.05	3.20	3.95	4.41	4.76	5.02	5.24	5.43	5.59	5.74
	.01	4.60	5.43	5.96	6.35	6.66	6.91	7.13	7.33	7.49
10	.05	3.15	3.88	4.33	4.65	4.91	5.12	5.30	5.46	5.60
	.01	4.48	5.27	5.77	6.14	6.43	6.67	6.87	7.05	7.21
11	.05	3.11	3.82	4.26	4.57	4.82	5.03	5.20	5.35	5.49
	.01	4.39	5.15	5.62	5.97	6.25	6.48	6.67	6.84	6.99
12	.05	3.08	3.77	4.20	4.51	4.75	4.95	5.12	5.27	5.39
	.01	4.32	5.05	5.50	5.84	6.10	6.32	6.51	6.67	6.81
13	.05	3.06	3.73	4.15	4.45	4.69	4.88	5.05	5.19	5.32
	.01	4.26	4.96	5.40	5.73	5.98	6.19	6.37	6.53	6.67
14	.05	3.03	3.70	4.11	4.41	4.64	4.83	4.99	5.13	5.25
	.01	4.21	4.89	5.32	5.63	5.88	6.08	6.26	6.41	6.54
15	.05	3.01	3.67	4.08	4.37	4.59	4.78	4.94	5.08	5.20
	.01	4.17	4.84	5.25	5.56	5.80	5.99	6.16	6.31	6.44
16	.05	3.00	3.65	4.05	4.33	4.56	4.74	4.90	5.03	5.15
	.01	4.13	4.79	5.19	5.49	5.72	5.92	6.08	6.22	6.35
17	.05	2.98	3.63	4.02	4.30	4.52	4.70	4.86	4.99	5.11
	.01	4.10	4.74	5.14	5.43	5.66	5.85	6.01	6.15	6.27
18	.05	2.97	3.61	4.00	4.28	4.49	4.67	4.82	4.96	5.07
	.01	4.07	4.70	5.09	5.38	5.60	5.79	5.94	6.08	6.20
19	.05	2.96	3.59	3.98	4.25	4.47	4.65	4.79	4.92	5.04
	.01	4.05	4.67	5.05	5.33	5.55	5.73	5.89	6.02	6.14
20	.05	2.95	3.58	3.96	4.23	4.45	4.62	4.77	4.90	5.01
	.01	4.02	4.64	5.02	5.29	5.51	5.69	5.84	5.97	6.09

(continued)

TABLE D

continued

(df_w)	α	\multicolumn{9}{c}{K = Number of Groups (Means)}
		2	3	4	5	6	7	8	9	10
24	.05	2.92	3.53	3.90	4.17	4.37	4.54	4.68	4.81	4.92
	.01	3.96	4.55	4.91	5.17	5.37	5.54	5.69	5.81	5.92
30	.05	2.89	3.49	3.85	4.10	4.30	4.46	4.60	4.72	4.82
	.01	3.89	4.45	4.80	5.05	5.24	5.40	5.54	5.65	5.76
40	.05	2.86	3.44	3.79	4.04	4.23	4.39	4.52	4.63	4.73
	.01	3.82	4.37	4.70	4.93	5.11	5.26	5.39	5.50	5.60
60	.05	2.83	3.40	3.74	3.98	4.16	4.31	4.44	4.55	4.65
	.01	3.76	4.28	4.59	4.82	4.99	5.13	5.25	5.36	5.45
120	.05	2.80	3.36	3.68	3.92	4.10	4.24	4.36	4.47	4.56
	.01	3.70	4.20	4.50	4.71	4.87	5.01	5.12	5.21	5.30
∞	.05	2.77	3.31	3.63	3.86	4.03	4.17	4.29	4.39	4.47
	.01	3.64	4.12	4.40	4.60	4.76	4.88	4.99	5.08	5.16

Source: This table is from Table 29 of E. S. Pearson and H. O. Hartley (Eds.), *Biometrika Tables for Statisticians,* Vol. 1, 3d ed., Cambridge University Press. Reprinted with permission of the Biometrika Trustees.

TABLE E

Critical Values of r
$df = N - 2$, *where* N *is the number of pairs of scores*

Degrees of Freedom (df)	5%	1%	Degrees of Freedom (df)	5%	1%
1	.997	1.000	24	.388	.496
2	.950	.990	25	.381	.487
3	.878	.959	26	.374	.478
4	.811	.917	27	.367	.470
5	.754	.874	28	.361	.463
6	.707	.834	29	.355	.456
7	.666	.798	30	.349	.449
8	.632	.765	35	.325	.418
9	.602	.735	40	.304	.393
10	.576	.708	45	.288	.372
11	.553	.684	50	.273	.354
12	.532	.661	60	.250	.325
13	.514	.641	70	.232	.302
14	.497	.623	80	.217	.283
15	.482	.606	90	.205	.267
16	.468	.590	100	.195	.254
17	.456	.575	125	.174	.228
18	.444	.561	150	.159	.208
19	.433	.549	200	.138	.181
20	.423	.537	300	.113	.148
21	.413	.526	400	.098	.128
22	.404	.515	500	.088	.115
23	.396	.505	1000	.062	.081

Source: This table is from Table VII of Fisher and Yates: *Statistical Tables for Biological, Agricultural and Medical Research,* published by Longman Group Ltd., London (previously published by Oliver and Boyd, Edinburgh). Reprinted by permission of Pearson Education Limited.

TABLE F

Critical Values of r_s

N	5%	1%	N	5%	1%
5	1.000	—	16	.506	.665
6	.886	1.000	18	.475	.625
7	.786	.929	20	.450	.591
8	.738	.881	22	.428	.562
9	.683	.833	24	.409	.537
10	.648	.794	26	.392	.515
12	.591	.777	28	.377	.496
14	.544	.714	30	.364	.478

Source: This table is adapted from E. G. Olds, Distribution of sums of squares of rank differences for small samples, *Annals of Mathematical Statistics, 9,* 1938, 133–148, and the 5% significance levels for sums of squares of rank differences and a correction, *Annals of Mathematical Statistics, 20,* 1949, 117–118, with permission of the editor.

TABLE G

Critical Values of χ^2

$df = K - 1$ *for the chi-square goodness-of-fit test. K is the number of categories.*

$df = (R - 1)(C - 1)$ *for the chi-square test of independence. R is the number of rows and C is the number of columns.*

Degrees of Freedom (*df*)	5%	1%	Degrees of Freedom (*df*)	5%	1%
1	3.84	6.64	16	26.30	32.00
2	5.99	9.21	17	27.59	33.41
3	7.82	11.34	18	28.87	34.80
4	9.49	13.28	19	30.14	36.19
5	11.07	15.09	20	31.41	37.57
6	12.59	16.81	21	32.67	38.93
7	14.07	18.48	22	33.92	40.29
8	15.51	20.09	23	35.17	41.64
9	16.92	21.67	24	36.42	42.98
10	18.31	23.21	25	37.65	44.31
11	19.68	24.72	26	38.88	45.64
12	21.03	26.22	27	40.11	46.96
13	22.36	27.69	28	41.34	48.28
14	23.68	29.14	29	42.56	49.59
15	25.00	30.58	30	43.77	50.89

Source: This table is from Table IV of Fisher and Yates: *Statistical Tables for Biological, Agricultural and Medical Research,* published by Longman Group Ltd., London (previously published by Oliver and Boyd, Edinburgh). Reprinted by permission of Pearson Education Limited.

TABLE H

Critical Values for the Mann–Whitney U

For a two-tailed test at the 10% level (roman type, $\alpha = .10$) and at the 5% level (boldface type, $\alpha = .05$). For a one-tailed test, halve the probabilities.

Dashes in the body of the table mean that no decision is possible at the given α.

N_2 \ N_1	1	2	3	4	5	6	7	8	9	10	11	12	13	14	15	16	17	18	19	20
1	—	—	—	—	—	—	—	—	—	—	—	—	—	—	—	—	—	—	0	0
																			—	—
2	—	—	—	—	0	0	0	1	1	1	1	2	2	2	3	3	3	4	4	4
	—	—	—	—	**0**	**0**	**0**	**0**	**0**	**0**	**0**	**1**	**1**	**1**	**1**	**1**	**2**	**2**	**2**	**2**
3	—	—	0	0	1	2	2	3	3	4	5	5	6	7	7	8	9	9	10	11
	—	—	—	—	**0**	**1**	**1**	**2**	**2**	**3**	**3**	**4**	**4**	**5**	**5**	**6**	**6**	**7**	**7**	**8**
4	—	—	0	1	2	3	4	5	6	7	8	9	10	11	12	14	15	16	17	18
	—	—	—	**0**	**1**	**2**	**3**	**4**	**4**	**5**	**6**	**7**	**8**	**9**	**10**	**11**	**11**	**12**	**13**	**13**
5	—	0	1	2	4	5	6	8	9	11	12	13	15	16	18	19	20	22	23	25
	—	—	**0**	**1**	**2**	**3**	**5**	**6**	**7**	**8**	**9**	**11**	**12**	**13**	**14**	**15**	**17**	**18**	**19**	**20**
6	—	0	2	3	5	7	8	10	12	14	16	17	19	21	23	25	26	28	30	32
	—	—	**1**	**2**	**3**	**5**	**6**	**8**	**10**	**11**	**13**	**14**	**16**	**17**	**19**	**21**	**22**	**24**	**25**	**27**
7	—	0	2	4	6	8	11	13	15	17	19	21	24	26	28	30	33	35	37	39
	—	—	**1**	**3**	**5**	**6**	**8**	**10**	**12**	**14**	**16**	**18**	**20**	**22**	**24**	**26**	**28**	**30**	**32**	**34**
8	—	1	3	5	8	10	13	15	18	20	23	26	28	31	33	36	39	41	44	47
	—	**0**	**2**	**4**	**6**	**8**	**10**	**13**	**15**	**17**	**19**	**22**	**24**	**26**	**29**	**31**	**34**	**36**	**38**	**41**
9	—	1	3	6	9	12	15	18	21	24	27	30	33	36	39	42	45	48	51	54
	—	**0**	**2**	**4**	**7**	**10**	**12**	**15**	**17**	**20**	**23**	**26**	**28**	**31**	**34**	**37**	**39**	**42**	**45**	**48**
10	—	1	4	7	11	14	17	20	24	27	31	34	37	41	44	48	51	55	58	62
	—	**0**	**3**	**5**	**8**	**11**	**14**	**17**	**20**	**23**	**26**	**29**	**33**	**36**	**39**	**42**	**45**	**48**	**52**	**55**
11	—	1	5	8	12	16	19	23	27	31	34	38	42	46	50	54	57	61	65	69
	—	**0**	**3**	**6**	**9**	**13**	**16**	**19**	**23**	**26**	**30**	**33**	**37**	**40**	**44**	**47**	**51**	**55**	**58**	**62**
12	—	2	5	9	13	17	21	26	30	34	38	42	47	51	55	60	64	68	72	77
	—	**1**	**4**	**7**	**11**	**14**	**18**	**22**	**26**	**29**	**33**	**37**	**41**	**45**	**49**	**53**	**57**	**61**	**65**	**69**
13	—	2	6	10	15	19	24	28	33	37	42	47	51	56	61	65	70	75	80	84
	—	**1**	**4**	**8**	**12**	**16**	**20**	**24**	**28**	**33**	**37**	**41**	**45**	**50**	**54**	**59**	**63**	**67**	**72**	**76**
14	—	2	7	11	16	21	26	31	36	41	46	51	56	61	66	71	77	82	87	92
	—	**1**	**5**	**9**	**13**	**17**	**22**	**26**	**31**	**36**	**40**	**45**	**50**	**55**	**59**	**64**	**67**	**74**	**78**	**83**
15	—	3	7	12	18	23	28	33	39	44	50	55	61	66	72	77	83	88	94	100
	—	**1**	**5**	**10**	**14**	**19**	**24**	**29**	**34**	**39**	**44**	**49**	**54**	**59**	**64**	**70**	**75**	**80**	**85**	**90**
16	—	3	8	14	19	25	30	36	42	48	54	60	65	71	77	83	89	95	101	107
	—	**1**	**6**	**11**	**15**	**21**	**26**	**31**	**37**	**42**	**47**	**53**	**59**	**64**	**70**	**75**	**81**	**86**	**92**	**98**
17	—	3	9	15	20	26	33	39	45	51	57	64	70	77	83	89	96	102	109	115
	—	**2**	**6**	**11**	**17**	**22**	**28**	**34**	**39**	**45**	**51**	**57**	**63**	**67**	**75**	**81**	**87**	**93**	**99**	**105**
18	—	4	9	16	22	28	35	41	48	55	61	68	75	82	88	95	102	109	116	123
	—	**2**	**7**	**12**	**18**	**24**	**30**	**36**	**42**	**48**	**55**	**61**	**67**	**74**	**80**	**86**	**93**	**99**	**106**	**112**
19	0	4	10	17	23	30	37	44	51	58	65	72	80	87	94	101	109	116	123	130
		2	**7**	**13**	**19**	**25**	**32**	**38**	**45**	**52**	**58**	**65**	**72**	**78**	**85**	**92**	**99**	**106**	**113**	**119**
20	0	4	11	18	25	32	39	47	54	62	69	77	84	92	100	107	115	123	130	138
		2	**8**	**13**	**20**	**27**	**34**	**41**	**48**	**55**	**62**	**69**	**76**	**83**	**90**	**98**	**105**	**112**	**119**	**127**

(continued)

TABLE H

continued

For a two-tailed test at the 2% level (roman type, $\alpha = .02$) and at the 1% level (boldface type, $\alpha = .01$). For a one-tailed test, halve the probabilities.
Dashes in the body of the table mean that no decision is possible at the given α.

N_2 \ N_1	1	2	3	4	5	6	7	8	9	10	11	12	13	14	15	16	17	18	19	20
1	—	—	—	—	—	—	—	—	—	—	—	—	—	—	—	—	—	—	—	—
2	—	—	—	—	—	—	—	—	—	—	—	—	0	0	0	0	0	0	1	1
													—	—	—	—	—	—	0	0
3	—	—	—	—	—	—	0	0	1	1	1	2	2	2	3	3	4	4	4	5
							—	—	0	0	0	1	1	1	2	2	2	2	3	3
4	—	—	—	—	0	1	1	2	3	3	4	5	5	6	7	7	8	9	9	10
					—	0	0	1	1	2	2	3	3	4	5	5	6	6	7	8
5	—	—	—	0	1	2	3	4	5	6	7	8	9	10	11	12	13	14	15	16
				—	0	1	1	2	3	4	5	6	7	7	8	9	10	11	12	13
6	—	—	—	1	2	3	4	6	7	8	9	11	12	13	15	16	18	19	20	22
				0	1	2	3	4	5	6	7	9	10	11	12	13	15	16	17	18
7	—	—	0	1	3	4	6	7	9	11	12	14	16	17	19	21	23	24	26	28
			—	0	1	3	4	6	7	9	10	12	13	15	16	18	19	21	22	24
8	—	—	0	2	4	6	7	9	11	13	15	17	20	22	24	26	28	30	32	34
			—	1	2	4	6	7	9	11	13	15	17	18	20	22	24	26	28	30
9	—	—	1	3	5	7	9	11	14	16	18	21	23	26	28	31	33	36	38	40
			0	1	3	5	7	9	11	13	16	18	20	22	24	27	29	31	33	36
10	—	—	1	3	6	8	11	13	16	19	22	24	27	30	33	36	38	41	44	47
			0	2	4	6	9	11	13	16	18	21	24	26	29	31	34	37	39	42
11	—	—	1	4	7	9	12	15	18	22	25	28	31	34	37	41	44	47	50	53
			0	2	5	7	10	13	16	18	21	24	27	30	33	36	39	42	45	48
12	—	—	2	5	8	11	14	17	21	24	28	31	35	38	42	46	49	53	56	60
			1	3	6	9	12	15	18	21	24	27	31	34	37	41	44	47	51	54
13	—	0	2	5	9	12	16	20	23	27	31	35	39	43	47	51	55	59	63	67
	—	—	1	3	7	10	13	17	20	24	27	31	34	38	42	45	49	53	56	60
14	—	0	2	6	10	13	17	22	26	30	34	38	43	47	51	56	60	65	69	73
	—	—	1	4	7	11	15	18	22	26	30	34	38	42	46	50	54	58	63	67
15	—	0	3	7	11	15	19	24	28	33	37	42	47	51	56	61	66	70	75	80
	—	—	2	5	8	12	16	20	24	29	33	37	42	46	51	55	60	64	69	73
16	—	0	3	7	12	16	21	26	31	36	41	46	51	56	61	66	71	76	82	87
	—	—	2	5	9	13	18	22	27	31	36	41	45	50	55	60	65	70	74	79
17	—	0	4	8	13	18	23	28	33	38	44	49	55	60	66	71	77	82	88	93
	—	—	2	6	10	15	19	24	29	34	39	44	49	54	60	65	70	75	81	86
18	—	0	4	9	14	19	24	30	36	41	47	53	59	65	70	76	82	88	94	100
	—	—	2	6	11	16	21	26	31	37	42	47	53	58	64	70	75	81	87	92
19	—	1	4	9	15	20	26	32	38	44	50	56	63	69	75	82	88	94	101	107
	—	0	3	7	12	17	22	28	33	39	45	51	56	63	69	74	81	87	93	99
20	—	1	5	10	16	22	28	34	40	47	53	60	67	73	80	87	93	100	107	114
	—	0	3	8	13	18	24	30	36	42	48	54	60	67	73	79	86	92	99	105

Source: This table is from Roger E. Kirk, *Elementary Statistics,* 2d ed. Copyright © 1984, 1978 by Roger E. Kirk. Adapted by permission of the author.

TABLE I

Critical Values of T

N	.05	.02	.01
6	0	—	—
7	2	0	—
8	4	2	0
9	6	3	2
10	8	5	3
11	11	7	5
12	14	10	7
13	17	13	10
14	21	16	13
15	25	20	16
16	30	24	20
17	35	28	23
18	40	33	28
19	46	38	32
20	52	43	38
21	59	49	43
22	66	56	49
23	73	62	55
24	81	69	61
25	89	77	68

Source: This table is from Table 1 of F. Wilcoxon, *Some Rapid Approximate Statistical Procedures,* American Cyanamid Company, 1949, p. 13.

APPENDIX **5**

Answers to Odd-Numbered Exercises

CHAPTER 1

1. Statistics was defined as (1) the summary numbers that result from the analysis of data and (2) a set of procedures and tools used to organize and interpret facts, events, and observations that can be expressed numerically. Studying statistics will make you a better everyday consumer of statistics, help you read and understand the literature in the behavioral sciences, and give you the tools to calculate and interpret data in your own research.

CHAPTER 2

1. **a.** The independent variable is the variable manipulated by the experimenter; the dependent variable is the measurement of behavior.
   b. A population is a complete collection of objects or individuals; a sample is a population subset.
   c. A parameter is a measurable characteristic of a population; a statistic is a measurable characteristic of a sample.
   d. In sampling with replacement, each subject chosen is returned to the population before the next selection. Subjects are not returned in sampling without replacement.
   e. Descriptive statistics is used to illustrate data or some feature of data; inferential statistics allows conclusions to be made about populations based on sample results.
3. From school rolls, you could obtain a list of all fifth-graders. This list would be your population. You could write the names on slips of paper and draw a sample from a container, either with or without replacement. Students in the sample would be contacted, and their body mass computed. From the indi-

vidual values, you could compute the average (a statistic, because it is a sample characteristic) and use this to estimate the population average (a parameter).

5. The independent variable is the type of reading instruction; the dependent variable is student reading performance.

7. The independent variable is the level of hypnosis (either hypnotized or unhyp-notized), whereas the dependent variable is the length of time participants can keep their hands in a bucket of ice water.

9. It would be a nonrandom sample because all college-age individuals do not have an equal chance of being enrolled there. For example, many would be excluded geographically and others financially.

CHAPTER 3

1.

X	f	Cum f	%age f	Cum %age
50	2	35	5.71	100.00
48	1	33	2.86	94.29
47	1	32	2.86	91.43
45	1	31	2.86	88.57
44	1	30	2.86	85.71
40	2	29	5.71	82.86
38	2	27	5.71	77.14
37	1	25	2.86	71.42
35	1	24	2.86	68.57
34	1	23	2.86	65.71
33	2	22	5.71	62.86
29	2	20	5.71	57.14
28	1	18	2.86	51.43
27	1	17	2.86	48.57
25	2	16	5.71	45.71
23	1	14	2.86	40.00
20	2	13	5.71	37.14
18	2	11	5.71	31.43
16	2	9	5.71	25.71
15	1	7	2.86	20.00
14	2	6	5.71	17.14
13	2	4	5.71	11.43
12	1	2	2.86	5.71
11	1	1	2.86	2.86

$$N = 35$$

Example of %age $= \dfrac{f}{N}(100) = \dfrac{1}{35}(100) = \dfrac{100}{35} = 2.86$

Example of Cum %age $= \dfrac{\text{Cum } f}{N}(100) = \dfrac{4}{35}(100) = \dfrac{400}{35} = 11.43$

3.

X	f	Cum f	%age f	Cum %age
14	1	23	4.35	100.00
13	2	22	8.70	95.65
12	2	20	8.70	86.96
11	3	18	13.04	78.26
9	5	15	21.74	65.22
8	3	10	13.04	43.48
7	2	7	8.70	30.43
6	1	5	4.35	21.74
5	1	4	4.35	17.39
4	2	3	8.70	13.04
3	1	1	4.35	4.35
	$N = 23$			

Example of %age $= \dfrac{f}{N}(100) = \dfrac{1}{23}(100) = \dfrac{100}{23} = 4.35$

Example of Cum %age $= \dfrac{\text{Cum } f}{N}(100) = \dfrac{3}{23}(100) = \dfrac{300}{23} = 13.04$

5.

X	Real Limits	f	Cum f	%age f	Cum %age
70	69.5–70.5	1	30	3.33	100.00
60	59.5–60.5	1	29	3.33	96.67
55	54.5–55.5	2	28	6.67	93.33
50	49.5–50.5	2	26	6.67	86.67
48	47.5–48.5	1	24	3.33	80.00
45	44.5–45.5	3	23	10.00	76.67
40	39.5–40.5	6	20	20.00	66.67
38	37.5–38.5	1	14	3.33	46.67
37	36.5–37.5	2	13	6.67	43.33
35	34.5–35.5	3	11	10.00	36.67
32	31.5–32.5	1	8	3.33	26.67
30	29.5–30.5	4	7	13.33	23.33
28	27.5–28.5	1	3	3.33	10.00
25	24.5–25.5	2	2	6.67	6.67
		$N = 30$			

$$\text{Example of \%age} = \frac{f}{N}(100) = \frac{2}{30}(100) = \frac{200}{30} = 6.67$$

$$\text{Example of Cum \%age} = \frac{\text{Cum } f}{N}(100) = \frac{3}{30}(100) = \frac{300}{30} = 10.00$$

7.

X	Real Limits	f	Cum f	Cum %age
60	59.5–60.5	1	30	100.00
58	57.5–58.5	1	29	96.67
57	56.5–57.5	2	28	93.33
56	55.5–56.5	2	26	86.67
55	54.5–55.5	1	24	80.00
53	52.5–53.5	1	23	76.67
52	51.5–52.5	2	22	73.33
51	50.5–51.5	3	20	66.67
49	48.5–49.5	5	17	56.67
48	47.5–48.5	3	12	40.00
46	45.5–46.5	2	9	30.00
45	44.5–45.5	1	7	23.33
44	43.5–44.5	1	6	20.00
43	42.5–43.5	2	5	16.67
42	41.5–42.5	1	3	10.00
41	40.5–41.5	1	2	6.67
40	39.5–40.5	1	1	3.33

$$N = 30$$

$$\text{Example of Cum \%age} = \frac{\text{Cum } f}{N}(100) = \frac{5}{30}(100) = \frac{500}{30} = 16.67$$

9. Cum f for 74 = 15; Cum f for 80 = 23.

11. a. A continuous variable is one whose measurement can take an infinite number of values; there are no gaps in its measurement, or the gaps are apparent rather than real. Height and weight are examples.

   b. A frequency distribution is an ordered listing of scores from highest to lowest with the number of times each score occurs given beside it.

   c. A discrete variable is one whose measurement results in a finite number of values. Examples are gender and the number of children in a family.

   d. Cumulative frequency is an accumulation of frequencies working from the bottom of the distribution to the top; to get each value, you add the frequency of a score to the sum of all the frequencies below it.

CHAPTER 4

1.

X	f
12	1
11	2
10	5
9	4
8	3
7	2
6	1

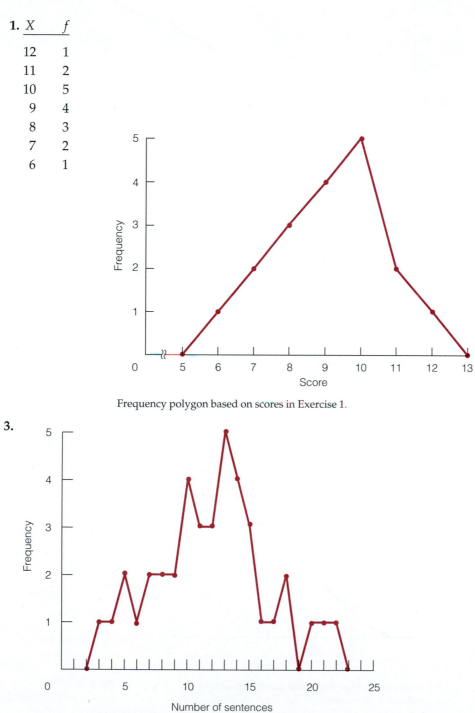

Frequency polygon based on scores in Exercise 1.

3.

Frequency polygon of number of sentences unscrambled in 10 minutes.

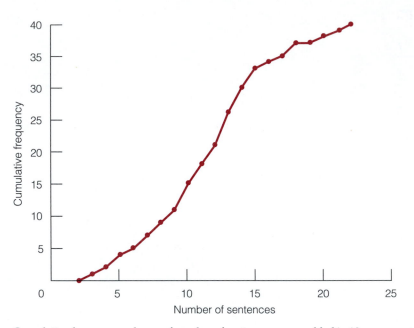

Cumulative frequency polygon of number of sentences unscrambled in 10 minutes.

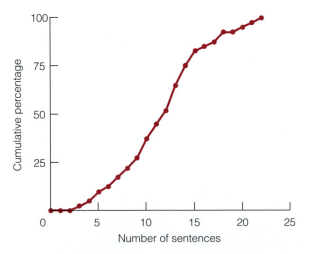

Cumulative percentage polygon of number of sentences unscrambled in 10 minutes.

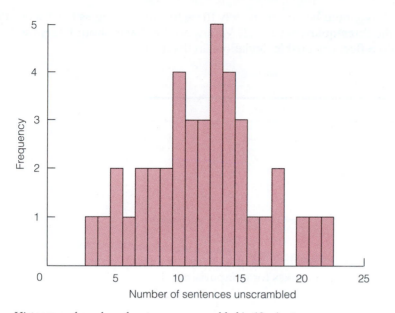

Histogram of number of sentences unscrambled in 10 minutes.

5.

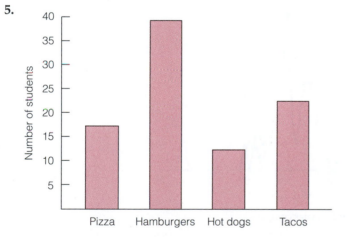

Fast food preferences of students.

7. a. A positively skewed curve is a distribution that has much smaller frequencies for large X values than it does for small X values; the resulting frequency polygon has a tail to the right.

b. A symmetrical curve results in a distribution whose left half would fold to precisely cover its right half.

c. A negatively skewed curve is a distribution that has smaller frequencies for small X values than it does for large X values; the resulting frequency polygon has a tail to the left.

9. (1) The Y axis should be approximately three fourths as long as the X axis; this is called the three-quarters rule. (2) Values on the Y axis should begin with 0 and should reflect reasonable deviations in the data.

11.

Stems	Leaves										
1	5	1	2	8	6	3	3	6	8	4	4
2	7	8	3	9	9	5	0	5	0		
3	7	4	3	8	5	3	8				
4	4	8	7	5	0	0					
5	0	0									

13. Because of unequal sample sizes, plot %age frequency polygons, with males and females on the same axes for comparison.

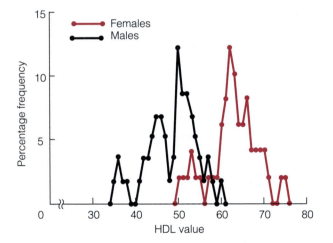

HDL values of males and females compared.

15. Monday—Cum f of 8 = 24
%age f of 8 = 15.15%
Cum %age of 8 = 72.73%

Wednesday—Cum f of 8 = 28
%age f of 8 = 6.45%
Cum %age of 8 = 90.32%

Friday—Cum f of 8 = 30
%age f of 8 = 3.13%
Cum %age of 8 = 93.75%

17.

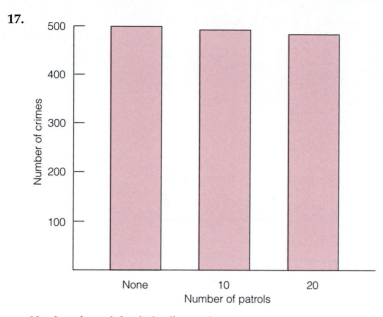

Number of patrols has little effect on the crime rate.

19.

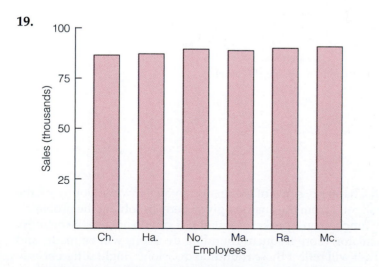

Total sales by employee; all are doing well.

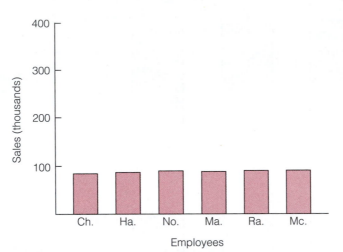

Total sales by employee; all are doing poorly.

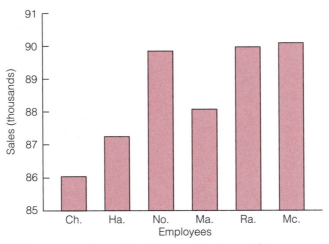

Total sales by employee; Charlie's not pulling his weight.

CHAPTER 5

Note: Beginning with Chapter 5, some of the answers you get when you work the exercises may differ slightly from the answers given here. In solving the problems, we used the memory function on a pocket calculator. If you do not use the memory function of your calculator, more frequent rounding decisions will be made, and the final answer you get will reflect these rounding decisions. Slight differences in answers can be overlooked.

1. $\overline{X} = 16.95$, $Md = 19$, $Mo = 19$; the median may be the most appropriate measure, as the distribution is rather negatively skewed.

3. **a.** $Md = 11$, $\overline{X} = 17$.

   b. $Md = 121.5$, $\overline{X} = 108.22$

   c. $Md = -0.5$, $\overline{X} = -4.9$

5. **a.** negatively

   b. positively

7. $Mo = 2$, $Md = 3$, $\overline{X} = 4$

9. $Mo = 36$, $Md = 35$, $\overline{X} = 35.57$

11. $Mo = 13$, $Md = 12$, $\overline{X} = 12.57$

13. $Mo = 7$, $Md = 6$, $\overline{X} = 6.17$; the Md is the most appropriate measure because of the arbitrary cutoff score.

15. $Mo = 6, 7$; $Md = 7$, $\overline{X} = 7.13$

17. $Mo = 2$, $Md = 3$, $\overline{X} = 3$

CHAPTER 6

1. $s^2 = 4.04$, $s = 2.01$

3. $s = 3.27$

5. $R = 8$, $s_{approx} = 2$, $\overline{X} = 6$, $s = 1.99$, $s^2 = 3.95$

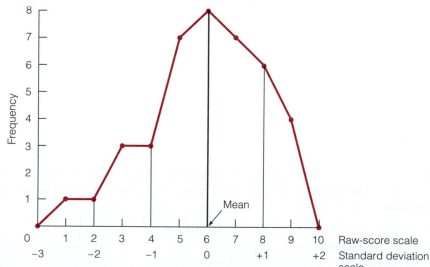

Frequency polygon showing standard deviation scale.

7. $R = 14, s_{approx} = 3.5, s^2 = 16.68, s = 4.08$

9. $R = 10, s^2 = 7.38, s = 2.72$

11. a. population variance

   b. population standard deviation

   c. population mean

   d. sample variance

   e. sample standard deviation

   f. range of a set of scores

13. $z = -0.53, z = 1.8; IQ = 116.5, IQ = 92.5$

15. $R = 112, s^2 = 1,009.96, s = 31.78$

17. $R = 4, s^2 = 1.06, s = 1.03$

19. $R = 11, s_{approx} = 2.75, s^2 = 8.18, s = 2.86$

CHAPTER 7

1. Without replacement, the probability is

$$(\tfrac{1}{52})(\tfrac{1}{51})(\tfrac{1}{50})(\tfrac{1}{49})(\tfrac{1}{48}) = .0000000032$$

3. $p = (\tfrac{1}{2})(\tfrac{1}{6})(\tfrac{1}{13}) = .0064$

5. $p = (\tfrac{4}{52})(\tfrac{3}{51})(\tfrac{2}{50})(\tfrac{1}{49}) = .0000036$

7. $p(\text{miss all 20 questions}) = \left(\dfrac{1}{2}\right)^{20} = .00000095$

9. a. .002   **b.** .004   **c.** .006   **d.** 0

11. .022

13. a. .42   **b.** .67   **c.** Yes, it increases the probability from .42 to .67.

CHAPTER 8

1. The normal curve is a unimodal, symmetrical curve whose tails never reach the X axis. The standard normal curve has a mean equal to 0, and its standard deviation is 1.

3. a. 72.57%

   b. 6.2, rounded to 6

   c. 11.34; 8.96

   d. $p = .0668$

5. **a.** 13.57%
   b. 14 students
   c. 1.6 or less, 6.86 or more
   d. 4; 3
   e. 5.2
   f. $p = .24$
7. **a.** 30.85%
   b. 7
   c. 62.34%
   d. 6.36 or less, 13.64 or more
9. 57.94 or less, 94.06 or more; $p = .011$
11. 0.912 or 1 meeting; $p = .0548$; 61 min or less, 159 min or more

CHAPTER 9

1. **a.** 99% CI: 88.81 to 111.19
   b. 95% CI: 96.73 to 103.27
3. 95% CI: 21.13 to 25.67, 99% CI: 20.32 to 26.48
5. $t(136) = 4.41$, $p < .01$. The rats took significantly longer than 11.5 sec to traverse the runway.
7. **a.** Power is defined as the probability of rejecting a false H_0 and is equal to $1 - \beta$.
   b. Rejecting a true H_0 is called an α error.
   c. A β error is failing to reject a false null hypothesis.
   d. A directional hypothesis is an alternative hypothesis that states the direction of the difference between a population parameter and the value assumed by H_0.
9. $t(9) = 4.25$, $p < .01$. Lack of sleep increases the average brainstem auditory response latency. Note: Less rounding substantially affects the value of t (e.g., 3.84), although the conclusion is the same.
11. $\mu_{\bar{X}} = 4 = \mu$; $\sigma_{\bar{X}} = 1.58$.
13. 95% CI = 255.39 to 312.01; 99% CI = 245.55 to 321.85
15. 95% CI = 3.45 to 3.61; 99% CI = 3.42 to 3.64. No, $\mu = 3.27$ is not in the 95% CI, nor is it in 99% CI. Yes, H_0 was rejected in Exercise 14.
17. $t(14) = 1.33$, $p > .05$. The null hypothesis is not rejected. Thus, there is no evidence for a change in the number of cents carried.
19. Assume the null hypothesis is that no attack has been launched. Failing to reject this hypothesis, if it is true, would be the correct decision. Rejecting the hypothesis by deciding that a Soviet strike has been launched (committing a Type I or α error) would lead to a counterstrike and thermonuclear war. On the other hand, if the null hypothesis is really false (the Soviets *have* launched an attack), then failure to reject it and thereby committing a Type II or β error would result in our annihilation, with no damage to the enemy.

CHAPTER 10

1. $t(18) = 2.26$, $p < .05$. Sleep deprivation resulted in slower cognitive performance.

3. $t(24) = 1.02$, $p > .05$. The speeches did not differ significantly in distractibility. The numerators of the t test are the same in Exercises 2 and 3. However, the denominator in Exercise 3 is much larger. This illustrates the gain in power and precision when a design is used in which the dependent t is appropriate.

5. $t(9) = 3.97$, $p < .01$. Order of presentation is important. The pattern discrimination is easier because the pilots have experience with the task after learning the brightness discrimination task.

7. $t(16) = -1.90$, $p < .05$, $t_{.05} = -1.7459$, $t_{.01} = -2.5835$; directional. Viewing the film significantly increased aggressiveness.

9. The assumptions are homogeneity of variance and sampling from normal populations. Both assumptions can be violated without affecting conclusions drawn from the test.

11. $t(5) = -7.86$, $p < .01$. The brain response to sound was increased by alcohol. Note that rounding can dramatically alter the value you obtain for t on this problem.

13. $t(28) = -4.89$, $p < .01$. Students responded more quickly to an "emergency" if they were alone than if they were in a group.

15. $t(28) = 2.24$, $p < .05$. The intruded-upon drivers took significantly longer to leave their parking spaces.

CHAPTER 11

1. $F(2, 21) = 6.48$, $p < .01$. The three hypnotic susceptibility groups differed significantly in their dream recall.
   Fisher LSD: $LSD_{.05} = 5.94$; $LSD_{.01} = 8.08$

Table of Differences

	Low HS 9.38	Medium HS 13.88	High HS 19.63
Low HS 9.38		4.50	10.25**
Medium HS 13.88			5.75
High HS 19.63			

*Note. *$p < .05$; **$p < .01$.*

Conclusion: Participants in the High Hypnotic Susceptibility group recalled significantly more dreams than participants in the Low Susceptibility group. Low HS = Medium HS < High HS.
Tukey HSD: $HSD_{.05} = 5.96$; $HSD_{.01} = 8.12$

Table of Differences

	Low HS 9.38	Medium HS 13.88	High HS 19.63
Low HS 9.38		4.50	10.25**
Medium HS 13.88			5.75
High HS 19.63			

Note. $*p < .05; **p < .01.$

Conclusion: Again, High HS participants recalled significantly more dreams than Low HS participants.

3. $F(2, 27) = 6.42, p < .01.$ The infant groups differ significantly in object permanence ability.

Fisher LSD: $LSD_{.05} = 2.19; LSD_{.01} = 2.95$

Table of Differences

	9 Months 4.2	12 Months 5.8	15 Months 8.0
9 Months 4.2	—	1.6	3.8**
12 Months 5.8		—	2.2*
15 Months 8.0			—

Note. $*p < .05; **p < .01.$

The 15-month infants show greater object permanence than either the 9-month infants or the 12-month infants, which do not differ significantly.

5. $F(3, 12) = 12.93, p < .01.$ Fatigue significantly affects performance on the data entry task.

Tukey HSD: $HSD_{.05} = 4.01, HSD_{.01} = 5.38$

Table of Differences

	1st 15 Minutes 8	2nd 15 Minutes 8	3rd 15 Minutes 12	4th 15 Minutes 16
1st 15 Minutes 8	—	0	4	8**
2nd 15 Minutes 8		—	4	8**
3rd 15 Minutes 12			—	4
4th 15 Minutes 16				—

Note. $*p < .05; **p < .01.$

There was a significant increase in errors at the 4th 15-minute interval relative to the 1st and 2nd intervals. In addition, the mean differences involving the 3rd interval nearly met the $HSD_{.05}$, which suggests an increase in errors at the 3rd interval relative to the 1st and 2nd intervals and an increase in the 4th interval relative to the 3rd. It also suggests that a more powerful test (e.g., the Fisher LSD) might be preferable for this analysis.

7. $F(2, 18) = 29.12$, $p < .01$, and we reject the null hypothesis as before, indicating a change in object permanence ability with age. With the smaller error term for the within-subjects ANOVA, the value computed for F is much larger, and the test is more powerful.

9. $F(3, 24) = 3.85$, $p < .05$. There is a significant difference in intrusive thoughts at different stages of therapy. Because of the smaller error term in the within-subjects ANOVA, the value computed for F was much larger in Exercise 4.

11. $F(2, 17) = 9.52$, $p < .01$. The size of the group affects performance response latencies.

Fisher LSD: $LSD_{.05}$ for the comparison of 1-person and 2-person groups $= 1.23$; $LSD_{.01}$ for the same comparison $= 1.69$. $LSD_{.05}$ for the comparisons with the 4-person group $= 1.28$; $LSD_{.01}$ for the same comparisons $= 1.76$.

Table of Differences

	1-Person 0.64	2-Person 1.62	4-Person 3.27
1-Person 0.64	—	0.98	2.63**
2-Person 1.62		—	1.65*
4-Person 3.27			—

Note. *$p < .05$; **$p < .01$.

The presence of three others (4-person group) caused longer response latencies relative to the other groups, which did not differ significantly.

CHAPTER 12

1. **a.** all nonsignificant

    b. significant A main effect; B main effect and interaction nonsignificant

    c. significant A and B main effects; no interaction

    d. A and B main effects nonsignificant; significant interaction

    e. A main effect nonsignificant; B main effect significant; significant interaction

3. The main advantage of the two-factor design is the ability to test for an inter-action of factors. A significant interaction is a mixed blessing because it makes the interpretation of results more complicated.

5. A significant interaction is usually revealed by crossing or converging lines on a graph.

CHAPTER 13

1. **a.** $r(7) = .82, p < .01$.
    b. $\hat{Y} = 0.73X + 1.13$.
    c. $\hat{Y} = 5.51$.

3. **a.** $r(8) = .64, p < .05$. There is a significant positive relationship between quiz scores from quizzes taken 2 weeks apart.
    b. $\hat{Y} = 0.67X + 0.51$.
    c. $\hat{Y} = 3.86$ or 4.

5. Ranked from most to least linear relationship, they are as follows: $-.98, +.95, +.85, +.57, -.37, +.08$.

7. $r(6) = .86, p < .01$. There is a high positive relationship between the IQ scores of pairs of identical twins; identical twins tend to have quite similar IQ scores.

9. $r(12) = .18, p > .05$. Order of completion and exam score are unrelated, accord-ing to these data. Assuming order of completion is rank-level measurement and computing r_s gives a similar result: $r_s = .16, p > .05$.

11. $r_s = .84, p < .01$. The ratings of the letters of recommendation by the two judges are quite similar.

13. $r_{pbis} = .37$. All of the computed correlation coefficients in Exercise 12 were larger than .37: $r = .52, r_s = .61$, and r computed from the ranks $= .59$.

CHAPTER 14

1. $\chi^2(2, N = 270) = 28.68, p < .01$. Liberals were more likely than conservatives to vote for the tax.

3. $\chi^2(1, N = 56) = 10.64, p < .01$. Help was less likely to be given to the shabbily dressed person.

5. $\chi^2(2, N = 90) = 18.78, p < .01$. Later-born students have a higher need for affiliation than first-born students, according to these data.

7. $\chi^2(1, N = 50) = 6.52, p < .05$. A higher percentage of the rural people were politically conservative.

9. $\chi^2(3, N = 134) = 31.99, p < .01$. Religious affiliation was related to voting practices, with Baptists and Catholics more likely to vote Republican, Methodists and Episcopalians more likely to vote Democrat.

11. $\chi^2(1, N = 3,195) = 364.36, p < .01$. The drug was effective in preventing relapse.

13. $\chi^2(2, N = 158) = 8.14, p < .05$. Consumption varied as a function of the tempo, with more sips the slower the tempo.

CHAPTER 15

1. $U = 1, p = .02$. Surrogate-reared monkeys exhibited more self-directed behavior.

3. The parametric test is normally more powerful; that is, it is more likely to result in rejection of the null hypothesis.

5. A vs. B, $U' = 1.5, p < .01$; Journal B has higher-rated articles than Journal A.
   A vs. C, $U' = 31.5, p > .10$; the ratings did not differ for Journals A and C.
   A vs. D, $U' = 1.5, p < .01$; Journal D had higher ratings than Journal A.
   B vs. C, $U = 4, p < .01$; Journal B had higher ratings than Journal C.
   B vs. D, $U = 20.5, p > .10$; the ratings did not differ for Journals B and D.
   C vs. D, $U' = 5, p < .01$; Journal D had higher ratings than Journal C.

7. $T = 31, p > .05$. There is no reason to believe that an attitude change resulted from watching the film.

9. $H = 0.63, p > .05$. The sales, delivery, and office personnel did not differ in self-rated personality.

MATH–ALGEBRA REVIEW

1. 0.0648
3. 0.0298
5. 25
7. 121
9. 8.50
11. -3.4
13. 21
15. 2

Index